CAPTURING THE CULTURE

RICHARD GRENIER, formerly film critic for *Commentary* and correspondent for the *New York Times,* writes for the *Washington Times.* He is also the author of *The Marrakesh One-Two* and *The Gandhi Nobody Knows.*

CAPTURING THE CULTURE

Film, Art, and Politics

Richard Grenier

Introduction by
Robert H. Bork

ETHICS AND PUBLIC POLICY CENTER

The **ETHICS AND PUBLIC POLICY CENTER,** established in 1976, conducts a program of research, writing, publications, and conferences to encourage debate on domestic and foreign policy issues among religious, educational, academic, business, political, and other leaders. A nonpartisan effort, the Center is supported by contributions (which are tax deductible) from foundations, corporations, and individuals. The authors alone are responsible for the views expressed in Center publications.

Library of Congress Cataloging-in-Publication Data

Grenier, Richard, 1926–
Capturing the culture : film, art, and politics / Richard Grenier ;
introduction by Robert H. Bork.
p.   cm.
Includes index.
    1. Motion pictures—Reviews.   2. Motion pictures—Political aspects—
United States.   3. Motion picture industry—Political aspects—United States.
I. Title.
PN1995.G684   1990   791.43'75—dc20   90-45303 CIP
ISBN 0–89633–149–0 (alk. paper)

Distributed by arrangement with:

National Book Network
4720 Boston Way
Lanham, MD 20706
3 Henrietta Street
London WC2E 8LU England

All Ethics and Public Policy Center books are produced on acid-free paper. The paper used in this publication meets the minimum requirements of American National Standard for Information Sciences—Permanence of Paper for Printed Library Materials, ANSI Z39.48–1984.   ∞™

Ethics and Public Policy Center
1030 Fifteenth Street N.W.
Washington, D.C. 20005
(202) 682–1200

Prince, porté soit des serfs Eolus
En la forest ou domine Glaucus;
Ou privé soit de paix et d'esperance:
Car digne n'est de posseder vertus
Qui mal vouldroit au royaulme de France!

François Villon
"Ballade Contre les Ennemis de la France"

For Arnaud
Qui l'a toujours su

With gratitude to my editors and publishers. In Europe: Claude Bourdet, Eric Rohmer, Lord Drogheda, and Peregrine Worsthorne; in America: Robert L. Bartley, William F. Buckley, Jr., John O'Sullivan, Martin Peretz, R. Emmett Tyrrell, Arnaud de Borchgrave, Norman Podhoretz, A. M. Rosenthal, and above all Ernest Lefever, without whom this book would not have existed.

Contents

Introduction

ROBERT H. BORK

ONE OF THE wonders of the modern world is that the intellectual and cultural elites of Western democracies are so overwhelmingly hostile to their own societies. That hostility is in no way diminished by the fact that these groups have never been as free and prosperous, as courted and admired, as cosseted and pampered as they are here and now.

A second wonder is that the public at large seems not to realize the full extent of the alienation of these elites, the extent to which they and their work have become politicized from the left. One does, to be sure, hear complaints about Dan Rather, and the press generally inspires a good deal of distrust. There are as well random laments about happenings on university campuses, as when someone like Jeane Kirkpatrick is prevented from speaking. But there seems no general appreciation of the degree to which leftish ideologies of both the hard and the soft varieties dominate so many of our institutions. When I occasionally speak of the condition of our most prestigious law schools, someone is likely to say, "Why, that sounds just like the so-and-so Divinity School," (or the literature or history department). And the law schools do resemble those and other departments because the same movement to the Left has enveloped most of our intellectual and cultural institutions.

Reading Richard Grenier's *Capturing the Culture* persuades me that I too never fully understood either the source of elite alienation or its magnitude. The political saturation of so many institutions seemed a phenomenon peculiar to the intellectual class, a class made up of people whose everyday work is with ideas or knowledge. Most of the prestigious universities, a majority of the print and electronic press, the publishing industry, the foundations, government bureaucracies, public interest organizations, and many of the mainline churches are, as every survey shows, well to the left of the American public. People in these occupations display vastly different voting patterns from the rest of us; they are much more likely to think America irredeemably racist and sexist and, as a result, to favor quotas as public policy; they are much more likely to oppose the United States's defense of its interests abroad, particularly where the use of force is required. The syndrome is well known.

The first and best explanation of all this had always seemed that offered by Joseph Schumpeter in his great book *Capitalism, Socialism, and Democracy*. Schumpeter argued that capitalism requires, and so inevitably produces, a large and free intellectual class. The members of this class are not usually creators of ideas nor are they necessarily noted for power of intellect or rigor of analysis. They are called intellectuals simply because their work involves dealing with ideas. Perhaps some less flattering term should be found to describe them.

Intellectuals' hostility to capitalism, said Schumpeter, was the manifestation of class struggle. In a capitalist regime prestige and goods accrue to businessmen. To the degree that capitalism can be weakened by regulation or perhaps displaced altogether by socialism, prestige and material rewards will be shifted toward members of the intellectual class. Or so the members of that class suppose. (Real socialist societies seem not to have showered rewards on their intellectuals, other than scientists and engineers.) Leftist ideas are therefore held by intellectuals not because those ideas have intrinsic merit but because they provide weapons with which the existing order may be attacked. In a basically egalitarian society, such as that of the United States, it is necessary to attack from the left rather than from the right. No one supposes that all of this is a conscious design by intellectuals as individuals, much less as a class. Schumpeter's theory was not about a conspiracy but about a natural hostility born of envy, and probably not even the envious are entirely conscious of their own motivations.

All of this still seems plausible and surely it is at least a partial explanation, but it overlooks an obvious fact. As Grenier reminds us, the theory hardly accounts, for example, for the Hollywood Left. No one, to my knowledge, has ever classified Edward Asner or Norman Lear as an intellectual. Jacques Barzun, in *The House of Intellect*, demonstrated that practitioners of the arts, classical or popular, are not engaged in intellectual occupations, though individual practitioners may, by happenstance, be intellectuals as well. Yet writers, painters, actors, and film producers seem to be as overwhelmingly to the left of the general public as are the intellectuals. That fact fits very awkwardly with Schumpeter's class struggle analysis. Surely actors and producers who are far more famous and who make more money than the chairman of the board of General Motors are not motivated by envy of his position. Nor does it seem likely that they expect a government like that of Fidel Castro or Daniel Ortega to be more generous in supporting the arts or to allow more artistic freedom than the United States. Something else must be at work, something that accounts for the fact that the intellectual and artistic classes, which often appear to have little else in common, are both well to the left of other Americans.

Grenier thinks he has found the answer in Max Weber's observation that as societies lose their belief in "ultimate and sublime values"—which means, first and foremost, the loss of religious belief—certain groups of people will seek salvation in other ways, ways that will endow their lives with "pervasive meaning." With God dead, the most readily accessible transcendent principle is politics. Among those groups Weber identified as most vulnerable to such transcendental longings were university professors, clergymen, government officials, poets, and journalists. Not a bad prediction, and it accounts for the susceptibility of artists along with intellectuals to the mood and the politics of alienation.

But Grenier has not written a book of sociological theory. The ideas briefly sketched here provide a context for the wonderful set pieces that follow. No one need fear being bored for a moment, though there are those who will be infuriated by the book and others of us who will delight in the wit, the insight, and the knowledge of history and culture that Grenier brings to the task of exposing and then skewering the cultural Left. But Grenier does much more than skewer: he informs, he educates, he offers a sane perspective on a politically crazed subject. The book's subtitle, *Film, Art, and Politics*, describes the work he sets out to do and so splendidly accomplishes. The movie criticism is masterful. "The Uniforms That Guard: Kipling, Orwell, and Australia's *Breaker Morant*" is by itself worth the price of admission. The contrast between the films dissected in "The Hard Left and the Soft: Hollywood Tests Its Radical Limits" and those analyzed in "The Clint Eastwood Phenomenon: How He Became the World's Favorite Movie Star" illustrates the enormous cultural divide we are experiencing. "My own observation," Grenier writes, "of the crowds that turn out to see a new Eastwood movie in small industrial or agricultural towns near liberal-arts colleges, compared with those that turn out in the same towns to see a new film with Jane Fonda, lead me to think that there are virtually two nations, each easily recognizable by manners and speech." But the two nations are divided by basic values as much as by manners and speech. Grenier notes that Eastwood denies that his films are at all political: "Perhaps Eastwood's patriotism, his belief in the legitimacy of force, and his determination to see predators punished are so deeply ingrained that he doesn't even think of them as political. Perhaps he thinks such fundamental assumptions should be beyond the realm of political debate. And the man might have a point."

But if we are two nations, with Clint Eastwood and the American Civil Liberties Union representing the ideal types at opposite poles, which nation is to prevail? That is hard to say. The extremely liberal intellectual and cultural elites are a minority and their candidates regularly lose presidential elections, where ideology is more visible to the electorate than in congressional races, and they usually lose by whopping margins. But cultural wars are not necessarily decided by numbers alone. The

Left commands the intellectual and cultural heights of our society—the most prestigious universities, most of the best-known newspapers and magazines, the three major television networks, the writers and producers of movies, much of the staffs of the mainline churches, and much more. The Left therefore has a disproportionate influence over the agenda for public discourse and over the symbols by which we define ourselves.

There are, of course, dissidents within the intellectual and cultural elites. Not long ago there were many fewer such persons to articulate and defend traditional values. G. K. Chesterton once wrote that a philistine is only a person who is right without being able to explain why. There are now people who can explain why. But they remain few in number and they have great difficulty breaking through the mass media to reach the American public. That is an additional reason why Richard Grenier is to be cherished and wished as broad an audience as possible.

The Back Story

FOR MANY YEARS the cinema has been the class act of the entertainment world. Television actors want to be movie actors. Television directors want to be movie directors. Television writers want to be screenwriters. And this not just because they would be paid more, but because they could lavish more time on their work, it would be shown to a more influential audience by a more majestic projection system, and because, in their view certainly, film is a higher and more compelling medium.

The other arts pay similar tribute. Movie people may or may not read novels or listen to rock music or go to shows of modern art, but all novelists and artists and rock musicians go to the movies. The theater, displaced by films some decades ago as the high-status dramatic art form, is in a sorry state. Whereas a generation back, Broadway plays were often too artistically ambitious to be made into movies, they are now usually too vulgar or simple-minded. The list is long of "smash" Broadway hits (and big literary best-sellers) that have come to ignominious ends in Hollywood. For American popular music, the shifting of major activity from New York to Los Angeles is significant in itself. *Playboy*'s Hugh Hefner, also moving to Los Angeles, declared enthusiastically, "The stars of Hollywood are my royalty."

Status is deeply important, for in certain areas of life people still tend to emulate what the Victorians called their "betters." The film industry, once the province of triple-plated American philistinism, is now dominated by a younger, college-educated generation—many of its leaders from fashionable universities, many former radical activists from the 1960s—while television, much of it in the hands of the same studios that control movie production, has to cinema something of the relationship that farm clubs have to the major leagues in baseball. We consequently see national television (which might be thought to be the realm of the common man) relentlessly diffusing, sometimes in diluted form, styles and attitudes which have established themselves in what television people consider their elite art, the movies.

And what of the American public? It has been acknowledged for some time that most people no longer get their information mainly from reading (schools, the printed press), but from television. Perhaps less thought is given to the fact that what young and old spend most of their time watching on television is not TV news, but TV dramas of one sort or another made by the movies' farm clubs. They watch TV series and movies, artful fictions, written, directed, and acted by people of an "artistic" temperament, subject to "artistic" estrangement, the famed alienation of intellectuals in a notably acute form. This highly refractive source is providing Americans with much of their information. The pressures of the marketplace are a brake, but only a partially effective one. A wag once said that Czarist Russia's form of government was "autocracy tempered by assassination," and I have said that the politics of American entertainment is now "utopianism tempered by greed." A confident autocrat easily convinces himself that he, at least, won't be assassinated, and wishful Hollywood producers are astonishingly adept at convincing themselves that their movie, at least— a bearer of great truth for mankind—will make money.

My central subject is the spiritual quest of the artistic class for a more meaningful world, and the estrangement of this class from the traditional values of its own society, which it finds unworthy. Historically this is a novelty, having its beginnings only in the eighteenth century. But what is even more novel and quite unprecedented is the influence, via modern technology (and the deference of subaltern to superior), that a small class of artists exercises over the American population at large and

over a vast array of American institutions. It is partly because
of its indirect influence that I focus disproportionately on the
cinema, the "elite" art, as these days ideas and attitudes which
have their origin in the estrangement of a quite small intellectual
and artistic class come spewing out of every TV set. Sometimes,
of course, although cherished by an educated elite, these ideas
do not "take" with the general public. Sometimes they merely
numb, but sometimes they soften up the viewer, which is an
achievement in itself as it makes manners of thinking that might
earlier have seemed outlandish familiar and even tolerable.
Sometimes, indeed, this same thinking is eventually heard coming out of the mouths of untold numbers of the country's
schoolteachers.

A guidebook for U.S. high-school teachers published in the
1980s by the National Council for Social Studies affirmed categorically that to regard our American definition of human rights
as superior to the Soviet definition was inexcusably "ethnocentric." The American news media in those years, to maintain
"balance," asserted time and again that Soviet human rights
included free health care, virtually free housing, freedom from
unemployment, freedom from inflation, freedom from want.
Now that these pious claims to attainment of "economic rights"
have been massively and angrily declared fraudulent throughout
Eastern Europe, and that the Soviet press itself is filled with
daily accounts of Soviet hunger, homelessness, street crime,
appalling health care, the extreme privileges of the elite, and
corruption at every level (without a bribe in hospitals, no surgery
or even clean sheets), one has a right to wonder at the curiously
induced predisposition that made certain Americans so gullible
about palpably delusionary notions.

Ordinary Americans, frankly, resist such notions as best they
can, but they receive little support from the nation's professional
intellectual class, of which the artistic class is only the most
demented and most estranged. People in most cultures throughout history, after all, have historically "stuck with their own,"
been "ethnocentric," thought their own culture best. People's
desire to hold a high opinion of themselves is considerable, and
traditionally this desire has led them to hold a high opinion of

most things with which they were associated, including their society, their country. But in the West we now have a class of people who have a high opinion of themselves, indeed, but think the society from which they emerged contemptible. They find this society morally wretched, in fact, miserably lacking in the shining values that give life meaning.

દે&

Two quotations, both from Germans, loom over these essays. Friedrich Nietzsche, in *The Will to Power*, predicted that a decline in religious faith would lead to a dramatic rise of "the millenarian urge in temporal form." Nietzsche's expectation showed far more understanding of human character than Karl Marx, for example, whose historical predictions have found little in recent times to support them. My second German thinker, equally perceptive, is one of the fathers of modern sociology, Max Weber, who wrote that artists and intellectuals have great difficulty giving their allegiance to states or political systems "from which the absolute and sublime values have been withdrawn."

We arrive swiftly at the heart of the matter: the dismay of most modern artists—among them film directors and even actors—at the loss of absolute and sublime values. In the long range of history, this is new.

The author of the *Song of Roland*, an early version of which was chanted to Norman troops before the Battle of Hastings, did not see himself as marginal, adversarial, or alienated in any way from his lord and sovereign, William the Conqueror. Nor did Taillefer, the celebrated Norman warrior and *trouvére*, who, singing of Roland, led William's army into battle. The author of the *Niebelungenlied* did not secretly think Siegfried was a putz. Homer did not think Achilles was a putz. Corneille did not think Le Cid was a putz. Cimabue and Fra Angelico were not secret atheists, painting this religious trash because the church paid them big commissions.

Dante, whose *Divine Comedy* pictures a changeless universe ordered by God, its theme the gradual revelation of God to man, was a nobleman and officer of the Florentine cavalry that routed the Ghibellines at the battle of Campaldino. Cervantes, for all his mockery of the medieval romance in *Don Quixote*, fought as an officer of Spain against the infidel Turk at Lepanto, one of the greatest sea battles of history. Spain's greatest playwright, Lope de Vega, for the true church and that most Christian king, Philip II, sailed to conquer England in the Spanish Armada.

In the time of Chaucer, who married a lady-in-waiting at the court of England's Edward III, there were two great movements of social turbulence, the fiery theological dissent of Wycliffe (a so-called Protestant *avant la lettre*) and the peasant rebellion of Wat Tyler, who stormed London and beheaded the Archbishop of Canterbury. As if by magic, not a hint of either movement appears in Chaucer's supposedly all-embracing tapestry of medieval life, the *Canterbury Tales*. In *King John*, Shakespeare broke some kind of record by omitting from his play the only truly major event of King John's reign, the signing of the Magna Carta, a curtailment—ominous in Queen Elizabeth's eyes—of the power of the crown.

Spenser's *The Faerie Queene*, to say the least, expresses no ambivalence about Queen Elizabeth. John Milton was secretary of state to Oliver Cromwell. Even Goethe (and this was historically quite late for a literary man) was chief minister of state of the German principality of Saxe-Weimar and loyally followed his duke, Charles Augustus, in the wars against revolutionary France. For earlier times the list could be extended indefinitely. There are no exceptions.

The simple fact is that, until the French Enlightenment, Romantic movement, and the American and French Revolutions of the eighteenth century, the artist saw himself as a celebrant of his society and all its values, which to him—if not to aesthetes of today—were noble and heroic. It was only with the modern state's progressive renunciation of claims to represent the absolute and sublime and the appearance of the liberal, bourgeois state of limited power, giving people more freedom than they had ever had in history (often more than they knew what to do with), that the artist was cut loose.

෧

In the middle of the 1980s I was assigned by the *New York Times* to cast my eye on the spiritual state of the arts in America, above all on its political drift—if I should discover any. I was sent to movies, the theater, art shows, to concerts (classical and rock), to opera, to ballet, to professional wrestling. I attended poetry readings. I read literature most diligently. I read essays, novels, interviewed writers and artists. I read art history and biographies of great artists and writers of the past. I watched rock videos. I watched television commercials.

I had written on related subjects before, and have written about them since, and a number of my essays, particularly on the motion picture, appear in this collection. But until now I have never brought it all together, neither in the *New York Times* nor elsewhere. My exploratory journalistic mission was exhaustive, and I was glad of it. Nor has the landscape changed since my exploration. *Vaut le voyage*, as French guide books say. It was worth the trip. He who would understand the present, of course, must understand the past. Recalling the social and spiritual history of the artistic class, and tying the motion picture to historical developments in all the arts, will provide the reader with a framework for my thinking.

The *New York Times* is in the heart of the city's theater district, and still leads its Sunday "Arts & Leisure" section with theater—as the dean of New York arts, I suppose. So, often only a few hundred yards from the newspaper's offices, it was at the theater that I began. Considering that these were economic boom years, I found the American theater full of despair—despair for our society, the world, life, the free-enterprise system, the American hero, the American spirit, the American dream.

In *Glengarry Glen Ross*, which won a Pulitzer Prize for drama, we see Chicago real estate salesmen lie, scheme, cheat, swindle, and rob from one end of the play to the other, and author David Mamet explained that his play, like his earlier *American Buffalo*, represents American capitalism in microcosm. Thieves and hoodlums are no worse, he said, than "stockbrokers or corporate lawyers who are the lackeys of business." David Rabe's *Hurlyburly*, another great success, has a somewhat different theme: not the villainy induced by greed, but—in depicting TV casting directors in the Hollywood Hills—the horror of life empty of meaning.

In Michael Weller's *The Ballad of Soapy Smith*, an off-Broadway production seen at the prestigious Public Theater, the profit motive comes under attack again, this time in the manner of the late Bertolt Brecht of East Germany. We had a notable revival of *Curse of the Starving Class* by Sam Shepard, who in forty-odd plays has imposed himself as the bard of rootlessness and lost values, as well as of Arthur Miller's celebrated *Death of a Salesman*, with Dustin Hoffman playing the Willy Loman who famously "had the wrong dreams"—which is to say he dreamed he and his sons could be happy in a salesman's America. We had still another Sam Shepard, *A Lie in the Mind*, the end of the American family again, a familiar theme for him. The year before *Glengarry Glen Ross*, the Pulitzer Prize went to Marcia Norman's *'Night, Mother*, in which an overweight woman with no friends or interests calmly, serenely, as if it were the sweetest and most natural thing in the world, blows her brains out.

It takes no remarkable feat of perception to realize that what we are dealing with here, in the upper, highly "serious" reaches of the American theater, is a culture of alienation. For the dissatisfaction with America and sometimes the world expressed in the works of these playwrights is so diffuse, so general, so undiscriminating, so lacking in citations of improvable conditions or circumstances, that it is hard to imagine what one could do to make them happy. Many are quite beside themselves in their attacks on "greed," the profit motive.

But recent developments in East European countries with collectivist economies—now desperately seeking to introduce material incentives and market mechanisms to improve what they freely admit are ruinously unproductive systems with deplorable standards of living—make it seem as if "greed" (i.e., material self-interest) isn't such a bad thing. To adapt a line from e. e. cummings, it sometimes seems the only solution for these alienated artists of ours would be to stop the world and let them get off. We find this estrangement, in any event, throughout all the arts.

Literature, which prides itself on "ideas," is even easier to interpret than the theater. In the year or so of my assignment from the *New York Times*, the alienated literary legions were on parade in full regalia. Robert Coover, a judge for the PEN/ Faulkner Awards, declared in the *New York Times Book Review* that awards should go to "the rebel, the iconoclast." Robert Stone *(Dog Soldiers)*, in the same periodical, expressed his vast admiration for Karl Marx as a man of "common sense." Norman Mailer, who had expressed for years his "protest, disgust, and rebellion" against exploitive American society, continued to do so in a new book, as did E. L. Doctorow *(Ragtime)* in two new books.

And on it went: the late Mary McCarthy, who once saluted Leon Trotsky as "the most romantic man in history"; Joseph Heller, who in *Catch-22* succeeded in "Vietnamizing" even World War II; Joan Didion, who found her Vietnam in *Salvador*. The American Book Award was won by Don Delillo, actually promoted as the "master of alienation." John Irving *(The World According to Garp)* devoted his new novel to the full, happy life of two American abortionists who finally discover their true vocation: Socialism.

A tremendous launching was given to *House of the Spirits*, the first novel of Isabel Allende, niece of Marxist Salvador Allende Gossens of Chile, last seen alive when troops of General Augusto Pinochet surrounded Santiago's presidential palace. Allende confessed to France's Régis Debray that his promises to preserve Chile's pluralistic democracy were merely a "tactical necessity," and openly admitted to several others his intention to make Chile a one-party Marxist state. His overthrow by Pinochet in 1973 received by referendum the overwhelming endorsement of the Chilean people, but the name "Allende" remained magic to the U.S. literary community. Inscribed across advertisements for the book by the new novelist were the proud words: *"Niece of the former president of Chile, Salvador Allende."*

The extent to which this literary community has removed itself from the real world became even more glaring with the free elections in Chile in December 1989. First, both candidates for the presidency, of the Left and of the Right, supported Allende's overthrow by Pinochet. Moreover, the "leftist" victor, Christian Democrat Patricio Aylwin, had strongly opposed Allende's Marxist policies while he was president and is widely reported (secretly meeting with military leaders many times during the crisis) to have urged the Pinochet coup, which he immediately endorsed publicly. Results for parliament's 120-seat lower house were, if anything, even more conclusive. In what the leader of the Socialist Party called a "punishment vote," the previously powerful Chilean Communist Party won no seats, was wiped out. A left-wing Socialist faction (pro-Allende) won two seats. And the rest of the political spectrum—moderate Socialists (anti-Allende), centrists, and conservatives—won all the rest. The score was: Allende opponents, 118; Allende supporters, 2.

Literary prizes are a faithful reflection of elite opinion in the literary world, and Hilton Kramer, editor of the *New Criterion*, has written: "The truth is, it would be easier for a camel to pass through the eye of a needle than for a serious conservative writer to win a major literary prize in this country today." A leading American publisher told me recently that the principal impediment to publishing literature of a conservative or patriotic bent—although he and others do publish some—is not the taste of the book-buying public but the politics of the literary establishment: prestige writers, critics, editors, professors of literature, publishers' readers, agents, reviewers (writers themselves), even buyers for chain stores, who all identify with the literary class. "I can't get the reputation of being a conservative publishing house," he said. "I'd be dead."

Painting and sculpture, serenely removed from worldly preoccupations in the earlier age of the Ivory Tower, have in our day become perhaps the most rabidly "revolutionary" of all. In a show held in the public mall of the Graduate School and University Center of City University of New York, a German painter-sculptor named Hans Haacke exhibited an eight-foot-square wooden box. Stenciled on its side were the words "Isolation Box as Used by U.S. Troops at Point Salines Prison Camp in Grenada." Haacke, unlike most citizens of Grenada itself, did not approve of the island invasion. The title of the show was "Artists Call Against U.S. Intervention in Central America," and it staged exhibitions, performances, and other "events" in twenty American cities. Art journals reported these events extensively. In an America where support for the Grenada invasion was enormous, the show's antagonistic poster, by Claes Oldenburg, was put on the cover of *Arts* magazine. And works of brazen anti-American sloganeering, whose artistic level is at best that of a deft advertising layout, have become a prominent part of the country's artistic mainstream.

The busiest promoter of this new "political" art, in which inspirational "content" dominates completely and aesthetic questions are apparently considered reactionary, has been New York's New Museum of Contemporary Art. It has been joined by the leading New York art schools, Cooper Union and the Pratt Institute, the fashionable galleries, and, if more tentatively, by New York's Museum of Modern Art. In Washington, the Hirshhorn Museum, running to catch up, opened 1990 with "Culture and Commentary: An Eighties Perspective," an extensive multi-media exhibition devoted to strident denunciations of an array of social ills: AIDS, racism, sexism, "advancing materialism." The whole political-art movement is decidedly odd since one of its goals appears to be the specific repudiation of artistic criteria. According to the director of the Blum Art Institute of Bard College, a leader in the field, these art works' principal function is to "jolt the viewer into a new awareness of today's most pressing social issues: nuclear war, unemployment, toxic waste, feminism, Reaganomics . . ."

One wonders, other than calling for the perfect world of their dreams, if these artists would necessarily have a solution to the problem of unemployment (actually reasonably low) or affordable housing. But the artists are outraged nonetheless. Unemployment is an outrage. Nuclear war is an outrage. Sexism is an outrage. Ronald Reagan was an outrage.

Yet it was the Reagan administration, in the 1980s, which chose the most ardent proponent of this specifically anti-American agitprop, the New Museum for Contemporary Art, to represent the United States at the Cannes Film Festival of the art world, the Venice Biennale. This was an action far more bizarre than the Corcoran Gallery's recent imbroglio over the Robert Mapplethorpe show and a federally funded arts council's controversial subsidy of Andres Serrano's "Piss Christ" (a crucifix immersed in the artist's urine).

Future historians might well wonder, in fact, in examining photographs of the venomously anti-American works at the U.S. exhibition at the Venice Biennale, if our artists were not suffering from a severe malfunctioning of their survival instinct. For no society in history has offered artists as much freedom as the one whose institutions they attack with such frenzy.

In his *History of Western Philosophy*, Bertrand Russell states categorically that before the American and French Revolutions and the Romantic movement "almost all large states were aristocratic." Apparently considering persons ignorant of this fact to be beyond the reach of civilized discourse, Russell does not even bother to document his case, simply affirming that in past eras "aristocracy was unquestioned." It was certainly unquestioned by the literary and artistic communities, and before the Enlightenment and the transition to Romanticism all artists celebrated in their art either aristocratic or religious values. The modern notion of the "artist as eternal revolutionary" is pure Romantic revisionism. Shelley, that "ineffectual angel," acutely distressed at Prometheus's condition in Aeschylus's *Prometheus Bound*, wrote his own happy ending, *Prometheus Unbound*, although in Greek myth Prometheus ultimately reconciles himself to the authority of Zeus.

During the late eighteenth and early nineteenth centuries the absolutist monarchies of Europe were gradually replaced by liberal bourgeois governments—"liberal" in the sense of John Locke, Adam Smith, and John Stuart Mill. The power of these bourgeois states was severely limited, conceived as they were mainly to allow men to live in freedom and enjoy such property as they could acquire—to become, in sum, as prosperous as they could. As it happened, countries living under this form of government became the richest in the history of the world. For the first time whole populations were lifted out of the numbing poverty thought to be the inescapable fate of man. But the artistic community had loftier criteria and found such societies ignoble, squalid, money-grubbing, entirely lacking in the transcendant values that had been the basis of earlier regimes. Artists did not give these societies their allegiance then, and they don't give them their allegiance now.

As is typefied by the life of Byron, initial hatred of bourgeois society was completely aristocratic, "from above," and throughout most of the nineteenth century the Right was the favorite refuge of the alienated artist and intellectual when such alienation took political form. It is now almost entirely forgotten that as late as the 1890s, at the time of the Dreyfus case, Paris was the capital of the intellectual Right, and that, despite Emile Zola, most of France's fashionable writers and artists, including Edgar Degas, Alphonse Daudet, Huysmans, and Edmond de Goncourt, were, like Paris's entire *beau monde*, ardently royalist, anti-republican, anti-Dreyfus, and, yes, anti-Semitic.

"Down with the republic of thieves!" they cried disdainfully, while the mobs cried, "Death to the Jews." This form of alienated artistic thinking, of course, led to Auschwitz. But those who feel that intellectuals and artists are more capable than ordinary people of detached, rational appraisal of political options should reflect that the great German universities—those centers of humanist idealism—were swept by Hitler long before he won over the rest of the German population.

Meanwhile, on a large scale only in the twentieth century, messianic Socialism became available as another alternative creed, and for a time the alienated Western artist had a choice between anti-democratic regimes of either Left or Right. It was only the cataclysmic disrepute brought upon Rightist thinking by the evil of Nazi Germany, in fact, that left Socialism without competition as a belief system for those who suffer from the oppressive feeling that our society has no exalting sense of purpose. The aristocratic position, moreover, has become increasingly difficult to sustain in a democratic age, so that all fundamental criticism of our society is now delivered as if "from beneath," in the name of "the people." But any examination of the taste and manner of living of our most severe critics, considering their scorn for polyester suits, sixpacks, and TV game shows as well as the fact that they absolutely never choose to live in the Marxist-Leninist countries they so often profess to admire, leads one to suspect that their model is still aristocratic, and that Byron lives.

Nothing so bedevils discussion of the politics of artists and intellectuals as the self-serving notion, put forth by intellectuals themselves, that since their actions are not primarily economic but dictated by "higher" criteria they are therefore more capable of impartial, disinterested, reasonable thinking in politics than other people. But, writing early in the century, Germany's Max Weber arrived at the classic formulation regarding intellectuals in a world from which, as he said, "ultimate and sublime values" have been withdrawn. He wrote:

> The salvation sought by an intellectual is always based on inner need, and hence it is at once more remote from life, more theoretical and systematic, than salvation from external distress, the quest for which is characteristic of non-privileged classes. The intellectual seeks in various ways, the casuistry of which extends to infinity, to endow his life with a pervasive meaning. . . . there is (consequently) a growing demand that the world and the total pattern of life be subject to an order that is significant and meaningful.

Many artists and intellectuals embrace their alienation enthusiastically, thinking it gives them a more detached, objective view of our society. We have, thus, two points of view: That of the artist himself, conveniently stated by novelist E. L. Doctorow: "Our perceptions are sharpest when we're estranged." And that of Max Weber, which holds that it is precisely this estrangement or alienation which, in conflict with empirical realities, produces what he called "the intellectual's characteristic flights from the world." Among these flights (again with some foresight) Weber includes a variety of escapes: into a life of contemplation, into "nature unspoiled by human institutions," and, of course, into "collective revolutionary transformation of the world towards a more ethical order."

In a report to the *New York Times* from Brazil, Warren Hoag, now an assistant managing editor, wrote matter-of-factly of intellectuals of the country's cultural capital, Rio de Janeiro: "To a man or woman, their political views are left-of-center." He added that Rio's intellectuals had recently gathered to "pay homage" to President Daniel Ortega of Nicaragua, which would suggest that their views were quite a bit left of center, and that they presumably favored transforming the world in the direction of Weber's "more ethical order." In France, with an election in the offing, a conservative politician was asked if a conservative government would use its very considerable powers of patronage to punish its artistic enemies. No, said the politician resignedly, apparently in recognition of a similar phenomenon. The artistic community was "on the Left." This simply had to be accepted. It was a fact of life.

Such sweeping statements are frowned on in the United States, a country where in political matters a spade is notoriously not called a spade. In France a celebrity playwright-novelist-philosopher like the late Jean-Paul Sartre darted about, proclaiming from the housetops his ideological devotion to Stalin's Soviet Union, then (after disenchantment) to Mao's Cultural Revolution, while in passing ardently supporting the PLO massacre of Israeli athletes at the Munich Olympics. He risked no penalty. In the United States such behavior was not possible for a cultural figure with a large audience, basically because such positions would have awakened violent hostility on the part of the American population.

In the smaller, more tolerant, intellectual world, on the other hand, it became habitual—to escape confrontation with Ameri-

can public opinion while still avoiding dread "McCarthyism"—
to befog the air with euphemisms and plain evasions to the point
that political terminology in the press and media became hope-
lessly blurred. A whole generation of Americans, in fact, has
been raised with dangerously warped political perceptions due
to these pious evasions. But the artistic community in America,
often quite at sea regarding precise distinctions, is no less
alienated and "Left" than it is in Brazil or France. Indeed, why
should it be?

Needless to say, a fair number of non-alienated American
writers and artists vote truly "left-of-center" for perfectly respectable reasons, through quite reasonable conviction. A pref-
erence for the moderate Left, however, is not the politics that
has come to dominate the arts. Artistic politics over the last
quarter century has become increasingly exalted, holistic, by its
limitless scope and soaring aspirations quite alien to the temper-
ate, gradualist politics of mutual accommodation heretofore
traditional in both major American parties. For many artists,
clearly, our society fails to satisfy the "need to believe."

Our question is whether any democratic society, with its
bewildering freedoms and inevitable loss of certainty and absolutes, can fill this need. The sobering answer appears to be that
for a large part of our artistic and intellectual classes it cannot.
When a society is deprived of its freedom, of course, the rallying
cry "Liberty!" is often enough to infuse life with a sense of
meaning. But once this liberty has been attained the cohesion
and sense of community that its pursuit inspired seems to
evaporate. Alexis de Tocqueville, writing some 150 years ago in
Democracy in America, was convinced that religion was necessary for democracy, insisting that the indispensable foundation
of the institutions of the free republic which he admired and so
lucidly analyzed was religious faith. In a passage interestingly
omitted from the abridged Oxford World Classics edition of
Democracy in America (introduction by Henry Steele Comma-
ger), Tocqueville writes: "How can a society avoid extinction if,
as political ties weaken, moral ties are not reinforced? What will
a people become if, master of themselves, they no longer serve
God?"

The question shows Tocqueville in a more religious light than customary, and illustrates once again the view that societies are founded on transcendental belief. When such belief is absent, artists and intellectuals—whose reputation as "free thinkers" appears largely undeserved—are precisely those most bereaved.

క

Nietzsche first wrote the words "God is dead" in 1882. But a quarter century earlier, well before the American Civil War, the poet Heinrich Heine had written, "Kneel down, they are bringing the sacraments to a dying God." And the precipitous decline in Western religions in our own century cannot be questioned. Fervent Christian belief, considered essential to democracy by Tocqueville and quite taken for granted in American history, is now considered in "sophisticated" circles to be grotesque when it is not dangerous. Examples are everywhere ranging from the solemn to the silly. At a New York critics' screening of a film about female "body builders"—a subject with many peculiar moments but containing its share of humanity and pathos—one young woman provoked repeated bursts of laughter when declaring that the most important thing in her life was Jesus. If she had declared she developed her muscles to serve as a "role model" for other women the critics might have found her heroic. But when she stood in defeat, eyes wet, and said her faith was in Jesus, New York critics found her ludicrous.

The gap left by religion has been filled by a great surging forward of Nietzsche's "millenarian urge in temporal form." Historian Christopher Lasch has written, "Radical politics filled many empty lives, provided a sense of meaning and purpose . . ." Among intellectuals of high social and economic standing most subject to longings for meaning, Max Weber listed, prophetically: university professors, clergymen, government officials, certain nobles, "coupon-clippers," and, at the time farther down on the social scale, journalists, school teachers, "wandering poets," and some self-taught proletarians, among them Jews. Drawn up a full half-century before the shock waves of political radicalism that swept through many of these exact social classes in America in the 1960s and early 1970s, this is a remarkable list.

Sociologist Paul Hollander has meticulously documented the follies of these Western intellectuals in their attempts to locate a better world in Moscow, Peking, Havana, Hanoi, and even Tirana (Albania). In his *Political Pilgrims*, he analyzes intellectuals' deep-rooted illusions about other societies and their "recurrent fantasies of new forms of liberation and collective gratification." The spectacular repudiation of collectivist systems in 1989 by the peoples of Eastern Europe—not to mention the student movement leading to the massacres around Tiananmen Square in China—make these collectivist fantasies appear more bizarre than ever. Yet they persist.

Little so discredits today's lovers of arts and letters as the mindless assumption that artistic figures of other periods were always "anti-establishment" or "on the Left." And it would probably come as a revelation to most of today's art lovers to learn that as recently as the 1930s, as I have indicated, European artists and intellectuals in pursuit of political fantasies were, depending on the country, as likely to swing to the revolutionary Right as the revolutionary Left, and some swung first one way and then the other.

After all, Hitler, too, offered a society with an exalting, transcendental sense of purpose, nothing less than a racist utopia—its main limitation being its particularism, which is to say it had a lot more to offer if you were a German than if you were not. But despite doctrines that are today universally considered inhumane, pernicious, and totally irrational, Hitler created such intellectual excitement at German universities that the entire German student movement passed under Nazi control in 1930—three years before Hitler was appointed chancellor. Other European Fascist movements, variants of the Nazi model (in Italy, Spain, Hungary, Romania, Bulgaria), had similar success.

The artists and intellectuals of France—historically the most eminent of the nations overrun by Nazi Germany—are an interesting case study. Considered by many the most brilliant prose writer of the period, Louis-Ferdinand Céline *(Journey to the End of Night)* was first a Communist, then a Fascist and rabid anti-Semite. Two of the country's most gifted young writers, Drieu La Rochelle and Robert Brasillach, were Fascists and pro-Nazi. Nobel Prize winner André Gide, as war approached in the 1930s, was typical enough. Wealthy, upper-class, Protestant, homosexual, vaguely royalist, anti-Semitic—and never having voted—Gide at sixty-three suddenly threw in his lot with the Communist-Socialist Popular Front, only to break with Communism after a trip to Moscow.

Novelist André Malraux, author of *Man's Fate*, had even more zigzags on his record. Regarding the Civil War in China (invoked in *Man's Fate*), he told some people he had been with Mao and the Communists, others he had been with Chiang Kai-Shek's Kuomintang. During the Popular Front—also never having voted—Malraux came close to joining France's Communist Party but, preferring to sit out the German Occupation in a Riviera villa being served by a valet with white gloves, he leapt into the Resistance movement's right wing once the Americans had landed, becoming in time General de Gaulle's minister of culture.

Jean-Paul Sartre—once again—had never voted when (his master Heidegger now a Nazi) he suddenly joined a supremely ineffectual Left-wing intellectual French Resistance unit and, after the war, became one of the few literary figures actually to designate himself a Communist "fellow traveller." After eulogizing Palestinian terrorism, including, as mentioned, the massacre of Israeli athletes at Munich, Sartre in his last days developed a strong sympathy for Israel.

Examples of such erratic extremism on the part of artists and writers could be continued ad infinitum. Americans and Britons were spared the ordeal by fire of a Nazi occupation, but Ezra Pound and Wyndham Lewis braved popular opinion and were pro-Fascist. P. G. Wodehouse, perhaps naively, made what was certainly taken at the time as a pro-Nazi radio broadcast from Germany. In post-war France, Pablo Picasso, having concerned himself with politics rather little in his life, suddenly became a fervent Communist supporter, summering with French Communist Party leader Maurice Thorez at a time when Picasso's paintings were vilified as decadent in the Soviet Union and hidden from sight in the vaults of Leningrad's Hermitage.

Among Germans, playwright Bertolt Brecht, although steadfast in his theoretical support of Communism, never put his theories to the test by staying in the world's first "workers' state," but, fleeing the Nazis, crossed the USSR like a shot and passed World War II admidst the capitalist rot of Pacific Palisades, California. In music, conductor Wilhelm Furtwangler and pianist Walter Gieseking lent prestigious support to the Nazi regime. Renowned Wagnerian soprano Kirsten Flagstad, a Norwegian, became the wife of that most famous Nazi collaborator of all, Vidkun Quisling.

Gabriele D'Annunzio, the most celebrated Italian writer of his time, was an ardent Fascist, as was Italy's most renowned playwright, Luigi Pirandello. Carlo Levi was a Communist. Ignazio Silone was also a Communist (but recanted). Hungary's Arthur Koestler *(Darkness at Noon)*, first a Communist, later one of the post-war period's most noted anti-Communists, slid off in his later years into the occult. Having excoriated Hindu mysticism in *The Lotus and the Robot*, he left funds at his death to study that alleged Hindu rising into the air known as "levitation," which he had earlier ridiculed.

In Britain again, poets W. H. Auden and Stephen Spender, never having read newspapers let alone voted, abruptly in the 1930s took up Communism, which they later repudiated. Auden rediscovered Christianity, while his friend Spender wrote one of the most important contributions to the celebrated anti-Communist confessional *The God That Failed*. For a time co-editor of the distinguished anti-totalitarian British journal *Encounter*, Spender a few years later again began to drift to the radical Left. Their elder, playwright G. B. Shaw, had at one point managed simultaneously to admire both Lenin and Mussolini.

I am not forgetting that some of these abrupt conversions to Communism occurred when Adolf Hitler seemed the greatest threat to Western civilization and when the Soviet Union had convinced many in the democratic West that Communism was "the leader in the fight against Fascism." But by no means all these new Western Communists fell away at news of the 1939 pact between Stalin and Hitler. And what of the Communists of Germany itself, who in the critical year 1933 deserted the Communist Party in droves for Hitler's Brown Shirts, constituting the so-called "roast beef Nazis," brown on the outside, red on the inside? There is little general recognition—confining ourselves now to the artistic and intellectual classes—that behind all this floundering about, these leaps and death-defying *volte-faces*, lay a certain thematic consistency, an attempt to find a system of absolutes to replace a painful spiritual void.

The great economist Joseph Schumpeter, in his one general historical work, *Capitalism, Socialism, and Democracy*, showed himself to be another of this century's seers who, however gloomily, acknowledged that capitalist society creates spiritual hungers it cannot gratify. Unlike other refugees from Hitler, who once in America often tended to see malign Fascist plotters around every corner, Schumpeter saw the danger to the democratic entrepreneurial system as coming from within itself. The system would continue to give rise to profound political attacks from intellectuals, he anticipated, but stressed that it would be a *fundamental error to believe that these attacks arose primarily from grievances of a material sort*. Criticism from this quarter, he wrote flatly, "cannot be met effectively by rational argument."

We should not deceive ourselves. Fascism provided an inspiring escape for any number of 1930s artists and intellectuals alienated by our lackluster society. It was finally only Hitler, the Antichrist, the Great Beast, who brought the Fascist Right into vast and seemingly irreversible disrepute, discredited as have been few political movements in history. In our day lost artistic souls, uneasy in Zion, burdened by freedom, made anxious by our lack of certitudes, desperate to give their lives a sense of purpose, a higher meaning, must flee to the glorious promises of messianic Socialism.

One might expect that a minimal level of rationality would

require artists seeking a "meaningful" alternative society to judge it by the same standards by which they judge their own. But this, alas, is one of their most consistent failings. They judge our society by the flaws and inadequacies they see all about them. But they tend to judge alternative societies, of which they often retain a peculiarly stubborn ignorance, by these societies' officially announced ideals, a practice Jean-Paul Sartre once defended as necessary to "preserve hope." Aleksandr Solzhenitsyn has reflected on such people. They have illusions, he says, which can only be destroyed by the "pitiless crowbar of events."

Messianic socialism did not present itself as a really sizeable political movement until the revolutionary Paris Commune of 1871 following France's defeat in the Franco-Prussian War. And it took hold more slowly than is commonly realized. Although Lenin today lies in Red Square enshrouded in the red banner of the Paris Commune, in 1871 the Commune attracted the active support of exactly one well-known artist, Gustave Courbet. Far more typical of the period were France's Impressionists.

Visitors to American art museums filing reverently through rooms devoted to this luminous group of painters might be shocked to learn their politics. Degas was the most extreme. Like most of the French literary establishment and social upper-crust, he was a flaming royalist, anti-Dreyfusard, and fierce anti-Semite. Edouard Manet, son of a high official of both the Bourbon and Orleans monarchies, also despised the "monied mediocrities" of his time. Like Delacroix before him and his close friend Baudelaire, Manet had a democratic spasm—in his case for the infant Third Republic—but soon returned to his distaste for the merchant class and patrician conservatism.

Auguste Renoir boasted, erroneously, of descent from an "orphan of the guillotine," a child of French aristocrats executed during the French Revolution, and his social attitudes were prodigiously conservative, objecting as he did to virtually everything modern. His utopia located firmly in the past, Renoir adamantly opposed the income tax, lending at interest, banks, railroads, electricity, sulphur matches, formal education, and even the new science of dentistry. He was vehemently hostile to feminism and a practicing xenophobe. Loyal of course to *la France réelle*, Renoir, Degas, and Manet all flocked to the colors at the outbreak of the Franco-Prussian War, Renoir serving in the cavalry.

Pissarro, from an upper-class Sephardic Jewish family but as hostile as the others to modern mercantile society, took the opposite rejection route and was an anarchist. Claude Monet rancorously refused membership in France's Legion of Honor. Degas was most outspoken about "the Jew" being responsible for what he considered France's moral and cultural decline, but even Emile Zola, notorious for defending Dreyfus, produced abundant negative, racist Jewish stereotypes in his fiction. He describes the owner of the big department store in his *Au Bonheur des Dames*, who is not Jewish, as "more Jewish than all the Jews in the world."

Hitler has made it hard for us to see that what these nineteenth-century artistic spirits didn't like about Jews was that they symbolized for them par excellence everything they deplored about the vulgar, mercantile world. Today, of course, with racism discredited, artistic spirits who yesterday would have been anti-Semites have risen to being socialists. And, whereas yesterday the community that symbolized for many the greed and materialism of the modern age was "World Jewry," today that position is obviously held by—America. It is there for all to see, go where you will, abroad or at home. You may try it for size on any exalted, artistic radical you meet, filled with loathing for our soulless, materialist, capitalist world. Yesterday's anti-Semite is today's anti-American.

A hundred years ago in France the indulgent judgment among the more educated supporters of the Left was that anti-Semitism was simply "the socialism of fools." Anti-Semites, perfectly consonant with this analysis, have today gone up-market, merely shifting their hate symbol. There is no need here for speculation. It has been pointed out in Europe many times. Take almost any piece of anti-capitalist, anti-American polemic produced by a highly charged modern radical movement such as West Germany's Greens. Wherever the words "America" or

"United States" appear, substitute "International Jewry." You will have in your hands a Nazi text.

Three examples might serve to give the "feel" of the modern artist alienated by our meaningless mercantile society. All three, it happens, have had connections with the theater and motion pictures. Gore Vidal has written many screenplays and spends half the year in Hollywood. Norman Mailer has written and directed three "underground" movies. The late Mary McCarthy was a long-time theater critic, her brother Kevin is a screen actor, and her novel *The Group* was made into a successful motion picture. All three have been highly visible. All three are admired in Hollywood. They are of course principally known as novelists and essayists, in pursuit of which calling they have had the opportunity to set forth their ideas more fully and systematically than any painter, playwright, or film director, which is why I have chosen them.

In addition to movies, television, and his literary career, Gore Vidal has had an active political life, running for Congress in Dutchess County, New York, and in California in 1982 for the Democratic nomination for the U.S. Senate. Although from a conservative, upper-class family, Vidal, as contributing editor of *The Nation*, is unlikely to object to being described as "left." Witty, urbane, and a complete Tory in manner, he combines his left-wing politics with a highly luxurious life style, maintaining homes on the Amalfi Coast, in Rome, and in the Hollywood Hills. He does not favor, he says, "unilateral socialism," which seems to imply that if multilateral socialism were to arrive he might, for example, be happy to surrender his palatial oceanside home in Ravello to the state as a refuge for unwed mothers.

Mary McCarthy went much farther on the road to equality. Celebrated in some circles for her opposition to the Vietnam War, she is not often remembered as having opposed the war against Nazi Germany as well. To be fair, she shifted her official position in the last days, because, she said: (1) we were winning anyway, and (2) "in her heart" she had been pulling for us all along.

One wonders if the United States had won in Vietnam whether Mary McCarthy might have realized that in her heart she'd been pulling for us there also. But her position on total economic equality is the most interesting. She realized, she admitted in an interview in her last years, that she enjoyed many material advantages denied to the masses, but declared she would willingly give them up in favor of a total economic leveling, confident that the "intellectual excitement" of such complete equality would be sufficient compensation.

Norman Mailer, too, is all for equality—presumably somewhere down the line. In the early 1950s, with even Mary McCarthy expressing qualified patriotism, Mailer felt nothing but hostility toward American society, which, he wrote, was driven toward war "as an answer to insoluble problems." "Great artists," he explained, "are almost always in opposition to their society." When similar spirits turned their hopeful thoughts of a better world toward Havana, Hanoi, Peking, and Managua, Mailer through thick and thin maintained complacent dreams about the Soviet Union itself, throughout, in fact, the entire Brezhnev regime—now entirely discredited in Moscow. The Soviet Union, Mailer said, was so lacking in the capacity to inflict harm on the United States that he saw no inconvenience if even Mexico became communist. What this would do to Mexico, or what we would do with the millions of refugees that might come flooding across the Rio Grande, he did not bother to consider.

But Mailer, even more than Gore Vidal and Mary McCarthy, has brought living in contradiction to his principles to the level of high art. Vidal and McCarthy, after all, have lived more or less in the manner of the class into which they were born, while Mailer, raised in a modest family in Brooklyn, has made relentless efforts to attach himself socially to the upper class by choice of wives, clothing, accent, summer residence, and all other available accoutrements. Mailer hated the Vietnam War, but at a recent West Point football game basked in the company of the man who commanded our forces, General Westmoreland. Although he hated the war, says Mailer, he loves the men who

THE BACK STORY xliii

fought it. The novelist considers capitalist tycoons rapists, furthermore, but is thrilled to be in their company.

I was at a small Manhattan dinner party when Mailer, having somehow failed to take this in before, suddenly realized that a young man sitting near him was the son of Stavros Niarchos, the Greek shipping tycoon. Mailer rose instantly, his face glowing, and, making a sound part moan, part gloating, reached out to embrace such greatness. So Mailer hates war but loves warriors, hates capitalism but loves capitalists.

Once again the key to the American spirit is provided by Tocqueville, in the concluding chapter of *Democracy in America*.

> There is little energy of character, but customs are mild and laws humane. If there are few instances of exalted heroism or of virtues of the highest, brightest, and purest temper, men's habits are regular, violence is rare, and cruelty almost unknown. Human existence becomes longer and property more secure; life is not adorned with brilliant trophies, but it is extremely easy and tranquil. Few pleasures are either very refined or very coarse, and highly polished manners are as uncommon as great brutality of tastes. Neither men of great learning nor extremely ignorant communities are to be met with; genius becomes more rare, information more diffused. The human mind is impelled by the small efforts of all mankind combined together, not by the strenuous activity of a few men. There is less perfection, but more abundance, in all the productions of the arts. The ties of race, of rank, and of country are relaxed; the great bond of humanity is strengthened.

One may find the above analysis slightly overdrawn and yet feel there is something in it. And the most cursory reflection on the style and values of the people I have described makes it perfectly clear that they have no intention whatever of repudiating glory, genius, the arts, great deeds, a brilliant society, elevation of the human spirit, and the hope of leaving an immense mark in history (all Tocqueville's words) just to assure "material wellbeing" and "tranquil habits."

History has played a dirty trick on these people. Everything about their taste, temperament, manner of living, and grand behavior marks them out as members or votaries of the aristocratic camp. In an earlier age they would have displayed undisguised contempt for the populist, equalitarian democracy that Alexis de Tocqueville so admired. But here they are marooned in the modern, democratic age, which offers so little support for aristocratic beliefs. By a dazzling leap that blinds them to their own hypocrisy, they have therefore contrived to turn everything on its head. They will prove their superiority to other people not by claiming blood lines, or in any of the old rank-differentiated ways, but by earnestly endorsing a *morally* superior principle, such as, let's say, reorganization of the world to ensure the total equality of all human beings.

This has the advantage of being quite unattainable, of course, so Gore Vidal will continue to enjoy his seaside mansion on the Amalfi Coast, as Mary McCarthy enjoyed her quail's eggs, unavailable in most peasant communes. Their faith in an ethical reordering of the universe has fulfilled their deep "need to believe," however, their need to give life significance. It is one of the oddities of our time that a peculiar combination of historical circumstances has led such people into a position diametrically opposed to their true beliefs, which are, obviously, not in the least democratic.

The most prescient analyst of the contemporary relationship of art and politics was the Italian Marxist Antonio Gramsci, who, it is worth noting, was drama critic of the Socialist organ *Avanti!* and regularly reviewed stage productions of the Fascist playwright Luigi Pirandello before being incarcerated and dying in one of Mussolini's prisons. A deviant from a Leninist (and even Marxist) point of view, Gramsci formulated in his *Prison Notebooks* the doctrine that those who want to change society must change man's consciousness, and that in order to accomplish this they must first control the institutions by which that consciousness is formed: schools, universities, churches, and, perhaps above all, art and the communications industry. It is these institutions that shape and articulate "public opinion,"

the limits of which few politicians can violate with impunity. Culture, Gramsci felt, is not simply the superstructure of an economic base—the role assigned to it in orthodox Marxism— but is central to a society. His famous battle cry is: *capture the culture*.

Gramscians, of course, would have no chance whatever of "capturing the culture" if it weren't for the spiritual estrangement of the artistic and intellectual classes. The culture, obligingly, might almost be seen as surrendering to the enemy without need of being captured, and what we are witnessing is certainly far less the result of a plot or conspiracy from outside than of a transformation from within. Yet it is not without interest that Gramscian doctrine exists, and that in Europe, far more than in the United States, great numbers of the principle participants, with varying degrees of deliberate intent, are trying to put it into practice.

The United States, in fact, is hardly aware of Gramsci. Half my life has been spent studying and working abroad. As a journalist I have reported on most of the world's cultural capitals. And wherever I go in the centers of intellectual life of Western Europe, at least, there is talk of Gramsci. Recently invited by the West German Foreign Ministry to lecture on American popular culture before a gathering of German intellectuals at the Friedrich Ebert Foundation, I heard German Socialists and Greens quoting, in addition to Gramsci's "Capture The Culture," the words of Gramsci's celebrated German disciple, the late German student leader Rudi Dutschke. An intellectual young German woman told me earnestly that she and her friends were engaged in what Dutschke called (*his* most famous expression) *the long march through the institutions*—meaning universities, arts, media, government agencies. . . .

Only in America, it seems, is it possible for a critic to be in the editorial offices of an influential organ of the press, receive compliments on a report he has written on film, television, or the theater, answer modestly, "It's just straight Gramsci," and have an editor say: "Who's Gramsci?" The critic answers in explanation, "capture the culture," which produces, frankly, a blank look. For the editors of the cultural pages of many a major

American news institution, "culture," apparently, is an opening-night party on Broadway, or Lincoln Center, or perhaps rubbing shoulders with rich patrons at the Museum of Modern Art.

The American motion picture industry, of course, had particularly humble social origins, unlike France, where Jean Renoir, a leading film director even in silent movie days, was the son of the great Impressionist painter Auguste Renoir. But one encounters a peculiar dead nerve in the American attitude toward not only motion pictures but toward other arts as well. With all the current folderol about "art," with a National Endowment for the Arts, state and municipal arts councils, and as, Jacques Barzun points out, more people with artistic aspirations than we can reasonably make use of, there are still vestiges of the old American artistic philistinism, a certain naivete about the "artist." Earlier, the American yahoo was indifferent to art, sometimes hostile. Now he is for it. It is great. Association with it gives social prestige. But what is it? Is it the carrier of values? Of attitudes which inform our whole society? That he is ill equipped to say.

This is particularly true of the motion picture, which is odd because the cinema—a fact which would have quite astonished its creators—has become such a high-status operation. In Gramsci's day the prestigious dramatic form was the theater itself (hence Pirandello). Today, there can be no question: it is the cinema. And yet old habits of thought hang on.

When Henry James died, in 1916, both D. W. Griffith and Charlie Chaplin had already produced films widely considered today to be masterpieces. Their authors are now often accorded the honorific "genius." Yet no character in a Henry James novel ever goes to the "flickers" or even a "cinematograph," nor does James once comment on the new art. In reading Marcel Proust (died 1922), or even James Joyce (died 1941), one would never discover that the cinema had been invented. When in the 1930s William Faulkner and F. Scott Fitzgerald went to Hollywood to earn a living they were felt to have fallen on evil times indeed and Faulkner expressed the greatest contempt for the medium. Nathanael West's *The Day of the Locust*, a major 1939 novel actually set in Hollywood, is suffused with a sense of degradation and ends in nightmare.

Edmund Wilson, probably the most influential writer of a whole generation in placing literature in its social and political context, despised "the movies" throughout his entire career. Although Wilson lived until 1972, and saw many a trashy play on Broadway, he never had anything but disdain for the cinema, and several times, when he encountered a novel so appalling it beggared description, said it was "as bad as a movie" and let it go at that, apparently feeling that in that nether world distinctions became meaningless. The long-established tradition of the American educated class was to treat the cinema with contempt.

In Petrograd, meanwhile, Vladimir Ilyich Lenin announced: "Of all the arts, for us cinema is the most important." As early as 1919, Lenin was deeply impressed by D. W. Griffith's *Intolerance* and proceeded to devote to the new art the full resources of the Soviet state. Already in the 1920s, Eisenstein (*The Battleship Potemkin, October*) and Pudovkin (*The Mother*, from Gorky) produced works still studied in film schools for their technical mastery. Eisenstein—inspired by Griffith's *Birth of a Nation*, although he was to use his camera for quite different purposes—declared that the motion picture was the most powerful means of political propaganda in world history.

In Europe, East as well as West, the cinema has had for a long time what the French call its *titres de noblesse* (titles of nobility), titles only recently acquired in America, and that amid much confusion. With Hollywood movies playing to vast audiences all over the world, it wasn't until fairly recently that *New York Times* film reviews began regularly mentioning the director's name. Before then, with some exceptions (Orson Welles, John Ford, Alfred Hitchcock), American film reviewers would no more identify the artistic creators of a movie than they would the artistic creators of a sausage.

❧

It is a sour irony that in the United States, of all places, most university presidents, "media barons," and others at the commanding heights of both the economy and government are serenely unaware that art in our time has become heavily and even ponderously ideologized. An explanation for this conspicuous lacuna that I used to offer fellow students and journalists in France was, despite the overuse of "ideology" as a buzzword, that America was not an ideological country, that it had little traditional acumen in analyzing ideology, and that it could stare straight at an ideological doctrine, particularly when embedded in "culture," and not even recognize it. Most Americans, I said, would not know an ideological concept if it punched them in the face.

This explanation, still plausible concerning much of the American population, is getting hard to sustain regarding the country's educated classes. In any event, I am tired of it. My goal is to alter the way these things are seen, both movies and all art. Simply that.

And so, on with the show.

Coming Attractions

A T THE TIME of its appearance in 1982, I wrote that *E.T.—The Extra-Terrestrial* might possibly become "one of the most successful films of all time." I erred on the side of moderation. According to the trade's rough rules of thumb, *E.T.* was estimated in 1989 to have been seen in U.S. movie houses by well over 100 million people (including repeaters), to which should be added further millions who have seen the film in their homes thanks to the exploding market for videocassette rentals, and still further millions who have seen it in foreign countries. With the tendency of show business to aggrandize, Hollywood gives its comparative box-office figures in inflated dollars, and *Gone with the Wind* (1939), which led *Variety*'s list of "All-Time Film Rental Champs" for decades, has consequently now sunk to twenty-second position. But the size of *E.T.*'s audience, which might in time reach a billion viewers, is impressive. Nor is director-producer Steven Spielberg ill-rewarded financially. He is the highest paid person in Hollywood, higher than Eddie Murphy, higher than Sylvester Stallone, seventeen times higher than the CEO of General Motors. His combined pre-tax income for 1988 and 1989 was $105 million.

Spielberg and his friend George Lucas are an unprecedented phenomenon, not only in motion pictures but in the whole history of story telling. What with Spielberg's *E.T.*, Lucas's *Star Wars* series, and the Lucas-Spielberg *Indiana Jones* series, the two of them, Lucas and Spielberg, either as director, producer, or twice working in tandem, have made eight out of the ten leading money-making films of all time. Even in inflated dollars, this is an imposing score. Whether Lucas and Spielberg have captured the culture, or the culture has captured them, could be debated, but something is going on. For Lucas and Spielberg have some rather clear ideas about the world and how we should conduct our lives, and they are not shy about presenting them in their chosen art, a very compelling medium of expression.

Given the stupefying size of the audience for these films, the comment of as intelligent an observer as Paul Johnson is curious: "Those who want to influence men's minds have long recognized that the theater is the most powerful medium." This was certainly not the opinion of Lenin, and Johnson's prime example is a play staged by the Earl of Essex—in 1601. Johnson goes on to conclude that in the 1960s and 1970s German playwright Bertolt Brecht (as abject a servitor as Stalin ever had) "was probably the most influential writer in the world." Since the audience of all Brecht's plays together, produced in all the languages into which they have been translated, is in the tens of thousands, while that of Lucas's and Spielberg's films is in the hundreds of millions, the point seems hardly worth discussing.

Johnson, who appears to be a modern avatar of Edmund Wilson, whose ossified disdain for "the movies" I have discussed earlier, would doubtless argue that Lucas and Spielberg are childish. But I met and knew Brecht in his last days in East Berlin, as well as knowing his plays, and I found Brecht very childish. And I do not hold him responsible for his mistress, Ruth Berlau, once chasing me down a staircase screaming *"filthy American pig!"* which, I suppose, can happen to anyone. Perhaps my essays on Lucas and Spielberg, and my short piece on Brecht, will throw some light on who is more influential, and even on who is worse for you, these California moviemakers or the man who in the early 1930s in pre-Hitler Germany was called the "bard of the KPD" (*Kommuniste Partei, Deutschland*). They appeal, I would suggest, to different childish audiences.

But another kind of audience I deal with in these essays, rambunctiously different in orientation, is that for the films of Clint Eastwood and another actor—who has replaced Eastwood even as Eastwood replaced John Wayne—Sylvester Stallone. For the views and attitudes of a certain cultivated elite, which find their way so easily into plays, novels, and movies, are often vigorously contested on a more popular level. And these popular views, too, find their way into movies, although when their popular character is embarrassingly *infra dig*—at least until proved beyond question to be the source of really big money— it is very much swimming against the stream. I recount in my essay on Clint Eastwood the truly freakish circumstances which led to his becoming, for many years, the world's leading movie star. But the story of Sylvester Stallone's big chance has never been told. In fact, he might not know the key part himself.

In 1975 an undistinguished young actor with an Italian name came to a team of independent producers named Chartoff and Winkler, and then to United Artists, with a script he'd written himself. It was about a prizefighter. The United Artists executives read it without excessive enthusiasm. Perhaps it was time for a new boxing movie, they thought reasonably. But this young actor wanted to play the leading role himself. Damn! Could he act? The actor sent along a well-received small movie he'd played in, *The Lords of Flatbush*, about a gang of young men in Flatbush, Brooklyn. The executives screened the film, thought the leading man, the only good-looking one in the gang, didn't look very Italian. But not bad, not bad. They felt lucky, drew up a contract, and signed. Then they caught sight of the new actor-writer-director they were betting their studio's money on. "My God!" one of the executives cried. "He's not the good-looking one at all! It's the wrong one!" Thus was born unto the world *Rocky*.

And the origins of *Rambo*, if slightly less eccentric, were unusual enough. Stallone had some disastrous failures (*F.I.S.T.*, *No Place To Hide, Paradise Alley*), and it was beginning to look as if moviegoers only liked him as Rocky. Later on, when *First Blood* (the first Rambo) became a runaway hit, hindsight specialists convinced themselves that the film had been a sure thing from the start, a certain blockbuster. But in the early 1980s, when *First Blood* went before the cameras—with Jane Fonda still riding high, winning an Academy Award for her anti-Vietnam War *Coming Home*—it was not at all certain that America was ready for a gut-patriotic movie vindicating American soldiers who had fought for their country in Vietnam. I quote two speeches from the film, first a Green Beret colonel:

It's going to look great in Arlington Cemetery. "John Rambo. Congressional Medal of Honor. Carried out countless missions behind the enemy lines in Vietnam. Shot for vagrancy in Jerkwater, U.S.A."

Second, Rambo himself, his last lines in the movie, delivered to his colonel:

I didn't want to go there! You sent me! We did our best to win! But somebody didn't want us to win! And then I come home and they call me a baby killer and I can't even get a job in a car wash!

Shortly before the inauguration of the Vietnam Veterans War Memorial, film critics called *First Blood*, which they hated with a passion, "stupid" and "implausible," the more reflective among them concluding that it sent a "mixed message" with respect to the military character. Whereas *First Blood* delivered one of the most *un*mixed messages I have ever seen in a movie. Vets understood it. Millions of moviegoers understood it. The film suggests that when a great nation commits itself to war, it must win or there will be the devil to pay. And it is a severe understatement of *First Blood*'s burden to say it conveyed the feeling that the black, tomb-like excavation on the Mall in Washington, which at the time had no flag, no statue, no inscription but the names of the 57,939 sent to their deaths, might in their honor at least bear the legend: *They died for their country.*

I do not want to make *First Blood* appear either more or less than it is. It is a popular, mass-market movie. The *Rambo* sequels, while still patriotic, became less realistic, and even more popular. Again, hindsight experts are now convinced that it was obvious from the start that the *Rambo* series would have a monstrous success. But it was far from obvious. On quite a few occasions (*Rambo* and *Rocky* are recent examples) popular culture and the masses have rebelled against elite views foisted on them in the name of entertainment, but the opportunity for such a rebellion is frequently the result of some accident, almost a fluke. After the millions start pouring in, of course, Eastwood and Stallone become pillars of the community, and all seems preordained.

For the moneybags of Hollywood are opened far more easily for a laudatory little film about old members of the violent Weather Underground like *Running on Empty* (1988, a terrific failure), than they are for some little film representing patriotic or traditional values. Hollywood of the 1930s, for example, during the Great Depression, produced an immensely successful series of movies on inventor heroes, on the men who created the electric light, telephone, steamboat, pasteurization (Louis Pasteur), a cure for syphilis (Paul Ehrlich), and even the gas-burning refrigerator. Whereas, although computers are changing the world, one of the most dynamic and promising elements in our society, I wonder how long we will have to wait for a film portraying, even as background, the life and work of the "computer hacker." Although if some screenwriter in the Hollywood Hills cooks up a plot about "big business" stealing Apple Computer from Steven Jobs, perhaps we might get a movie after all.

The following essays and short pieces are reprinted (with permission) from *Commentary*, the *New York Times*, and the *Washington Times*. Barring alterations of tense and elimination of "now's," "recently's," and a handful of topical references of transient interest, they are as I first wrote them. No judgments are changed. My speculations as to the dubious future of the *Star Wars* series, written after the second installment, are presented intact. After a meteoric trajectory of three films, the series came to a crashing end with *Return of the Jedi*. The tone of my pieces is varied, some solemn, some flippant. What the articles selected for this present book have in common is a focus on the politics of culture, particularly the politics of film culture.

Feature Films

1

The True Child: George Lucas and the Star Wars *Series*

IN *The Empire Strikes Back*, a continuation of the *Star Wars* saga, George Lucas made an original movie: the first space fantasy heralding the demise of Western civilization. Originally aimed at an audience of twelve-year-olds (literally), the series— for such it became—in time showed unmistakable signs of aspirations to the deepest "relevance" and "significance," drawing its ideology, although this might surprise some of its viewers, straight from the radical utopianism of the sixties, widely thought to be quiescent.

In the opening scene of the original *Star Wars*, an imperial Death Star commanded by the Dark Lord of the Sith, Darth Vader himself, halts and boards in outer space a vessel carrying Princess Leia (Carrie Fisher). Leia somehow manages to be, at the same time, a princess of the royal family, a senator of a republic overthrown by the wicked Empire of which Darth Vader is a kind of shogun, and a leader of the rebel Alliance to Restore the Republic. She is the daughter of Bail Organa, viceroy and first chairman of the Alderaan System. Leia's claim to the appellation "royal," the quaintness of giving her the seemingly contradictory twin titles of princess and senator, and the problem of what a viceroy's daughter (retaining her royal title) is doing leading a rebellion to restore a republic are left zanily foggy. In any event, Vader takes Leia prisoner.

Meanwhile, on another planet, no less, our "farm-boy" hero, the young Luke Skywalker (Mark Hamill), is tooling around in an outer-space equivalent of a beat-up old Chevy. Via some very human robot chums, Luke intercepts a holographic distress signal from Princess Leia to a certain Obi-Wan Kenobi, appealing to Kenobi to extricate her from her predicament and join the struggle against wicked Darth Vader. "Say, I wonder if he could be referring to old Ben Kenobi . . . who lives somewhere out on the fringe of the Western Dune Sea?" says Luke, and proceeds to the Western Dune Sea, where he promptly finds Alec Guinness, dressed in a cowl rather like that of a Christian monk, living a life of monastic asceticism.

In classical mythology, when the young hero encounters the essential mystery or problem at the heart of the tale, he conveniently finds close at hand a seer of some sort who both explains the problem to him and instructs him how to solve it. Ben Kenobi serves this traditional double function, filling in the young Luke on all he needs to know about the world and history, on who is good and who is bad. He informs Luke forthrightly that his father, like Kenobi himself, was a Jedi knight, who was betrayed and murdered by Darth Vader. (Unlike other elite military castes, from Praetorian Guards and Janissaries to Samurai and Ivan the Terrible's *Oprichniki*, all of whom served absolutist autocracies, the Jedi knights, curiously, are the defenders and custodians of *Star Wars'* ancient republic.) Kenobi gives Luke his father's "light-sword," the Jedi emblem he had been keeping for him (he knew he'd happen by some day), and Luke is off to do battle with Darth Vader.

Once Luke has teamed up with Han Solo (Harrison Ford), a World War II "hot-pilot" type who serves as an older-brother figure, the adventures of the two are, in essence, those of *The Rover Boys in Space*. There are ups and downs, setbacks, obstacles to overcome. But basically the story is of two red-blooded American boys, pure-hearted, valiant, sure of their values and the justice of their cause, who trounce the villain. At the film's climax Luke and Han Solo destroy the Empire's Death Star and apparently Darth Vader with it, and in the last scene they are decorated with medals by Leia, our republic's well-known royal princess.

The only element of the story that seriously clashes with

traditional boys' adventure fiction is the character and personality of Princess Leia, whose dialogue seems to have been vetted by the National Organization for Women and whose personality would have chilled the blood of centuries of male "action" writers from Sir Thomas Malory to Ian Fleming. Whether Princess Leia's obstreperousness was introduced to increase *Star Wars'* appeal to young females, or to mollify the women's movement specifically, or Lucas's own wife, or perhaps even because Lucas has a personal weakness for obstreperous women, I do not know. But her character, plus the replacement of the devoted retainers of inferior race—a staple of an earlier age of adventure fiction—by Luke Skywalker's robots R2-D2 and C-3PO and Han Solo's "Wookie" Chewbacca (an ape-like creature of surprisingly high intelligence in that he can both pilot a rocket ship and repair electronic equipment) are *Star Wars'* only concessions to recent social developments. They are signs, however, of things to come.

Between *Stars Wars* and *The Empire Strikes Back,* two things overtook George Lucas that had earlier overtaken his friend and mentor Francis Ford Coppola. He became intellectually more ambitious. And he became more "relevant," offering profound comment on the times in which we live.

It is noteworthy that the decade of the seventies, which saw network television scrub from its programming the last remote allusions to the high culture (studies having shown that uneducated audiences actively resented references to a culture they did not themselves possess), witnessed the further consolidation of the cinema as the most "intellectual" of the popular theatrical arts. Taken seriously by critics, thrown into the company of Picasso and Solzhenitsyn and Alban Berg by arts-section editors of major publications, American filmmakers have had an increasing tendency to take themselves seriously as well, casting off the cloying conventions of the old "masscult" Hollywood and grappling with intellectually challenging material.

This has produced substantial numbers of American films of an artistic and dramatic sophistication unthinkable in the old Hollywood, whose upper reaches stopped fairly abruptly at Louisa May Alcott and Raymond Chandler. Sadly, it has also induced numerous successful filmmakers of essentially popular gifts to embark on enterprises for which they are plainly not intellectually equipped. There is nothing that makes more ludicrous the whole last section of *Apocalypse Now* than Coppola's daft attempt to integrate into the Joseph Conrad story his own ill-grasped readings in Sir James Frazer's *The Golden Bough* and Jessie K. Weston's *From Ritual to Romance*. (So proud was Coppola of his newly acquired erudition that he even displayed copies of the books in the film itself—presumably to prove to a doubting world that he had read them.) With the cheers of the critics in his ears, with vast sums earned from earlier hits, Coppola, now his own producer, would hardly have been amenable to suggestions from lesser men that he was living beyond his intellectual means. Who was there to say to him nay? So too with Lucas.

By and large *Star Wars* is a technically extremely accomplished rendition of the world of the adventure comic books of George Lucas's childhood. (His first commercial success, *American Graffiti*, was a celebration of his adolescence.) But with *Star Wars* the biggest financial hit in movie history (in inflated dollars since passed by Steven Spielberg's *E.T.*), Lucas was now out in the adult world of big money, and a hit this big called inexorably for a sequel. How to extend the story in time? The first segment had almost taken form of itself. The Princess in Distress. The bad Darth Vader. The seer Ben Kenobi explaining the perilous situation to young Luke (Lucas?) and telling him what to do. Luke doing it. The story had been told so many times that Lucas, unassumingly, considered the film more of a composite than anything else.

But now what? Unable to resist the impulse to "upgrade" his work intellectually, what Lucas did, of course, was to give himself a crash course in mythology, anthropology, and psychology, reading ancient myth, classical epics, folk tales, the Arthurian cycle, *chansons de geste*, tales of all the ancient heroes, mythic or legendary, throwing in lumps (no doubt from secondary sources) of *Paradise Lost, Sohrab and Rustam*, Freud, Jung, Yoga, Zen (California school), drawing from what the press manual for *The Empire Strikes Back* calls a rich "miasma" of cultural sources.

Lucas claims that well before making *Star Wars* he wrote a series of nine sequential movie treatments (synopses) covering the whole *Star Wars* cycle, of which he felt most "secure" with Part IV, or the first section of the Second Trilogy. This he consequently made first as *Star Wars*. (In this age of cultural inflation, even a vulgar twenty-four part television series might some day be referred to as "eight trilogies," or perhaps "six tetralogies.") Unfortunately, the press material handed out on the First Trilogy no longer jibes with the *Star Wars* prologue. And, more grave, at least one conspicuous element of *The Empire Strikes Back* no longer even jibes with the main body of the earlier film.

Star Wars tells us quite unequivocally that Luke's father was a Jedi knight betrayed and killed by Darth Vader. But in *The Empire Strikes Back* we learn to our astonishment that Luke's father was not killed by Darth Vader at all and is still alive. In fact, he *is* Darth Vader. This is the Dark Secret that critics are enjoined not to reveal to their readers. I am not certain how great a thrill is felt by the audience when it receives this information, but I have a suspicion of how thrilled George Lucas was when the new concept burst upon him. What vistas it opens: Zeus and Cronus! Oedipus and Laius! The stirring prospect of generational conflict!

I have unearthed the tape of a curious unpublished interview Lucas gave before the release of *Star Wars* and in which, modest and unaffected, he makes no bones about his intended audience. *Star Wars* is "something for kids"—specifically twelve-year-olds. It is not science fiction and not about the future, but his attempt to do a "young person's adventure film" providing a "wholesome fantasy life like we used to have when we were kids." He lists the favorites of his childhood, the spirit of which he has attempted to capture, condensing them all in one film: Westerns, pirate movies, *Gunga Din, Treasure Island, Flash Gordon, Robin Hood,* King Arthur, the Walt Disney "classics," early John Wayne, the *Odyssey*.

On the tape Lucas chats freely about three earlier *Star Wars* scripts he wrote before choosing to make the fourth into the final film. He talks of his hope of sequels if *Star Wars* is successful, which would keep him going financially while he indulged his penchant for "little, tiny, experimental movies." "My directing tendencies are so radical. They're not commercial," he says. It is odd to hear Lucas—whose earlier success with *American Graffiti* surprised him—say in his shy voice: "*Graffiti* was as successful as I could ever hope a movie of mine to be. I don't think anything I'll ever do could be more successful than that." This, from the man who had just finished *Star Wars*, whose dollar earnings were in weeks to rocket it past every other motion picture ever made.

It is not widely known that Lucas, before *Star Wars*, worked four years on the *Apocalypse Now* project and was never able to raise the financing, finally turning it over in despair to his friend Coppola, who could. The world will never know what George Lucas would have done with *Apocalypse Now*; he says his version would have been "angry" and "esoteric," a kind of "*Dr. Strangelove in Vietnam.*" But monied tyrants deemed that Lucas should make "this movie for kids." (The history of the cinema is replete with stories of this sort, Coppola himself having been dragged with some reluctance into *The Godfather*— generally considered his best film—because he needed the money.) But if Lucas was denied his chance to indict the United States for the Vietnam war, the success of *Star Wars* gave him the opportunity to make up for the lost opportunity in a new and unexpected way.

The original *Star Wars*, to stress the point again, is boys' fiction of a perfectly conventional and traditional sort. Although set in an exotic locale (outer space), it contains an endless string of feats of intrepid derring-do by our boy-man heroes and ends with their smashing victory over villainy and their adversaries. There is no questioning, no casting about for "new values." The old ones are good enough for them. By contrast, *The Empire Strikes Back* consists of an extensive series of defeats, disasters, humiliations, almost as if our heroes were being punished for the sin of pride (or cultural arrogance) they displayed in *Star Wars*.

The reversals, in fact, are well under way even before *The Empire Strikes Back* starts, and the new movie opens with the leaders of our rebel Alliance to Restore the Republic very much down on their luck, holed up in a hideout on the ice-planet Hoth (actually shot in Norway). In the first scene, Luke Skywalker is mauled by an abominable Hoth snowman. But trouble begins in earnest when the Empire, having spotted the rebel hideaway via space probes, sends out an expeditionary force consisting of a squadron of giant, death-belching tanks that walk like enormous camels. In the debacle that follows the destruction of their Hoth hideaway, the friends split up, and one of the tedious things about *The Empire Strikes Back* is that from this point on it keeps cutting back and forth between two separate stories, which are never fully reentwined even at the end of the picture.

Princess-Senator Leia, pilot Han Solo, his Wookie Chewbacca, and C-3PO (the walking robot with an English accent) set off in the Millennium Falcon, their beat-up intergalactic Buick. They are rather swiftly trapped and captured by Darth Vader, C-3PO is dismantled for scrap, and Han Solo is put into "carbon freeze," a kind of suspended animation, in which state he remains suspended, in a stunning non-climax, as the final credits crawl up the screen.

Meanwhile, Luke Skywalker—accompanied by R2-D2 (the wheeled robot that beeps)—has been having experiences of a far more significant nature. A holographic vision of Alec Guinness sends Luke, in his dark night of the soul, off to apprentice himself to an Oriental-style guru named Yoda on the planet Dagobah, which for variety is all tropical swamp. Now in *Star Wars* Ben Kenobi, dressed in his monk-like cowl, could for all the futurist rigamarole and Japanese-sounding name have almost been a knight of the monastic Order of Saint John of Jerusalem, the so-called Knights of Malta, sworn to defend Christian Europe against the infidel Saracen or Turk. Yoda, however, is another matter.

The actual Yoda (yoga?), in fact a twenty-six-inch Muppet manipulated by the same man who does Miss Piggy, puts Luke on an idiot's version of an Oriental mystic discipline. Yoda's Orientalism is only Muppet-skin deep, his basic belief system being a lot less close to the sound of one hand clapping than it is to *The Little Engine That Could.* But even the most ignorant members of the audience (in fact, especially the ignorant members of the audience) are plainly intended to see that Luke is reaching outside his corpus of traditional (Western) belief for some new, mystical, "Oriental" understanding of the universe. At the start of his training Yoda says of Luke to the holographic Alec Guinness, "I cannot instruct him. The boy has no patience. . . . All his life has he looked away—to the horizon, to the sky, to the future. . . . Adventure, excitement. A Jedi craves not these things."

The absurdity of applying such admonishments to the hero of a futurist comic-book series hardly needs stating, but it is worth noting that Irvin Kershner, whom Lucas delegated to direct this installment of the series, is an adept of Zen and has had what the parapsychology crowd calls "out of body" experiences, while Lucas himself, it turns out, subscribes to a rich array of occultist beliefs, literally believing, of all things, in *Star Wars'* "The Force." "If you use [The Force] well," he says solemnly, "you can see the future and the past. You can sort of read minds and you can levitate and use that whole netherworld of psychic energy." Lucas humbly admits he cannot yet do any of these exhilarating things personally, but it is evident that we are dealing here with a card-carrying member of the occultist sub-culture.

Warned by Yoda that he is not yet ready, that his training is not yet complete, Luke Skywalker nonetheless sets forth to do battle with Darth Vader. We are treated to a long *Three Muske-teers*-like duel with light-swords, in the time-out moments of which Vader alternately taunts Luke ("You're not a Jedi yet!") and, Mephistopheles-like, tempts him to join the Forces of Darkness. Luke remains uncorrupted, however, continues the sword fight, and is soundly defeated by Vader, who strikes off his right hand, his symbolic sword arm, and again tempts Luke to join him. It is only when Luke refuses that Vader reveals that he is his father. "Join me and together we will rule the galaxy as father and son!" he appeals to him majestically. "Never!" cries Luke and—death before dishonor—casts himself into the void.

A suicide attempt by a comic-book hero is another first. But Luke doesn't really die, of course. He catches onto an external weather vane of the space station and, not seeming to lose any blood to speak of from his severed arm, happily breathes the non-air of intergalactic space until the Millennium Falcon, receiving an SOS via ESP, nips by to rescue him. With a new sword arm for Luke hitched on by futuristic surgeons aboard the rebel flagship, conveniently cruising in the vicinity, we arrive at a thumping non-ending.

In the final scene, half of our little group of lovable subhumans and intergalactic adolescents sets off to free Han Solo from his state of carbon freeze, while the other half waves them goodbye over an almost visible "To Be Continued." It is a most extraordinary conclusion to a piece of popular entertainment, with the heroes still all in dire straits, and the villain not only winning, but way out in front.

The obvious defense for this non-ending is that the *Star Wars* films have been converted from a "series" (in which every episode is self-contained) to a "serial" (each segment merely an installment, with conflicts unresolved). But the concept of a movie serial to be made over a projected time span of some twenty-seven years (at current rate of production) is in itself rather stunning, suggesting that Lucas fell victim to lurking delusions of grandeur. Personally quiet and self-effacing, he nonetheless admitted, "*The Empire* is as complicated as any movie, and it says a lot of things," adding only, "But I don't like to come out with a big sign and say, *This is significant*." It doesn't seem to have occurred to him that when he undertakes a gargantuan epic blatantly plucking themes from classical mythology and some of the greatest works of world literature he is doing just that.

Lucas, moreover, has given out that, if he identified in *Star Wars* with Luke Skywalker, in *The Empire Strikes Back* he identifies with our Muppet mystic, Yoda. This bodes ill for the ideology of the rest of the serial, at least of the concluding episode of the current trilogy. For in the opening sequences of the episode Luke is doomed to return for a graduate course in Yoda's brand of Dale Carnegie mysticism. With his parchment in his pocket, as it were, Luke will battle once again with Darth Vader, a combat from which Lucas has promised all interviewers that "only one will walk away." The betting, obviously, is favoring Luke heavily. Those confident of his eventual triumph assume that in *The Empire Strikes Back* Luke is passing through the time of testing and trials faced by all mythic heroes as they confront demons, monsters, magicians, the dark forces of the cosmos, as well as those within themselves, a contest from which Luke, like them, will emerge victorious.

But I am not so sure. During a scene in *The Empire Strikes Back* in which Ben Kenobi says to Yoda, "The boy [Luke] is our last hope," my ear was caught by yoda's cryptic answer: "No. There is another." My sense of George Lucas's thinking is that Luke—the old Luke, that combination of Rover Boy, Captain Marvel, and Mr. America—can no longer be allowed to triumph in the old gung-ho, self-justifying way. To win, if he is to win, he must be transformed into someone representative of George Lucas's own, superior ideals. If I were to take a wild flyer at plotting for this increasingly meaning-laden space fantasy, I might guess that Darth Vader will conquer Luke, but that Luke will be discovered to have a "purer" twin brother (the bad self and the good self), or conceivably even son (who could play Galahad to his Lancelot).

In any case, whoever triumphs, Lucas's heavy emphasis on the "Oriental" wisdom of Yoda leads me to doubt very much that the victory will be shown as one for "our side." If Yoda is the key—and everything indicates that he is—*Star Wars'* way ahead for humankind will be founded on the Four Pillars of the Lucas world: (1) superficial Orientalism: (2) profound occultism; (3) pop Freudianism; and (4) a hodgepodge of "anti-materialist" pieties salvaged from the detritus of the counterculture.

To give a balanced view, I should point out that some intellectual analysts hailed with enthusiasm the greater complexity of *The Empire Strikes Back*, Lucas's jettisoning of the simple black-and-white ethics of his earlier picture, and Luke Skywalker's "internalization" of evil. Dr. Weyler Greene, a Los Angeles Jungian psychologist, feels a clean break between good and evil may not be something we want our children to learn these days.

"Can we afford this kind of purity?" he asks. "In *Star Wars* they were able to go in—bombs away—and be successful. In this one, that approach no longer works. That's what's wrong with America in this Iranian situation. [American hostages were still being held in Tehran.] We want to operate in a traditional, rational, strong-guy hero way, and somehow it doesn't work any more."

The only comment called for here is that the reason the traditional, rational way doesn't work any more might be that so many Americans have been going about "internalizing evil," like Dr. Greene and George Lucas, and that perhaps a Jungian might not be a very good choice for secretary of state. Dr. Greene and I plainly saw the same movie, however. We merely feel differently about where it leads us.

Let there be no mistake. George Lucas has real gifts. He is a superb film craftsman, and, although *The Empire Strikes Back* was directed by Kershner and its full screenplay was fleshed out by Lawrence Kasdan and the late Leigh Brackett, the whole concept was Lucas's, he reviewed the production footage day by day, and his mark is on it. *The Empire Strikes Back* is a particularly obvious example of the falsity—at least in America—of the currently wildly popular notion that the director is the "author" of a film. Although Lucas has courteously affirmed, "It's Kershner's movie," Irving Kershner is hardly more the author of *The Empire Strikes Back* than Elia Kazan is the author of *A Streetcar Named Desire*, which he directed on Broadway. American movies are group undertakings made under the leadership of whoever has effective control. Great battles have been fought for artistic control of a film, but not in this case. *The Empire Strikes Back* was completely under the control of George Lucas. Lucas is also far too modest when he describes the original *Star Wars* as merely a "composite." He is remarkably fertile in the invention of those near-human doll characters on which the appeal of a certain kind of children's fiction so much depends; his creations equal or surpass the Tin Man, Scarecrow, and Cowardly Lion of L. Frank Baum's *The Wizard of Oz* and that whimsical bunch of familiars surrounding Christopher Robin in A. A. Milne's *Winnie the Pooh*. Lucas's Droids

R2-D2 and C-3PO and the Wookie Chewbacca, along with the magical suprahuman adversaries Ben Kenobi and Darth Vader, are far more responsible for the vast success of *Star Wars* than the movie's nominal central characters, Luke, Han Solo, and Princess Leia.

In *The Empire Strikes Back* Lucas seems to be at the top of his form in this department. At this writing, Amy Carter, the president's twelve-year-old daughter, has already been allowed to see the new movie twice, and her favorite is Yoda. [Miss Carter's subsequent career shows that she is indeed a disciple of Yoda.] "I just loved him and the way his ears wiggled!" she says. Indeed, the comradeship of Droids, Wookies, Muppets, and other such is one of the real *trouvailles* of the *Star Wars* movies, replacing such fixtures of earlier generations as Gunga Din, Nigger Jim, and Robinson Crusoe's Man Friday. Relationships of this sort are now unacceptable to our modern notions of social equality (though they offer deep pleasure and comfort to the mind of the child). Change Gunga Din into R2-D2, however, and the proprieties are preserved.

It only remains to explain how it is that George Lucas, who just a few short years ago thought "wholesome" fantasies for children were Westerns, pirate movies, the warlike knights of the Round Table, military tales by Kipling, and Classic Comics—all representing rather extreme patterns of aggressivity and cultural assertiveness—should, when given his head on his own epic, suddenly find such models unwholesome, apparently preferring to inculcate a quietism aimed at undermining them. The question is critical, and the answer clear-cut.

George Lucas lives in the dream world of the child, where the relationship of action to consequence is fuzzy at best—a state of impaired perception widespread in the so-called counterculture. Lucas, in fact, is the counterculture in a nutshell, a charter member of that extraordinary "youth" generation which took absolutely for granted all the affluence and freedoms which came its way so effortlessly, and wanted not less, as it claimed, but more. In addition to effortless ease it wanted moral superiority, admiration, power. It is ironic, now that so many of the radical and revolutionary leaders of the sixties and early seventies have scampered back into the political mainstream, that their attitudes are now being voiced by a True Child, in what is after all the appropriate medium of a children's story. Many have fallen away, but Lucas, with his particularly intimate feeling for the joys and longings of the juvenile mind, is still engaged in the vast enterprise of proving that the world of the child is superior to the world of the adult.

Note: By the time of *Return of the Jedi* (1983), the third and last episode of the *Star Wars* series, three years had passed, the country had gone from Jimmy Carter's hostage crisis in Iran to the middle of the first Reagan administration, and George Lucas did some scampering of his own, returning, somewhat halfheartedly, to his earlier style. In *Return of the Jedi*, Luke's planned graduate work in Yoda's oriental mysticism is cut, he does battle with Darth Vader, and triumphs, giving Darth Vader, his father, the opportunity for a deathbed repentance: "Luminous beings are we, Luke, not this crude matter." And then, Luke to the Emperor: "Never! Never will I turn to the Dark side! I am a Jedi as my father before me!"

But, as I suspected, Luke *does* turn out to have a twin. Not a twin brother, as it happens, but a twin sister. She is Leia, our old friend the Princess-Senator, who is destined to save the Alliance if Luke should "go over to the Dark side" (the bad self and the good self, after all). *Perhaps it will be left to Leia to carry on the struggle. Perhaps she will know a way. Perhaps she will find a path beyond the darkness. Leia is our last, unflagging hope.* "Leia felt like a creative spark, dancing about in the fires of life, dancing behind a furtive, pudgy midget bear. It was this, then, that the Alliance was fighting to preserve, furry creatures in mammoth forests." Leia, there is no doubt about it, was intended to accomplish great things, perhaps to be the feminist-environmentalist woman hero of episode four of the *Star Wars* series.

But there never was an episode four. *Return of the Jedi*, episode three, was the third biggest moneymaker of all time. Lucas was the true originator of both the *Star Wars* series and the *Indiana Jones* series. But he got divorced and, for whatever reason, the fire went out. Perhaps George Lucas grew up, which given his special gifts, meant the end.

2

The Uniforms That Guard:
Kipling, Orwell, and Australia's
Breaker Morant

When you're wounded and left on Afghanistan's plains,
And the women come out to cut what remains,
Just roll to your rifle and blow out your brains
And go to your God like a soldier.

Rudyard Kipling
The Young British Soldier

"MAKING MOCK OF uniforms that guard you while you
sleep" was a phrase of Kipling's that caught in George
Orwell's mind. And there were patent reasons why the line
should have nagged at his conscience, for in the dramatic years
that preceded the writing of his celebrated essay on Kipling in
the middle of World War II, Orwell—a more complex and far
less consistent man than is commonly thought—had undergone
an abrupt and profound reorientation of his political thinking.
His view of Soviet totalitarianism (the attitude for which he is
best known) did not change. He learned to despise Stalinism
during the Spanish Civil War, and to his death the intensity of
this loathing remained unimpaired. But his feelings toward the
liberal "bourgeois" states, particularly those possessing colonies, were another matter. His hostility toward the social injus-
tices of these states was so strong that he thought them not
worth defending against even such as Hitler, and consequently
was a fervent supporter of the antiwar party during the Munich

17

crisis of 1938 and sneered most contemptuously at the Socialist "warmongers" who felt that Hitler had to be stopped. In January 1939, eight months before the German attack on Poland, he wrote to Herbert Read: "I believe it is vitally necessary for those of us who intend to oppose the coming war to start organizing for illegal antiwar activities."

In July in *Adelphi*, he wrote: "What meaning would there be. . . in bringing down Hitler's system in order to stabilize something that is far bigger and in its different way just as bad? . . . Nothing is likely to save us except the emergence within the next two years of a real mass party whose first pledges are to refuse war and to right imperial injustice." In the last issue of *Left Forum* to be published before the German attack in the East, Orwell was still fulminating against "left-wing jingoes," saying if their eyes were open they must be aware that "their [anti-Hitler] version of 'defense of democracy' leads directly *away* from democracy. . . ."

On September 1, the German *Blitzkreig* against Poland was launched, and France and his own country declared war. Orwell was silent. We know that he tried repeatedly to join the army and was rejected each time as medically unfit, but no article or dispatch or personal letter issued from his pen to explain the change in his thinking. September: silence. October: silence. November: silence. December: silence. On January 8, 1940, with no transition, explanation, or *peccavi* of any sort, Orwell wrote earnestly to Victor Gollancz, his publisher: "What worries me at present is the uncertainty as to whether the ordinary people in countries like England grasp the difference between democracy and despotism well enough to defend their liberties. . . . The intellectuals who are at present pointing out that democracy and fascism are the same thing etc. depress me horribly." Two days later, to his close friend Geoffrey Gorer, he wrote: "I have so far completely failed to serve HM government in any capacity, though I want to, because it seems to me that now we are in this bloody war we have got to win it & I would like to lend a hand. They won't have me in the army, at any rate at present, because of my lungs." (Orwell was tubercular.) In April, a month before the German attack in the West, he wrote, in a review of a book by Malcolm Muggeridge, who had just joined the army: "I know very well what underlies these [deeply moving] closing chapters. It is the emotion of the middle-class man, brought up in the military tradition, who finds in the moment of crisis that he is a patriot after all. It is all very well to be 'advanced' and 'enlightened,' to snigger at Colonel Blimp and proclaim your emancipation from all traditional loyalties, but a time comes when the sand of the desert is sodden red and what have I done for thee, England my England?"

The German onslaught began. France fell. Belgium fell. Holland. The British army was cut off, but, abandoning all its weapons and equipment, was evacuated at Dunkirk. And Orwell, soon to be admitted to the Home Guard, wrote his extraordinary essay, "My Country Right or Left." "The night before the Russo-German pact was announced I dreamed that the war had started. It was one of those dreams which . . . sometimes reveal to you the true state of your feelings. It taught me . . . that I was patriotic at heart, would not sabotage or act against my own side, would support the war, would fight in it if possible." He confesses that "To this day it gives me a faint feeling of sacrilege not to stand to attention during 'God Save the King.' " He pities people "whose hearts have never leapt at the sight of the Union Jack." And he closes with a ringing affirmation of the "spiritual need for patriotism and the military virtues, for which, however little the boiled rabbits of the Left may like them, no substitute has yet been found." When a man says things like this, can Kipling be far behind?

I write in such detail of Orwell's astounding reversal of attitudes toward patriotism and "military virtues" once his own country was placed in deadly peril because we seem at present to be living through a substantial shifting of opinion on these same subjects in this country; and because two significant new movies have appeared about these "uniforms that guard you while you sleep" (a subject obsessional with Kipling and of deep significance for Orwell also), the two films displaying sharply contrasting attitudes toward everything these uniforms stand for.

The first is Australia's *Breaker Morant,* a story of Australian soldiers in the Boer War. Beyond its international success and a top prize at the 1980 Cannes Film Festival, the movie is the biggest commercial money-maker in Australian history and, in America, without a known name connected to it and competing with works by celebrity directors like Polanski, Resnais, and Truffaut, it is proving one of the leading foreign box-office attractions of 1981. The second film is about wearers of another sort of uniform that even more obviously "guards us while we sleep": policemen. *Fort Apache, The Bronx,* protested against and picketed by offended South Bronx residents, was nonetheless the number-one commercial film in the country for many weeks. Hence: two successful, strong, highly ideological films about men in uniform.

The Boer War was a nasty piece of business, resembling in many ways our war in Vietnam. Even some of the statistics were similar. The British, at the end, had almost half a million men there under arms, imperial, colonial, and even a few local African—the Africans being attracted to the British because of their more liberal racial policies. Boers fought on both sides (one-fifth of them siding with the British). Africans died on both sides. Much of the veldt was a great free-fire zone. The British practiced defoliation, burned crops and houses and everything that might give the Boer guerrillas support, did not have "strategic hamlets" but built thousands of blockhouses, herded the families and retainers of the guerrillas (including over 100,000 blacks) into vast concentration camps—a dazzling novelty of the period. Both sides killed prisoners, the Boers, at least partly because guerrillas cannot take many prisoners, doing so first and most systematically. They openly admitted killing armed Africans whenever they captured them and there is abundant evidence that they killed unarmed ones as well. A leading British missionary in the Transvaal wrote privately of the commandos led by General Jan Smuts, one of the most respected of the Boer leaders: "The Boers under Smuts captured this post last month and when afterwards a column visited the place they found the bodies of all the Kaffirs murdered and unburied. . . . They look upon the Kaffirs as dogs and the killing of them as hardly a crime. . . ." The British forces suffered over 100,000 casualties, the death roll of whites on both sides together being in the vicinity of 50–60,000. The number of black dead was not even estimated.

It was the twentieth century's first anti-colonial war, with a modern army bogged down in battle with fierce and determined nationalist guerrillas on the guerrillas' own terrain. In his more morbid moments, the British commander Lord Kitchener felt the only way to win the war was to "exterminate" every last one of them. The expression "body count" had not yet been invented, the British talking, instead, about the daily "bag." Enlightened opinion on the Continent condemned the British almost universally, but, unlike the United States during the Vietnam war, morale in Britain remained comparatively high; Kipling, needless to say, backed the war to the hilt. And support for the war among the self-governing members of the Empire, such as Australia and Canada, remained surprisingly enthusiastic, the only episode sticking in the craw of the Australians—whose combat units displayed much valor—being the affair of the so-called Bush Veldt Carabineers, a special anti-commando unit formed to fight in enemy territory in the wild northern Transvaal. Six of its officers were court-martialed for killing Boer prisoners, and two of them, "Breaker" Morant and Peter Handcock, were executed by firing squad.

The execution caused an uproar of protest in Australia as the Boers had been killing prisoners from the beginning and it was no secret that the British, particularly the colonial deep-penetration units, were retaliating in kind. ("Hold up your hands, men!" called the second-in-command of a unit of Canadian Scouts after coming upon the bullet-riddled body of its commanding officer, shot after capture. "I want you to take an oath with me not to take another prisoner!" Recalled a sergeant solemnly long afterward, "We held up our hands.") But Germany was intervening diplomatically on behalf of the Boers, peace feelers were out to end the war, and many thought that Morant and Handcock were offered up by Kitchener as scapegoats to international opinion. Thomas Pakenham, author of the excellent study, *The Boer War,* feels that this is a "misconception," but offers no supporting evidence and grants that the view is "still current."

On the face of it, the scapegoat interpretation seems far from

implausible and, in any event, it is still widely believed in
Australia and played for all it's worth in the present movie.
Breaker Morant is the only film I can recall whose press material
includes a detailed historical bibliography—an invitation to the
critic, if he doesn't like the film's view of history, to run the
facts down himself in the major sources. Unfortunately this is a
thing which film critics, sometimes for practical reasons, sometimes from sheer psychological submission to the entrancing
world of make-believe presented on the screen, seldom do.

Breaker Morant is a superbly made film. The rolling veldt.
The horses. The period uniforms and faces. The patrols coming
in over the ridgeline against glorious skies. Bruce Beresford, the
director, uses a wonderful mix of long establishing shots and
tight close-ups of faces. They are faces worthy of a Fellini—
except of course they are from a different world. These are the
faces of Australian roughnecks and stiff British soldiers, with
pomaded hair and black handlebar mustaches. And the stiffest
faces are some of the best of all, with, behind the stiffness,
ghost-like but palpable, the thoughts of the characters plainer
than if printed in ink. Men's blue eyes, whether filled with rage,
or duplicity, or even cautious decency, have rarely been used to
such dramatic effect.

The frame of the story is the court-martial of three of the
Carabineer officers, with deft flashbacks to the key moments of
their story—cut usually on the "off-beat" (not in the wooden,
old-fashioned manner which seemed a clumsy attempt to repro-
duce narrative). Morant (Edward Woodward), who owes his
nickname "Breaker" to having been the best horse breaker in
Australia, is curiously enough a black-sheep English gentleman
who went out to Australia at nineteen and has been recommended for a DSO for valor in South Africa. Handcock (Bryan
Brown) joined up because he was jobless during a depression,
and Witton (Lewis Fitz-Gerald), the youngest, because his father, an old soldier, said it would make a man of him. They are
all lieutenants. We see the engagement during which their commanding officer, Captain Hunt, is wounded and captured, and
later the scene when they come upon his body, savagely muti-
lated by the Boers before they killed him. Morant, who was

engaged to marry Hunt's sister, had up to this point never killed a prisoner, but when the next one falls into the unit's hands, his instructions from an English captain, delivered in an icily quiet voice, are, "Avenge Hunt." When a whole batch of prisoners comes in, and there is no place they can be kept or guarded with the unit on the move in enemy country, we hear the same icy, cold voice, the same order: "Execute them. This is guerrilla war, not a debutante's ball."

We see Kitchener at his headquarters. It is an unattractive portrait. Germany has protested against the execution of a German missionary, and Kitchener says sanctimoniously, "The Kaiser is our late Queen's grandson you know," and then more practically, "The Germans would like any excuse to come in on the side of the Boers. They don't give a damn about the Boers, of course. All they want is the gold and diamonds." To which a staff officer replies, "They lack our altruism, sir." Considering its subject matter, there is much humor in the film. During the court-martial, when another soldier gives transparently false evidence against them, Handcock bursts out at the witness, "You couldn't lie straight in bed, Donaldson!" When Donaldson invites him outside to settle the matter, Handcock, ready to go, cries, "Any time, mate!" at which the presiding officer of the court warns him, "Control yourself, Lieutenant, or you'll find yourself in serious trouble." This brings a laugh of genuine, if bitter, amusement to Handcock, who is already, of course, on trial for his life.

In the middle of the court-martial there is a Boer attack on the barracks in which it is being held. Morant, Handcock, and Witton are served out weapons and fight gallantly to repel the attack. When the court-martial resumes, their defense counsel, Major Thomas (played by Australia's leading film star, Jack Thompson), pleads that British army tradition since Wellington calls for prisoners who fight bravely against the enemy to be pardoned. But there is no pardon. Biased ruling after biased ruling is made against the defendants. A key witness for the defense is transferred to India before he can testify. Thomas, who has had only twenty-four hours to prepare his case, destroys the credibility of witness after witness, but the court remains unmoved. Everything indicates that the three men are being railroaded.

Thomas rises at last for his final summation, delivered with great eloquence. "War changes men's natures," he says. "The barbarities of war are seldom committed by abnormal men, but by normal men under abnormal circumstances. They live every day with fear and anger and blood and death, and when rules are departed from by one side, they will be departed from by the other. Soldiers at war are not to be judged by civilian rules. Their actions, viewed calmly afterward, often seem un-Christian and brutal, but if all men who committed barbarous acts in war were court-martialed, courts-martial would be in permanent session." He closes quietly, with the stunning statement, "We ourselves are not fit to judge such men."

This speech won, first gasps, then great cheers at the Cannes Film Festival, where the audience tends to cheer, not artistry, but sentiments it agrees with, and where Thompson's performance also won him the top acting prize. The speech also earned cheers when I saw the film in Paris, and even, they tell me, at the first performances in New York. The events portrayed in the film, of course, took place long, long before the Nuremberg Trials, where it was decided that the fact that a soldier was "following orders" did not exonerate him from responsibility for actions contrary to the Geneva Convention. Consideration of the Nuremberg principle would naturally have been a gross anachronism in 1902, and a substantial part of *Breaker Morant*'s court-martial is devoted to whether Kitchener had in fact given "secret orders" to kill Boer prisoners, later to disavow the orders publicly—a proposition for which the film establishes at least a plausibility. But Morant, Handcock, and Witton are all sentenced to death. Two of the judges recommend mercy, but Kitchener orders that the death sentence be carried out on all but Witton, the youngest, whose sentence is commuted to life imprisonment.

The mood of the film's last scenes is extraordinary. There is gallows humor to the end. "Live every day as if it's to be your last, lads," says Morant. "One day you're certain to be right." He reflects that perhaps they'd been fighting "on the wrong side" after all, and drinks to—"The Bush Veldt Carabineers! The best fighters in a bad cause." Somberly he says, "This is what comes of empire building." Earlier, at headquarters, Kitchener has said to a staff officer, "The sacrifice of these Australians wouldn't seem an unreasonable price to pay for a peace conference," to which the officer replies, "No, sir. Although the Australians might see the matter somewhat differently." Now, when the defense counsel makes his last desperate plea for the three men, the same staff officer tells him, "Forget it, Major. It's a sideshow of the war. Good news, by the way. It looks as if we're going to have a peace conference."

The night before their execution, Morant pens a poem. It is high-flown. Men marching off to war, patriotism, high hopes, and to what end? Handcock writes a long letter to his wife, saying no matter what he has done, he has always loved her. The letter's last line is "*Australia forever!*"

In the light of dawn, Morant is asked what he wants written on his tombstone and he says Matthew 10:36—"*And a man's foes shall be they of his own household.*" Both Morant and Handcock spurn the consolation of the padre. Both spurn the blindfold. They hold hands for a moment as they march out in front of the firing squad, and then go to their death like soldiers.

In 1970, almost seventy years after the event (a scene now shown in the film), the British officer who commanded the firing squad, then a very old gentleman, remembered Handcock as a "charming young man." Handcock had given him his cigarette case, and he had kept it those many years.

What is this film about? It is anti-British, up to a point, anti-imperialist, anti-colonialist ("the wrong side," "this is what comes of empire building"). It has bitterness of a particularly acute kind against senior officers, "brass," who cold-heartedly treat their men like cannon fodder, to be sacrificed, declared expendable, occasionally offered up as scapegoats. But on the most profound level, it is about something even larger. It burns with a white rage against societies as a whole, from military leaders and chiefs of state to (more common in our time) comfortable civilians in easy chairs, who send rough men out to serve their interests brutally, murderously (what is war?), and then—when circumstances change and in the exquisite safety and fastidiousness of their living rooms they suddenly find these rough men's actions repugnant—disown them.

There is deep hypocrisy and injustice here and *Breaker Morant*'s director, Bruce Beresford, makes no bones about his feelings. He declares openly that one of the main things that drew him to the film's subject was its parallels to the war in Vietnam and to the story of—yes—William Calley. That a motion picture made in conscious defense of William Calley should be receiving ovations today is a historic event in itself. Badgered by an interviewer from the *New York Times* who suggested that the film could be seen as an "apologia for war crimes" and "for dangerously reactionary behavior," Beresford stood fast. (Who actually *approves* of the killing of prisoners?) "If you're stuck with a charge of atrocity," said Beresford, "it's not that simple; it's not just a case of being a madman with a gun in your hand. The film says that in this kind of situation you can't simply turn around and condemn the people who've done the deed." Jack Thompson (the defense counsel), who has served in the Australian army himself, was even more emphatic. His great speech in the film, he said, tells us mainly that "people behave desperately in desperate situations. Others who sit in judgment and call them criminals *are the ones who put them in that situation—and are highly suspect*" (emphasis added). The statement could hardly be more clear. It is not difficult to infer that Beresford and Thompson feel that the uneducated young Americans who answered their country's call and did its dirty work in Vietnam deserved better on their return than jeers like, "You were in Vietnam? How many kids did you kill?"—particularly when these jeers came from sons of the liberal, privileged elite which had sent them to Vietnam to begin with, and whose heroism during the war was confined to performing prodigies of draft evasion. There was no honor in this; and no amount of cheering for returned Teheran hostages, some of whom endured rigors rather less severe than what an ordinary Marine goes through in boot camp, will wipe out the stain.

Breaker Morant, of course, plunges us into a world of undiluted Kipling:

> For it's Tommy this, an' Tommy that, an' "Tommy, wait
>   outside";
> But it's "Special train for Atkins" when the trooper's on the
>   tide.

It brings back the peculiar quality of Kipling's soldiers, stoical, hard-bitten, unconcerned with political objectives or lofty ideals:

> "What was the end of all the show, Johnnie, Johnnie?"
> Ask my Colonel, for I don't know, Johnnie, my Johnnie, aha!
> We broke a King and we built a road—
> A court-house stands where the Reg'ment goed.
> And the river's clean where the raw blood flowed
> When the Widow gives the party.

Given the many decades during which Kipling was looked on with disfavor by the literary intelligentsia, it is remarkable how many writers of refined literary sensitivity found him so fascinating they felt compelled to write about him: not only Orwell but Edmund Wilson, T. S. Eliot, W. H. Auden, Lionel Trilling, Randall Jarrell, Angus Wilson, C. S. Lewis. Many of these wrote to pay Kipling a sometimes grudging tribute. There are numerous reasons for disliking Kipling, as all these writers are aware. Among others, he identified totally, and with relish, with coarse men of action against liberal humanists, which many intellectuals saw as a betrayal of his own class and calling. But as set out by Orwell—the intensity of whose love-hate for Kipling perhaps gave him the deepest perceptions—Kipling "sees clearly that men can only be highly civilized while other men, inevitably less civilized, are there to guard and feed them." Lewis echoes the same theme: "It is a brutal truth about the world that the whole everlasting business of keeping the human race protected and clothed and fed could not go on for twenty-four hours without the vast legion of hard-bitten, technically efficient, not-over-sympathetic men, and without the harsh processes of discipline by which this legion is made. It is a brutal truth that unless a great many people practiced the Kipling *ethos* there would be neither security nor leisure for any people to practice a finer *ethos*."

I have no doubt that all the writers I have mentioned knew this to be true, whence their dark fascination with Kipling. In times of ease and security such ideas as Kipling's have not been wildly popular in the intellectual class. When the very survival of their culture is seen as in jeopardy, however, then liberal humanists rejoin the nation, and, as Victoria Crosses and Congressional Medals of Honor are handed out to harsh, not always very lovable men, they consider themselves lucky to count such men as compatriots, and toast their Rangers, and Green Berets, and Blue Light, and, indeed, their Handcocks and Morants and Bush Veldt Carabineers.

Auden wrote that for Kipling civilization was "a little citadel of light surrounded by a great darkness full of malignant forces and only maintained through the centuries by everlasting vigilance, will power, and self sacrifice." Kipling's peculiarity, according to Auden, was that he was obsessed exclusively with dangers threatening civilization from outside, whereas there were also dangers which threatened it from within. Auden was thinking of corruption and "the *ennuis* of the cultured mind," whereas in our own time one of the dangers threatening American civilization from the inside presents itself in startlingly Kiplingesque terms like the external dangers of old—as the title *Fort Apache, The Bronx* so clearly suggests—and the "hard-bitten," "not-over-sympathetic" men who protect us while we sleep are policemen.

Needless to say, when the enemy is within a society the battle lines are never as clearly drawn as when it is without, and since *Fort Apache* has well-made, exciting action scenes, Paul Newman's best performance in many years, and detailing and niceties of construction not normally encountered in network police dramas on television, great numbers of viewers have been issuing from movie houses under the impression that they have seen simply a "good cop movie." But *Fort Apache*, without being so absurd as to suggest that police forces should be disbanded, is deeply and systematically hostile to the police, to the way they are compelled to do their job, and, perhaps most of all, to the rough kind of men willing to do this work. It misrepresents the police. It misrepresents crime. And it even misrepresents the South Bronx.

The film begins with a double cop killing. Before the titles, a black prostitute, "whacked out of her mind" on Angel Dust, weaves across a street toward a halted police squad car. Two rookie cops, lulled into a false sense of security by her drugged state, watch the prostitute with amusement as she approaches, invites them seductively to "party" with her, and then fumbles in her bag. From the bag she draws a pistol and empties it into the two policemen. After the titles, back at the station house, we meet Patrolman Murphy (Paul Newman), who has what even his patrol partner designates as an "anti-authority" streak. With eighteen years on the force, he has been broken twice from sergeant, once for protesting against what he considered trivial disciplinary spit-and-polish. As the film proceeds we will see that the only good cop is an anti-authority cop.

But a change of command is taking place in the South Bronx's Precinct 41. The easygoing Captain Dugan is being replaced by the firm, authoritarian Captain Connolly (Edward Asner). Connolly is critical of the state of affairs in the precinct and Dugan defends himself indignantly: "Sure. Let the politicians and everybody else off the hook. Blame Dugan, that's the easy way. You got a forty block area with 70,000 people packed in like sardines, living like cockroaches. And that's Dugan's fault, right? You got the lowest per-capita income and the highest rate of unemployment in the city. That's my fault. Why aren't I out gettin' all these people jobs? Largest proportion of non-English speaking population. Dugan's fault. Why ain't he out there teachin' 'em English? Families that have been on welfare for three generations. Youth gangs, winos, junkies, pimps, hookers, maniacs, cop killers. Dugan's fault."

But two cops have been killed and Connolly calls for draconian measures. All criminals in the district are to be pulled in, he tells his patrolmen sternly. No more looking the other way. "We're going to bring them in, book them, toss them, and see what they spit out. And we won't quit until we get a lead!" Murphy, before all the other patrolmen, somewhat incredibly, objects. "If we all go around with our noses buried in the penal code we could make a hundred bum collars a day. The jails would be full, the neighborhood would be empty, and we wouldn't be one step closer to clearing these killings." Murphy spells his humane doctrine out even more explicitly to his partner while on patrol: "You don't go turnin' this neighborhood upside-down every time somebody gets killed. Not even a cop."

For someone who knows anything about the behavior of policemen when other policemen are killed, particularly in their district, this is a truly breathtaking statement. And as for Murphy's remark that the jails "would" be full, the jails are full already, as everybody knows (most especially policemen), they are in fact *over*-full—two men to a one-man cell—which is why dangerous criminals are being paroled, a considerable part of the problem in itself. In any case, Connolly's orders are followed. Hundreds of small-time criminals, all black or Puerto Rican, are run into the precinct house, plus a few members of the "South Bronx People's Party," and soon a jeering crowd is forming outside, chanting, "Let the brothers out! Let the brothers out." Murphy is standing by a window, cupping his hands, joining in the chant. When he sees Captain Connolly's angry eye on him, he continues the chant defiantly, "Let the brothers go!" Later, when Connolly orders him to take a black leader of the crowd into custody, Murphy, ever a friend of the oppressed, says to the man quietly when he resists: "Hey, man, we don't want you in here. You just cool it, and let us book you, and you'll be out on the street in an hour."

Another key scene occurs later on when fire engines answer a call and neighborhood youths start bombarding the firemen with bricks from the roofs. Police squad cars come to the firemen's aid and are bombarded in their turn, and a particularly tough cop named Morgan (brilliantly played by Danny Aiello), rushes to a rooftop with his partner, spots a Puerto Rican we know to be innocent (but he does not), and brutally throws him from the roof into the alley. The scene is witnessed from a nearby roof by Murphy, and a crisis of conscience ensues: should he rat on a fellow cop?

Murphy, of course, is given ample opportunity throughout the movie to demonstrate that he is the kind of humane, compassionate, "caring" person policemen should be, but, alas, are usually not. He delivers a baby. He beguiles a homicidal maniac into surrendering his weapon to him without the senseless force so often used on such poor creatures. He saves a hysterical transvestite, a "jumper," from plunging to his death from a rooftop after a fight with his roommate over a Donna Summer wig. There are a few wicked people in the South Bronx too, of course. How could one deny it? José and Hernando (played with imposing authenticity by Miguel Pinero, distinguished off-Broadway playwright and ex-convict, author of *Short Eyes*) are heroin pushers who, trapped in a neighborhood hospital, take doctors, nurses, and patients hostage—which gives Officer Murphy, assisted by a Puerto Rican colleague, the opportunity to prove his heroic qualities as well by descending from the roof in a harness, entering a back window, and gunning down the evildoers.

The plot also manages to work in a love affair for Murphy with a hospital nurse (Puerto Rican, of course). To Murphy's grief he discovers that she is a heroin user, if not quite an addict. By her definition "smack" is her equivalent of a vacation. She dies of an overdose, administered to her deliberately and cold-bloodedly by Hernando, who sees danger in her relationship with Murphy (this before he is blown away by this same Murphy).

We have heard Murphy's partner warn him that a policeman who informs openly on another policeman—by testifying against him in a murder trial, for example—is ostracized and must leave the force. But Murphy, in his grief at the loss of the woman he loves, decides that he must turn Morgan in for murder nonetheless, though the connection between the two events is murky. The only causal link I can see between the nurse's death and this momentous decision is that Murphy feels that, after all the evil perpetrated by White Society upon the poor suffering residents of the South Bronx, to let a murderous white cop go unpunished would be too much (although if someone can find a better explanation I will be delighted to hear it). The film ends in a blaze of virtue. In the last scene, Murphy's urge to preserve the law proves too strong to resist, and he, implicitly but unmistakably, reverses himself and decides to stay on the force after all. Presumably he and his partner walk off together into a good cop's sunset, ostracized but happy.

The story of *Fort Apache* is organized around a series of deaths. The first is the murder of the two rookie cops by the black prostitute whacked out on Angel Dust. This surely is a tragedy. But who is responsible? The point could be debated in this first case, but my view is that what this movie is telling us, by and large, is that if White Society had only provided this unfortunate black prostitute with a good job downtown she wouldn't be wandering around zonked out of her mind on Angel Dust murdering cops.

We now have killing number two (arranged in order of logical sequence). The black prostitute is knifed to death by José, the partner of Hernando, the two of them drug pushers. Since Hernando and José, not visibly under the influence of drugs, behave like truly vicious people, in the simple terms of the movie it would be implausible to claim they are portrayed as victims of White Society. But every ethnic group has its bad apples, does it not? Hernando and José are villains. But, lo, in killing number three, Hernando and José, having taken hostages at the hospital, are shot to pieces by Murphy and his partner. Of all the killings in the film, this is the most conventional, the film's offering to accepted piety: good destroys evil. But with the death of the nurse, Murphy's love, we approach the film's moral center. *Who killed the nurse?* Now, "mechanically" speaking, it was Hernando who killed the nurse by deliberately giving her an overstrength, undiluted sachet of heroin. But if the nurse didn't shoot heroin, she wouldn't have been exposed to this sort of viciousness. And why does the nurse shoot heroin? If there is perhaps some ambiguity about what drove the black prostitute into prostitution and taking Angel Dust (since we never learn what they call in Hollywood her "back story"), I submit that what we are being told by every scene in this movie, every shot, every foot, every frame, is that if White Society hadn't erected a wall of both racial and economic prejudice against the nurse (whom we come to love and admire) she would have been able to take *real* vacations in the Bahamas and wouldn't have been driven to surrogate vacations by means of heroin.

The last killing, of course, is also central to the film's meaning. Officer Morgan, a racist white man, throws an innocent Puerto Rican youth from a rooftop to his death. Considering the chorus of apologetics the film has given us for every kind of criminal behavior committed by nonwhites in the South Bronx—even declaring that the police had no right to turn a neighborhood upside-down every time "even a cop" is killed—we hear not a word in extenuation of Morgan's action. No one tells us he was an abused child or had a cruel father. No one reminds us that the fire engines have come into the precinct to help it, and that they have been greeted by a hail of bricks—which can kill very easily. Remember, also, that two cops have just been killed. A cop killer is on the loose. But, no. Morgan is a white man and is condemned utterly.

Near the end of the film, Captain Connolly makes a speech to Murphy at the moment Murphy announces his intention of resigning. Connolly says with great gravity: "I want this neighborhood to know there are cops up here to protect them when they're in trouble, and arrest them when they're wrong. I want them to know that this precinct isn't a clubhouse or a freak show, but the house of law. And that the law means something in their lives!" The speech is well written, and delivered with strong feeling by Asner. But Murphy (Newman) rejects it flatly and bitterly: "You've run this district into the ground in two fuckin' weeks. Look outside at your domain, Captain Connolly. Blood's been runnin' like sewer water in the streets. Riots and homicides and who knows what else is laying out there that we haven't found. But nothing's changed."

It must be obvious that what we are dealing with here is nothing less than the full "liberal" doctrine on crime. Crime is caused by poverty. If poverty is not somehow abolished, nothing can be done about it. Punishment of crime, since it does not attack the root of the problem, can have no effect. Another idea associated with the liberal view is that since prison demonstrably fails to rehabilitate prisoners, and since these people lead such miserable lives anyway, what is the point of aggressive police and judicial action against them? (This view is much easier to maintain if the speaker lives in Scarsdale, New York, or New Canaan, Connecticut.) And indeed, cozily conforming to this attitude, all the native South Bronx evildoers in *Fort Apache* are conveniently wiped out: the black prostitute, the two drug pushers, all neatly done in by their environment. In the normal course of human events in the South Bronx, truly dangerous criminals are tidily destroyed, you see, so why all the commotion?

As a description of big-city crime, the above analysis has drifted so far from the reality of recent years as to read like some kind of liberal fairy tale. In fact, most street criminals are *not* punished. In fact, on the odds, it is extremely rare when a street criminal *is*. What with the tiny proportion of violent street felons who are apprehended, of apprehended felons who are indicted, of indicted felons who are convicted, and of convicted felons who are actually sent to prison, the chances of a violent street criminal spending even a day in jail are almost microscopic. Criminals, to all appearances pragmatic people, are acting accordingly, and crime continues to increase. Second— very disturbing to liberal orthodoxy—as welfare programs and aid to non-white inner city ghettos have risen to historic proportions in this country in the past two decades, crime has not dropped, as it theoretically should have, but continues to rise.

We have on our hands a case of profound social pathology concerning which Orwell (since I have been quoting him) offers a clue. In *Down and Out in Paris and London* he points out that people who live on the dole, when this is offered in a depersonalized, institutional, way, are not grateful. If anything, although they speedily accept what is given, they demonstrate an active resentment toward their benefactors. (Orwell was describing tramps, who did not even want to work, so he was dealing with a pure case.) What seems to be involved is a psychological quirk. Common sense should tell those on the dole that if it weren't for the compassion of others they might be starving. But they have also accepted a state of dependence, and this is an offense to their pride and self-esteem, and they resent it.

The most clear-cut manifestation of this today, in my opinion, occurs when firemen who enter ghetto districts to extinguish fires, or policemen to apprehend murderers or violent robbers, are welcomed by storms of stones, bricks, and even ashcans thrown from the rooftops. Sometimes there are gunshots. To my knowledge such scenes are unprecedented in history. They have nothing in common with Sicilian neighborhoods cowed into submission by the Mafia and *omertà*, the law of silence. Nor do they have much to do with oppressed populations who, repeatedly in history, of course, have risen against their oppressors. It is hard to see how a fireman on his way to put out the flames in a neighbor's home is oppressing you. *Some* nonwhite ghetto residents have shown again and again and again their tendency to feel that a fellow ghetto nonwhite can do no wrong. A ghetto resident murders another ghetto resident? The neighborhood youths throw bricks at the policemen who come to arrest him. He's a soul brother. They don't want him arrested. A community in which behavior of this sort is standard has lost not only its sense of law, but its sense of survival.

As it happens, most people living in the ghetto communities— as we know from polls and other evidence—are against this kind of behavior. They are the ones who are victimized by it, and they repeatedly call for more police protection, not less, and tougher enforcement of the law. The irony is that most of the intended recipients of *Fort Apache*'s benevolence—in effect a kind of "benign racism"—reject it vehemently.

As for Murphy's reaction to a cop-killing—regretful but unvindictive, kindly, unwilling to disturb the South Bronx's forgivably illegal folkways just because two comrades have been murdered—this is the fairy tale of fairy tales. Cops often feel lonely, they often feel society (above all the judiciary) isn't backing them up, and they're the only ones who even care about catching criminals. But they take care of their own. Unlike a liberal-minded actor *playing* a cop, a real cop's life is on the line. Criminals who kill cops are normally resisting arrest, desperate, and half-crazed. Their life expectancy can usually be counted in seconds. In 1976 Tom Walker, a former police lieutenant in the same 41st Precinct, wrote a book of memoirs also called *Fort Apache*. A passage concerning the mere "stomping" of a police officer is worth quoting (Officer Marsh was in trouble and had radioed for support): "Marsh was being unmercifully beaten when the responding unit knocked down the door. They were followed by another unit and together they did a job on the three men. Marsh lay still, his face already swollen, his arm broken. Infuriated by the sight of him lying on the floor, the officers evened the score . . . you can't allow precedents. Word gets around and the next thing you know cops are being stomped on street corners."

So we are back among Kipling's rough, hard-bitten, not-over-sympathetic men without whose willingness to administer harsh justice and brutal discipline the refined, humanitarian culture of more civilized men would not last a day.

How is it that the authors of the movie *Fort Apache, The Bronx* do not see this? I return to Orwell—whose changing attitudes in a time of crisis are relevant here also. In April 1940, during the so-called "Phony War," when Orwell himself had already rallied to the flag but when it was still unclear what was in the heart of the mass of Britons, so recently believers in Neville Chamberlain's appeasement policy, Orwell wrote: "The truth is that it is impossible to discover what the English people are really feeling and thinking. . . . One cannot be sure until something of a quite unmistakable nature—some great disaster, probably—has brought home to a mass of the people what kind of world they are living in." One month later German panzer divisions broke through in the West, the Allied armies collapsed, and Britain stood alone against a totalitarian world stretching from the English Channel to the Bering Strait. The British people learned at last the kind of world they were living in and rose, it must be said, to their "finest hour."

In international affairs, in a piecemeal fashion, a long string of events from Pol Pot and the Boat People in Southeast Asia, through Afghanistan and the Ayatollah Khomeini, to growing awareness that most of the world's vital oil supplies are under the control of none-too-friendly powers, has led the American people, and some other nations of the West, to glimmerings of the "kind of world they are living in." Hence the making, and the triumph, of *Breaker Morant*. But when the enemy is within the gates the problem is murkier. I personally feel there is a mounting tide of feeling in this country to repress criminal and lawless elements, but this tide has yet to reach the liberals of Hollywood—who, naturally, do not live in or anywhere near the South Bronx. What's more, in this area of public policy, I can imagine no "disaster of a quite unmistakable nature," no Dunkirk or Pearl Harbor, capable, in one dramatic stroke, of bringing these liberals back to reality.

I refer once more to Orwell—the post-Dunkirk Orwell—and again to his essay on Kipling. Orwell continued to think Kipling a "jingo imperialist" and "morally insensitive," but Orwell had a perception of genius. Kipling's notorious identification with authority and the ruling power, so distasteful to later intellectuals, conferred upon him one tremendous advantage, a "sense of responsibility," which was the secret of his strength and influence. "The ruling power," wrote Orwell, "is always faced with the question 'in such and such circumstances what would you *do*?'—whereas the opposition is not obliged to take any real decisions. Where it is a permanent and pensioned opposition . . the quality of its thought deteriorates accordingly."

Some wealthy Hollywood entertainers, along with many of the tenured professors in our universities, are members of our "permanent and pensioned" opposition, and the quality of their thought has, indeed, deteriorated appallingly. For all I know, the authors of *Fort Apache, The Bronx* think themselves perfectly capable of making "real" decisions, and even preeminently suited to take over command of New York's Police Precinct 41. If so, I would like to see them tell a muster room filled with cops about to go out on patrol in the South Bronx that two of their comrades have just been shot to death but that they shouldn't give the incident undue importance. I would like to witness the scene.

All that remains to be said about *Fort Apache, The Bronx* is that the people who made it had talent and it ran away with them. Excellent casting, acting, exciting action. Real Puerto Ricans. Real-looking cops and pimps and hookers and pushers. Real garbage. The nightmare vision of the South Bronx, crime and vice, death and putrescence. If ex-President Carter made a tourist's circuit of this new zone of horrors, why shouldn't

American moviegoers want to make it as well? The film's didactic message (and I have quoted chapter and verse) plainly went sailing over the audiences' head, just so much verbiage between the action scenes. If the public had responded to the didactic conclusions the film's authors were so earnestly trying to convey, I suspect most theaters would have been empty.

Note: This essay was published in early 1981, in the first months of the Reagan presidency.

3

Bolshevism as the Politics of Intent: Warren Beatty's Reds

I FIRST MET Warren Beatty in the transit lounge at the Copen-
hagen airport in 1969. He was on his way to Russia, already
embarked on a project to make a film called *Ten Days That
Shook the World*, based on the celebrated work of a boyhood
hero of his, John Reed. When Warren Beatty was a boy, and for
many years afterward, the only biography of Reed available was
the one by Granville Hicks—written when Hicks was a member
of the Communist party, a work whose proofs had been vetted
by Earl Browder and which Hicks called "as important a contribution to the cause of Communism as I was likely to make."
And it can be supposed that Beatty's view of Reed even in 1969
was not highly critical.

In the presidential campaign of 1972, Beatty, who seemed at
the time to have political ambitions of his own, vigorously
supported George McGovern. But more recently he has
chummed up, I understand, to Senator Daniel P. Moynihan—
rather closer to the opposite end of the Democratic party. Such
a change of heart left him the problem of what to do with this
movie, which had already swallowed up millions of dollars.

We will never know what *Reds* would have been if Beatty had
made it when his enthusiasm for McGovern was at its height.
But even after the crushing McGovern defeat, with Nixon in
office, détente was the watchword. Beatty put in many hours
reading through the John Reed collection in the Widener Library
at Harvard, and in 1976, with Nixon gone but détente still the

39

cry, commissioned a talented British playwright, Trevor Griffiths (*The Comedians*), to do a screenplay. History, however, would still not lie down and play dead. I will not summarize the international developments of those years, but I am sure that Warren Beatty more than almost anyone else was aware that relations between the United States and the Soviet Union since the invasion of Afghanistan were—to be succinct—chillier, and that he was stuck with a hero who was a member of the first Executive Council of the Comintern and the most famous American Communist of all time.

Now it is perfectly clear that at no point did Warren Beatty, who is *Reds*'s producer, director, co-scriptwriter, and star, ever intend to convey the total and unqualified admiration for a Communist state expressed in *Ten Days* by John Reed. But Beatty must have thought that there was something, as they say, that Reed was doing right. And what he was "doing right" has been honed down for Beatty by the cruel events of the years. The Bolsheviks, we all know, brought into being a system of government that has comparatively few avowed advocates in the West these days. But Reed, boyish, romantic, sublimely ignorant of the theories of the Bolsheviks before their seizure of power, convinced that he was taking the side of the earth's insulted and injured against their malign and only oppressor, capitalism, celebrated the Bolshevik triumph as a millennium. What are we to think of that?

The film's answer was most clearly illustrated to me by the words of a well-known fellow film critic as, his face illuminated, we walked together out of one of *Reds*'s early screenings. He had loved it. "What was so great about the film," he said emotionally, "was that it shows that all John Reed's wonderful idealism was *still* a good thing, no matter what happened afterward." He glowed for perhaps half a minute with the virtue of this idea, and then, an unexpected thought coming along, turned to me in genuine curiosity and asked, slightly troubled: "What went wrong over there in Russia anyway?" This was one of the critics who, at the annual meeting of the New York Film Critics Circle, voted *Reds* the best movie of 1981.

So even though *Reds* hardly endorses the Bolshevik Revolution (in fact at the end, in gentle tones, it even condemns it), the movie, it turns out, has politics after all. They are what can be called the "politics of intent," as opposed to the politics of achievement. If one has noble intentions, and means well toward one's fellow man, and one's heart is pure, and generous, and filled with love, then that is what matters. If one's ideas are unworkable, bring social disruption, disaster, and even tragedy on a colossal scale—one can't be expected to foresee all that, can one?

The commercial success of *Reds* was only moderate. Early reports had it successful in the affluent neighborhoods of big cities, but doing poorly in the South, heartland America, and even most suburbs. The film's greatest triumph by far was unquestionably with the critics (and with the members of the Motion Picture Academy who gave it twelve Academy Award nominations), and it is hard for me to avoid thinking that some of them love the movie so passionately precisely because it exonerates them from responsibility for some follies and unworkable nostrums to which they subscribed in the sixties and seventies. Their heart, after all, was in the right place. That, *Reds* tells them, is what counts.

And indeed, *Reds* evokes quite a number of themes of the 1915–20 period that make a link with recent decades: the counterculture (then called "bohemianism"), the sexual revolution (then called "free love"), advocacy journalism (a variety of which was known as "muckraking"), and in a very large way feminism, which entirely takes over major parts of *Reds* through the love story of John Reed and Louise Bryant. In fact, it was mainly by putting that story into the foreground and pushing the strictly political issue into the background that Beatty hoped to overcome the problem of a movie with a Communist hero being released in the unfavorable climate of the early 1980s.

John Reed's life is rather better known than that of Louise Bryant. Reed's family, or at least his mother's family, was one of the richest in the state of Oregon. In his maternal grandparents' mansion, in which he grew up, he was an isolated rich boy, a dreamer. The closest he ever came to the laboring classes of this world, aside from servants (Chinese and romantically exotic), was Portland's shanty Irish, of whom he lived in mortal dread. Whenever he saw an Irish kid coming he ran for his life.

In one sense, however, Reed came by his radicalism honestly. His father lined up with Lincoln Steffens in supporting Theodore Roosevelt's conservation movement, and since one of the movement's principal targets was the timber interests, the basis of Oregon's major fortunes, he suffered for it financially. Nor was there any lack of radicalism about at Harvard when young Reed got there in 1910, and Reed—in a fairly novel approach for the time—made strong efforts to establish himself as both a radical and an aristocrat. When his Harvard classmate Walter Lippmann later crossed swords with Reed, he wrote him a singularly disdainful letter saying: ". . . I have known you too long and I know too much about you. I watched you at college when a few of us were taking our chances. I watched you trying to climb into clubs and hang on to a position by your eyelids, and to tell you the truth, I have never taken your radicalism the least bit seriously."

Reed first came to public notoriety by organizing the Madison Square Garden pageant to raise funds for the IWW silk workers on strike in Paterson, New Jersey. The strike also marked the beginning of his love affair with Mabel Dodge, who maintained the most brilliant salon in Greenwich Village, and who, it was said, had enough money to endow all of Greenwich Village forever. Mabel sponsored the Paterson pageant, and the following day, without waiting to discover the fate of their silk strikers (they were crushed), or even to see if the pageant had turned a profit (it had not), scooped up the poor, exhausted Reed and carried him off to Europe where he recuperated in a villa in Florence, bathing in a fountain designed by Michelangelo. Upton Sinclair called Reed "the playboy of the Revolution," and, although he apologized for the remark, there was, as can be seen, some truth in it.

For the wider American public, Reed became an overnight celebrity with his reporting as a war correspondent on the Mexican Revolution, during which he attached himself to Pancho Villa's brigand-guerrillas. His tales of wild cavalry charges amidst a hail of bullets and of colorful, illiterate peon-generals festooned with cartridge belts quite captured the imagination of U.S. readers. Reed admitted even at the time to "rearranging" his stories, and there is now substantial skepticism about his overall integrity, particularly regarding his account of close calls with death when, aside from the Mexican pointing the gun, Reed was the only witness.

When World War I broke out, Reed was inevitably sent as a correspondent, but after the turbulent excitement and exoticism of Mexico, with simple, savage men swooping down from the hills on their horses in daring attacks, singing afterward around campfires, Britain, France, and Italy were a big let-down: nations about as materially developed as his own (hence not romantic), engaged in a grim, static war of attrition.

Reed had no great enthusiasm for either party in what he called this "trader's war," but since Washington sympathized with the Western allies, most Greenwich Village radicals leaned somewhat to the other side, viewing Germany as the "underdog," and when Reed journeyed around to the German side of the line (the United States then being neutral), his reports on the German occupation of French territory were largely favorable. One day in the trenches, handed a Mauser by a German officer, he even fired two shots at the French lines. When this action was reported in the press, the French, needless to say, did not consider the matter a joke and barred Reed from France for the remainder of the war.

He next appeared in Russia. Since he had written playfully in his U.S. passport, "I am a German and an Austrian spy. I do it for money. Reed," the Russians immediately threw him in jail. Released, Reed found himself surrounded by a vast population almost as backward, emotional, and disorderly as his beloved Mexicans, and became an instant Russophile.

Disappointed in himself as a war correspondent, Reed returned to the United States, had a bad kidney removed, and published a volume of bad poetry. On learning that the Czar had fallen, Reed's spirits lifted again and he immediately sought an assignment to Russia. With funds provided by a wealthy Park Avenue lady, he arrived in Petrograd barely in time to catch the

October Revolution, his eyewitness record of which, in *Ten Days That Shook the World*, was to write his name into history.

Before leaving New York, he had written in an unpublished introspective essay: "I wish with all my heart that the proletariat would rise and take their rights. . . . I cannot give up the idea that out of democracy will be born the new world—richer, braver, freer, more beautiful." And now here it was happening before his eyes. Reed had no, or next to no, Russian. As Bertram Wolfe said: "Of the awesome disputations of Russia's intelligentsia he knew nothing. Of Lenin's authoritarian party structure and organization machine even less: so much the freer was his fancy to endow the conflict and chaos he was to witness with the form and substance of his own dream." Even his illustrator, Boardman Robinson, once complained to Reed, "But it didn't happen that way!" To which Reed replied, "What the hell difference does it make!"

As can be seen, John Reed was a rather free-wheeling adept of the "New Journalism" (which of course was no more "new" in his time than it was when it reemerged in America in the 1960s). He nonetheless left a book that, for all its "rearrangements," lacunae, and unabashed partisanship, provides the most vivid eyewitness account of one of the great events in modern history.

Almost ironically, perhaps in accordance with the principle that "those who know don't write," early Soviet leaders found *Ten Days That Shook the World* the most coherent rendition of those October days written by anybody of any nationality, including Russian, and it became, for a time, one of their sacred books. Stalin later suppressed it because of the huge role it gives to Trotsky (hardly mentioning Stalin at all), and in the Soviet Union it remained a non-book for over twenty-seven years. As for Reed himself, he died of typhus in a Russian hospital in 1920 at the age of thirty-three, and was accorded the singular honor of burial under the Kremlin wall.

Whatever his failings, John Reed is by any measure a far more imposing figure than the petulant young woman whose love affair with Reed has been pushed so alarmingly to the fore in Warren Beatty's movie.

Louise Bryant was a sexual adventuress, a chronic liar, a self-styled "writer" who hardly wrote, an ambitious social climber described as "very eager to get on," a thrill seeker, a character more out of Emile Zola than Theodore Dreiser. While using Reed's connections to the fullest, she deceived him at every turn, usually with men either famous or handsome. After Reed's death in Moscow she made a society marriage with none other than diplomat William Bullitt, Franklin D. Roosevelt's first ambassador to the Soviet Union and U.S. ambassador to Paris at the fall of France in 1940. Their divorce papers were sealed permanently at Bullitt's request.*

She had actually had a brief career as a journalist, reporting from Europe for the Hearst press after Reed's death, her major scoop being an interview with Mussolini. But she took to drink, then to narcotics. One of the last sightings of her was in the mid-thirties in Paris by an American writer who had known her while she was married to Bullitt. A "terrifying figure" rose "literally out of the gutter." Emma Goldman saw her being carried out of the Sélect Café by two drunken Corsican soldiers. Within a few months she was dead.

Charitable souls have attributed Louise's rather spectacular final decline to mourning for Reed, her true love. But her seven-year marriage to Bullitt, who maintained palatial homes in New York and Paris, would not at first glance seem an act of mourning. The plain fact is that Louise, along with her ambition, had always given clear signs of a dark, destructive, "mucker" strain in her personality. On her first trip to Europe in 1917, the U.S. passport official, who knew nothing about her, wrote resignedly on her application, "I suppose I will have to issue a passport to this wild woman." The passport picture has been described as

---

*I have been reproached by members of Louise Bryant's generation for concealing what I knew perfectly well at the time I wrote this essay: that Louise Bryant was living openly in her last years as a lesbian, and that there is little doubt it was because of her lesbian activities that Ambassador Bullitt had their divorce papers sealed. I have been assured by numerous people that "everyone" in the Paris of the period knew Louise Bryant was a lesbian, and since it has never been reported and these people will not be with us forever, I note their assurances here as part of the historical record.

showing "an unkempt young woman, hollow-cheeked, with dark rings under her eyes, mouth agape. . . ." She was twenty-nine years old.

Why should John Reed fall in love with and marry such a creature? A fragment of an unpublished piece of fiction written by Reed and called *Story About Celia* offers a significant clue:

> Celia belongs to a race of women who are the world's great lovers. They seem less of the earth than of the spirit of the earth. . . . They respire habitually in the thin, high atmosphere that artists sometimes breathe. They see Truth, not in flashes, but as a steady white light; Truth often at variance with the world's ideas. . . . They are as innocent as a swallow in mid-air, for even when they know evil, they cannot understand it. They are always beautiful.
>
> Such a woman is created for love alone. Although by breeding and delicacy, she shrinks from vulgarity, yet she will give herself to a beast among men if she loves him. . . . Deliciously human, they desire human love above all else. They are brimful of the joy of the world, shifting colors, jewels, robes, the pageant of lights and moving people. They are like chalices filled with unbounded passion and infinite faith in the love of men.

This fragment suggests, first, that literature, which was Reed's first love (and to which he hoped eventually to return), suffered no great loss when he abandoned it for journalism and politics. Second, it would seem to indicate that sharp perceptions of female character were not Reed's strong point. Neither Mabel Dodge, nor Louise Bryant, nor any other woman with whom Reed is known to have been connected bore the slightest resemblance to "Celia"; indeed, one has the right to wonder if such a woman has ever walked the earth. But it appears evident that this description of "Celia" captures the inner essence of what Reed imagined an attractive woman to be. When he met Louise Bryant in Portland, he wrote to a friend: "I think I've found her at last. She's wild, brave, and straight—and graceful and lovely to look at. In this spiritual vacuum, this unfertilized soil, she has grown . . . into an artist."

The plain fact seems to be that Reed saw women through an idealistic haze. And I will carry the point further. Having read in Reed's writings of the new life that would spring up on earth with the advent of socialism ("richer, braver, freer, more beautiful"), I am inclined to think that the idealistic haze through which he saw women was the same idealistic haze through which he saw the socialist future.

The bitter irony of all this is that there is a marked parallel (fastidiously avoided by Warren Beatty) between the ultimate destinies of John Reed's two great loves. The political love of his life was the infant Bolshevik Republic, viewed in 1917, when hearts were young, hopes were high, and the brightest dreams seemed possible. This euphoric paradise degenerated into the Soviet Union we know today, which whatever a few persistent admirers may think of it, John Reed would unquestionably have loathed. The female love of Reed's life, Louise Bryant, after her splendid time in the sun, degenerated into a moral derelict, a drug addict, a human wreck in the gutters of Paris. She died the very year of the first Moscow Trials. Where was that "Truth," that "innocence," that "joy," that "steady white light"? Gone, alas, with the rest of John Reed's hazy illusions.

Now many eminent men in history have had relationships with women of slender substance. Literature abounds with examples, and even recent political affairs offer us, on varying levels of respectability: Pierre and Margaret Trudeau, Nelson Rockefeller and Megan Marshak, Wilbur Mills and Fanne Foxe. But stories like this, while not without their fascination, do not—cutting to what I think is the heart of the matter—offer attractive "role models" to the new woman of today. If the romantic hero John Reed was in love with Louise Bryant (Warren Beatty's reasoning clearly went), the historic Louise Bryant must be pumped up to be worthy of the love of the romantic hero John Reed. Louise's act, in short, would have to be cleaned up quite a bit. This pumping up of Louise with an eye to feminine audiences corresponds in my view to a phenomenon of recent years that could be called Zelda-ization, after Nancy Milford's highly successful book on the wife of F. Scott Fitzgerald.

The technique is a slippery one. American history hardly lacks for colorful folk heroines, ranging from Susan B. Anthony to Annie Oakley, not to mention the quite incredible Claflin sisters, Tennessee Claflin and Victoria Woodhull, perhaps the most flamboyant and beautiful women ever to come out of Ohio, who preached free love, socialism, and women's suffrage as early as 1870, were supported for a time by Cornelius Vanderbilt, published *The Communist Manifesto*, and both married rich, Victoria managing meanwhile in 1872 to be the first woman candidate for U.S. president—with Frederick Douglass as her running mate. But the Zelda school sternly ignores these women who achieved distinction on their own merits, preferring to select the wife or woman companion of some male celebrity, puffing her up to an unconscionable degree, and leaving the final impression that if she was less important than this celebrated masculine mate, it was only by a hairsbreadth, and then perhaps because she was forced to sacrifice her own talents to his.

In the apotheosis of Louise Bryant in *Reds*, this calculated strategy to flatter the female public is what we are dealing with, and it involves distortion of the historical facts and suppression of some of the gamier details about Louise.

Louise Bryant told various friends at different times that her grandfather was the young son of an Irish lord, that her father was an officer in the British army, and that she was related to Oscar Wilde. She was born, in fact, Anna Louise Mohan, and her father, a one-time Pennsylvania Irish coal miner named Hugh Mohan, abandoned her mother, "a very plain, unremarkable woman" of Spanish origin, soon after the child's birth. The mother remarried a railroad conductor on the Southern Pacific named Sheridan Bryant, and most of Louise's youth was spent at desolate rail junctions in Nevada.

Ambition, certainly not scholarship, finally took Louise to the University of Oregon in Eugene, where she cast a veil of mystery over her earlier life. Upon arrival in Portland after graduation, she promptly sought the company of her well-to-do university sorority sisters and with their help secured a job as a society reporter on a local newspaper. Louise soon made a "good match," marrying a handsome young dentist of good family named Paul Trullinger in an Episcopal ceremony (she was born Catholic). On a miniature scale, she followed much the same new line John Reed was taking in the fashionable East, mixing life among the well-born with "advanced" ideas, both political and sexual. Her husband allowed her to maintain a separate artist's studio in downtown Portland where, tiring of reporting, she first did sketching, then wrote poetry, meanwhile carrying on a series of love affairs.

When she heard that Portland's native son, John Reed—now a national celebrity thanks to his coverage of the Mexican Revolution—was about to pay a visit to his family, she calmly laid plans to ensnare him. Always supremely confident of her sexual attractiveness, Louise arranged a dinner through mutual friends. As it happened, they met before the dinner. The love affair—if that was what it was—took fire almost instantly. Reed invited her to come live with him in New York and, since this was Louise's intention from the beginning, she did not need much convincing. In exactly three days, she was off to Greenwich Village. Within two years of her arrival there she was to become the wife of John Reed and the mistress of Eugene O'Neill, to get to know many of the most celebrated people in America, and to witness the October Revolution in Russia. Given that her assets were almost entirely sexual, and that this was all a long way from rail junctions in Nevada, it was a rather good score.

Reds sets out to give us something of the romantic sweep of the period 1915 to 1920, to be something of a *Gone With the Wind* of the American radicalism of those years. It has an excellent supporting cast: Maureen Stapleton as Emma Goldman, novelist Jerzy Kosinski as Grigori Zinoviev (first head of the Comintern), Paul Sorvino as Louis Fraina (Reed's rival as head of the contending wing of the American Communist party), Gene Hackman and George Plimpton as different sorts of editors, and Edward Herrmann as Max Eastman. (It should be pointed out, in passing, that both the writing and casting of the Eastman character completely falsify the Reed-Eastman relationship, as the historical Max Eastman was not only more brilliant than Reed but, as it happened, far more handsome.) But the most extraordinary figure in the "supporting" cast is Jack Nicholson as Eugene O'Neill, who in my view walks away with the movie.

As for the principal characters, Diane Keaton is completely out of her depth as the upgraded Louise Bryant: fretful and peevish at her dignified moments, superficial and nervous when supposedly projecting emotion. If you want to see *Annie Hall Takes the Winter Palace*, this is the movie for you.

Warren Beatty, an actor far from without resources, is up against a different sort of problem. The trouble with *Reds* as a *Gone With the Wind* is that the average American moviegoer knows more or less what the Civil War was about, but when it comes to the Smolny Institute and Grigori Zinoviev, it is doubtful if one U.S. filmgoer in a thousand has ever heard of them. What's worse, there are those doctrinal problems, as between the Communist party of America and the Communist Labor party, the AFL and IWW, etc., etc. Though for revolutionaries ideology is of supreme importance, Beatty proceeds in terror that the audience might be bored stiff by all the political doctrine or, even more dangerous, that it might actually focus on the violent upheaval being proposed and take fright.

Hence whenever Reed talks politics in the film—and a certain amount is unavoidable—Beatty's voice is rapid, light, high; he trips along at such a rate that the viewer could hardly follow him if he wanted to. Time and again irrelevant distractions are introduced to lead the mind away. When Beatty can think of nothing else, the camera dwells on the face of Louise Bryant to see how Annie Hall is taking all this: anything to get away from what is being said.

In dealing with the love story, and Reed's personal life, Beatty uses a different technique. Since one of the main purposes of the film is to show that even though his revolutionary ideas didn't pan out too well, Reed was still a warm, idealistic, lovable fellow, Beatty's performance, I am sorry to report, suffers from a horrible case of the cutes.

Jack Nicholson, on the other hand, doesn't seem the least bit reticent about what he's got to say. Unlike his friends, the real O'Neill—and I understate—never fell under the spell of the promised Bolshevik utopia. True to this, when he and Louise meet in the film after her return from Petrograd, Nicholson, faintly smiling, a glass in his hand, drawls out, taking his own sweet time: "Russia. Russia. Ah, Russia. Russia's been good to you and Jack. It's given you a means of leaving home, meeting people, lecturing. . . ." Agitated and indignant, Louise sputters, "Are you really that cynical?" Calmly, his eyes cold, but still smiling faintly, O'Neill answers, "I'm really that cynical." On the printed page, the line seems unremarkable. But I have seen *Reds* twice, once at a fancy invitational screening on New York's East Side, the second time a month later with a popular audience in Times Square, and on both occasions the line brought down the house. Most movies have only a single line that will have this effect, and for *Reds*, explain it as you will—Nicholson's delivery, the thought, astringency amid so much soppiness— this is the one.

The film actually begins with a series of elderly people reminiscing about John Reed and Louise Bryant. First we hear only reedy old voices: "I'm beginning to forget." . . . "Were they Socialists?" . . . "I'd forgotten all about them." . . . "There was Mabel, then another gal, then Louise." . . . We begin to see the faces as they speak. In all, there are about thirty real persons in this series and they reappear periodically throughout the film as a kind of chorus. Although never identified, they include a number of quite distinguished people, some no longer living: Roger Baldwin, founder of the ACLU; the old Hamilton Fish; Dame Rebecca West; Lady Dora Russell; Henry Miller; George Jessel.

Almost all the critics have testified to the feeling of authenticity provided by these real witnesses, and regretted their not being identified. I myself, although I agree as to their effectiveness, feel a little hocus pocus has been practiced upon the audience. Each of these people, it has been reported, was interviewed for something like four hours, but we only get them for two or three sentences at a time, on an average of about twice apiece. Four hours of Rebecca West out of which we are given a grand total of perhaps thirty seconds; what did she say in the other three hours and fifty-nine minutes? We hear her disparagement of Beatrice Webb, for example, but nothing about Jack Reed.

The snippets have obviously been edited very artfully. There are contradictions here and there to give an impression of heterogeneity. When a dignified old lady says, "In those days men respected women," we cut straight to raffish old Henry Miller debunking, "There was as much fucking then as there is today!" But by and large, not surprisingly, the elderly chorus has been edited to leave very much the impression that the film as a whole is intended to leave. It all happened in another age. It was romantic. They were free souls, free spirits, a romantic couple. In politics, they were idealistic. They meant well.

The main body of *Reds* begins in Portland at about the time local beauty Louise Bryant meets the famous journalist John Reed. She takes him to her studio for an all-night interview. He rattles on with boyish excitement about one radical cause after another (there are lots of quick cuts in mid-sentence; you are not supposed to listen). Cup after cup of coffee is poured and in the morning light Louise, still pure, rushes the dismayed Reed out of the house.

Their second meeting leads to sexual union, but when Reed invites her to join him in New York, Louise is suddenly indignant, each word filled with biting scorn: "What would I go as, your *girl friend*? Your *mistress*? Your *paramour*? Your *concubine*?" The historical Louise Bryant, as I have already indicated, had no objection at all to such a position, and in fact had been plotting and scheming and deploying all her wiles to get Reed to bring her to New York in just that capacity.

Reds contains dozens of examples of artistic license taken with the lives of its two principal characters, but I shall only mention a few which suggest how the basic traits of these characters have been altered, particularly that of the heroine. When Reed in the film considerately introduces Louise to an important editor ("I'd like you to meet Louise Bryant. She's a very talented writer"), she attacks Reed furiously afterward: "I don't need that! I don't need that kind of patronizing introduction!" The movie also gives the impression that Louise was a crackerjack newswoman—at the front, under enemy artillery fire, even earning Reed's accolade, "You're a hell of a journalist." And when Reed urges her to come with him to Russia, she imposes strict conditions: "I want my own byline. And I want to be known as Miss Bryant, not Mrs. Reed!'' Yet the real Louise wrote so little as to have a very weak claim to this professional description. When she went to France as a ''war correspondent'' during World War I, entirely through Reed's connections, she wrote exactly one piece, which was deemed unusable, and returned to America without a single published story to her credit.

The movie, then, gives us a feminist Louise Bryant, independent, successful, and successful *in her own right*, whereas the historical Louise Bryant was almost the pure prototype of a woman who achieved her success entirely by getting her hooks into one man, then another, then another. When the line of men ran out, it was the end.

Louise's most interesting relationship was the one with Eugene O'Neill, perhaps because it was part of the most notorious ''triangle'' in American letters, but also because it was such a shameless, sometimes comic example of Louise at work. Here again the movie distorts by showing O'Neill taking the lead in the affair, whereas it was actually Louise. Good looks played a part. Even John Reed's friend, Max Eastman, described his face affectionately as ''rather like a potato,'' whereas the looks of Eugene O'Neill as a young man—black-eyed, brooding, romantic—have been called ''breathtaking.'' One day at Provincetown (which the whole gang of them put on the map), while Reed was away on some assignment or other, Louise sent O'Neill a note slipped between the pages of a book of poetry: ''Dark eyes. What do you mean?''

It didn't take. O'Neill considered Reed one of his closest friends. Reed helped him tremendously to get a start. To deceive him with Louise would be the vilest treason. So Louise tried again, another note: ''I must see you alone. I have to explain something, for my sake and Jack's. You have to understand.'' When O'Neill came, as he felt he must because of Jack, Louise told him that Jack, despite his apparent cheerfulness, was preparing himself for death because of his coming kidney operation. His sickness prevented their having sexual relations and they were living together as ''brother and sister.'' She loved Jack and could never leave him, she said, and was helping him to resign himself to death, but her own state was desperate. She was turning to O'Neill for consolation and for love. Jack, she assured him, understood.

It was said that the only person in Provincetown who believed this story was O'Neill (and strong evidence of his belief is that he used different parts of the story in two of his greatest Broadway successes, *Strange Interlude* and *Beyond the Horizon*). But it worked. She got him.

When Reed came back from his trip, he was chipper, gregarious, not at all like a man preparing himself for death. He acted lovingly toward Louise, comradely and admiring toward O'Neill, as ever. Great numbers of people considered it the most scandalous *ménage à trois* in America, but their closest friends were convinced that Reed didn't have a clue. The final irony was that Reed wrote a one-act farce for the Provincetown Players called *The Eternal Quadrangle* to parody the current Broadway vogue for triangle plays, which he considered ridiculous.

Soon Reed and Louise were off to Russia for the October Revolution. The movie shows them returning to New York together, but in actual fact Louise had abandoned Reed in Russia two months earlier. This time she actually succeeded in publishing a number of newspaper articles, covering the Bolshevik Revolution from "the woman's angle," and, having spent *four* months in Russia, collected them together in a book entitled *Six Red Months in Russia.*

As soon as she arrived in New York, she wrote O'Neill in Provincetown a series of passionate love letters, saying she had crossed three thousand miles of frozen steppes to come back to him, her lover, and pleaded with him to join her in New York and live with her, displacing Reed. As it happened, O'Neill at this point was living with another lady, whom he was about to marry. Accommodatingly, however, he offered to meet Louise halfway, literally, in Fall River, Massachusetts. Louise, indignant, wrote that she had better things to do than go to Fall River, Massachusetts. They never met again.

In actual fact, then, the scenes in *Reds* between Louise Bryant and Eugene O'Neill after her return from Russia obviously never took place. Nonetheless, one of them is among the best things in the film: because it is grounded on what I think was O'Neill's real character, because it is stunningly performed by Jack Nicholson, and because it provides a note of skepticism in what is otherwise a very syrupy movie. It is the scene in which O'Neill confesses he's "that cynical," and then goes on coolly pressing his point. "Something in me tightens," he says drily, "when an American intellectual's eyes shine at the mention of Russia. I say to myself, 'Watch out. I am being offered a new version of Irish Catholicism.' " He concludes with ironic sadness, "It's too bad, Louise. You had a lighter touch when you were touting free love."

The degree to which these lines reflect Warren Beatty's own feelings could be debated, but by the time we get to the film's last sequences it is plain that Beatty is laying down *Reds*'s definitive view of Bolshevism. At a meeting with Reed in Moscow in 1920, Emma Goldman says in great distress: "The dream we had is dying, Jack. The centralized state has all the power. They're putting anarchists like me in jail, exterminating all dissenters. I want no part of it. Nothing works. There's starvation. Four million Russians have died." Reed answers promptly, at first full of the old fight: "Those four million died because of the Allied blockade. What did you think anyway? It was all going to work right away? It's a war, Emma! And we have to fight it with discipline, terror, firing squads—or give up." Reed pauses, as if the seeds of doubt have been sown in his mind too, and turns to Emma Goldman, his face filled with childlike uncertainty: "Otherwise, what has your whole life meant?"

Nonetheless he is soon off with Zinoviev, Radek, and other leaders of the Comintern for the Congress of Oriental Nations at Baku on the Caspian. This Congress, called to foment anti-imperialism, was thronged with Persians, Turks, Caucasians, and Arabs, and the goal of Reed's speech (the historical transcript of which shows few doubts) was to warn them that while they already hated the British and French colonialists, they should not think Americans were any better. "Don't trust American capitalists. There is but one road to freedom. Unite with the Russian workers and peasants. . . . Follow the red star of the Communist International!"

In the movie, startled by a sudden roar from the mob with great brandishings of swords at his words "class war," Reed persists in his confusion until he is informed that this expression has been translated for the audience as "holy war."

The actual train trip to and from Baku was one of the first glimpses some of the foreign members of the Comintern were to get of just how rapidly the Bolshevik bureaucracy had adapted itself to its position as the new privileged class: expensive foods, rare wines, beautiful Caucasian prostitutes. According to a report attributed to Reed, old Muslim women boarded the train and stripped their charges, lovely girls, some barely fourteen years old, before the delegates—these idealists dedicated to destroying the rotten structure of capitalism and building a better world. It all ended, said Reed, in a drunken sex orgy led by Radek, all in an armored train riding through a countryside whose population was starving. What seemed to disgust Reed was mainly that the girls had been paid for. Now if they had been fine Russian girls who had freely chosen to engage in sexual intercourse with the delegates, he said, that would have been something else.

This whole historical episode is naturally far too raw for a movie that is edging into soft focus for its final sequences. In the film, we get only Zinoviev, Radek, and company, well dressed, rather like modern corporate executives, eating good food off white tablecloths on the train. If it is a point, it is not exactly a lethal one. There are no shots of starving peasants.

In the train scene, on the way back to Moscow, Reed squabbles with Zinoviev over the translation of his "class" into "holy" war. "Nobody changes my text," he exclaims righteously, as if arguing with one of his editors in New York. Zinoviev, unperturbed, confident, acts as if Reed is making a mountain out of a mole hill. Reed brings out hurriedly, "My text is the truth! When you separate a man from the truth, you separate him from what he loves the most, from what is unique. You purge dissent. And when you purge dissent, you purge the Revolution!" At which point Reed is saved, literally, by the cavalry. White troops are attacking the train. A Red Cavalry unit, riding in the train's cattle compartments, disembarks and gives chase. Reed runs after them, tries to board a horse-drawn cart bearing machine guns, but fails.

An obvious allegory is intended here. In an earlier "memory" shot of Reed in his Pancho Villa days, we have seen him running after a similar Mexican cart and joyously catching it. This time he runs and runs, runs and runs, but the cart of the Red Revolution disappears into the dust and mist. Gone. At the train's arrival in Moscow, the Comintern leaders disembark with some pomp at the station. But Reed is not with them. Symbolically, no doubt, he slinks off the train by another door, wasted by exhaustion, and perhaps also by disillusionment (who can tell?), to find to his amazement Louise, to whom he murmurs, "Please don't leave me."

And that, politically speaking, is it. From there on, the film is simply the end of their tragic love story, with Reed dying in a Russian hospital of "the movie disease," sometimes known as "malady X"—with no conspicuous symptoms, the patient remaining pretty—the same disease Ali McGraw died from in Erich Segal's *Love Story*. The real Reed was stricken by typhus, one of the dread killers. Paralyzed on his right side, unable to speak, at the end he was fighting for every breath, and died at two o'clock in the morning on October 18, 1920.

There has been extensive debate as to whether John Reed, America's most famous Communist, was disillusioned with Communism when he died. With few exceptions, those hostile to Communism have been convinced that he was (Reed's published letters to Max Eastman being particularly persuasive), while Communist sympathizers have tended to resist this view one way or another and, when they could, to ignore it.

The only real issue is whether Reed was disillusioned enough to make an actual break, for which there is evidence on both sides. I am prepared to accept the balanced judgment of Bertram Wolfe: "If disillusionment means a final accounting with the Communist movement and its ideology, there is room for differences of opinion. . . . But if disillusionment is understood intellectually and emotionally rather than organizationally, Reed was probably as disillusioned as it was possible to be and still remain in the movement." To which he adds: "His disillusionment was cumulative, and it was headed toward a break on both sides if he had persisted in his course . . . the reins were tightening almost visibly month by month. If Reed had gone on fighting the new line and the old leadership, the Comintern would probably have saved him the trouble of resigning."

Taking the long view, the statistics are eloquent. To my knowledge every single member of the first Comintern Executive Committee who was not physically present in the Soviet Union—such as its first secretary, Angelica Balabanoff, or Reed's American colleague, Louis Fraina—became a bitter anti-Communist. Of those who actually lived in the USSR, few survived. Zinoviev was the chief defendant in the first of Stalin's show trials and was executed in 1936. Radek was tried in 1937 and died in the camps. Bukharin was tried in 1938 and executed. Béla Kun died in 1939 in Lefortovo prison. It is a grim list.

In Warren Beatty's *Reds*, Reed's disillusionment with Communism is nothing if not tactfully handled. A look of uncertainty on Reed's face. A quibble with Zinoviev over a translated word. A grand thought, hastily delivered in time for the cavalry. A symbolic cart run after and not caught. And a separate descent from the train's back door. As disillusionments go, you can't accuse Beatty of going overboard.

After Reeds' death, the film closes on quavering old voices, again, for the last time calling up the shades of the past. "It was October, I think. Someone told me Jack Reed died. You can imagine how I felt." . . . "I'd forgotten all about them. Were they Socialists?" . . . "They were a couple. You always spoke of Jack Reed and Louise Bryant." . . . "Lenin said to him, 'Are you an American?' And Reed said yes. And Lenin said, 'An American American?' Reed said yes." And then *Reds*'s last lines, its last nostalgic old voice, its very last words: *"Grand things are ahead. Worth living, and worth dying for. Jack himself said that."*

Well, we now know what lay ahead. According to the most recently published estimate, evenly reported by the *New York Times*'s Harrison Salisbury, during the Russian Civil War and from related famine and forceful repressions: 18 million dead. In the Soviet forced collectivization of agriculture and associated imprisonments and executions: 22 million dead. In the great Soviet purges of the 1930s: 19 million dead. In Soviet executions after World War II: 9 million dead. Other authorities estimate that of Russia's 30 million dead during World War II, at least half, or 15 million, died at the hands of the Soviet state in massacres of labor camp populations and various ethnic groups during retreats, mass deportations, and continuing deaths in the Gulag. In all, no fewer than 83 million deaths. The fruits of Bolshevism. Grand things, indeed.

One report of John Reed's last days had it that he was "terribly afraid of having made a serious mistake in his interpretation of a historical event for which he would be held accountable before the judgment of history."

But he needn't have worried. In the world of Warren Beatty's *Reds*, where men are judged by good intentions alone, Jack's as clean as a hound's tooth.

4

Is It a Cuddly Universe?
Spielberg's E.T. *and Scott's*
Blade Runner

WITH ALL THE attitudes and institutions that the great Western nations have in common, there are still sharp differences among them in matters of daily living. The French, for example, almost close down their film business in summer. Movie houses are nearly empty, showing mainly reruns, old hits, holdovers from the spring. For a new film to be scheduled to open in Paris in midsummer is considered a virtual death sentence. In America, on the other hand, as everyone knows, summertime is the big season, sometimes the go-for-broke season, when major Hollywood studios often learn whether they will end up the year in the red or in the black. Americans turn out in their millions to see the big summer movies, particularly young Americans, and many other Americans nominally adult in whom warm weather seems to trigger a regression to a state of emotional immaturity.

Now the received wisdom of the U.S. film industry is that what adolescents of all ages want in the summer is escapism: adventure, "action," horror movies, broad comedies. There are fashions in escapism as in all things, of course. In the summer of 1981 the "socko" film for immature minds, *Raiders of the Lost Ark*, seemed to be a retreat to an imagined golden age of immature minds, when an aggressive, culturally assertive style of behavior was permissible because the story was set, after all, some fifty years ago—thereby neatly avoiding today's mixed

61

and shifting attitudes. The summer movies of 1982, not altogether surprisingly, were split into widely diverging streams.

Steven Spielberg's *E.T.* ("The Extra-Terrestrial"), which has been called by the country's leading reviewers "miraculous," "magical," "radiant," a "triumph," a "masterpiece," and a work of "genius," is so mawkish that I can barely manage to write about it. It is the story of an adorable little creature from outer space—a $1.5-million toy resembling a shell-less turtle—who is stranded on earth when his spaceship departs prematurely. He wins the hearts of three children in the Los Angeles hills and they save him from bullying grown-ups, one of the children saying feelingly, *"E.T., I love you,"* when a team of doctors almost kills the little fellow, presumably by proceeding too aggressively in trying to save his life. "Leave him alone! Can't you see you're killing him!" cries the child, who later, the doctors gone, brings E.T. back to life with his simple declaration of love. Not much else happens in the film, E.T. departing by spaceship to his heavenly home at the end, promising the children that he will always be with them: "I'll be right here."

All the reviewers noticed that the children in the film "understand" E.T. better than the adults, but none of them, to my knowledge, noticed how specifically American these menacing adults are shown to be. While at least one of the children wears a "No Nukes" T-shirt, the domineering adults, shot in a variety of ways to make them appear as menacing as possible, almost all represent American authority, two of them even dressed in silver suits with the Old Glory shoulder patches of U.S. astronauts—once a fearless nation's blue-eyed pride.

The message of *E.T.*—which pervades every frame of the film—is that except for us, it is a benign, cuddly universe. Gentle, loving E.T. arrives from gentle, loving space on a gentle, loving spaceship. He is treated roughly by a bunch of insensitive, aggressive Americans who think that everything outside their narrow world is dangerous. And the sooner we give up that sort of attitude the better. One leading New York critic wrote: "It's been years since I've been this caught up in the emotions of a movie." Later, concerning the film's emotional climax, when the regenerative power of love brings the adorable toy back to life and E.T. leaves this vale of aggression on his peaceful spaceship, the critic affirmed: "I have never seen so many grown men weeping at a screening." I personally have never noticed grown men weeping at screenings at all and can only say that when I saw the film there was not a humid eye in the house.

Since the same critic compared *E.T.* to Walt Disney and classic animal films, and since I am probably one of comparatively few people in America to have seen the kind of animal films the Soviet state shows *its* citizens, the reader, in passing, might be interested in learning what they are like. Boa constrictors swiftly wrap themselves around trapped rabbits (seen in close-up), pause, and then squeeze. The rabbit's head bulges hideously as he dies. Swamp animals swim desperately across lakes to excape a predator but are—not sometimes but always—caught and promptly eaten. A baby fox which strays from the litter is caught and eaten. Hunt, pursue, kill, eat. Kill, eat. Kill, eat. Nature is merciless in a Soviet animal movie. When I first saw a whole series of these quite extraordinary films, and reflected on their impact on a Soviet audience, I felt that their thrust was essentially Hobbesian: men, left to themselves, would be in a state of constant war with each other, like animals, and any form of government at all is preferable to anarchy. Let us say it is unlikely that a spectator would emerge from a Soviet animal film with the impression that we live in a benign universe.

E.T., in any event, is expected to be not only the giant hit of the season but possibly one of the most successful films of all time. And the *E.T.* phenomenon is particularly interesting with respect to what I can only call anti-national films in recent American cinema. Openly pro-Soviet or pro-revolutionary films have never done well in the United States. The "neutralist" movie, with the United States and the USSR either equally bad or equally good, certainly had its day during détente, the James Bond *The Spy Who Loved Me* being a conspicuous example. But the most interesting genus is a film that is militantly anti-American without being *for* anybody in particular. This is by far the most popular kind of anti-national film, has many variants, and promises to be with us for some time. It corresponds to a whole attitude toward the United States which has been compared with watching a boxing match with only one prizefighter visible. There is America thrashing away in the middle of the ring. But why? At whom? How pointless it all seems. In this group we have most anti-CIA movies, the interesting fact here being that none of them has been successful, at least in the United States. Robert Redford's *Three Days of the Condor*, made at the height of the anti-CIA fever in Washington, was a commercial disaster in the United States (although a great hit among our critics abroad, so all was not in vain). The treacherous thing about making a movie against the CIA, it seems, is that the very existence of the CIA seems to imply an adversary. The logic of the situation suggests that there is a second fighter in the ring after all, and that the filmmaker is concealing him. So the trick, if one wants to make a film showing American society as brutal and aggressive, is to concoct a story without the faintest hint of an adversary, revealing a tranquil, peaceful universe in which we, only we, disturb the loving order of nature. I give you *E.T.*, which might be rather extraordinary after all.

Steven Spielberg learned the hard way. His ponderous and hugely expensive *1941*, a resounding fiasco (in the United States), was an alleged comedy treating with sneering ridicule the sudden war spirit which arose in Los Angeles during a false air alert immediately following Pearl Harbor. The problem with the movie was that there were these Japanese, who had just sunk a large part of the U.S. Pacific Fleet. There was a real war. Hundreds of thousands of Americans were killed. Spielberg had forgotten about that. He is not likely to make that same mistake again, although his heart, I should expect, is in exactly the same place.

E.T., of course, represents a reversion to the same luminous, benevolent, wondrously sweet, little creatures from outer space that Spielberg already used to such commercial effect in *Close Encounters of the Third Kind*. It seems oddly simple, but for traditionalists and conservatives, science-fiction creatures from outer space are malevolent. For the new utopian liberals, they are sweet, mean us no harm, and really might be an example to us all.

But by far the best and most interesting of 1982's summer movies was *Blade Runner*. The leading role is played by Harrison Ford (of *Raiders of the Lost Ark*). It cost some $30 million. It is "futuristic." But above all it is directed by England's Ridley Scott, who the previous time out created *Alien*, with its eponymous Alien, an outer-space creature of quite astonishing malevolence. The film ended up in the year's big four (in the company, coincidentally, of Clint Eastwood, Sylvester Stallone, and *Superman*). Scott is a director with a dazzling visual technique, an undisputed virtuoso manner in the handling of colossal subjects, and how he managed to combine these skills with a smashing entry into the big money without becoming one of the cinema's household names is a mystery I have yet to plumb.

Even if I had not seen Scott's earlier pictures (*Alien* and his superb *The Duellists*), I think I might have suspected from a few advance hints I picked up that *Blade Runner* was not going to be just another summer kid movie. I knew that Scott was not very attracted to science fiction as a genre and avoided the expression entirely, going so far as to say, "Anybody on this set who uses the word 'android' gets his head broken with a baseball bat" (thereby also making it unlikely that Scott is a Quaker). I knew that what he disliked about most films set in the future was their juvenile fantasy quality, what he has called "all silver hair and diagonal zippers." I knew that he was by vocation a realist, however stunning his skills of composition and montage. And, perhaps not entirely irrelevantly, I knew that his producer was Michael Deeley, who also produced *The Deer Hunter*.

The opening shot of *Blade Runner* is simply staggering. The scene is Los Angeles in the year 2019. (At an earlier stage Scott had planned to set his film in New York or Chicago, but I suspect the new vision came when he saw Los Angeles from the heights of the Hollywood Hills, which is one of the strange sights of this world.) The aerial perspective still suggests Los Angeles of the early 1980s, but all has changed. Where today flourishes that endless archipelago of suburbs, in the film all is dark and ominous, the cityscape lit only by occasional flareups of burning gas as at oil refineries. A drastic energy shortage has arrived and the suburban areas seem half empty, but as we approach the central city we see first the splendor—giant truncated pyramids in a kind of high-tech Babylonian—and then the squalor of the streets: slime, consumer detritus of all kinds, incessant rain, presumably the result of a pernicious change in the earth's atmosphere. On the roofs of old buildings, shabby wind-energy generators turn desultorily. The colonization of outer space is well advanced, and we see an electrified dirigible cruising above the streets as part of a high-pressure media blitz exhorting viewers, not to "Come to Sunny California," of course, but to join the new colonists "off-world." The advertising blitz has a menacing ambiguity to it, suggesting that perhaps the earth's best have already gone to settle in outer space, leaving only the dregs, while at the same time planting skepticism: if it's so wonderful out there, why are they advertising so frantically?

Meanwhile, on the streets, the citizens of what was once the greatest automobile city in the world peddle bicycles in what now looks like Tokyo's Ginza district. And if this picture of the technological future is disturbing, the picture of the future of the American population—at least of the mass population of the cities—comes as something of a shock, for the Anglo-American civilization seems to have been submerged. The blare of music in the streets is sometimes Arab, sometimes Japanese. Physically the people are a mix of Chicanos, Chinese, Japanese, riff-raff whites, some dressed in "punk" derivatives. They talk "Streetspeak," a mixture of "Spanish, Japanese, German, whatever." An absolutely gigantic electrical bas relief of a Japanese woman's head urges viewers in Japanese to drink Coca-Cola. On the sleazy streets and in the garish bars there are, curiously, very few blacks—one of the film's many departures, in its construction of the future, from straight-line extrapolations of present trends.

The reviewer from *Variety*, the show-business trade journal, while showering Ridley Scott with praise for his spectacular mastery of his craft (also given high praise by Jack Kroll of *Newsweek* and others), felt that he had presented an exceedingly "depressing" view of the future. I offer this critic at least one reason why this may be so. Ridley Scott's view is not a realistic projection of things to come. It is, I suspect, his nightmare vision of what our society would become if it were overrun by what we call the Third World.

In addition to being swamped by alien peoples not absorbed into the national culture (Scott has called the "splitting into faction groups" explicitly "alarming"), the America of *Blade Runner* has lost all sense of community. Individuals in this Los Angeles of the future, and most unmistakably the film's hero, Deckard (Harrison Ford), lead lives of agonizing loneliness. Deckard has no friends, no lover, no family. What has brought about this bleak state of affairs? If this were a vision of George Orwell the cause would probably be totalitarianism, but the world of *Blade Runner* is not a highly controlled police state. If this were the vision of Jean-Luc Godard, the cause would no doubt be capitalism, but, although capitalism has evidently survived in *Blade Runner*, we see very little of the power structure. The film's burden seems to be the opposite of Marshall McLuhan's panglossian concept of a "global village." The world is too vast and too variegated to become a global village. Smaller, more cohesive social units will have been destroyed and there will be nothing to replace them.

But, curiously, *Blade Runner* is not primarily political at all. *Caveat emptor.* It is a film about the human condition, about mortality, and ends with a startling burst of Christian symbolism.

A skimpy summary of *Blade Runner*'s plot emphasizes the science-fiction origins of a film whose merits reside in texture and detailing. By 2019 the earth is decayed and millions of people have been forced to colonize other planets. Those who remain behind live in huge cities, a mixture of new buildings four-hundred stories high and the dilapidated remains of our own and earlier periods. The streets team with Orientals, Hare Krishnas, men in fezzes, all lit by a lurid blaze of flashing neon. Police patrol in "Spinners," flying cars that hover above the swarming streets. Genetic engineering has become one of the earth's major industries. When most of the world's animals became extinct, genetic engineers first produced artificial animals, and then, to do the hard, hazardous, and often tedious work necessary in the colonies on other planets, artificial humans called "replicants."

The Tyrell Corporation, the world's leading manufacturers of replicants, has recently introduced the "Nexus 6," with far greater strength and intelligence than human beings. These latest-model replicants represent an obvious potential danger to human society and their introduction on earth has been strictly outlawed, an offense calling for the death penalty. The replicants who somehow make their way back to earth are systematically exterminated (not "killed" since they are not human), the special detectives trained to track down and liquidate the infiltrating replicants being known as "blade runners."

The replicants, then, are a kind of super-slave race, closely resembling human beings (and of course played in the film by thoroughly human actors), but with no rights or, in fact, feelings—which is how they are detected, by a special "Voight-Kampff empathy/response test." As a safety factor they have been given only a four-year life span, and are, in a sense, mortal: the germ of the story.

Once upon a time, when the world was new, which is to say in 1921, Karel Capek's *R.U.R.*, "Rossum's Universal Robots" (a play which originated not only the idea of robots but the very word "robot," a derivative of the Czech and Russian words for "work"), was easily seen as an anti-Communist play: the robot revolution slaughtering the creators of robots, everyone who doesn't work with his hands; the attempt to make "nationalist" robots to fight the "revolutionary" robots. The political allegory that attached to the original artificial humans washed away a long time ago, however, and contemporary science fiction now gives us synthetic humanlike creatures in all shapes and sizes.

In the opening of *Blade Runner*, police receive an emergency report that four Nexus-6 replicants—two male and two female—have killed the crew of a space shuttle and returned to earth. The blade runner assigned to track them down and "terminate" them is Deckard. It is one of Ridley Scott's consistent traits that, whatever the locale or setting, he seeks to make his stories as credible and realistic as possible, avoiding, in this case, what he calls the "pristine, austere, clean look" in his sets and the childlike fantasy quality in general story line. Scott has reached back to the forties, for example, for the suggestion of some of the women's costumes. The year 2019 isn't that far ahead, he says. And Deckard himself is straight out of the forties, a Raymond Chandler character, a Philip Marlowe.

So it is in the tones of that hardbitten Raymond Chandler voice we have heard in a thousand movies that we hear the story of this decayed, atomized, loveless world of the future. It is a calculated stroke, daring, slightly surrealistic, nutty, but in my view works. "The replicants have no feelings. The blade runners have no feelings," muses the joyless Deckard, adding bleakly that the rest of humanity isn't much better.

But desolate and hopeless as is his view of the world, Deckard, like his Chandlerian antecedents, still does his duty. Like a combatant who no longer remembers the ideals for which a war is being fought, hates the suffering, but still continues to fight, Deckard soldiers grimly on. His cynical tone doesn't prevent him from engaging in absolutely spectacular battles with, interestingly, the two (particularly warlike) female Nexus-6 replicants, with one of his antagonists hurtling through a whole series of shattering plate-glass windows and the other producing an electrifying death rattle of shocking violence. I would not want to leap to conclusions and infer that this is Ridley Scott's final statement on the female "assertiveness training" going around, and on the coming aggressive feminist millennium, but I can only note that I have never seen anything even resembling a woman blown to such bloody bits as in *Blade Runner*.

A fifth replicant, however, has infiltrated the Los Angeles area, another female, Rachael (Sean Young), this one much more peaceful. In fact, she is so socially adapted that she doesn't even know she's a replicant, but Deckard subjects her to lengthy sessions with his Voight-Kampff equipment (rather like our lie-detector apparatus) and concludes that she is not human. Yet so desperate is his loneliness that even suspecting she is a soulless artifact and that all her rather bland emotional responses have been "implanted," he proceeds to fall in love with her.

But the film's central encounter is between Deckard and the

chief of the four warrior replicants, the silver-blond Roy Batty (played by Holland's Rutger Hauer of *Soldier of Orange* and of Sylvester Stallone's *Nighthawks*). A strange shift takes place in the movie when we realize that the "combat-model" replicants, murderous though they may be, have a stronger sense of community than the human beings on earth (where they get this from is mysterious). They are a cohesive group. They are loyal to each other. The next step is when we learn the nature of Batty's mission. With his three other partners now destroyed by explosive bullets, Batty succeeds in finding his way to Tyrell himself, the master of the Tyrell Corporation and the genetic-engineering genius who actually designed him. Batty wants to have his genetic code altered to extend his assigned four-year life span. He wants simply: to live. This proves impossible and Batty, condemned to die, kills Tyrell in a despairing rage, calling him (as Zeus to Cronos) "Father." And we are soon into the final combat between Deckard and Batty on the rooftops of this mad, futuristic, Ginza-Los Angeles.

At the battle's climax, Batty, who has been growing more human every minute, bests Deckard, who at the end is entirely at Batty's mercy, hanging by his fingertips from a ledge, ready to drop hundreds of feet into the street below. But Batty spares him, saying, "Now you know what it's like to live in fear," and plucks him back from the abyss. Then, his time come, Batty sits down on the roof in the rain. His head slumps forward. "There was nothing I could do but watch him die," says Deckard. Earlier, feeling increasing sympathy for the replicants, Deckard has reflected, "They're not that different from us really," and wondered, "Where do we come from? Where are we going? How much time have we got?" During the Deckard-Batty combat, Batty drives a spike into his own hand, and in the very last phase a white dove—for centuries the symbol of the Holy Ghost—suddenly appears in his other hand. As he slumps dying on the roof the dove stays with him, until, at his last breath, the white bird takes wing and flies into the heavens.

In a panic Deckard rushes to find the beautiful Rachael. When he asks a fellow blade runner how she is, he gets the answer, "She's going to die, but aren't we all?" Deckard finds her, and in the last sequence the two of them fly to the north to escape (breathtaking aerial shots), seeking a place to hide where Rachael can live out her time, neither of them knowing how long that time will be, the other blade runner's words still echoing in Deckard's mind: "She's going to die, but aren't we all?" Their plane sweeps over the California coastal range, between heaven and earth. This is the end of the picture.

Where do we come from? Where are we going? How much time have we got? Reviewers have expressed admiration for Ridley Scott's technical virtuosity, praising the film as a visual festival, but a number of them have admitted puzzlement as to what it is "about." Now I can understand *Blade Runner* being called insanely ambitious, pretentious, anguished, violent, mystical, incoherent, or simply mad. But when a movie features the lines I have italicized, and shows the holy spirit mounting to heaven at the death of a mortal creature, I should think it would be plain what it is about.

In my view this is a very strange and highly original movie. While using a vast array of materials from popular culture, it seems to me to have been made in something of an ontological pop frenzy about the meaning of existence. As the film advances no occasion is missed to stress that the condition of replicants is, in fact, the human condition. Replicants are made by a creator they cannot comprehend. They want to live, but know they must die. They, like men, crave life everlasting.

Ridley Scott did not come out of nowhere. *Blade Runner* is his third film. His first, made when he was thirty-eight, was *The Duellists*, based on a rather obscure Joseph Conrad short story, "The Duel," originally called "A Point of Honor." It is a tale of two officers in Napoleon's Hussars who cross each other and somewhat absurdly, fight a whole series of bitter duels from one end of Europe to the other while nominally concerned with fighting their country's enemies in the service of the Emperor. The costumes, setting, and feeling for the period are extraordinary, the faces sweaty, the officers with braided hair. French critics (a hard audience when it comes to watching Harvey Keitel and Keith Carradine play Frenchmen) were utterly swept away. The film won the Special Jury Prize at the Cannes Film Festival and Scott's career as a director was off to a flying start.

Most critics who admired *The Duellists* were probably under the impression that it was an "antiwar" movie, strongly condemning the military mentality, but I believe Scott's attitude, indeed like Conrad's, was much more nuanced. While granting the insanity of dueling, Conrad, like most men of his age, was in some awe of the martial spirit, and it is unlikely that Scott would have been browsing through Conrad to begin with if he had not felt something of the same response. "Those were violent times," Scott has said about the Napoleonic wars. "And violent men."

Aside from a truly sumptuous shooting style, Scott's most consistent trait as a director is probably his flair for realistic detailing, which makes whatever setting he chooses, no matter what the period, past or present, so peculiarly convincing. In *The Duellists* the tense sword fights, which take place everywhere from a gentle valley in the Dordogne to the snows of Russia, are likely to be counterpointed by the bleating of sheep, the lowing of cows, the snort of a horse. Flapping geese waddle to get out of the hussars' path as they savagely thrust and parry. In *Alien* the crew members of the spaceship argue about pay rates. The spaceship's passageways are filled with sweating pipes, littered with greasy rags. Even in as wildly imaginative a work as *Blade Runner*, Deckard is not served the noodles he orders in a Japanese diner but the wrong kind of noodles. The computer terminal in his home (whose decor is copied from that of a famous Frank Lloyd Wright house in Los Feliz in the L.A. area) is suitably worn and battered. The Bradbury Building, where Deckard and Batty have their last battle, is a real building in downtown Los Angeles, built in 1893 and shown, over a century later, in appropriate disrepair.

Ridley Scott studied at the Royal College of Art in London. After a brief stint as a television director in Britain he found he was given bigger budgets, and received higher pay, to make television commercials, which he proceeded to do for more than a decade. It is not generally realized that European directors almost without exception do television commercials between movies, and that even in the United States many major filmmakers (Michael Cimino) have done the same kind of work, although it is rare that they advertise the fact. Ridley Scott is something of a prodigy in this area. He has directed over 3,000 television commercials, for everything from Levis to Chanel perfume. And, perhaps most interesting, for more than ten years he ran his own thriving company, employing five directors to work under him full time. He is, oddly enough, a successful business man.

One of my long-standing complaints about most of the stars of Hollywood (both the star actors and the star directors) is that they are the highest paid people in the world who still think of themselves as workers. They have little experience of hierarchical authority, nor do they often identify with it, and when they have authority they frequently exercise it capriciously. When they start their own film companies (Francis Coppola), they usually run them like children. I am entertained by the notion that Ridley Scott's realistic touch might have been conditioned to some extent by the fact that year after year, in the most humdrum way imaginable, he has been required, as they say, to meet a payroll. It is a requirement that inculcates different habits of thought, one of which might be realism. On the other hand, I am probably reversing cause and effect. Scott probably became a success in business because he had that practical aptitude to begin with.

Although most reviewers found the tone of *Blade Runner* ominous, Ridley Scott is cheerful. The film is "good fun," he says, "not too serious," "not a warning in any sense." He says suggestively that he doesn't choose to adopt the warning mode "at the moment." It all leaves me wondering what Ridley Scott has on his mind to warn us about. Having polished off mortality, the life eternal, and all that, what will he have to say when he gets serious?

Note: E.T., as of 1989, had become far and away the biggest moneymaker in film history, at least in inflated dollars. The Ridley Scott–Harrison Ford *Blade Runner* finished an honorable but undistinguished twenty-fifth in the year of its release—but with the videocassette after-life films developed in the 1980s has become a great "cult" movie favorite, the scale of the film industry being so enormous that *Blade Runner* has now been seen by more people than have read all the works of Franz Kafka put together. At the Academy Awards that year, *E.T.*, although it had received many award nominations, won nothing. The "peace vote," it was said, went for *Gandhi*.

5

Fassbinder, Germany, and the Bloomingdale's Factor

MIKE FRANKOVICH, the veteran Hollywood film producer, used to say, "Everybody's got two businesses: his own, and the movie business." By this he meant that, wherever he went in Beverly Hills, people with no connection with the film industry whatsoever were always telling him that he should have known that film A was going to be a blockbuster at the box office and film B a turkey, that star X wasn't worth a plugged nickel but that star Y was dynamite. These experts, of course, all went to the movies, but they also all used toothpaste and they would never have presumed to deliver themselves of rash opinions to executives of the toothpaste industry. A problem was that most of these outside experts also read a fair amount about films, without ever seeming to realize that almost all of what passes for entertainment journalism is for all practical purposes a branch of the public-relations arm of the entertainment industry itself. Most people start thinking about whether a movie is potentially successful when it has already been reviewed and released, and there are either long lines standing waiting to buy tickets or there are not. At this point, all seems preordained to them, predestined. *They,* at least, would have known.

It is quite hard to convince outsiders that time and again during the making of *Jaws* the production was swept by panic. *A plastic shark: who's going to believe it?* George Lucas, on the eve of the release of *Star Wars,* gave an interview in which he hoped that, with luck, it would become a modestly successful little "kid movie" so that he could make a living doing juvenile sequels as a bread-and-butter account while devoting his main energies to more important projects. When Steven Spielberg's *Close Encounters of the Third Kind* was already finished and "in the can," the executives of Columbia Pictures were very nervous, had no idea what was in store for them, and "sneaked" the film in Texas to get some kind of advance notion of what the public reaction was likely to be. It was their misfortune that *New York* magazine sent a financial reporter to Texas to catch the sneak preview. He gazed upon the screen, saw what he thought anyone could tell was going to be a failure, and said as much in his magazine. The stock of Columbia Pictures, many of whose assets and hopes were tied to *Close Encounters*, sank sickeningly on Wall Street. But the film went on to become what was then the seventh most successful movie of all time—in the hall-of-fame list in which *Star Wars* and *Jaws* stood, respectively, one and three.

Now, on the strength of *Jaws*, you would think that Zanuck-Brown, the film's producers, had a pretty good sense of what the public wanted in a big-budget popular movie, and consequently when the team bought *The Island*, the new bestseller by Peter Benchley, author of *Jaws*, hearts were high. The film cost $22 million to produce. According to a *Variety* estimate, *The Island* earned in domestic rentals exactly 31 percent of the amount it should have brought in if it were to break even. In short, it was a fiasco. In 1979, Michael Cimino had a big win with *The Deerhunter*. Hailed as the new genius director, Cimino set out for Montana the following year to make *Heaven's Gate*. The atmosphere was festive. When the film's budget went over $30 million, passing that of *Apocalypse Now* and becoming the most expensive film in history (it was ultimately to reach $36 million), Cimino gave a big party. Until the movie was finished, he refused to show a single foot of it to the producers, who were not happy about this, but accepted, firm in the faith that they had a winner. When the film was released, the proportion of domestic rentals it actually earned to those it should have earned to break even was almost exactly 3 percent—something of a record.

But perhaps you are thinking *Jaws* and *The Deerhunter* were flashes in the pan. Perhaps *The Island* and *Heaven's Gate* didn't have big enough stars. Consider, then, the fate of Irwin Allen, the man who gave the world the "disaster movie" (*Towering Inferno, The Poseidon Adventure*). In 1980 he decided to make the disaster movie to end all disaster movies, one of the provisional titles for which was *Volcano.* Irwin Allen was prudent. He didn't take chances. The film would have a volcanic eruption, an earthquake, a tidal wave. It would take place on a beautiful Hawaii-like island in the Pacific, because people like movies that take place in nice locations. As an "insurance policy," he said, Allen signed Paul Newman, Jacqueline Bisset as the female lead, and William Holden. Even the character parts were played by actors like Ernest Borgnine, Burgess Meredith, Valentina Cortesa, Red Buttons. I visited the set of the movie when it was being shot—in Hawaii, in fact. Morale was high. Allen was sure that the picture was foolproof, that it couldn't miss. Warner Brothers, whatever it thought, forked over $22 million. When the film opened, under the title *When Time Ran Out*, its domestic rentals, compared to those it would have needed in order to reach "the break," were 5 percent.

So films over which producers have wrung their hands have made them and their descendants rich for life, while others, on which the handicappers were quoting very good odds indeed, have gone, as they say quaintly in Hollywood, straight down the toilet. "There's a lot of luck in this business," I once said to a senior Hollywood executive. "A *lot*?" he answered scornfully. "It's *all* luck." Another executive, whom I had just congratulated on a string of winners, answered sardonically, "Dear Mom, I am making a good living shooting craps here in Vegas." Hard as it is for Mike Frankovich's hindsight experts to credit, if they habitually saw even finished movies in a deserted screening room in Burbank with just two or three other executives, and had to put down their money—preferably a lot of money—at this point, months before the movie's release, they might rather abruptly discover that, curiously, the public's reaction to movies is harder to predict than they had thought.

Parlor experts on the movies are a strangely obdurate lot,

meanwhile, far more so than Monday-morning quarterbacks— who at least know who won Sunday's game. It might be that these experts are infected by the make-believe mentality of the movies themselves, for quite often they hold grossly mistaken views on which movies are successes or failures long after the returns are already in. A new film receives good or bad reviews and gets off to a good or bad start on Third Avenue in Manhattan and, for them, that's it. I have difficulty in convincing some people that Steve Martin's *The Jerk*—which got bad notices and had a halting start in New York—finished the 1980 season in the number-three position, on the heels of *Kramer vs. Kramer*. In the opposite direction, many movie buffs, remembering the initial lines and hoopla, remain stubbornly convinced that the following recent pictures—among others—were highly success- ful: Sidney Lumet's *Prince of the City*, the Candice Bergen- Jacqueline Bisset *Rich and Famous*, Louis Malle's *Atlantic City* with Burt Lancaster (which received some high-sounding critics' prizes), and two films from Australia—the pacifist World War I *Gallipoli* and the romantico-feminist *My Brilliant Career*. The first four finished the year, respectively, 75th, 79th, 94th, and 104th—which is to say, way out of the money. *My Brilliant Career* finished no less than 122nd, between *Vampire Playgirls* and *The Swinging Barmaids*. All this is by way of demonstrating that perceptions of the movie business are often quite unreal, and sometimes oddly resistant to fact.

When it comes to foreign films, and the cinematic interchange between the United States and foreign countries, the mispercep- tions frequently approach the grotesque, which is regrettable because, in my judgment, the actual relations between the United States and, say, France or Germany are rich in instruc- tion. America's foreign-language film market has historically been dominated by France, with Italy in second place. In the 1970s, however, Germany came up fast, with critics crying that the late Rainer Werner Fassbinder was the "Godard of the seventies." But just how big a thing is it to be the Godard of the seventies, or even the eighties, and just how much impact do these foreign films have on American moviegoers? At the end of every year *Variety* lists all films released in the domestic American market whose rentals came to a million dollars or more (a modest figure). In 1981, based on this list, all foreign films together accounted for 0.5 percent of the American domestic market, half of 1 percent. In 1988, the figure was 0.7 percent.

This is not a very large figure. In France, by contrast, despite a flourishing local movie industry, foreign films accounted in the same year for over 50 percent of the market (with the lion's share going to the United States). In West Germany, foreign films reached 84 percent. In 1980, American films alone accounted for 55 percent. This was not in the grand old days of American self-confidence and cultural assertiveness, you will notice, but in the eighties. The figures give an unmistakable picture of American popular culture—to this day—possessing vast international appeal. The appeal that foreign popular cultures exercise in America, on the other hand, is almost microscopic.

I do not take all this as simply a worldwide tribute to the preeminence of what used to be called the American Way of Life—although that is definitely part of the explanation. Another very large factor is that Americans, even moviegoing Americans, after over four decades of the deepest involvement in world affairs, are still not very interested in societies other than their own. To judge by their moviegoing patterns (and book-reading patterns are comparable), the bedrock American cultural insularity, or isolationism—call it what you will—is far from extinct. American moviegoers, in proportions that dwarf other societies, are absorbed in their own ways of doing things and their own country, and ill-informed, unconcerned, and incurious about others.

I should point out, furthermore, that moviegoers, compared to the audiences for television and even Broadway, are considered an elite group, disproportionately young, active, affluent, and educated. It was moviegoers who demonstrated against the war in Vietnam, and later for a nuclear freeze. Their quite remarkable lack of interest in other countries could, arguably, go either way politically, either toward the Mansfield Resolution and "global unilateralism," or, out of sheer ignorance of the nature of Soviet society (they certainly avoid Russian films like the plague), toward benign indulgence. In any event, if movie-goers are an "elite" (given *Vampire Playgirls* and *The Swinging Barmaids* the term will be understood as relative), people who see foreign films regularly are clearly the tiniest elite within that elite.

Considering the small and commercially insignificant size of the American audience for foreign films, how then did they attain the towering position of prestige they now enjoy? Why, on a visit to my native city of Boston, was I greeted by an old friend, a highly successful lawyer, with the cry, "Fassbinder's dead!"? He'd never seen a Fassbinder film, mind you, but he had been given the impression that we were witnessing a major turning point in our cultural history, something comparable to the death of Picasso, perhaps, or Bartok.

I ascribe this in large measure to what I call the Blooming-dale's Factor. Before explaining what I mean by this, having already noted the trade's minute scale, I must make an obser-vation about the quality and nature of foreign films imported into the United States. France, to take the most prominent example, has a large and successful film industry. It makes big, vulgar adventure movies, gross, implausible cops-and-robbers tales, broad farces, "women's" films of love and feminine nobility. Hardly any of these films are brought to the United States. Of Paris's ten top movies for 1981, only two have opened in New York: one because it had an American star (James Caan), and the other because one of its leading players had become known here through an earlier, cult film (Michel Serrault from *La Cage aux Folles*). Both new movies failed in America. The 1982 season's most successful French films in the United States, by way of comparison, have been a wildly pretentious, stylized art movie called *Diva*, and the latest film by François Truffaut, *The Woman Next Door*, whose commercial rankings in their own country were, respectively, 25 and 33.

So, while there is hardly a Frenchman alive who does not know Clint Eastwood, Paul Newman, and Robert Redford, France has a pop-cinema galaxy that has a huge market in Japan but that the movie houses of Manhattan's Third Avenue know not. The man reputed to be France's most successful and richest film star, who reigned over French popular movie comedies for over two decades, an institution, is named Louis de Funès. But while the French rave about Mel Brooks, Americans don't even know who Louis de Funès is.

A result of all this is that New York's purveyors of high cinema art have chosen to import from France, Germany, Italy, or wherever, a hand-picked selection of those countries' intimate, unconventional, or intellectually ambitious movies. There is certainly nothing wrong with a nothing-but-the-best policy for that American elite within the elite which enjoys foreign films. But this has given rise to the notion in a certain American class that Europe produces more subtle, sensitive, mature, intelligent, sophisticated, artistic, culturally elevated films in general (an idea which, if the American viewers were exposed to the common run of French and other European movies, would evaporate in days). And if the same American class were to approach the foreign films shown in the United States with the prior assumption that Europe was a culturally more elevated place to begin with, this assumption would most assuredly be left undisturbed.

For those who know neither New York nor the retail trade, I should perhaps explain that Bloomingdale's is a fashionable department store on Manhattan's East Side dedicated to the proposition—at least in its clothing departments—that foreign is better. In the floor devoted to women's luxury apparel the brand names of the great houses of European couture are lined up one after the other: Yves Saint Laurent, Valentino, Missoni, Chanel, Givenchy, Kenzo, Christian Dior, Giorgio Armani (interestingly, all French and Italian houses). Now at about the same time that Bloomingdale's was embarking upon its mission of bringing European culture to our shores, the future operator of Cinema I and Cinema II, who was embarking on a mission of his own—to show European films in New York with more pizzazz than ever before—deliberately chose the lot directly across Third Avenue from Bloomingdale's as the location for his new theaters. "When they're tired of shopping," he said, "those are the kind of people who'll come to my movies." It seems almost comically simple, but it turned out to be an extraordinarily astute judgment. It caught on. It snowballed. With the decline of the Times

Square area, Third Avenue became not only the choicest place to open a foreign movie, but the choicest place to open any kind of movie: *The Exorcist, M*A*S*H, Saturday Night Fever, Stir Crazy, Kramer vs. Kramer, The Deerhunter, Reds, On Golden Pond.* The invasion of big Hollywood productions probably contributed somewhat to the confusion. I suspect that the person who sees *Piaf, The Early Years* at Cinema I, with Richard Gere's *An Officer and a Gentleman* playing next door at the Coronet, is imperfectly aware that the former is drawing only $25,000 a week while the latter, showing simultaneously at seventy-six other houses in the New York area in a "wide break," is pulling in a fast $1.6 million. The view from Third Avenue can be misleading.

I think that if Cinema I and Cinema II had been located elsewhere on the East Side I might still have detected the Bloomingdale's Factor in the American reaction to foreign movies. Nevertheless, it is a historical fact that the operator who for many years was the leading promoter of foreign films in New York deliberately and consciously sought the Bloomingdale's connection. It will be seen, in any event, that the whole phenomenon is very much in the American grain. For if the American masses over the long course have been overwhelmingly self-absorbed and isolationist, there has always been a small American "upper crust"—formerly of birth and money, now more often of education and money—convinced in their bones that Europe was a culturally superior place that America could never match. Lenny Bruce used to tell a joke that Hitler had at last been found in Greenwich Village—where he was a "big hit." It wasn't the anti-Semitism part, Bruce explained, "It was that he'd been to Europe!"

When we turn from France, which has had a thriving film industry since the invention of the motion picture, to Germany, whose cinema has never really recovered from the rise of the Nazis over fifty years ago, we come upon an imbalance in trade with the United States that is truly stunning. Three facts: (1) The ten top moneymaking films in West Germany since World War II have been American, every one. (2) In 1980, as already mentioned, American movies held 55 percent of the German market—quite overwhelming the Germans' share of their own market: 9 percent. (On the U.S. market German films accounted for the smallest fraction of 1 percent). (3) In 1981, the same year which saw massive "peace," antinuclear, and anti-American demonstrations in West Berlin, Bonn, and elsewhere in West Germany, nine of the leading fifteen moneymaking movies at German box offices were American, including the top four. As opposed to France, moreover, which in the past has had a weakness for American films critical of the United States (the E. L. Doctorow–Milos Forman *Ragtime* and Costa-Gavras's *Missing*), the American films popular in Germany are in the old-fashioned, overpoweringly pro-American mode. The number-one film of 1982 in Germany was Burt Reynolds's *Cannonball Run* (which the French did not like), and the number-two film was the James Bond, *For Your Eyes Only*, whose villains are Communists, Cubans, and East Germans—which must have struck rather close to home. The most evil, malevolent person in the movie is an East German. (I apologize to British readers, but from the start the James Bond films have been written and produced by Americans, and they are considered by the trade, and most of the public, as American movies.)

Although I have not spent more than a few weeks in Germany recently, I have the impression that there has been a marked shift away from the West, and toward neutralism, in West German opinion, particularly among the young. But it would be hard to prove this by studying the German movie business. John Vinocur, whose coverage of Germany in the *New York Times* for five years was, in my opinion, extremely perspicacious, has remarked that in Germany (as opposed to other countries) films are treated as "comparatively low culture." That might be part of the explanation. But in Germany, as elsewhere, the moviegoing public is disproportionately young, educated, and affluent, which leads one to suspect that many of the demonstrators and moviegoers might be the same people, which in turn suggests a society in a state of quite considerable confusion.

But if there is one subject in Germany about which there has been little confusion, it is Rainer Werner Fassbinder. Until very recently the German public has quite unequivocally loathed him. An American enthusiast, writing recently in the scholarly *Quarterly Review of Film Studies*, said that among Fassbinder's great assets were his "absurd or grotesque esotericism," the "sheer number of his films" (over forty in thirteen years), and "just as importantly perhaps—his flamboyantly marketable personality: an outspoken, homosexual, leftist critic of modern capitalist society." To this glowing personality sketch we can add, from the police reports at the time of his death, that he was a drug addict.

But the above writer's appraisal notwithstanding, it is not everyone who would find an outspokenly homosexual drug addict with radical, revolutionary politics to be flamboyantly marketable. And, in actual fact, until about the last three years of his life, he was hardly marketable at all, at least in his own country. Another contributor to the same issue of the *Quarterly Review of Film Studies*, with more knowledge of the German scene, wrote that in the Federal Republic until the mid- and even the late seventies, Fassbinder and his friends were "scorned, ridiculed, and rarely exhibited," and that Fassbinder himself was "increasingly shunned." How then did Fassbinder survive, plunking out three or four films per year from 1969 on?

The filmmakers of Germany's *Neue Welle* ("New Wave") represented a kind of "underground" cinema, by which I mean that the slovenliness of much of their work, combined with its counterculture flavor and (though there are exceptions) tediously anti-materialist, anti-bourgeois, anti-consumer-society themes, recalled many American noncommercial films made when the word "underground" was still in vogue. It should be clearly understood, however, that in the case of Germany this was a *subsidized* underground cinema. For without lavish government funding this New German Cinema would not only never have survived, it would never have been born.

The *Bundesrepublik*'s film-subsidy system is one of the marvels of the world. Government subsidies are available to worthy German filmmakers at three levels, federal, state, and municipal, and of course the supplementary subsidizers of last resort are the state-owned regional television networks. A number of the

West German *länder* (states) came under Socialist control before the federal government in Bonn, and television has been called, simply, the "patron saint" of the New German Cinema. But the Federal Film Board *(Filmforderungsanstalt)* is of an extraordinary solicitousness as well. If a new film it has sponsored cannot find a distributor, it will pay a distributor to handle the film. And if the distributor cannot find an exhibitor, it will pay the exhibitor. *Variety*, which calls this system "cradle to grave" security for filmmakers, has written that a German producer "who knows how to play the complex but bountiful subsidy game can totally finance his film without personal risk," and it protested editorially against a system that takes taxpayers' money and "channels it to *auteurs* who can make a risk-free living cranking out turkeys." But the question is, which *auteurs* get to make a risk-free living cranking out turkeys, and which do not?

Now, from Fassbinder's verbal statements, which I find abundantly illustrated in his films, I think it fair to say that he was irremediably and viscerally hostile to the society in which he found himself. He was not a very coherent thinker, but his political philosophy, as clearly as I can sum it up, was Marxism tempered by anarchy. He believed in "the Revolution" and "the class struggle," but also managed to get himself attacked as a misogynist and an anti-Semite. "The really terrible thing about oppression," he said, "is that you can't show it without showing the person who's being oppressed and who also has his faults. For example, you can't talk about the German treatment of the Jewish minority without evoking the Jews' connection with money. . . ." He liked Jerry Lewis because he was "very destructive" and showed that material goods were worthless. He adored director Douglas Sirk (a Hollywood hack) because he "destroyed the very life-style [the studios] wished to exemplify." Fassbinder thought that television was an "interesting medium" but that owning a color TV set was contemptible. It was observed that he took a "romantic view of terrorism." Now why should a man with such a sanguinary attitude toward his own society have been funded by public monies to make movies which the public of that society did not want?

Here all I can say is that this tells us something about the politics of people drawn to become cultural bureaucrats, dispensing taxpayers' money for the public edification. In our own country, under a Republican administration, we have seen on the Public Broadcasting Service a "documentary" on the Sandinistas that should have been paid for by the Nicaraguan Information Ministry, and a "documentary" on the Algerian-sponsored Polisario Front that should have been paid for by the Algerian Information Ministry. They were both funded by American taxpayers. Under the Carter administration we had, also on PBS, a "documentary" on the CIA whose architect and star witness was Philip Agee. So if sufficient funds were available at the Corporation for Public Broadcasting, for example, I see no reason why its personnel would not gladly finance films by an American Fassbinder. And in Germany, of course, Socialist governments had been in power for thirteen years. In fact, Fassbinder's entire career took place, and was promoted by the state, under Socialist governments. He made his first feature film in 1969, the year Willy Brandt became Chancellor.

The defense of German cultural officials would obviously be that Fassbinder represented High Art and deserved protection from the philistine laws of the marketplace. Should a government refuse support to a Kafka, a Rilke, a Proust, a Joyce, just because he does not sell like Vicki Baum or Harold Robbins? The flaw here, on the evidence, is that these cultural bureaucrats would not know a Kafka if they saw one, and that what I find politically objectionable in Fassbinder they plainly like. For if you take away Fassbinder's politics and *Weltanschauung* there is not much left. Fassbinder was self-confident and enterprising (what role drugs played here I do not know), but he did not have a shred of film talent. His taking drugs or dressing like a Hell's Angel or being a homosexual would not prejudice me one way or another with respect to his artistic talent. His politics, since they loom large in his work, would pose more of a problem, but I believe myself capable of admiring the artistry of men to whose doctrinal beliefs I am unremittingly hostile. (To take only one example, I am an admirer of the prose of Louis-Ferdinand Céline, author of *Journey to the End of Night*, who was a fanatic anti-Semite.)

But Fassbinder's films are an institutionalized amateur night. They are inept, wooden, stilted. The characters are walking ideas or allegorical symbols. His typical films are made up of endless tableaux with static camera in which inexperienced actors improvise lifelessly, "acting adjectives," as Stanislavsky would have said. The scenes often approach complete stasis. The frame does not move. Actions do not develop. Emotions do not change. It was Fassbinder's conviction that life under capitalism was alienated and stunted, so in his films characters begin scenes alienated and stunted, and they end scenes beyond his capacity to show the alienating and stunting processes at work. The early Warhol-Morrissey films (*Flesh, Heat, Trash*), to which Fassbinder's could technically be compared, also used static camera and were of an even more ostentatious slovenliness, but they had an idiosyncratic vitality which Fassbinder films do not possess. In the last years of his life, when he was given bigger budget and sets and period costumes for such movies as *The Marriage of Maria Braun* and *Lili Marleen*, Fassbinder was completely beyond his depth. There was rather more to look at, but the films were really no better.

On the set of Fassbinder's posthumous *Querelle de Brest*, actors Brad Davis and Franco Nero were reportedly "surprised at the apparent scarcity of direction they got." Fassbinder himself has been described as "hiding in corners and acting almost like a visitor on the set and not the director." But to anyone who knows anything about the way motion pictures are made, the most revealing fact of all is that Fassbinder almost never looked at his "dailies"—formerly called "rushes." I have never heard of such a thing. I have known directors who considered their art as that of "provoking accidents," but I have never known a director not to take a look at the accidents he'd managed to provoke. A man who makes a film like that might have written the screenplay (as Fassbinder did more or less), and he might be responsible for having brought the whole thing about in the way a theatrical producer might be responsible for staging a happening, but I am not certain I would consider such a film as under his control. To my way of thinking, Fassbinder's movies—and they look it—are virtually undirected.

During the seventies, unappreciated by audiences in their native Germany, Fassbinder and the other lonely, subsidized directors of the New German Cinema set out on their *Wanderjahre*, specializing in the film-festival circuit, where they began to earn considerable kudos. Fassbinder won the International Critics Prize at the Cannes Film Festival in 1974, and other foreign honors. By general agreement the Big Four of the new cinema were Fassbinder, Werner Herzog, Wim Wenders, and Volker Schlöndorff (one of whose films was the fervently pro-PLO *Circle of Deceit*). In varying groupings they dominated attention at the 1975 film festivals in both London and New York (*Village Voice:* "The Germans are coming! The Germans are coming!") And so it went. I trust all this foreign peer-group acclaim produced great gratification among German cultural officials, but it did not translate into noticeably stronger box-office returns for German films even abroad. Foreign movies in the United States hardly matter commercially, but France, as I have explained, is very open to the cinema of foreign countries. In 1972, when the *Old* German Cinema was still firmly in the saddle, the German share of the French market was 3.3 percent. By 1980, with the New German Cinema riding high, as it were, this figure had dropped to 1.8 percent. There is some irony in that fact that when Germany finally cracked the French and even the American markets in 1981 and 1982, it was with two films that owed little to the New German Cinema. To everyone's astonishment the unprepossessing *Christina F.* outdid Robert Redford's *Brubaker* in France, while *Das Boot*, the story of a German U-boat in World War II, was the biggest film success in German history, both here and in Germany.

Based on a huge German bestseller, *Das Boot* is directed by Wolfgang Petersen, who has gone about saying it is "antiwar" and that it shows that war makes beasts of men, and so on. Perhaps he felt obliged to make statements of this sort to avoid giving the impression he approved of World War II, or perhaps thought the Nazis' cause was just. Possibly it is lost from the memory of the race that even such men as our own Theodore Roosevelt, who believed in the tonic effects of war, never claimed it was pleasant or agreeable. The fact is that *Das Boot—*

and I suspect Petersen knows this quite well—shows military men, fighting in a cause that was not only doomed but diabolical, behaving with the most extreme stamina and courage. Along with Australia's *Breaker Morant* and Hollywood's *An Officer and a Gentleman* (set in peacetime), it was the most pro-military movie to be made in the West since the great upheavals of the late sixties. The cause, in such stories, is almost immaterial. The outcome is most certainly so. The Alamo was lost, after all. But William James felt that the qualities men showed during such ordeals were necessary for a nation's survival. If nations did not produce such men, they succumbed.

At the German Film Prize festivities in June 1982, where the awards are made by special jury, *Das Boot* was of necessity very much in the running. Also in competition were a new Fassbinder, a new Herzog, a film based on *The Magic Mountain* by Thomas Mann, and the latest from Margarethe von Trotta (Volker Schlöndorff's wife), *Die Bleierne Zeit*. Called *Marianne and Juliane* when it played briefly in New York, it is a work of naked apologetics for Baader-Neinhof terrorism, and since it is not at all allegorical it seems even more extreme than Fassbinder. The surprise isn't that *Marianne and Juliane* carried off the top prize, which is about what I would expect from a German film jury these days (or for that matter Italian, since it had already won the top award at Venice), but that someone let slip that during the six months of *Das Boot*'s triumphal runs in Germany an apparent majority of the jury had never even seen it. This is a degree of narrowness rarely met, even among custodians of a nation's culture.

In an essay published in the *American Sociologist*, Paul Hollander points out that in recent times the structure and institutions of society have come to be held responsible, not only for social and racial justice, the pattern of distribution of wealth, and economic misery and deprivation, but for the highly personal problems of the individual. In this new style of thought, the individual is seen to be less and less responsible for his own happiness. If he does not attain personal fulfillment and self-realization, it is the fault of "society." Examining statements by young Americans who joined the Venceremos Brigade in

Cuba, Hollander observes that it is hard to imagine Robespierre, Bakunin, Lenin, or Trotsky voicing such sentiments as the following: "I am all fucked up. Too many problems that I have to deal with. I am amazingly selfish . . . that's certainly how we are taught in a capitalist society, and I am a child of capitalism." Or: "I am beginning to understand how very thin is the line between neurosis and oppression, and consequently how in the most profound way the solution to what formerly seemed our most personal problems is deeply political." Or: "Amerika does a lot of ugly things to people. It puts walls between them. . . ." And so on.

As it happens, this kind of thing is the core of the politics of Rainer Werner Fassbinder. His films show an endless stream of people in advanced stages of neurosis, social apathy, alienation, and anomie. And both the films and Fassbinder's explicit statements make it clear that all this neurosis and anomie are caused by the "capitalist system," often referred to more murkily and forebodingly (as indeed it was at the time of pre-Hitler Weimar) as *das System*. Of course, Fassbinder had available to him within his own linguistic culture—as most alienated Western artists do not—a state, East Germany, which is organized according to a completely different system, Communism, but he displayed singularly little interest in investigating whether the Communist system, despite its lower economic efficiency and bracing absence of freedom of expression, also produces neurosis, alienation, and social apathy. It is a question that did not stimulate Fassbinder's artistic imagination.

Almost all Fassbinder's films have what he proudly proclaimed to be "fatalistic" endings, usually accompanied by ringing declarations that the more fatalistic they were the more optimistic they were. What lay behind these seemingly nonsensical statements was that Fassbinder, in his own frazzled way, was a social determinist. As long as *das System* was in place, people would be unhappy. His approach, as I have indicated, was not comparative. He did not explore how happy people were under other systems. Nor was he programmatic. His films express criticism of capitalism, of course, of Communists living in the West, and even of anarchists, but they give no indication of the manner in which deliverance might come. Subsumed in all Fassbinder's films is the belief that there could be a far, far better world, where there would be no neurosis, or oppression, or perhaps even pain. But Fassbinder did not seem to think it was his role to lay out a plan of action to help bring this better world about. The world we live in is debased and worthless. Fassbinder, subsidized by German cultural officials, did his best to bring it low. Others would take it from there.

One of Fassbinder's quainter traits was his preoccupation— evident in his films—with "domination," a word particularly meaningful for someone coming, as he did, from the homosexual culture. "Sure, I liked this," he once said. "I like to dominate." But later when he reflected on what he was doing he would "feel grieved and end this dependency" (by which he meant, end the relationship). It was capitalism, he would explain, that gave us this lust. Although Fassbinder once defined Marxism as a "good idea formulated in an inhuman manner," I am not aware that he ever expanded on whether anyone "dominated" anyone else east of the Elbe. One of his deepest beliefs was that the will to dominate was engendered by capitalism. Once we get rid of capitalism, all men will live on terms of perfect equality, and no man will lift his hand against another. And sin will fall away, and we will be clad in white raiment, and all stand pure and shining in the light Socialism.

Fassbinder asked to be judged by his *oeuvre* in its entirety, so I am obliged to give some account of those first thirty-odd movies which established his reputation at international film festivals and among movie critics, if not with the German public. There is wide consensus on Fassbinder's objectives among critics, including Ruth McCormick, a left-wing film scholar, who published a long study on Fassbinder's work in the late seventies in *Cinéaste*. By way of introduction, McCormick writes that most talented U.S. directors seem "strangled by the demands of the marketplace," a number of them "in the corporate dog-houses for having hatched multimillion dollar turkeys." It was "happily obvious" to American radicals, on the other hand, she says, that "almost all the German newcomers were critical of the status quo, some even attempting to challenge with their

aesthetics the established bourgeois view of the world." Of
Fassbinder she writes: "His anger at the prevailing order is all-
pervasive"; his goal is to make potential revolutionaries "see
clearly into the social and economic forces that keep them
down" as well as to "root out the psychological structures of
domination within themselves." "Abominated by all good, conservative Germans," she assures us, Fassbinder "totally destroys the bourgeois notion of the independent individual." He
shows that we are unable to change our social relations "because of the ideologies we have been fed, like slow poison, since
infancy." McCormick ardently supports the demands of Fassbinder, and others, for government subsidies to express this all-
pervasive anger at the prevailing order.

Now, the movies:

Katzelmacher (1969), Fassbinder's second feature film, set in
Munich, is a group portrait of nine or ten young, lower-middle-
class people suffering from anomie. They are listless, petty,
unhappy. In their midst suddenly erupts a lovable, warm-hearted
Greek *Gastarbeiter* ("guest worker"). Since these foreign
"guest workers" are subject to appreciable social discrimination
in Germany, it has been an article of faith of the New German
Cinema that they are not only as good as Germans, but better.
This particular Greek (played by Fassbinder himself) brings
with him the vitality and vibrancy of the Mediterranean, so
different from the cold glumness of the young Germans. I give
McCormick's summation: "unloving couples, 'friends' who
never really communicate, sexual relations undertaken out of
boredom or for money, conformity in the face of group pressure,
worries about money, unlikable but not totally unsympathetic
people dominated by the unseen forces of internalized repression and a marketplace society. . . ." Everything ends badly, of
course. This is Fassbinder's picture of the Federal Republic of
Germany the year Willy Brandt became chancellor.

In *Gods of the Plague* (also 1969), a crime movie, McCormick
says "the crooks are seen to be victims of society, and certainly
more honest than the cops." *Why Does Herr R. Run Amok?*
(Fassbinder's fourth film of 1969) is vintage Fassbinder. Herr R.

is a draftsman, married, and the father of a small son with a speech impediment. His job is dull, his boss domineering, his friends boring. One night, without warning, Herr R. bludgeons his wife, his son, and a visiting friend to death. But why should Herr R. commit such a horrible series of actions? No student of Fassbinder will ponder long over the answer. It was *das System*, of course. It was all that slow poison, dripping, dripping.

The Merchant of Four Seasons (1971, two years and eight films later) is still another tale of alienation. Hans Epp, a humble fruit peddler, is the family failure. He is a nice man, who wants only a simple life, but our repressive society does him in, too. He has a heart attack. His wife cuckolds him. (These things apparently do not happen in socialist societies.) To help him on the job, he hires an old friend, who makes a go of the business for him. Finding that he is unnecessary and unwanted, Hans drinks himself to death. McCormick writes that Hans Epp "is a prisoner of the society in which he lives," and that the film proves that "there is no place for the autonomous individual in today's world."

To plop out movies like this was as easy for Fassbinder as breathing. *The Bitter Tears of Petra von Kant* (1972) never leaves the apartment of the eponymous Petra, a successful fashion designer. It is a lesbian story, all about domination, which we learn is bad. In *Jail Bait* (also 1972), a nineteen-year-old chicken plucker named Franz is jailed for statutory rape. When he is released, his fourteen-year-old mistress, Hanni, persuades him, out of fear, to murder her reactionary father. But they are caught. Again, McCormick: "She, coming out of a stuffy, over-furnished home full of religious icons and he, out of the bloody alienation of the chicken factory, were doomed from the start."

Effi Briest is the literary masterpiece of Theodor Fontane, considered Germany's first master of the realistic novel. It is a brilliant work of literature, set entirely among the Prussian artistocracy. There are fashionable marriages, grand estates, an adulterous liaison, a spectacular duel, the adulterer killed on the field of honor. All this is far, far too much sparkle for Rainer Werner Fassbinder, and in his movie adaptation (1974) we consequently see almost none of it. The story is reduced to what McCormick calls "a series of tableaux depicting the oppressive reality of the woman's everyday life." It shows "the crushing of a lively spirit" by "an unresponsive world concerned only with unquestioning conformity." This is not how the novel ends, of course. Like most people in real life, Effi has more spunk than is allowed in the world of R. W. Fassbinder, and ends her days not crushed but comfortable and happy.

It took some doing, but Fassbinder's aristocratic Effi has much in common with the modern, middle-class protagonist of his *Fear of Fear* (1975): "Little by little, her life is revealed—the routine housework, the neat apartment, the whining kids, the nosy mother-in-law, the indifferent husband—that make her uneventful life a trap."

As the reader will have gathered, Fassbinder is a somewhat monotonous storyteller. He tells the same tale again and again, and he tells it badly. His style is nil. The acting is usually appalling. There is nothing to look at. There is nowhere to hide. If you've seen it all before, and do not vibrate to his message, the experience can be excruciating.

It is a strange comment on the New German Cinema that in 1979, after making no fewer than thirty-one feature films, Fassbinder at last had what even a recent publicity release described as his "first commercial success in Germany": *The Marriage of Maria Braun*. Fassbinder had a lifelong ambition to make a "subversive cinema for a mass audience," and I can only assume that this was it. A director who through 1975 had never spent as much as a quarter-of-a-million dollars on a movie (a pittance in these times), Fassbinder was given a multimillion-dollar budget. He had crowd scenes, complicated sets, pretty costumes. He framed, and cut, and edited, just like a grown-up (or someone did it for him). The camera moved; he panned and zoomed. It was all very clumsily done, and the acting was as stilted as ever, but the product was a passable facsimile of a real movie. Fassbinder's formula for subverting a mass audience was to give it all these costumes and sets, all this movement and action and plot to whet its appetite, and then convert it to revolutionary socialism by imposing on the plot a didactic allegory. *Maria Braun* turned out to be the first of three films on the same theme, a denunciation of the Germany of Konrad Adenauer. This was basically the fifties, called in most textbooks the years of Germany's "astonishing postwar recovery" or "economic miracle." They were also years in which democratic institutions, extinguished in Germany during a very dark period, were reestablished. But for Fassbinder the fifties (which ended when he was thirteen) were entirely a time of repression and debased materialism.

Maria Braun's husband is a Wehrmacht soldier, evidently representing the Old Germany. Maria, who works her way up from bar girl to the ranks of the corporate rich, is to all appearances the New Germany. She becomes the mistress of the head of her company, a Frenchman, the two of them constituting the New Europe. The Frenchman dies, leaving Maria his fortune (Germany triumphant), and she remarries her old husband, who has been in prison for the murder of Maria's American lover. So the New Germany reunites with the Old Germany, and Hitler rules the world, I suppose, or perhaps precipitates a new calamity. Frankly I wouldn't be the least surprised to hear that German audiences, unaccustomed to allegory, saw in the film a simple success story.

Fassbinder's *Lili Marleen* (1981), with a budget of $10 million, also did well in Germany (though far less well than *Das Boot*). Shot and written with the director's usual awkwardness, it is nonetheless the least typical of his movies, with Fassbinder's usual political message somehow going adrift. Although *Lili Marleen* is nominally anti-Hitler (hardly a novel attitude), and while it is his only film set in the Nazi period, I can only say that the director's hostility to the Nazis is not nearly so intense as his hatred of the Nazis' successor regime in the Federal Republic. *Lili Marleen*'s Nazis do such things as torturing a prisoner by playing the song "Lili Marleen" to him over and over again— not exactly the worst atrocity that has ever been attributed to the Gestapo or the SS. The movie is the story of a famous singer (played by Fassbinder standby Hanna Schygulla, who in Schlöndorff's *Circle of Deceit* plays the German heroine in love with a

PLO officer). The public at large no doubt took this singer to be a sympathetic character since she has a Jewish lover (Giancarlo Giannini) and the role is fuzzily rendered at best. Perhaps I, alone—since I have at hand the code book constituted by Fassbinder's interviews—know that she is a bad person, because she falls into raptures at the luxurious appointments of her new living quarters ("nice apartments" were singled out time and again by the director as the cleft hoof of materialism). She is also very pleased to meet Hitler, ascending a ceremonial staircase into dazzling radiance as if going to meet God.

Clearly Fassbinder would have found much that was congenial to him in the Nazi regime. It was not materialistic. It preached an exalting creed that lifted men out of themselves. It was cruel (there is tremendous unavowed cruelty in Fassbinder's films), and it was consecrated to strength, the power of will. I have no difficulty whatever in reading Fassbinder as a Nazi personality type with just a few inversions. He could quite easily be seen as a lost spiritual Nazi, adrift, despairing, with nothing left to believe in. In *Lili Marleen*, which deals with Nazism, he certainly shows nothing of the absolutely obsessive hatred displayed throughout his entire work for *das System*, the pluralistic, liberal, democratic society in which he lived. *Lili Marleen* came in for explicit criticism for its unattractive portrait of a rich Swiss Jew (Mel Ferrer), who springs Jews from the Nazis' grasp by using his financial resources. But of course Fassbinder reminded us that we should never discuss the Nazis' treatment of the Jews without recalling the Jews' "connection with money." Vincent Canby of the *New York Times* wrote that there was a suggestion in a film Fassbinder made in 1980 that the director "might be moving from the far Left to the far Right." In Fassbinder's case—as indeed in many others—I would not consider this a very great distance.

Fassbinder worked with such speed, and carelessness, that at his death he left behind three movies, none of which had yet been released in the United States, two of them not even in Germany. *Querelle de Brest* is a homosexual love story by France's Jean Genet, in whose works homosexuality and crime are seen as rebellions against the established order. The other two were *Lola* and *Veronika Voss*, the second and third films of Fassbinder's trilogy of philippics against Adenauer's Germany. (He was also planning to make a film on Rosa Luxemburg, to be played by Jane Fonda.)

The germ of *Lola* was *The Blue Angel* by Josef von Sternberg, a film masterpiece of pre-Hitler Germany based on the novel by Heinrich Mann. It is the story of the enslavement and degradation of a respectable *Gymnasium* professor by a low cabaret singer named Lola Lola, played by Marlene Dietrich. (*"Ich bin die fesche Lola, der Liebling der Saison. . . ."*) Fassbinder, of course, politicizes the story (the film opens and closes with the portrait of Konrad Adenauer). The *Gymnasium* professor becomes a provincial building commissioner. Lola remains a cabaret singer. But the cabaret itself becomes a grand and gaudy place, a combination night club and whorehouse, where all the local wheeler-dealers meet to discuss their corrupt projects while pawing the women. It is 1955, and West Germany is being reconstructed under the free-enterprise system, so it is all very corrupt. Now the city's leading building contractor, it just so happens, owns the cabaret-bordello, and is also Lola's lover, and he wants something out of the new commissioner, and that something is building permits. Since the contractor is, naturally, very corrupt, he puts his girlfriend up to enslaving the commissioner, an idealistic ninny, who swallows the bait whole. The contractor gets his permits, and Lola's share of the take is ownership of the cabaret-bordello. For good measure, she marries the commissioner (as in *The Blue Angel*), promptly cuckolds her new husband (as in *The Blue Angel*) with her old friend the contractor. And that's about it. That's the way things work in that big old whorehouse, capitalism.

Something odd happens in Fassbinder's *Lola*. The title role is played by Barbara Sukowa (who played with feeling the Ulrike Meinhof–Kathy Boudin-type terrorist in *Marianne and Juliane*). In *Lola*, Sukowa, historically speaking, is going up against Marlene Dietrich in what I consider Dietrich's one truly great role, and it is a sorry spectacle. She is also a frightful singer.

But the true oddity of the film is Mario Adorf, who plays Schuckert, the contractor. It must surely be clear that Schuckert is intended to be the villain of this movie. He is capitalism, domination, corruption made flesh. The problem is that, unlike the usual Fassbinder road company, a gang of resolutely luster-less performers who stalk through his films like the living dead, Mario Adorf is an absolutely first-rate actor. Given a role to play, he tried to make the character as plausible and human as he could. Schuckert is beefy, witty, cynical—as engaging a rascal as you're likely to meet. His performance threw off a number of critics. One wrote that the film suggests a certain "mellowing" of Fassbinder's attitude toward our society, another that it has "almost a happy ending." The simple fact is that while Fassbinder was hiding in a corner, cleaning his nails, or otherwise engaged, Mario Adorf, as the saying goes, ran away with his movie, almost rehabilitating capitalism. My guess is that Fassbinder didn't even notice.

Beyond politics, beyond Left, beyond Right, beyond a secular millennium, I have a private view of Rainer Werner Fassbinder. In the French literary description of the romantic character, I was always struck by one defining trait: a romantic had *le dégoût de la vie*, translated crudely, "Disgust with life." After long exposure to Fassbinder's films, I cannot avoid thinking that he had the most profound "disgust with life." I know no social prescriptions for this malady. The French also say that the romantics loved death. And so Fassbinder died, on June 10, 1982, at the age of thirty-six, from what was described as the combined effect of alcohol and drugs. To which I can only say, *Ainsi soît-il*, which means both "So be it," and "Amen."

6

The Gandhi Nobody Knows

I HAD THE singular honor of attending an early private screening of *Gandhi* with an audience of invited guests from the National Council of Churches. At the end of the three-hour movie there was hardly, as they say, a dry eye in the house. When the lights came up I fell into conversation with a young woman who observed, reverently, that Gandhi's last words were "Oh, God," causing me to remark regretfully that the real Gandhi had not spoken in English, but had cried, *Hai Rama!* ("Oh, Rama"). Well, Rama was just Indian for God, she replied, at which I felt compelled to explain that, alas, Rama, collectively with his three half-brothers, represented the seventh reincarnation of Vishnu. The young woman, who seemed to have been under the impression that Hinduism was Christianity under another name, sensed somehow that she had fallen on an uncongenial spirit, and the conversation ended.

At a dinner party shortly afterward, a friend of mine, who had visited India many times and even gone to the trouble of learning Hindi, objected strenuously that the picture of Gandhi that emerges in the movie is grossly inaccurate, omitting, as one of many examples, that when Gandhi's wife lay dying of pneumonia and British doctors insisted that a shot of penicillin would save her, Gandhi refused to have this alien medicine injected in her body and simply let her die. (It must be noted that when Gandhi contracted malaria shortly afterward he accepted for himself the alien medicine quinine, and that when he had appendicitis he allowed British doctors to perform on him the alien outrage of an appendectomy.) All of this produced a wistful mooing from an editor of a major newspaper and a recalcitrant, "But still. . . ." I would prefer to explicate things more substantial than a wistful mooing, but there is little doubt it meant the editor in question felt that even if the real Mohandas K. Gandhi had been different from the Gandhi of the movie it would have been *nice* if he had been like the movie-Gandhi, and that presenting him in this admittedly false manner was beautiful, stirring, and perhaps socially beneficial.

An important step in the canonization of this movie-Gandhi was taken by the New York Film Critics Circle, which not only awarded the picture its prize as best film of 1982, but awarded Ben Kingsley, who played Gandhi (a remarkably good performance), its prize as best actor of the year. But I cannot believe for one second that these awards were made independently of the film's content—which, not to put too fine a point on it, is an all-out appeal for pacifism—or in anything but the most shameful ignorance of the historical Gandhi.

Now it does not bother me that Shakespeare omitted from his *King John* the signing of the Magna Charta—by far the most important event in John's reign. All Shakespeare's "histories" are strewn with errors and inventions. Shifting to the cinema and to more recent times, it is hard for me to work up much indignation over the fact that neither Eisenstein's *Battleship Potemkin* nor his *October* recounts historical episodes in anything like the manner in which they actually occurred (the famous march of the White Guards down the steps at Odessa— artistically one of the greatest sequences in film history—simply did not take place). As we draw closer to the present, however, the problem becomes more difficult. If the Soviet Union were to make an artistically wondrous film about the entry of Russian tanks into Prague in 1968 (an event I happened to witness), and show them being greeted with flowers by a grateful populace, the Czechs dancing in the streets with joy, I do not guarantee that I would maintain my serene aloofness. A great deal depends on whether the historical events represented in a movie are intended to be taken as substantially true, and also on whether— separated from us by some decades or occurring yesterday—

they are seen as having a direct bearing on courses of action now open to us.

On my second viewing of *Gandhi*, this time at a public showing, I happened to leave the theater behind three teenage girls, apparently from one of Manhattan's fashionable private schools. "Gandhi was pretty much an FDR," one opined, astonishing me almost as much by her breezy use of initials to invoke a president who died almost a quarter-century before her birth as by the stupefying nature of the comparison. "But he was a religious figure, too," corrected one of her friends, adding somewhat smugly, "It's not in our historical tradition to honor spiritual leaders." Since her schoolteachers had clearly not led her to consider Jonathan Edwards and Roger Williams as spiritual leaders, let alone Joseph Smith and William Jennings Bryan, the intimation seemed to be that we are a society with poorer spiritual values than, let's say, India. There can be no question, in any event, that the girls felt they had just been shown the historical Gandhi—an attitude shared by Ralph Nader, who at last account, had seen the film three times. Nader has conceived the most extraordinary notion that Gandhi's symbolic flouting of the British salt tax was a "consumer issue" which he later expanded into the wider one of Indian independence. A modern parallel to Gandhi's program of home-spinning and home-weaving, another "consumer issue" says Nader, might be the use of solar energy to free us from the "giant multinational oil corporations."

As it happens, the government of India openly admits to having provided one-third of the financing of *Gandhi* out of state funds, straight out of the national treasury—and after close study of the finished product I would not be a bit surprised to hear that it was 100 percent. If Pandit Nehru is portrayed flatteringly in the film, one must remember that Nehru himself took part in the initial story conferences (he originally wanted Gandhi to be played by Alec Guinness) and that his daughter Indira Gandhi is [in 1983], after all, prime minister of India (though no relation to Mohandas Gandhi). The screenplay was checked and rechecked by Indian officials at every stage, often by the prime minister herself, with close consultations on plot and even casting. If the movie contains a particularly poisonous portrait of Mohammed Ali Jinnah, the founder of Pakistan, the Indian reply, I suppose, would be that if the Pakistanis want an attractive portrayal of Jinnah let them pay for their own movie. A friend of mine, highly sophisticated in political matters but innocent about filmmaking, declared that *Gandhi* should be preceded by the legend: *The following film is a paid political advertisement by the government of India.*

Gandhi, then, is a large, pious, historical morality tale centered on a saintly, sanitized Mahatma Gandhi cleansed of anything too embarrassingly Hindu (the word "caste" is not mentioned from one end of the film to the other) and, indeed, of most of the rest of Gandhi's life, much of which would drastically diminish his saintliness in Western eyes. There is little to indicate that the India of today has followed Gandhi's precepts in almost nothing. There is little, in fact, to indicate that India is even India. The spectator realizes the scene is the Indian subcontinent because there are thousands of extras dressed in dhotis and saris. The characters go about talking in these quaint Peter Sellers accents. We have occasional shots of India's holy poverty, holy hovels, some landscapes, many of them photographed quite beautifully, for those who like travelogues. We have a character called Lord Mountbatten (India's last viceroy); a composite American journalist (assembled from Vincent Sheehan, William L. Shirer, Louis Fischer, and straight fiction); a character called simply "Viceroy" (presumably another composite); an assemblage of Gandhi's Indian followers under the name of one of them (Patel); and of course Nehru.

I sorely missed the fabulous Annie Besant, that English clergyman's wife, turned atheist, turned Theosophist, turned Indian nationalist, who actually became president of the Indian National Congress and had a terrific falling out with Gandhi, becoming his fierce opponent. And if the producers felt they had to work in a cameo role for an American star to add to the film's appeal in the United States, it is positively embarrassing that they should have brought in the photographer Margaret Bourke-White, a person of no importance whatever in Gandhi's life and a role Candice Bergen plays with a repellant unctuousness. If the filmmakers had been interested in drama and not hagiography, it is hard to see how they could have resisted the awesome confrontation between Gandhi and, yes, Margaret Sanger. For the two did meet. Now *there* was a meeting of East and West, and *may the better person win!* (She did. Margaret Sanger argued her views on birth control with such vigor that Gandhi had a nervous breakdown.)

I cannot honestly say I had any reasonable expectation that the film would show scenes of Gandhi's pretty teenage girl followers fighting "hysterically" (the word was used) for the honor of sleeping naked with the Mahatma and cuddling the nude septuagenarian in their arms. (Gandhi was "testing" his vow of chastity in order to gain moral strength for his mighty struggle with Jinnah.) When told there was a man named Freud who said that, despite his declared intention, Gandhi might actually be *enjoying* the caresses of the naked girls, Gandhi continued, unperturbed. Nor, frankly, did I expect to see Gandhi giving daily enemas to all the young girls in his ashrams (his daily greeting was, "Have you had a good bowel movement this morning, sisters?"), nor see the girls giving him *his* daily enema. Although Gandhi seems to have written less about home rule for India than he did about enemas, and excrement, and latrine cleaning ("The bathroom is a temple. It should be so clean and inviting that anyone would enjoy eating there"), I confess such scenes might pose problems for a Western director.

Gandhi, therefore, the film, this paid political advertisement for the government of India, is organized around three axes: (1) anti-racism—all men are equal regardless of race, color, creed, etc.; (2) anti-colonialism, which in present terms translates as support for the Third World, including, most eminently, India; (3) nonviolence, presented as an absolutist pacifism. There are other, secondary precepts and subheadings. Gandhi is portrayed as the quintessence of tolerance ("I am a Hindu and a Muslim and a Christian and a Jew"), of basic friendliness to Britain ("The British have been with us for a long time and when they leave we want them to leave as friends"), of devotion to his wife and family. His vow of chastity is represented as something selfless and holy, rather like the celibacy of the Catholic clergy.

But, above all, Gandhi's life and teachings are presented as having great import for us today. We must learn from Gandhi.

I propose to demonstrate that the film grotesquely distorts both Gandhi's life and character to the point that it is nothing more than a pious fraud, and a fraud of the most egregious kind. Hackneyed Indian falsehoods such as that "the British keep trying to break India up" (as if Britain didn't give India a unity it had never enjoyed in history), or that the British *created* Indian poverty (a poverty that had not only existed since time immemorial but had been considered holy), almost pass unnoticed in the tide of adulation for our fictional saint. Gandhi, admittedly, being a devout Hindu, was far more self-contradictory than most public men. Sanskrit scholars tell me that flat self-contradiction is even considered an element of "Sanskrit rhetoric." Perhaps it is thought to show profundity.

Gandhi rose early, usually at three-thirty, and before his first bowel movement (during which he received visitors, although possibly not Margaret Bourke-White) he spent two hours in meditation, listening to his "inner voice." Now Gandhi was an extremely vocal individual, and in addition to spending an hour each day in vigorous walking, another hour spinning at his primitive spinning wheel, another hour at further prayers, another hour being massaged nude by teenage girls, and many hours deciding such things as affairs of state, he produced a quite unconscionable number of articles and speeches and wrote an average of sixty letters a day. All considered, it is not really surprising that his inner voice said different things to him at different times. Despising consistency and never checking his earlier statements, and yet inhumanly obstinate about his position at any given moment, Gandhi is thought by some Indians today (according to V. S. Naipaul) to have been so erratic and unpredictable that he may have delayed Indian independence for twenty-five years.

For Gandhi was an extremely difficult man to work with. He had no partners, only disciples. For members of his ashrams, he dictated every minute of their days, and not only every morsel of food they should eat but when they should eat it. Without ever having heard of a protein or a vitamin, he considered himself an expert on diet, as on most things, and was constantly experimenting. Once when he fell ill, he was found to have been living on a diet of ground-nut butter and lemon juice; British doctors called it malnutrition. And Gandhi had even greater confidence in his abilities as a "nature doctor," prescribing obligatory cures for his ashramites, such as dried cow-dung powder and various concoctions containing cow dung (the cow, of course, being sacred to the Hindu). And to those he really loved he gave enemas—but again, alas, not to Margaret Bourke-White. Which is too bad, really. For admiring Candice Bergen's work as I do, I would have been most interested in seeing how she would have experienced this beatitude. The scene might have lived in film history.

There are 400 biographies of Gandhi, and his writings run to eighty volumes, and since he lived to be seventy-nine, and rarely fell silent, there are, as I have indicated, quite a few inconsistencies. The authors of the present movie even acknowledge in a little-noticed opening title that they have made a film only true to Gandhi's "spirit." For my part, I do not intend to pick through Gandhi's writings to make him look like Attila the Hun (although the thought is tempting), but to give a fair, weighted balance of his views, laying stress above all on his actions, and on what he told other men to do when the time for action had come.

Anti-racism: The reader will have noticed that in the present-day community of nations South Africa is a pariah. So it is an absolutely amazing piece of good fortune that Gandhi, born the son of the Prime Minister of a tiny Indian principality and received as an attorney at the bar of the Middle Temple in London, should have begun his climb to greatness as a member of the small Indian community in, precisely, South Africa. Natal, then a separate colony, wanted to limit Indian immigration and, as part of the government program, ordered Indians to carry identity papers (an action not without similarities to measures under consideration in the United States today to control illegal immigration). The film's lengthy opening sequences are devoted to Gandhi's leadership in the fight against Indians carrying their identity papers (burning their registration cards), with for good measure Gandhi being expelled from the first-class section of a railway train, and Gandhi being asked by whites to step off the sidewalk. This inspired young Indian leader calls, in the film, for interracial harmony, for people to "live together."

Now the time is 1893, and Gandhi is a "caste" Hindu, and from one of the higher castes. Although, later, he was to call for improving the lot of India's Untouchables, he was not to have any serious misgivings about the fundamentals of the caste system for about another thirty years, and even then his doubts, to my way of thinking, were rather minor. In the India in which Gandhi grew up, and had only recently left, some castes could enter the courtyards of certain Hindu temples, while others could not. Some castes were forbidden to use the village well. Others were compelled to live outside the village, still others to leave the road at the approach of a person of higher caste and perpetually to call out, giving warning, so that no one would be polluted by their proximity. The endless intricacies of Hindu caste by-laws varied somewhat region by region, but in Madras, where most South African Indians were from, while a Nayar could pollute a man of higher caste only by touching him, Kammalans polluted at a distance of twenty-four feet, toddy drawers at thirty-six feet, Pulayans and Cherumans at forty-eight feet, and beef-eating Paraiyans at sixty-four feet. All castes and the thousands of sub-castes were forbidden, needless to say, to marry, eat, or engage in social activity with any but members of their own group. In Gandhi's native Gujarat a caste Hindu who had been polluted by touch had to perform extensive ritual ablutions or purify himself by drinking a holy beverage composed of milk, whey, and (what else?) cow dung.

Low-caste Hindus, in short, suffered humiliations in their native India compared to which the carrying of identity cards in South Africa was almost trivial. In fact, Gandhi, to his credit, was to campaign strenuously in his later life for the reduction of caste barriers in India—a campaign almost invisible in the movie, of course, conveyed in only two glancing references, leaving the audience with the officially sponsored if historically astonishing notion that racism was introduced into India by the British. To present the Gandhi of 1893, a conventional caste

Hindu, fresh from caste-ridden India where a Paraiyan could pollute at sixty-four feet, as the champion of interracial equalitarianism is one of the most brazen hypocrisies I have ever encountered in a serious movie.

The film, moreover, does not give the slightest hint as to Gandhi's attitude toward blacks, and the viewers of *Gandhi* would naturally suppose that, since the future Great Soul opposed South African discrimination against Indians, he would also oppose South African discrimination against black people. But this is not so. While Gandhi, in South Africa, fought furiously to have Indians recognized as loyal subjects of the British empire, and to have them enjoy the full rights of Englishmen, he had no concern for blacks whatever. In fact, during one of the "Kaffir Wars" he volunteered to organize a brigade of Indians to put down a Zulu rising, and was decorated himself for valor under fire.

For, yes, Gandhi (Sergeant-Major Gandhi) was awarded Victoria's coveted War Medal. Throughout most of his life Gandhi had the most inordinate admiration for British soldiers, their sense of duty, their discipline and stoicism in defeat (a trait he emulated himself). He marveled that they retreated with heads high, like victors. There was even a time in his life when Gandhi, hardly to be distinguished from Kipling's Gunga Din, wanted nothing so much as to be a Soldier of the Queen. Since this is not in keeping with the "spirit" of Gandhi, as decided by Pandit Nehru and Indira Gandhi, it is naturally omitted from the movie.

Anti-colonialism: As almost always with historical films, even those more honest than *Gandhi*, the historical personage on which the movie is based is not only more complex but more interesting than the character shown on the screen. During his entire South African period, and for some time after, until he was about fifty, Gandhi was nothing more or less than an imperial loyalist, claiming for Indians the rights of Englishmen but unshakably loyal to the crown. He supported the empire ardently in no fewer than three wars: the Boer War, the "Kaffir War," and, with the most extreme zeal, World War I. If Gandhi's mind were of the modern European sort, this would seem to suggest that his later attitude toward Britain was the product of unrequited love: he had wanted to be an Englishman; Britain had rejected him and his people; very well then, they would have their own country. But this would imply a point of "agonizing reappraisal," a moment when Gandhi's most fundamental political beliefs were reexamined and, after the most bitter soul-searching, repudiated. But I have studied the literature and cannot find this moment of bitter soul-searching. Instead, listening to his "inner voice" (which in the case of divines of all countries often speaks in the tones of holy opportunism), Gandhi simply, tranquilly, without announcing any sharp break, set off in a new direction.

It should be understood that it is unlikely Gandhi ever truly conceived of "becoming" an Englishman, first, because he was a Hindu to the marrow of his bones, and also, perhaps, because his democratic instincts were really quite weak. He was a man of the most extreme, autocratic temperament, tyrannical, unyielding, even regarding things he knew nothing about, totally intolerant of all opinions but his own. He was, furthermore, in the highest degree reactionary, permitting in India no change in the relationship between the feudal lord and his peasants or servants, the rich and the poor. In his *The Life and Death of Mahatma Gandhi*, the best and least hagiographic of the full-length studies, Robert Payne, although admiring Gandhi greatly, explains Gandhi's "new direction" on his return to India from South Africa as follows:

> He spoke in generalities, but he was searching for a single cause, a single hard-edged task to which he would devote the remaining years of his life. He wanted to repeat his triumph in South Africa on Indian soil. He dreamed of assembling a small army of dedicated men around him, issuing stern commands and leading them to some almost unobtainable goal.

Gandhi, in short, was a leader looking for a cause. He found it, of course, in home rule for India and, ultimately, in independence.

We are therefore presented with the seeming anomaly of a Gandhi who, in Britain when war broke out in August 1914, instantly contacted the War Office, swore that he would stand by England in its hour of need, and created the Indian Volunteer Corps, which he might have commanded if he hadn't fallen ill with pleurisy. In 1915, back in India, he made a memorable speech in Madras in which he proclaimed, "I discovered that the British empire had certain ideals with which I have fallen in love. . . ." In early 1918, as the war in Europe entered its final crisis, he wrote to the viceroy of India, "I have an idea that if I become your recruiting agent-in-chief, I might rain men upon you," and he proclaimed in a speech in Kheda that the British "love justice; they have shielded men against oppression." Again, he wrote to the viceroy, "I would make India offer all her able-bodied sons as a sacrifice to the empire at this critical moment. . . ." To some of his pacifist friends, who were horrified, Gandhi replied by appealing to the *Bhagavad Gita* and to the endless wars recounted in the Hindu epics, the *Ramayana* and the *Mahabharata*, adding further to the pacifists' horror by declaring that Indians "have always been warlike, and the finest hymn composed by Tulsidas in praise of Rama gives the first place to his ability to strike down the enemy."

This was in contradiction to the interpretation of sacred Hindu scriptures Gandhi had offered on earlier occasions (and would offer later), which was that they did not recount military struggles but spiritual struggles; but, unusual for him, he strove to find some kind of synthesis. "I do not say, 'Let us go and kill the Germans,' " Gandhi explained. "I say, 'Let us go and die for the sake of India and the empire.' " And yet within two years, the time having come for *swaraj* (home rule), Gandhi's inner voice spoke again, and, the leader having found his cause, Gandhi proclaimed resoundingly: "The British empire today represents Satanism, and they who love God can afford to have no love for Satan."

The idea of *swaraj*, originated by others, crept into Gandhi's mind gradually. With a fair amount of winding about, Gandhi, roughly, passed through three phases. First, he was entirely pro-British, and merely wanted for Indians the rights of Englishmen (as he understood them). Second, he was still pro-British, but with the belief that, having proved their loyalty to the empire,

Indians would be granted some degree of *swaraj*. Third, as the home-rule movement gathered momentum, it was the *swaraj*, the whole *swaraj*, and nothing but the *swaraj*, and he turned relentlessly against the crown. The movie to the contrary, he caused the British no end of trouble in their struggles during World War II.

But it should not be thought for one second that Gandhi's finally full-blown desire to detach India from the British empire gave him the slightest sympathy with other colonial peoples pursuing similar objectives. Throughout his entire life Gandhi displayed the most spectacular inability to understand or even really take in people unlike himself—a trait that V. S. Naipaul considers specifically Hindu, and I am inclined to agree. Just as Gandhi had been totally unconcerned with the situation of South Africa's blacks (he hardly noticed they were there until they rebelled), so now he was totally unconcerned with other Asians or Africans. In fact, he was adamantly *opposed* to certain Arab movements within the Ottoman empire for reasons of internal Indian politics.

At the close of World War I, the Muslims of India were deeply absorbed in what they called the "Khilafat" movement—"Khilafat" being their corruption of "Caliphate," the caliph in question being the Ottoman sultan. In addition to his temporal powers, the sultan of the Ottoman empire held the spiritual position of caliph, supreme leader of the world's Muslims and successor to the Prophet Muhammad. At the defeat of the Central Powers (Germany, Austria, Turkey), the sultan was a prisoner in his palace in Constantinople, shorn of his religious as well as his political authority, and the Muslims of India were incensed. It so happened that the former subject peoples of the Ottoman empire, principally Arabs, were perfectly happy to be rid of this caliph, and even the Turks were glad to be rid of him, but this made no impression at all on the Muslims of India, for whom the issue was essentially a club with which to beat the British. Until this odd historical moment, Indian Muslims had felt little real allegiance to the Ottoman sultan either, but now that he had fallen, the British had done it! The British had taken away their Khilafat! And one of the most ardent supporters of this Indian Muslim movement was the new Hindu leader, Gandhi.

No one questions that the formative period for Gandhi as a political leader was his time in South Africa. Throughout history Indians, divided into 1,500 language and dialect groups (India today has 15 official languages), had little sense of themselves as a nation. Muslim Indians and Hindu Indians felt about as close as Christians and Moors during their 700 years of cohabitation in Spain. In addition to which, the Hindus were divided into thousands of castes and sub-castes, and there were also Parsees, Sikhs, Jains. But in South Africa officials had thrown them all in together, and in the mind of Gandhi (another one of those examples of nationalism being born in exile) grew the idea of India as a nation, and Muslim-Hindu friendship became one of the few positions on which he never really reversed himself. So Gandhi—ignoring Arabs and Turks—became an adamant supporter of the Khilafat movement out of strident Indian nationalism. He had become a national figure in India for having unified 13,000 Indians of all faiths in South Africa, and now he was determined to reach new heights by unifying hundreds of millions of Indians of all faiths in India itself. But this nationalism did not please everyone, particularly Tolstoy, who in his last years carried on a curious correspondence with the new Indian leader. For Tolstoy, Gandhi's Indian nationalism "spoils everything."

As for the "anti-colonialism" of the nationalist Indian state since independence, Indira Gandhi, India's present prime minister, hears an inner voice of her own, it would appear, and this inner voice told her to justify the Soviet invasion of Afghanistan as produced by provocative maneuvers on the part of the United States and China, as well as to be the first country outside the Soviet bloc to recognize the Hanoi puppet regime in Cambodia. So everything plainly depends on who is colonizing whom, and Mrs. Gandhi's voice perhaps tells her that the subjection of Afghanistan and Cambodia to foreign rule is "defensive" colonialism. And the movie's message that Mahatma Gandhi, and by plain implication India (the country for which he plays the role of Joan of Arc), have taken a holy, unchanging stance against the colonization of nation by nation is just another of its hypocrisies. For India, when it comes to colonialism or anti-colonialism, it has been *Realpolitik* all the way.

Nonviolence: But the real center and *raison d'être* of *Gandhi* is *ahimsa*, nonviolence, which principle when incorporated into vast campaigns of noncooperation with British rule the Mahatma called by an odd name he made up himself, *satyagraha*, which means something like "truth-striving." During the key part of his life, Gandhi devoted a great deal of time explaining the moral and philosophical meanings of both *ahimsa* and satyagraha. But much as the film sanitizes Gandhi to the point where one would mistake him for a Christian saint, and sanitizes India to the point where one would take it for Shangri-la, it quite sweeps away Gandhi's ethical and religious ponderings, his complexities, his qualifications, and certainly his vacillations, which simplifying process leaves us with our old European friend: pacifism. It is true that Gandhi was much impressed by the Sermon on the Mount, his favorite passage in the Bible, which he read over and over again. But for all the Sermon's inspirational value, and its service as an ideal in relations among individual human beings, no Christian state which survived has ever based its policies on the Sermon on the Mount since Constantine declared Christianity the official religion of the Roman Empire. And no modern Western state which survives can ever base its policies on pacifism. And no Hindu state will ever base its policies on *ahimsa*. Gandhi himself—although the film dishonestly conceals this from us—*many times* conceded that in dire circumstances "war may have to be resorted to as a necessary evil."

It is something of an anomaly that Gandhi, held in popular myth to be a pure pacifist (a myth which governments of India have always been at great pains to sustain in the belief that it will reflect credit on India itself, and to which the present movie adheres slavishly), was until fifty not ill-disposed to war at all. As I have already noted, in three wars, no sooner had the bugles sounded than Gandhi not only gave his support, but was clamoring for arms. To form new regiments! To fight! To destroy the enemies of the empire! Regular Indian army units fought in both the Boer War and World War I, but this was not enough for

Gandhi. He wanted to raise new troops, even, in the case of the Boer and Kaffir Wars, from the tiny Indian colony in South Africa. British military authorities thought it not really worth the trouble to train such a small body of Indians as soldiers, and were even resistant to training them as an auxiliary medical corps ("stretcher bearers"), but finally yielded to Gandhi's relentless importuning. As first instructed, the Indian Volunteer Corps was not supposed actually to go into combat, but Gandhi, adamant, led his Indian volunteers into the thick of battle. His physical bravery is beyond question. When the British commanding officer was mortally wounded during an engagement in the Kaffir War, Gandhi—though his corps's deputy commander—carried the officer's stretcher himself from the battlefield and for miles over the sun-baked veldt. The British Empire's War Medal did not have its name for nothing, and it was generally earned.

Anyone who wants to wade through Gandhi's endless reminations about *himsa* and *ahimsa* (violence and nonviolence) is welcome to do so, but it is impossible for the skeptical reader to avoid the conclusion—let us say in 1920, when *swaraj* (home rule) was all the rage and Gandhi's inner voice started telling him that *ahimsa* was the thing—that this inner voice knew what it was talking about. By this I mean that, though Gandhi talked with the tongue of Hindu gods and sacred scriptures, his inner voice had a strong sense of expediency. Britain, if only comparatively speaking, was a moral nation, and nonviolent civil disobedience was plainly the best and most effective way of achieving Indian independence. Skeptics might also not be surprised to learn that as independence approached, Gandhi's inner voice began to change its tune. It has been reported that Gandhi "half-welcomed" the civil war that broke out in the last days. Even a fratricidal "bloodbath" (Gandhi's word) would be preferable to the British.

And suddenly Gandhi began endorsing violence left, right, and center. During the fearsome rioting in Calcutta he gave his approval to men "using violence in a moral cause." How could he tell them that violence was wrong, he asked, "unless I demonstrate that nonviolence is more effective?" He blessed the Nawab of Maler Kotla when he gave orders to shoot ten Muslims for every Hindu killed in his state. He sang the praises of Subhas Chandra Bose, who, sponsored by first the Nazis and then the Japanese, organized in Singapore an Indian National Army with which he hoped to conquer India with Japanese support, establishing a totalitarian dictatorship. Meanwhile, after independence in 1947, the armies of the India that Gandhi had created immediately marched into battle, incorporating the state of Hyderabad by force and making war in Kashmir on secessionist Pakistan. When Gandhi was assassinated by a Hindu extremist in January 1948 he was honored by the new state with a vast military funeral—in my view by no means inapposite.

But it is not widely realized (nor will this film tell you) how much violence was associated with Gandhi's so-called "nonviolent" movement from the very beginning. India's Nobel Prize-winning poet, Rabindranath Tagore, had sensed a strong current of nihilism in Gandhi almost from his first days, and as early as 1920 wrote of Gandhi's "fierce joy of annihilation," which Tagore feared would lead India into hideous orgies of devastation—which ultimately proved to be the case. Robert Payne has said that there was unquestionably an "unhealthy atmosphere" among many of Gandhi's fanatic followers; and that Gandhi's habit of going to the edge of violence and then suddenly retreating was fraught with danger. "In matters of conscience I am uncompromising," proclaimed Gandhi proudly. "Nobody can make me yield." The judgment of Tagore was categorical. Much as he might revere Gandhi as a holy man, he quite detested him as a politician and considered that his campaigns were almost always so close to violence that it was utterly disingenuous to call them "nonviolent."

For every *satyagraha* true believer, moreover, sworn not to harm the adversary or even to lift a finger in his own defense, there were sometimes thousands of incensed freebooters and skirmishers bound by no such vow. Gandhi, to be fair, was aware of this, and nominally deplored it—but with nothing like the consistency shown in the movie. The film leads the audience to believe that Gandhi's first "fast unto death," for example, was in protest against an act of barbarous violence, the slaughter by an Indian crowd of a detachment of police constables. But in actual fact Gandhi reserved this "ultimate weapon" of his to interdict a 1931 British proposal to grant Untouchables a "separate electorate" in the Indian national legislature—in effect a kind of affirmative action program for Untouchables. For reasons I have not been able to decrypt, Gandhi was dead set against the project, but I confess it is another scene I would like to have seen in the movie: Gandhi almost starving himself to death to block affirmative action for Untouchables.

From what I have been able to decipher, Gandhi's main preoccupation in this particular struggle was not even the British. Benefiting from the immense publicity, he wanted to induce Hindus, overnight, ecstatically, and without any of these British legalisms, to "open their hearts" to Untouchables. For a whole week Hindu India was caught up in a joyous delirium. No more would the Untouchables be scavengers and sweepers! No more would they be banned from Hindu temples! No more would they pollute at sixty-four feet! It lasted just a week. Then the temple doors swung shut again, and all was as before. Meanwhile, on the passionate subject of *swaraj*, Gandhi was crying, "I would not flinch from sacrificing a million lives for India's liberty!" The million Indian lives were indeed sacrificed, and in full. They fell, however, not to the bullets of British soldiers but to the knives and clubs of their fellow Indians in savage butcheries when the British finally withdrew.

Although the movie sneers at this as being the flimsiest of pretexts, I cannot imagine an impartial person studying the subject without concluding that concern for Indian religious minorities was one of the principal reasons Britain stayed in India as long as it did. When it finally withdrew, blood-maddened mobs surged through the streets from one end of India to the other, the majority group in each area, Hindu or Muslim, slaughtering the defenseless minority without mercy in one of the most hideous periods of carnage of modern history.

A comparison is in order. At the famous Amritsar massacre of 1919, shot in elaborate and loving detail in the present movie and treated by post-independence Indian historians as if it were Auschwitz, Ghurka troops under the command of a British officer, General Dyer, fired into an unarmed crowd of Indians defying a ban and demonstrating for Indian independence. The crowd contained women and children; 379 persons died; it was all quite horrible. Dyer was court-martialed and cashiered, but the incident lay heavily on British consciences for the next three decades, producing a severe inhibiting effect. Never again would the British Empire commit another Amritsar, anywhere.

As soon as the oppressive British were gone, however, the Indians—gentle, tolerant people that they are—gave themselves over to an orgy of bloodletting. Trained troops did not pick off targets at a distance with Enfield rifles. Blood-crazed Hindus, or Muslims, ran through the streets with knives, beheading babies, stabbing women, old people. Interestingly, our movie shows none of this on camera (the oldest way of stacking the deck in Hollywood). All we see is the aged Gandhi, grieving, and of course fasting, at these terrible reports of riots. And, naturally, the film doesn't whisper a clue as to the total number of dead, which might spoil the mood somehow. The fact is that we will never know how many Indians were murdered by other Indians during the country's Independence Massacres, but almost all serious studies place the figure over a million, and some, such as Payne's sources, go to *4 million*. So, for those who like round numbers, the British killed some 400 seditious colonials at Amritsar and the name Amritsar lives in infamy, while Indians may have killed some 4 million of their own countrymen for no other reason than that they were of a different religious faith, and people think their great leader makes an inspirational subject for a movie. *Ahimsa*, as can be seen, then, had an absolutely tremendous moral effect when used against Britain, but not only would it not have worked against Nazi Germany (the most obvious reproach, and of course quite true), but, the crowning irony, it had virtually no effect whatever when Gandhi tried to bring it into play against violent Indians.

Despite this at best patchy record, the filmmakers have gone to great lengths to imply that this same principle of *ahimsa*—presented in the movie as the purest form of pacifism—is universally effective, yesterday, today, here, there, everywhere. We hear no talk from Gandhi of war sometimes being a "necessary evil," but only him announcing—and more than once—"An eye for an eye makes the whole world blind." In a scene very near the end of the movie, we hear Gandhi say, as if after deep reflection: "Tyrants and murderers can seem invincible at the time, but in the end they always fall. Think of it. Always." During the last scene of the movie, following the assassination, Margaret Bourke-White is keening over the death of the Great Soul with an English admiral's daughter named Madeleine Slade, in whose bowel movements Gandhi took the deepest interest (see their correspondence), and Slade remarks incredulously that Gandhi felt that he had failed. They are then both incredulous for a moment, after which Slade observes mournfully, "When we most needed it [presumably meaning during World War II], he offered the world a way out of madness. But the world didn't see it." Then we hear once again the assassin's shots, Gandhi's "Oh, God," and last, in case we missed them the first time, Gandhi's words (over the shimmering waters of the Ganges?): "Tyrants and murderers can seem invincible at the time, but in the end they always fall. Think of it. Always." This is the end of the picture.

Now, as it happens, I have been thinking about tyrants and murderers for some time. But the fact that in the end they always fall has never given me much comfort, partly because, not being a Hindu and not expecting reincarnation after reincarnation, I am simply not prepared to wait them out. It always occurs to me that, while I am waiting around for them to fall, they might do something mean to me, like fling me into a gas oven or send me off to a Gulag. Unlike a Hindu and not worshipping stasis, I am also given to wondering who is to bring these murderers and tyrants down, it being all too risky a process to wait for them and the regimes they establish simply to die of old age. The fact that a few reincarnations from now they will all have turned to dust somehow does not seem to suggest a rational strategy for dealing with the problem.

Since the movie's Madeleine Slade specifically invites us to revere the "way out of madness" that Gandhi offered the world at the time of World War II, I am under the embarrassing obligation of recording exactly what courses of action the Great

Soul recommended to the various parties involved in that crisis. For Gandhi was never stinting in his advice. Indeed, the less he knew about a subject, the less he stinted.

I am aware that for many not privileged to have visited the former British Raj, the names Gujarat, Rajasthan, and Deccan are simply words. But other names, such as Germany, Poland, Czechoslovakia, somehow have a harder profile. The term "Jew," also, has a reasonably hard profile, and I feel all Jews sitting emotionally at the movie *Gandhi* should be aprised of the advice that the Mahatma offered their coreligionists when faced with the Nazi peril: they should commit collective suicide. If only the Jews of Germany had the good sense to "offer their throats willingly" to the Nazi butchers' knives and throw themselves into the sea from cliffs they would arouse world public opinion, Gandhi was convinced, and their moral triumph would be remembered for "ages to come." If they would only pray for Hitler (as their throats were cut, presumably), they would leave a "rich heritage to mankind." Although Gandhi had known Jews from his earliest days in South Africa—where his three staunchest white supporters were Jews, every one—he disapproved of how rarely they loved their enemies. And he never repented of his recommendation of collective suicide. Even after the war, when the full extent of the Holocaust was revealed, Gandhi told Louis Fischer, one of his biographers, that the Jews died anyway, didn't they? They might as well have died significantly.

Gandhi's views on the European crisis were not entirely consistent. He vigorously opposed Munich, distrusting Chamberlain. "Europe has sold her soul for the sake of a seven days' earthly existence," he declared. "The peace that Europe gained at Munich is a triumph of violence." But when the Germans moved into the Bohemian heartland, he was back to urging nonviolent resistance, exhorting the Czechs to go forth, unarmed, against the Wehrmacht, *perishing gloriously*—collective suicide again. He had Madeleine Slade draw up two letters to President Eduard Beneš of Czechoslovakia, instructing him on the proper conduct of Czechoslovak *satyagrahi* when facing the Nazis.

When Hitler attacked Poland, however, Gandhi suddenly endorsed the Polish army's military resistance, calling it "almost nonviolent." (If this sounds like double-talk, I can only urge readers to read Gandhi.) He seemed at this point to have a rather low opinion of Hitler, but when Germany's panzer divisions turned west, Allied armies collapsed under the ferocious onslaught, and British ships were streaming across the Straits of Dover from Dunkirk, he wrote furiously to the viceroy of India: "This manslaughter must be stopped. You are losing; if you persist, it will only result in greater bloodshed. Hitler is not a bad man. . . ."

Gandhi also wrote an open letter to the British people, passionately urging them to surrender and accept whatever fate Hitler had prepared for them. "Let them take possession of your beautiful island with your many beautiful buildings. You will give all these, but neither your souls, nor your minds." Since none of this had the intended effect, Gandhi, the following year, addressed an open letter to the prince of darkness himself, Adolf Hitler.

The scene must be pictured. In late December 1941, Hitler stood at the pinnacle of his might. His armies, undefeated—anywhere—ruled Europe from the English Channel to the Volga. Rommel had entered Egypt. The Japanese had reached Singapore. The U.S. Pacific Fleet lay at the bottom of Pearl Harbor. At this superbly chosen moment, Mahatma Gandhi attempted to convert Adolf Hitler to the ways of nonviolence. "Dear Friend," the letter begins, and proceeds to a heartfelt appeal to the Führer to embrace all mankind "irrespective of race, color, or creed." Every admirer of the film *Gandhi* should be compelled to read this letter. Surprisingly, it is not known to have had any deep impact on Hitler. Gandhi was no doubt disappointed. He moped about, really quite depressed, but still knew he was right. When the Japanese, having cut their way through Burma, threatened India, Gandhi's strategy was to let them occupy as much of India as they liked and then to "make them feel unwanted." His way of helping his British "friends" was, at one of the worst points of the war, to launch massive civil disobedience campaigns against them, paralyzing some of their efforts to defend India from the Japanese.

Here, then, is your leader, O followers of Gandhi: a man who thought Hitler's heart would be melted by an appeal to forget race, color, and creed, and who was sure the feelings of the Japanese would be hurt if they sensed themselves unwanted. As world-class statesmen go, it is not a very good record. Madeleine Slade was right, I suppose. The world certainly didn't listen to Gandhi. Nor, for that matter, has the modern government of India listened to Gandhi. Although Indian politicians of all political parties claim to be Gandhians, India has blithely fought three wars against Pakistan, one against China, and even invaded and seized tiny, helpless Goa, and all without a whisper of a shadow of a thought of *ahimsa*. And of course India now has atomic weapons, a *satyagraha* technique if ever there was one.

I am sure that almost everyone who sees the movie *Gandhi* is aware that, from a religious point of view, the Mahatma was something called a "Hindu"—but I do not think one in a thousand has the dimmest notion of the fundamental beliefs of the Hindu religion. The simplest example is Gandhi's use of the word "God," which, for members of the great Western religions—Christianity, Judaism, and Islam, all interrelated—means a personal god, a godhead. But when Gandhi said "God" in speaking English, he was merely translating from Gujarati or Hindi, and from the Hindu culture. Gandhi, in fact, simply did not believe in a personal God, and wrote in so many words, "God is not a person . . . but a force; the undefinable mysterious Power that pervades everything; a living Power that is Love. . . ." And Gandhi's very favorite definition of God, repeated many thousands of times, was, "God is Truth," which reduces God to some kind of abstract principle.

Like all Hindus, Gandhi also believed in the "Great Oneness," according to which everything is part of God, meaning not just you and me and everyone else, but every living creature, every dead creature, every plant, the pitcher of milk, the milk in the pitcher, the tumbler into which the milk is poured. . . . After all of which, he could suddenly pop up with a declaration that God is "the Maker, the Law-Giver, a jealous Lord," phrases he had probably picked up in the Bible and, with Hindu fluidity, felt he could throw in so as to embrace even more of the Great

Oneness. So when Gandhi said, "I am a Hindu and a Muslim and a Christian and a Jew," it was (from a Western standpoint) Hindu double-talk. Hindu holy men, some of them reformers like Gandhi, have actually even "converted" to Islam, then Christianity, or whatever, to worship different "aspects" of the Great Oneness, before reconverting to Hinduism. Now for Christians, fastidious in matters of doctrine, a man who converts to Islam is an apostate (or vice versa), but a Hindu is a Hindu is a Hindu. The better to experience the Great Oneness, many Hindu holy men feel they should be women as well as men, and one quite famous one even claimed he could menstruate (I will spare the reader the details).

In this ecumenical age, it is extremely hard to shake Westerners loose from the notion that the devout of all religions, after all, worship "the one God." But Gandhi did not worship the one God. He did not worship the God of forgiveness. And this for the simple reason that the concepts of mercy and forgiveness are absent from Hinduism. In Hinduism, men do not pray to God for forgiveness, and a man's sins are never forgiven— indeed, there is no one out there to do the forgiving. In your next life you may be born someone higher up the caste scale, but in this life there is no hope. For Gandhi, a true Hindu, did not believe in man's immortal soul. He believed with every ounce of his being in *karma*, a series, perhaps a long series, of reincarnations, and at the end, with great good fortune: *mukti*, liberation from suffering and the necessity of rebirth, nothingness. Gandhi once wrote to Tolstoy (of all people) that reincarnation explained "reasonably the many mysteries of life." So if Hindus today still treat an Untouchable as barely human, this is thought to be perfectly right and fitting because of his actions in earlier lives. As can be seen, Hinduism, by its very theology, with its sacred triad of *karma*, reincarnation, and caste (with caste an absolutely indispensable part of the system) offers the most complacent justification of inhumanity of any of the world's great religious faiths.

Gandhi, needless to say, was a Hindu reformer, one of many. Until well into his fifties, however, he accepted the caste system *in toto* as the "natural order of society," promoting control and discipline and sanctioned by his religion. Later, in bursts of zeal, he favored moderating it in a number of ways. But he stuck by the basic *varna* system (the four main caste groupings plus the Untouchables) until the end of his days, insisting that a man's position and occupation should be determined essentially by birth. Gandhi favored milder treatment of Untouchables, renaming them Harijans, "children of God," but a Harijan was still a Harijan. Perhaps because Gandhi's frenzies of compassion were so extreme (no, no *he* would clean the *Harijan*'s latrine), Hindu reverence for him as a holy man became immense, but his prescriptions were rarely followed. Industrialization and modernization have introduced new occupations and sizable social and political changes in India, but the caste system has dexterously adapted and remains largely intact today. The Sudras still labor. The sweepers still sweep. Max Weber, in his *The Religion of India*, after quoting the last line of the *Communist Manifesto*, suggests somewhat sardonically that low-caste Hindus, too, have "nothing to lose but their chains," that they, too, have "a world to win"—the only problem being that they have to die first and get born again, higher, it is to be hoped, in the immutable system of caste. Hinduism in general, wrote Weber, "is characterized by a dread of the magical evil of innovation." Its very essence is to guarantee stasis.

In addition to its literally thousands of castes and sub-castes, Hinduism has countless sects, with discordant rites and beliefs. It has no clear ecclesiastical organization and no universal body of doctrine. What I have described above is your standard, no-frills Hindu, of which in many ways Gandhi was an excellent example. With the reader's permission I will skip over the Upanishads, Vedanta, Yoga, the Puranas, Tantra, Bhakti, the *Bhagavad-Gita* (which contains theistic elements), Brahma, Vishnu, Shiva, and the terrible Kali or Durga, to concentrate on those central beliefs that most motivated Gandhi's behavior as a public figure.

It should be plain by now that there is much in the Hindu culture that is distasteful to the Western mind, and consequently is largely unknown in the West—not because Hindus do not go on and on about these subjects, but because a Western squeamishness usually prevents these preoccupations from reaching print (not to mention film). When Gandhi attended his first Indian National Congress he was most distressed at seeing the Hindus—not laborers but high-caste Hindus, civic leaders—defecating all over the place, as if to pay attention to where the feces fell was somehow unclean. (For, as V. S. Naipaul puts it, in a twisted Hindu way it is *unclean to clean*. It is unclean even to notice. "It was the business of the sweepers to remove excrement, and until the sweepers came, people were content to live in the midst of their own excrement.") Gandhi exhorted Indians endlessly on the subject, saying that sanitation was the first need of India, but he retained an obvious obsession with excreta, gleefully designing latrines and latrine drills for all hands at the ashram, and, all in all, what with giving and taking enemas, and his public bowel movements, and his deep concern with everyone else's bowel movements (much correspondence), and endless dietary experiments *as a function* of bowel movements, he devoted a rather large share of his life to the matter. Despite his constant campaigning for sanitation, it is hard to believe that Gandhi was not permanently marked by what Arthur Koestler terms the Hindu "morbid infatuation with filth," and what V. S. Naipaul goes as far as to call the Indian "deification of filth." (Decades later, Morarji Desai, a Gandhian and one-time Indian prime minister, was still fortifying his sanctity by drinking a daily glass of urine.)

But even more important, because it is dealt with in the movie directly—if of course dishonestly—is Gandhi's parallel obsession with *brahmacharya*, or sexual chastity. There is a scene late in the film in which Margaret Bourke-White (again!) asks Gandhi's wife if he has ever broken his vow of chastity, taken, at that time, about forty years before. Gandhi's wife, by now a sweet old lady, answers wistfully, with a pathetic little note of hope, "Not yet." What lies behind this adorable scene is the following: Gandhi held as one of his most profound beliefs (a fundamental doctrine of Hindu medicine) that a man, as a matter of the utmost importance, must conserve his *bindu*, or seminal fluid. Koestler (in *The Lotus and the Robot*) gives a succinct account of this belief, widespread among orthodox Hindus: "A man's vital energy is concentrated in his seminal fluid, and this is stored in a cavity in the skull. It is the most precious substance in the body . . . an elixir of life both in the physical and mystical sense, distilled from the blood. . . . A large store of *bindu* of pure quality guarantees health, longevity, and supernatural powers. . . . Conversely, every loss of it is a physical and spiritual impoverishment." Gandhi himself said in so many words, "A man who is unchaste loses stamina, becomes emasculated and cowardly, while in the chaste man secretions [semen] are sublimated into a vital force pervading his whole being." And again, still Gandhi: "Ability to retain and assimilate the vital liquid is a matter of long training. When properly conserved it is transmitted into matchless energy and strength." Most male Hindus go ahead and have sexual relations anyway, of course, but the belief in the value of *bindu* leaves the whole culture in what many observers have called a permanent state of "semen anxiety." When Gandhi once had a nocturnal emission he almost had a nervous breakdown.

Gandhi was a truly fanatical opponent of sex for pleasure, and worked it out carefully that a married couple should be allowed to have sex three or four times *in a lifetime*, merely to have children, and favored embodying this restriction in the law of the land. The sexual-gratification wing of the present-day feminist movement would find little to attract them in Gandhi's doctrine, since in all his seventy-nine years it never crossed his mind once that there could be anything enjoyable in sex for women, and he was constantly enjoining Indian women to deny themselves to men, to refuse to let their husbands "abuse" them. Gandhi had been married at thirteen, and when he took his vow of chastity, after twenty-four years of sexual activity, he ordered his two oldest sons, both young men, to be totally chaste as well.

But Gandhi's monstrous behavior to his own family is notorious. He denied his sons education—to which he was bitterly hostile. His wife remained illiterate. Once when she was very sick, hemorrhaging badly, and seemed to be dying, he wrote to her from jail icily: "My struggle is not merely political. It is religious and therefore quite pure. It does not matter much whether one dies in it or lives. I hope and expect that you will also think likewise and not be unhappy." To die, that is. On another occasion he wrote, speaking about her: "I simply cannot bear to look at Ba's face. The expression is often like that on the face of a meek cow and gives one the feeling, as a cow occasionally does, that in her own dumb manner she is saying something. I see, too, that there is selfishness in this suffering of hers. . . ." And in the end he let her die, as I have said, rather than allow British doctors to give her a shot of penicillin (while his inner voice told him that it would be all right for him to take quinine). He disowned his oldest son, Harilal, for wishing to marry. He banished his second son for giving his struggling older brother a small sum of money. Harilal grew quite wild with rage against his father, attacked him in print, converted to Islam, took to women, drink, and died an alcoholic in 1948. The Mahatma attacked him right back in his pious way, proclaiming modestly in an open letter in *Young India*, "Men may be good, not necessarily their children."

If the reader thinks I have delivered unduly harsh judgments on India and Hindu civilization, I can refer him to *An Area of Darkness* and *India: A Wounded Civilization*, two quite brilliant books on India by V. S. Naipaul, a Hindu, and a Brahmin, born in Trinidad. In the second, the more discursive, Naipaul writes that India "has little to offer the world except its Gandhian concept of holy poverty and the recurring crooked comedy of its holy men, and . . . is now dependent in every practical way on other, imperfectly understood civilizations."

Hinduism, Naipaul writes, "has given men no idea of a contract with other men, no idea of the state. It has enslaved one quarter of the population [the Untouchables] and always has left the whole fragmented and vulnerable. Its philosophy of withdrawal has diminished men intellectually and not equipped them to respond to challenge; it has stifled growth. So that again and again in India history has repeated itself: vulnerability, defeat, withdrawal." Indians, Naipaul says, have no historical notion of the past. "Through centuries of conquest the civilization declined into an apparatus for survival, turning away from the mind . . . and creativity . . . stripping itself down, like all decaying civilizations, to its magical practices and imprisoning social forms." He adds later, "No government can survive on Gandhian fantasy; and the spirituality, the solace of a conquered people, which Gandhi turned into a form of national assertion, has soured more obviously into the nihilism that it always was." Naipaul condemns India again and again for its "intellectual parasitism," its "intellectual vacuum," its "emptiness," the "blankness of its decayed civilization." "Indian poverty is more dehumanizing than any machine; and, more than in any machine civilization, men in India are units, locked up in the straitest obedience by their idea of their *dharma*. . . . The blight of caste is not only untouchability and the consequent deification in India of filth; the blight, in an India that tries to grow, is also the overall obedience it imposes, . . . the diminishing of adventurousness, the pushing away from men of individuality and the possibility of excellence."

Although Naipaul blames Gandhi as well as India itself for the country's failure to develop an "ideology" adequate for the modern world, he grants him one or two magnificent moments— always, it should be noted, when responding to "other civilizations." For Gandhi, Naipaul remarks pointedly, had matured in alien societies: Britain and South Africa. With age, back in India, he seemed from his autobiography to be headed for "lunacy," says Naipaul, and was only rescued by external events, his reactions to which were determined in part by *"his experience of the democratic ways of South Africa"* [my emphasis]. For it is one of the enduring ironies of Gandhi's story that it was in South Africa—*South Africa*—a country in which he became far more deeply involved than he had been in Britain, that Gandhi caught a warped glimmer of that strange institution of which he would never have seen even a reflection within Hindu society: democracy.

Another of Gandhi's most powerful obsessions (to which the movie alludes in such a syrupy and misleading manner that it would be quite impossible for the audience to understand it) was his visceral hatred of the modern, industrial world. He even said, more than once, that he actually wouldn't mind if the British remained in India, to police it, conduct foreign policy, and such trivia, if it would only take away its factories and railways. And Gandhi hated, not just factories and railways, but also the telegraph, the telephone, the radio, the airplane. He happened to be in England when Louis Blériot, the great French aviation pioneer, first flew the English Channel—an event which at the time stirred as much excitement as Lindbergh's later flight across the Atlantic—and Gandhi was in a positive fury that giant crowds were acclaiming such an insignificant event. He used the telegraph extensively himself, of course, and later would broadcast daily over All-India Radio during his highly publicized fasts, but consistency was never Gandhi's strong suit.

Gandhi's view of the good society, about which he wrote *ad nauseam*, was an Arcadian vision set far in India's past. It was the pristine Indian village, where, with all diabolical machinery and technology abolished—and with them all unhappiness—contented villagers would hand-spin their own yarn, hand-weave their own cloth, serenely follow their bullocks in the fields, tranquilly prodding them in the anus in the time-hallowed Hindu way. This was why Gandhi taught himself to spin, and why all the devout Gandhians, like monkeys, spun also. This was Gandhi's program. Since he said it several thousand times, we have no choice but to believe that he sincerely desired the destruction of modern technology and industry and the return of India to the way of life of an idyllic (and quite likely non-existent) past. And yet this same Mahatma Gandhi hand-picked as the first prime minister of an independent India Pandit Nehru, who was committed to a policy of industrialization and for whom the last word in the politico-economic organization of the state was (and remained) Beatrice Webb.

What are we to make of this Gandhi? We are dealing with two strangenesses here, Indians and Gandhi himself. The plain fact is that both Indian leaders and the Indian people ignored Gandhi's precepts almost as thoroughly as did Hitler. They ignored him on sexual abstinence. They ignored his modifications of the caste system. They ignored him on the evils of modern industry, the radio, the telephone. They ignored him on education. They ignored his appeals for national union, the former British Raj splitting into a Muslim Pakistan and a Hindu India. No one sought a return to the Arcadian Indian village of antiquity. They ignored him, above all, on *ahimsa*, nonviolence. There was always a small number of exalted *satyagrahi* who, martyrs, would march into the constables' truncheons, but one of the things that alarmed the British—as Tagore indicated—was the explosions of violence that accompanied all this alleged nonviolence. Naipaul writes that with independence India discovered again that it was "cruel and horribly violent." Jaya Prakash Narayan, the late opposition leader, once admitted, "We often behave like animals. . . . We are more likely than not to become aggressive, wild, violent. We kill and burn and loot. . . ."

Why, then, did the Hindu masses so honor this Mahatma, almost all of whose most cherished beliefs they so pointedly ignored, even during his lifetime? For Hindus, the question is not really so puzzling. Gandhi, for them, after all, was a Mahatma, a holy man. He was a symbol of sanctity, not a guide to conduct. Hinduism has a long history of holy men who, traditionally, do not offer themselves up to the public as models of general behavior but withdraw from the world, often into an ashram, to pursue their sanctity in private, a practice which all Hindus honor, if few emulate. The true oddity is that Gandhi, this holy man, having drawn from British sources his notions of nationalism and democracy, also absorbed from the British his model of virtue in public life. He was a historical original, a Hindu holy man that a British model of public service and dazzling advances in mass communications thrust out into the world, to become a great moral leader and the "father of his country."

Some Indians feel that after the early 1930s, Gandhi, although by now world-famous, was in fact in sharp decline. Did he at least "get the British out of India"? Some say no. India, in the last days of the British Raj, was already largely governed by Indians (a fact one would never suspect from this movie), and it is a common view that without this irrational, wildly erratic holy man the transition to full independence might have gone both more smoothly and more swiftly. There is much evidence that in his last years Gandhi was in a kind of spiritual retreat and, with all his endless praying and fasting, was no longer pursuing (the very words seem strange in a Hindu context) "the public good." What he was pursuing, in a strict reversion to Hindu tradition, was his personal holiness. In earlier days he had scoffed at the title accorded him, Mahatma (literally "great soul"). But toward the end, during the hideous paroxysms that accompanied independence, with some of the most unspeakable massacres taking place in Calcutta, he declared, "And if . . . the whole of Calcutta swims in blood, it will not dismay me. For it will be a willing offering of innocent blood." And in his last days, after there had already been one attempt on his life, he was heard to say, *"I am a true Mahatma."*

We can only wonder, furthermore, at a public figure who lectures half his life about the necessity of abolishing modern industry and returning India to its ancient primitiveness, and then picks a Fabian Socialist, already drawing up Five-Year Plans, as the country's first prime minister. Audacious as it may seem to contest the views of such heavy thinkers as Margaret Bourke-White, Ralph Nader, and J. K. Galbraith (who found the film's Gandhi "true to the original" and endorsed the movie wholeheartedly), we have a right to reservations about such a figure as a public man.

I should not be surprised if Gandhi's greatest real humanitarian achievement was an improvement in the treatment of Untouchables—an area where his efforts were not only assiduous, but actually bore fruit. In this, of course, he ranks well behind the British, who abolished *suttee*—over ferocious Hindu opposition—in 1829. The ritual immolation by fire of widows on their husbands' funeral pyres, *suttee* had the full sanction of the Hindu religion, although it might perhaps be wrong to overrate its importance. Scholars remind us that it was never universal, only "usual." And there was, after all, a rather extensive range of choice. In southern India the widow was flung into her husband's fire-pit. In the valley of the Ganges she was placed on the pyre when it was already aflame. In western India, she supported the head of the corpse with her right hand, while, torch in her left, she was allowed the honor of setting the whole thing on fire herself. In the north, where perhaps women were more impious, the widow's body was constrained on the burning pyre by long poles pressed down by her relatives, just in case, screaming in terror and choking and burning to death, she might forget her *dharma*. So, yes, ladies, members of the National Council of Churches, believers in the one God, mourners for that holy India before it was despoiled by those brutish British, remember *suttee*, that interesting, exotic practice in which Hindus, over the centuries, burned to death countless millions of helpless women in a spirit of pious devotion, crying for all I know, *Hai Rama! Hai Rama!*

I would like to conclude with some observations on two Englishmen, Madeleine Slade, the daughter of a British admiral, and Sir Richard Attenborough, the producer, director, and spiritual godfather of the film, *Gandhi*. Slade was a jewel in Gandhi's crown—a member of the British ruling class, as she was, turned fervent disciple of this Indian Mahatma. She is played in the film by Geraldine James with nobility, dignity, and a beatific manner quite up to the level of Candice Bergen, and perhaps even the Virgin Mary. I learn from Ved Mehta's *Mahatma Gandhi and his Apostles*, however, that Madeleine Slade had another master before Gandhi. In about 1917, when she was fifteen, she made contact with the spirit of Beethoven by listening to his sonatas on a player piano. "I threw myself down on my knees in the seclusion of my room," she wrote in her autobiography, "and prayed, *really* prayed to God for the first time in my life: 'Why have I been born over a century too late? Why hast Thou given me realization of him and yet put all these years in between?' "

After World War I, still seeking how best to serve Beethoven, Slade felt an "infinite longing" when she visited his birthplace and grave, and, finally, at the age of thirty-two, caught up with Romain Rolland, who had partly based his renowned *Jean Christophe* on the composer. But Rolland had written a new book now, about a man called Gandhi, "another Christ," and before long Slade was quite literally falling on her knees before the Mahatma in India, "conscious of nothing but a sense of light." Although one would never guess this from the film, she soon (to quote Mehta's impression) began "to get on Gandhi's nerves," and he took every pretext to keep her away from him, in other ashrams, and working in schools and villages in other parts of India. She complained to Gandhi in letters about discrimination against her by orthodox Hindus, who expected her to live in rags and vile quarters during menstruation, considering her unclean and virtually untouchable. Gandhi wrote back, agreeing that women should not be treated like that, but adding that she should accept it all with grace and cheerfulness, "without thinking that the orthodox party is in any way unreasonable." (This is as good an example as any of Gandhi's coherence, even in his prime. Women should not be treated like that, but the people who treated them that way were in no way unreasonable.)

Some years after Gandhi's death, Slade rediscovered Beethoven, becoming conscious again "of the realization of my true self. For a while I remained lost in the world of the spirit. . . ." She soon returned to Europe and to serving Beethoven, her "true calling." When Mehta finally found her in Vienna, she told him, "Please don't ask me any more about Bapu [Gandhi]. I now belong to van Beethoven. In matters of the spirit, there is always a call." A polite description of Madeleine Slade is that she was an extreme eccentric. In the vernacular, she was slightly cracked.

Sir Richard Attenborough, however, isn't cracked at all. The only puzzle is how he suddenly got to be a pacifist, a fact which his press releases now proclaim to the world. Attenborough trained as a pilot in the RAF in World War II, and was released briefly to the cinema, where he had already begun his career in Noel Coward's super-patriotic *In Which We Serve*. He then returned to active service, flying combat missions with the RAF. Richard Attenborough, in short—when Gandhi was pleading with the British to surrender to the Nazis, assuring them that "Hitler is not a bad man"—was fighting for his country. The viceroy of India warned Gandhi grimly that "We are engaged in a struggle," and Attenborough played his part in that great struggle, and proudly, too, as far as I can tell. To my knowledge he has never had a *crise de conscience* on the matter, or announced that he was carried away by the war fever and that

Britain really should have capitulated to the Nazis—which Gandhi would have had it do.

Although the present film is handsomely done in its way, no one has ever accused Attenborough of being excessively endowed with either acting or directing talent. In the fifties he was a popular young British entertainer, but his most singular gift appeared to be his entrepreneurial talent as a businessman, using his movie fees to launch successful London restaurants (at one time four), and other business ventures. At the present moment [1983] he is chairman of the board of Capital Radio (Britain's most successful commercial station), Goldcrest Films, the British Film Institute, and deputy chairman of the BBC's new Channel 4 television network. Like most members of the *nouveaux riches* on the rise, he has also reached out for symbols of respectability and public service, and has assembled quite a collection. He is a trustee of the Tate Gallery, pro-chancellor of Sussex University, president of Britain's Muscular Dystrophy Group, chairman of the Actors' Charitable Trust and, of course, chairman of the Royal Academy of Dramatic Art. There may be even more, but this is a fair sampling. In 1976, quite fittingly, he was knighted, by a Labor government, but his friends say he still insists on being called "Dickie."

It is quite general today for members of the professional classes, even when not artistic types, to despise commerce and feel that the state, the economy, and almost everything else would be better and more idealistically run by themselves, rather than these loutish businessmen. Sir Dickie, however, being a highly successful businessman himself, would hardly entertain such an antipathy. But as he scrambled his way to the heights perhaps he found himself among high-minded idealists, utopians, equalitarians, and lovers of the oppressed. Now there are those who think Sir Dickie converted to pacifism when Indira Gandhi handed him a check for several million dollars. But I do not believe this. I think Sir Dickie converted to pacifism out of idealism.

His pacifism, I confess, has been more than usually muddled. In 1968, after twenty-six years in the profession, he made his directorial debut with *Oh! What a Lovely War*, with its superb parody of Britain's jingoistic music-hall songs of the "Great War," World War I. Since I had the good fortune to see Joan Littlewood's original London stage production, which gave the work its entire style, I cannot think that Sir Dickie's contribution was unduly large. Like most commercially successful parodies— from Sandy Wilson's *The Boy Friend* to Broadway's *Superman, Dracula*, and *The Crucifier of Blood—Oh! What a Lovely War* depended on the audience's (if not Littlewood's) retaining a substantial affection for the subject being parodied: in this case, a swaggering hyper-patriotism, which recalled days when the empire was great. In any event, since Littlewood identified herself as a Communist and since Communists, as far as I know, are never pacifists, Sir Dickie's case for the production's "pacifism" seems stymied from the other angle as well.

Sir Dickie's next blow for pacifism was *Young Winston* (1973), which, the new publicity manual says, "explored how Churchill's childhood traumas and lack of parental affection became the spurs which goaded him to . . . a position of great power." One would think that a man who once flew combat missions under the orders of the great war leader—and who seemingly wanted his country to win—would thank God for childhood traumas and lack of parental affection if such were needed to provide a Churchill in the hour of peril. But on pressed Sir Dickie, in the year of his knighthood, with *A Bridge Too Far*, the story of the futile World War II assault on Arnhem, described by Sir Dickie—now, at least—as "a further plea for pacifism."

But does Sir Richard Attenborough seriously think that, rather than go through what we did at Arnhem, we should have given in, let the Nazis be, and even—true pacifists—let them occupy Britain, Canada, the United States, contenting ourselves only with "making them feel unwanted"? At the level of idiocy to which discussions of war and peace have sunk in the West, every hare-brained idealist who discovers that war is not a day at the beach seems to think he has found an irresistible argument for pacifism. Is Pearl Harbor an argument for pacifism? Bataan? Dunkirk? Dieppe? The Ardennes? Roland fell at Roncesvalles. Is the *Song of Roland* a pacifist epic? If so, why did William the

Conqueror have it chanted to his men as they marched into battle at Hastings? Men prove their valor in defeat as well as in victory. Even Sergeant-Major Gandhi knew that. Up in the moral never-never land which Sir Dickie now inhabits, perhaps they think the Alamo led to a great wave of pacifism in Texas.

In a feat of sheer imbecility, Attenborough has dedicated *Gandhi* to Lord Mountbatten, who commanded the Southeast Asian Theater during World War II. Mountbatten, you might object, was hardly a pacifist—but then again he was murdered by Irish terrorists, which proves how frightful all that sort of thing is, Sir Dickie says, and how we must end it all by imitating Gandhi. Not the Gandhi who called for seas of innocent blood, you understand, but the movie-Gandhi, the nice one.

The historical Gandhi's favorite mantra, strange to tell, was *Do or Die* (he called it literally that, a "mantra"). I think Sir Dickie should reflect on this, because it means, *dixit* Gandhi, that a man must be prepared to die for what he believes in, for, *himsa* or *ahimsa*, death is always there and, in an ultimate test, men who are not prepared to face it lose. Gandhi was erratic, irrational, tyrannical, obstinate. He sometimes verged on lunacy. He believed in a religion whose ideas I find repugnant. He worshipped cows. But I still say this: he was brave. He feared no one.

On a lower level of being, I have consequently given some thought to the proper mantra for spectators of the movie *Gandhi*. After much reflection, in homage to Ralph Nader, I have decided on *caveat emptor*, "buyer beware." Repeated many thousand times in a seat in the cinema it might with luck lead to *om*, the Hindu dream of nothingness, the Ultimate Void.

Note: Gandhi swept the Academy Awards in the spring of 1983, winning in all eight awards, including best film, best actor, best director, and best screenplay.

7

The Hard Left and the Soft: Hollywood Tests Its Radical Limits

" "IVE FILMS WITH POLITICAL STATEMENTS DUE IN FALL."
There it was, in a headline right on the front page of the
New York Times, so it must have been true. The point had
already been amply covered, in any event, in the pages of
Variety, the trade journal of the entertainment business, which,
for those who can translate its eccentric linguistic constructions
into English, is an excellent historical source. Of course, the
cinema is becoming an increasingly ideologized medium, a process under way (not surprisingly) since the late sixties. But I
admit that the fall of 1983 brought out a particularly large crop
of blatantly didactic movies—substantially more than five, in
fact. How have they fared commercially? The nakedly political
ones have done badly, as it happens, ranging generally from
failures to humiliating failures. Why then all this brouhaha? And
why in 1983?

The simplest way of explaining the timing is by referring to
the Democratic gains in the off-year congressional elections of
1982. For the movie industry has become so highly politicized
that, allowing for the nine-to-twelve-month lead time between
the studio green light and the appearance of a film in movie
houses, the political films we have seen in the fall of 1983
correspond to Hollywood's reading of the election returns of the
preceding year. The nationalistic revival of the latter part of the
Carter administration and the first two years of the Reagan
administration gave us a whole string of patriotic, pro-military,

135

anti-Soviet movies (*The Deer Hunter, Firefox, An Officer and a Gentleman, First Blood*); but unlike Clint Eastwood and Sylvester Stallone (stars of *Firefox* and *First Blood*), most of the "bankable" stars of Hollywood these days are liberal Democrats. Now in this year of "primary politics," liberal Democrats throughout the country have in the opinion of many analysts been "re-McGovernized," and they have been re-McGovernized nowhere more emphatically than in Hollywood. Hence this barrage of films from the Left.

First off the mark was Sidney Lumet, the director, fresh from his box-office triumph with *The Verdict* starring Paul Newman. A radical in his youth, Lumet chose for this leftist film season E. L. Doctorow's *The Book of Daniel*, a lightly fictionalized version of the life and death of Julius and Ethel Rosenberg in which the Rosenbergs are totally innocent victims of a straight frame-up by J. Edgar Hoover and the FBI. In *Daniel*, the movie version, starring Ed Asner (television's Lou Grant, known politically in his own person for his ardent support of the Marxist-Leninist rebels in El Salvador), we are given "the romance of Jewish Communism." I have been told that at the time of the Rosenberg trial in 1951 patriotic American Jews were considering placing an advertisement in newspapers announcing that, although the Rosenbergs were Communists, most American Jews were not and were loyal to their country. They commissioned a study, however, and discovered that ordinary heartland Americans didn't even know the name "Rosenberg" was Jewish—and cancelled their plans for the advertisement.

From this point of view, I can only say that *Daniel* has certainly blown the Rosenbergs' cover. In the film, the "Isaacsons" (as they are called) are both extravagantly Jewish and extravagantly Communist. They eat Jewish food, speak with strong Yiddish inflections. Every detail of their everyday lives identifies them unequivocally as members of an exclusively Jewish community—and of a Jewish Communist community. They sing "The Peat Bog Soldiers," talk of "the Scottsboro boys," take buses to hear Paul Robeson at the famous pro-Soviet Progressive-party rally in upstate New York. In the present preposterous age, in which I fully expect that if Joseph

Stalin were to return from the grave he would be introduced on CBS as a "liberal activist," I had strongly suspected that the "Isaacsons" would be presented as good liberals. But, no. Even though the film-makers are clearly more comfortable when their cast refers less provocatively to "the party," the word "Communist" is heard also, so there is no doubt what "party" is being talked about.

Daniel was done substantial damage by being released shortly after the publication of Ronald Radosh's and Joyce Milton's *The Rosenberg File*, which would convince anyone but the most fossilized old Stalinist that the Rosenbergs were guilty. The book also makes clear the unappealing contempt the Rosenbergs felt for their fellow Americans and their lust for martyrdom as the "first victims of American fascism." But even without the Radosh-Milton book, I strongly suspect that *Daniel* would have failed.

I am, first, not at all certain that American moviegoers (although an elite audience compared to the mass movie public of the age before television) are prepared to lavish their sympathies on people who so openly believe in the political system of the Soviet Union. The style for some time now has been to find alternative utopias in Havana, Hanoi, Beijing, Santiago (under Allende), Luanda, Maputo, and, of course, Managua. But Moscow is a no-no. In the 1983 mayoral elections in Boston, one-third of the voters (mostly black and Hispanic) cast their ballots for a candidate who declared that he preferred the government of Fidel Castro to that of Ronald Reagan. But I do not think he could have done that well by preferring the government of Yuri Andropov. Further, I feel Sidney Lumet made a gross miscalculation in estimating that America shares his narcissistic passion for warm, lovable Communist Jews—or perhaps even Jews, period. If a Pitchfork Ben Tillman or any other such anti-Semitic demagogue ever arises again in the land, in fact, he could use selected clips from *Daniel* in his campaign commercials. Nor would a future Pitchfork Ben be likely to miss *Daniel*'s young Stalinist Jewish children growing up to be militants in the antiwar movement of the Vietnam years and the antinuclear "peace" movement. For their part, I should think a Stalinist connection would be the last thing many of the supporters of these movements would want, but to Sidney Lumet Jewish Stalinism is so adorable that he gives them such a connection anyway.

Costa-Gavras's *Hannah K.*, next out of the starting gate, was an even greater fiasco than *Daniel*. In the film, Jill Clayburgh plays a Jewish woman from Middle America who, after a stopover in Paris during which she picks up a rich French husband, emigrates to Israel where she learns Hebrew (presumably), gets a law degree, becomes a lawyer, and acquires a Jerusalem district attorney as a lover. Fate decrees that she should defend in court the right of a Palestinian Arab—and, she admits under questioning, that of two million other Palestinian Arabs—to return to their homeland in Israel. A rich French husband, an illegitimate child by an Israeli lover (the D.A.), a new Arab lover (the Palestinian), a law degree, a noble cause—what else could a Jewish girl from Middle America want? Costa-Gavras explained to me personally that the film's secret asset was that the Palestinian was a "Gandhian"—a Palestinian sect which has not been very conspicuous in the Middle East up to this point. Possibly this explains why the film had to be withdrawn in three weeks.

No less a personage than Peter Bogdanovich (*The Last Picture Show*), who should know, once said that Hollywood allowed you three flops, after which they took you down from your pedestal. Jill Clayburgh has now had four flops running. *Luna*, *It's My Turn*, *I'm Dancing as Fast as I Can*, and now *Hannah K.* At this rate she might soon be camping out on Greenham Common with ex-star Julie Christie, or joining the Nicaraguan support staff at the United Nations with ex-actress Bianca Jagger.

Richard Gere, following his giant success in *An Officer and a Gentleman* and a sharp failure in a Los Angeles remake of Jean-Luc Godard's *Breathless*, has now brought in another failure by following what he might have imagined to be the winds of change. *Beyond the Limit*, in which he co-stars with Michael Caine, is a film version of Graham Greene's *The Honorary Consul* and gives the most extraordinarily sympathetic account of Latin American terrorists who attempt to kidnap a U.S.

ambassador. We have a lapsed priest, now a terrorist, who tells us, "Sometimes we have to leave God for men!" The same lapsed priest, when an objection is raised to Paraguayan terrorists operating in Argentina, proclaims joyfully, "But Latin America is our country!" (So much for those who think that doings in El Salvador might not spill over into Guatemala, then Mexico.) All this is mixed in with Graham Greene's variety of Catholicism, which is becoming hard to distinguish these days from that of the Maryknollers. I have always held Graham Greene to be a shoddy writer, from his first book to his last, but it is sometimes only when people see a writer's work blown up on the screen (however creditably acted and directed), that they realize just how shoddy he actually is.

Saturday Night Live's Chevy Chase, probably still best remembered as the man who imitated Gerald Ford falling down, and Sigourney Weaver, remembered for nothing in particular, joined hands this fall to give us *The Deal of the Century*, an alleged comedy intended to demonstrate that wars break out in Third World nations because Western arms merchants from the United States, Britain, France, and Israel "dump" weapons on these poor little countries. The Soviet Union, well known for never exporting weapons (to Syria, for example, or to Cuba), is somehow or other never mentioned. This movie, too, flopped at the box office.

But perhaps the most astonishing of the fall's radical-Left films is *Under Fire*, starring Gene Hackman and Nick Nolte. Well acted, and well shot by Roger Spottiswoode, it is the story of American journalists in Nicaragua deliberately falsifying the news they are sending back home so as to bring a wavering Jimmy Carter into the camp of the Sandinistas, the movie's heroes. These deceitful journalists are heroes, too, actually, because for the authors of *Under Fire* being on the side of the good and the beautiful (which is to say the Sandinistas) is obviously more important for a journalist than reporting the truth to the best of his ability. The movie ends with the triumphal entry of the Sandinistas into Managua in 1979, after which one is supposed to assume that everything in Nicaragua has gone swimmingly.

If the authors know that the Sandinistas proceeded to lay the foundations for a totalitarian regime in Nicaragua, they display no uneasiness about this development. But what astounds me most about *Under Fire* is that the people who made it did not realize that the prestige press—already shown by many studies to be suspected by its readers of having a leftward bias in reporting the news—would be virtually compelled to attack the film. Did they really think the *New York Times* could praise a movie making heroes of journalists who consciously and deliberately falsify events in their reporting? The *Times*, in actual fact, gave *Under Fire* a thorough drubbing, not once, but twice. For the last two of the film's four weeks of "showcasing" in the New York area, its distributor would not even release its rental figures, a practice resorted to only to avoid humiliation.

Testament, with Jane Alexander, is your ordinary low-budget movie about everyone dying of radiation poisoning in a small town in California, a poor man's version, in short, of ABC's hotly debated *The Day After*. Distributed by Paramount Pictures, and produced by an independent company with grants from both the National Endowment for the Arts and the Corporation for Public Broadcasting (a three-way mingling of taxpayers' money and private venture capital I have never noticed before and which might not even be legal), *Testament* is a miserably pious little film and has attracted precisely the audience this sort of thing gets when people have to pay for their entertainment: very small.

In sum: six films, six failures, all from the radical Left, or at least its environs. That is, these films have all failed in the United States. Following what has become a sparkling new Hollywood tradition, they may of course turn handsome profits abroad, appealing, as they well might, to the followers of Neil Kinnock in Britain, Willy Brandt and Petra Kelly in West Germany, Olaf Palme in Sweden, and many more. Exporting anti-American movies is a real Hollywood growth industry.

But does this mean that the Left has run out of steam in its appeal to down-home American movie audiences? Not at all. It is only the radical or "hard" Left that has run out of steam—if, indeed, it ever had much. A film embodying the ideas of Congressman Ted Weiss of Manhattan and the members of the Black Caucus, all of whom want to impeach President Reagan for the invasion of Grenada, would face almost certain ruin. The "soft" Left, however, is alive and well, and *The Big Chill*, almost a walking embodiment of the soft Left in its present phase, is one of the biggest hits of the fall season.

Now the expression "soft Left" is fairly new in the language, and I had some difficulty recently in explaining the concept to French readers, citizens of a highly ideologized society in which people who move from one school of political thought to another are usually sharply aware of their change in affiliation. The soft Left is far more woolly than the hard, its members floating lightheadedly from one notion to the next, often without any clear idea that these various political belief systems have clear-cut precepts, sometimes quite incompatible. The defining element of the soft Left, in my view, is a kind of persistent utopianism, in the name of which some shining social ideal or other, no matter how unworkable, will always be honored.

The Big Chill is set on a beautiful country estate in South Carolina. The occasion is a gathering of seven graduates of the University of Michigan for the funeral of an eighth, who has committed suicide, some fifteen years or so after their salad days as young "revolutionaries" (their word) during the brave and radical sixties. The film is well directed by Lawrence Kasdan (*Body Heat*), the acting ranges from competent to excellent—my top awards going to William Hurt, Jeff Goldblum, Kevin Kline, and Meg Tilly. *The Big Chill* has entertaining dialogue, charm, mood, atmosphere. It is a first-rate film of its kind. But just what kind of film is it?

It is a monument to the sixties, to the dreams and hopes of that wondrous decade. As the seven survivors reminisce, comparing their present selves with what they had planned to be, they convince themselves that even if the world in its gross way has not lived up to their expectations, it was still all worthwhile. Their lives are still illuminated by an inner grace, a grace which those untouched by the vibrant idealism of those early years will never know. The film is, yes, a trifle narcissistic. It is also marvelously hypocritical.

The Big Chill does not have much plot, and the substance of the movie consists mainly of delineating these old sixties radicals in their present incarnation. We must remember that these seven people were plainly all once members of the SDS [Note to the young: Students for a Democratic Society] or affiliated in some more informal way with what was at the time called "the Movement." But the film (one of its many hypocrisies) goes to extraordinary lengths to avoid recalling just what the program of the Movement was. So there is no yardstick to measure just how far these characters have departed from their original goals. There is no discussion of issues, either of the sixties or of now: no Vietnam, no Central America, no draft, no socialism, no equality, no "participatory democracy," no affirmative action, no nuclear power, no peace movement, no ecology, no darter snail, nothing. Moreover, the whole crowd is lily-white and straight as a die. None of the seven is black and not one is a homosexual.

The first thing that strikes the viewer about these old Ann Arbor revolutionaries is how affluent they all are now: lucrative jobs, expensive automobiles, a sumptuous estate. (This distinguishes the movie from John Sayles's low-budget *The Return of the Secaucus Seven*, another sixties memory film.) As we get to know these survivors, we realize that not a single one has failed to "betray" (in the language of the period) the revolutionary objectives of his youth. Yet somehow it is all right. Harold (Kevin Kline) is a young tycoon who manufactures and distributes running shoes. A real capitalist, he has twenty-seven or twenty-eight shops, and his estate is the scene of the story. Sam (Tom Berenger) is the star actor of a successful television series. Nick (William Hurt) is a narcotics trafficker—not a very respectable profession, but he drives a Porsche. Michael (Jeff Goldblum) is a senior writer for *People* magazine, another disreputable profession (by their lights), but he knows many of the great and famous and "does most of his work in limousines." Sarah (Glenn Close), the tycoon's wife, is a successful doctor. Meg (Mary Kay Place) started out as a public defender but is now a successful real-estate lawyer, "raping the land," as she puts it ruefully. Karen (JoBeth Williams) has abandoned her poems and short stories to marry a successful businessman and have children. But her husband is not the "right" kind of businessman (as is Harold, touched by the grace of having been a campus revolutionary), he is just an ordinary businessman who has provided a good home for his family. An eighth major character is Chloe (Meg Tilly), a mere chit of a girl (the younger generation), who was the mistress of Alex, the friend who committed suicide.

Alex's suicide admittedly gets the film off to an acerbic start. We never do find out why Alex killed himself, which some might take as an act of despair, but one of his friends remarks feelingly, "Alex was too good for this world." One is tempted to infer the same attitude toward Alex's surviving comrades, at least during their revolutionary period. They were not impractical, or unrealistic, or spoiled, or subject to ecstatic fits, but transfigured by some vision of a better world. The only question is, since they have all violated their earlier beliefs, why are we supposed to find these people wonderful now?

There are little things, of course. Harold, the running-shoe tycoon, gives his friends an insider tip that his company is about to be acquired by a conglomerate, so if they buy in now they will triple their money. It is by behavior like this that one can recognize an ex-revolutionary (or Wall Street operator). Sam, the TV star, always tries to work "something of value" into each episode of his series. But this sort of piffle cannot be kept up for long and the screenwriters soon have to resort to sex. Karen, atoning for her husband and child-raising, proves her loyalty to the old ideals by fornicating with Sam on the grass. We learn that Sarah, Harold's wife, had a love affair with the dead Alex some five years before and we see her nude, slumped in the shower, sobbing as the terrible reality of his death is borne in upon her. Chloe, the late Alex's more recent mistress, gives the come-on to Nick, the drug trafficker, but he's been to the war, you see (Vietnam), and like Hemingway's Jake in *The Sun Also Rises*, has come back impotent. At the end, Nick and sweet Chloe go off together hand in hand, impotence or no impotence, providing one of the film's upbeat touches. All this takes place to the steady thump of sixties rock ("I Heard It Through the

Grapevine") and amidst constant volleys of *I love you guys!* and *God, I loved you guys!* and *I don't care what you say, I'm going to love you guys until the day I kick!* Apparently a great deal of bonding took place back there at Ann Arbor.

But by far the most extended and significant plot-sex development in the film is the destiny of Meg, the real-estate lawyer who rapes the land. Now I have known for some time, since his appalling *The Continental Divide* (one of the late John Belushi's last films), that Lawrence Kasdan is a doctrinaire, card-carrying feminist. So I might well have suspected that when Meg decided to have a baby he would contrive for her to have it all by herself, with no husband or boyfriend in sight. For by such things does one know a true feminist. Now you will have noticed that Karen and Sarah have both committed adultery, almost ritually. And it would clearly be an infringement of Meg's independence as a woman for her to have such an antique notion as to associate childbearing in any way with marriage or "cohabitation." So in her best *God, I love you guys* spirit she has decided to get herself fertilized by one of her old Michigan comrades. Meg first makes advances to Nick, but he gets off with his "Don't you know what happened to me in Vietnam?" Then she tries Sam, the actor, but he is just too damn decent. "God, I really love you all the more!" cries Meg. Of course there's always Michael, the *People* man, with whom, now that you mention it, Meg has already has sex. "Remember the march on Washington?" he reminds her. But Michael really is *too* cynical—or is the plot creaking here a bit? Because I think we all know the intended result. Nick out, Sam out, Michael out, Alex dead. Why that leaves only Harold, Sarah's husband! Meg confides her troubles to Sarah, perforce, and Sarah, with a smug radiance that makes you want to punch her in the face, offers Meg her own husband for purposes of fertilization. Greater sacrifice maketh no feminist.

Nick, Sam, Michael, Harold, Sarah, Meg, Karen. Meg, Karen, Sarah, Harold, Sam, Michael, Nick. What, other than their overweeningly high opinion of themselves, separates this gang of ex-campus revolutionaries from the common run of mankind? For someone not engaged in a comparable exercise of self-congratulation, the answer is not that obvious. Without explicitly repudiating a single one of their former revolutionary beliefs (for that would imply error), they have all accepted the free-enterprise system, private property, wealth. Police are no longer "pigs" but valued as protectors of property and order (and one of the group is reprimanded for not realizing this). Early in the film the Rolling Stones' "You Can't Always Get What You Want" comes up very loud on the sound track, and during one of the group's heavy rap sessions about the meaning of it all there seems to be a general consensus that although devotion and love might not be able to "save" another person, "I do think you can *help* people"—which is like reinventing the wheel.

We have all heard of the nuclear family, and the extended family, and the commune—the old-fashioned, cohabiting "nuclear" commune, I suppose. But *The Big Chill* offers us an exhilarating new concept—the extended commune, extending from Atlanta to Los Angeles, in fact. This, it seems, is what the "soft" Left has salvaged from the hostility to the family that was so salient an element of the Movement in the sixties. Is the extended commune a more noble construction than the traditional family? As a social-support system, would it work? I don't think so, but such a criterion has never deterred adepts of the soft Left yet.

By what can only be a highly unusual coincidence, one of Europe's most interesting young directors, Italy's Marco Bellocchio, has almost simultaneously made a film exploring the same material as *The Big Chill*: the fall-out of the radical sixties— where are those revolutionaries now? Bellocchio's *Gli Occhi, La Bocca* ("The Eyes, The Mouth") begins with a suicide, fraught with symbolism, just like *The Big Chill*. In the American film, the man who commits suicide is a fellow member of the Ann Arbor commune. In the Italian, he is the twin brother of the movie's protagonist, Giovanni. The opening scenes of both movies consist of the ingathering of clans, in *The Big Chill* of the commune (to all appearances Alex is a sibling-free orphan), in *Gli Occhi* of the dead man's relatives. In both films, the dead man has been having a love affair with a much younger woman, a member of the "successor generation," completely out of touch with, and ignorant of, the turbulent sixties. In both films a survivor of the earlier period takes up the love affair with the dead man's mistress. In *The Big Chill* it is Nick, the drug trafficker (William Hurt). In *Gli Occhi* it is the man's twin brother, Giovanni (Lou Castel).

This is a remarkable series of parallels, but here the resemblances end. *Gli Occhi* is superior to *The Big Chill* in every way. It is more imaginative, more realistic. It is not hypocritical or self-congratulatory. It offers no "role models." Among its advantages might be that Giovanni returns to his native Bologna from Rome at his brother's death and encounters his real family. And his brother's mistress Wanda (Angelina Molina) has a real family, too. Perhaps it is that real Bologna families are more interesting than communes. They are certainly more interesting than the *God, I love you guys* commune in *The Big Chill*.

Marco Bellocchio first gained attention with his *Fists in the Pocket*, made in 1965. The film is almost pure nihilism. In its most notorious scene, the hero leads his mother to her death by enticing her forward until she falls off a cliff (Abbie Hoffman, who once proclaimed that a true revolutionary must be prepared to kill his father and mother, would surely have approved). *Fists in the Pocket*, for whatever reason, became a great success, and something of a *film fétiche* for nihilistic elements of the European youth movement.

In *Gli Occhi* Bellocchio uses a device I have never seen in a movie before. He takes as the hero of his tale the *actor* who played the lead in the earlier film. The story is heavily fictionalized, of course. He gives Giovanni a twin brother, a home in Bologna (the actual actor Lou Castel, was originally Swedish). But there are biographical elements as well. Giovanni's career as an actor has dwindled considerably. Here he had been famous, his face known to millions, intensely associated with the period's revolutionary youth. Now he is a thirty-five-year-old has-been, his ideas, as well as his character, gone out of style. The film makes no attempt to disguise the fact that Giovanni has become something of a misfit. Wanda asks him if he has an apartment in Rome, and it turns out that he spends a while here, a while there. He doesn't even have a home. This is where all that dazzling nihilism has lead.

The older generation, conspicuously absent in *The Big Chill*, is very much present in *Gli Occhi*. Giovanni's mother (Emmanuele Riva) is hysterical with grief over her son's death, but, far from wanting to push her off a cliff, Giovanni can't bear to separate himself from her. His uncle (magnificently played by Michel Piccoli) is scathingly contemptuous of the pretensions of youthful revolutionaries. Giovanni hates him ("Confident! Rationalist! Progressive!"), but such a character would not have been allowed on the set of Lawrence Kasdan's movie. Giovanni is buffeted from both sides, in fact, both by the older generation and the younger. In *The Big Chill*, Chloe, the dead man's young mistress, is docile, respectful of her elders. But in *Gli Occhi* Wanda is rambunctious, not respectful in the least. "Why have all the rebellions failed?" asks Bellochio, commenting on his own film. He might not have the answer, but he is working on it.

When in bed with Wanda, Giovanni muses at one point, "Your generation doesn't even know who I am." To which he adds without self-pity, "*E giusto*," which I would translate in the context, "And they're right" (or, more literally, "That is as it should be"). For some reason, the "*E giusto*" is not translated in the subtitles, although it is one of the most important lines in the movie. Giovanni, says Bellochio, must separate himself from the "crippling ties of the past."

When it comes to separation from the crippling ties of the past, something quite interesting just might be happening in America. I am extremely cautious about drawing large conclusions from the success or failure of individual motion pictures, but consider, for what it may be worth, the list of the three biggest commercial hits in the United States in the fall of 1983. They are, in order: (1) *Risky Business*, (2) *Never Say Never Again* (the latest James Bond), and (3) *The Big Chill*. Now films in Hollywood today are more often than not aimed at specific age groups. The median American moviegoer is scarcely over twenty years old, and, not having a study at hand, I would guess that a James Bond picture, from the point of view of age, is aimed at the entire filmgoing public, average age about twenty. *The Big Chill*, however, is obviously aimed principally at moviegoers in their thirties. But what is this *Risky Business?* Who went to see that? Here the target audience was not just the teenage group, but, even more specifically, the fifteen-to-seventeen-year-olds, as is evident from the film's subject matter, high-school students who are trying to get into a "good" college.

Risky Business is a comedy. It is not very realistic, but it is not without meaning. A quite engaging young actor named Tom Cruise [three years later to star in the country's number-one blockbuster movie, *Top Gun*] plays the shyest member of a group of upper-middle-class high-school students in the Chicago area who (although all this is spoofed affectionately) are quite consumed with ambition. They want to be successful. They want to be rich. They want to have sex with beautiful women. What do they discuss when they gather together in the school lunchroom? Why, an M.B.A. from Harvard business school starts at $40,000 a year, but an M.D. from Harvard *medical* school starts at $60,000 a year. When Joel (Cruise) is asked what he wants to do with his life, and he suggests tentatively that he would like to do something "for his fellow mankind" (*sic*), his cronies all jeer and bombard him with bread pellets. This is all done humorously, as I say, but these are not represented as rotten, corrupt kids. They are good, *normal*, American kids. Joel, in any event, applies for admission to Princeton. At which point his well-to-do parents take off for a holiday in a warm climate, possibly the Bahamas, leaving him alone in the house.

Well, a combination of circumstances brings Joel into contact with an attractive young call girl. Further circumstances lead to her abandoning her pimp and thrusting herself on Joel. She has a dozen call-girl friends. They all join her and descend on Joel's family home. And the next thing you know, Joel—dressed like a pimp himself now, cool, with shades and a punk jacket—is running the best little whorehouse in Illinois. Disaster strikes. The interviewer from Princeton arrives as hookers career out of every bedroom—but he stays to spend the night. In the last scene of the movie the letter arrives admitting Joel to the freshman class at Princeton. This kid has leadership qualities.

I was a trifle leery of *Risky Business* before I saw it, thinking that with the prominent place given to prostitution, an equation was being suggested between any kind of business and human "exploitation." But a viewing in the midst of a delighted young audience persuaded me that the prostitution (very unrealistically presented) is merely a titilating comic device and that the film is quite benign, an innocuous little comedy about kids who want to get ahead in life. And it is hammering *The Big Chill* at the box office, beating it two to one.

A sixteen-year-old in 1984, we must remember, was barely born at the time of the Tet offensive in Vietnam in 1968. And those who still think of the generation of the sixties as "young" might be entertained to realize that from the point of view of American teenagers (and they do have their point of view), the characters in *The Big Chill* are a band of sentimental oldsters nursing their pathetic memories of days lost now in the mists of time.

This new generation is entering college. A recent survey conducted by the American Council on Education found that, whereas in 1972 those college freshman considering themselves "far Left" or "liberal" numbered 52 percent, by 1982 this figure had plummeted to 21 percent. So a new age might be on its way.

Note: This essay was published in 1984, the year Ronald Reagan took forty-nine out of fifty states in the presidential election.

8

The Feminization of Henry James: Vanessa Redgrave and The Bostonians

The whole generation is womanized; the masculine tone is passing out of the world; it's a feminine, a nervous, hysterical, chattering, canting age, an age of hollow phrases and false delicacy and exaggerated solicitudes and coddled sensibilities, which, if we don't soon look out, will usher in the reign of mediocrity, of the feeblest and flattest and the most pretentious that has ever been.

THUS Basil Ransom, one of the three major protagonists—and certainly the conqueror—of Henry James's *The Bostonians*, which has reached the screen in one of the most singularly perverse adaptations of a classic I have ever encountered.

Ransom is a cousin of Olive Chancellor, the second of the novel's dominant triad and its most sharply delineated figure, and he has been invited to visit her on Charles Street in her native Boston. The scene is the early 1870s, just after the end of Reconstruction in the South (and shortly after the period in which James still lived in the Boston-Cambridge area). Ransom is a Southerner, from Mississippi. He has fought for the Confederacy and lost everything—the war, his wealth, home, plantation, slaves, friends, relatives—while his third cousin Olive has conveniently retained her fortune and, if her blood is not absolutely the bluest, is one of Boston's leading philanthropic heiresses. The great struggle for the abolition of slavery having been won, she is now—still a reformer—a passionate feminist. Her own sister says of her: "A radical? She's a female Jacobin—

she's a nihilist. Whatever *is*, is wrong. . . . She would reform the solar system if she could get hold of it." But here is James, speaking in his own voice, of Olive Chancellor:

> The curious tint of her eyes was a living color; when she turned it upon you, you thought vaguely of the glitter of green ice. She had absolutely no figure, and presented a certain appearance of feeling cold. . . . She smiled constantly at her guest, but from the beginning to the end of the dinner, though [Ransom] made several remarks that he thought might prove amusing, she never once laughed. Later, he saw that she was a woman without laughter; exhilaration, if it ever visited her, was dumb. Once only, in the course of his subsequent acquaintance with her, did it find a voice; and then the sound remained in Ransom's ear as one of the strangest he had heard.

After their dinner at her luxurious house on the edge of Beacon Hill, Olive invites Ransom to a small gathering of people "interested in new ideas." Although Ransom has tasted in full the bitterness of defeat, and has left the South for New York, where he is a penniless young lawyer, he has retained his virility, his stoicism, and his wit. When Olive asks him, "Don't you care for human progress?" he answers breezily, "I don't know—I never saw any. Are you going to show me some?" And when she presses him passionately, "Don't you believe then, in the coming of a better day—in its being possible to do something for the human race?" he wonders what in God's name he's gotten himself into, but answers drily, "Well, Miss Olive, what strikes me most is that the human race has got to bear its troubles." Basil Ransom, this tall, muscular young Southerner, is, in short, a profound conservative.

The two ill-assorted cousins nonetheless make their way to Boston's South End to the sparsely furnished, ascetic home of Miss Birdseye for an evening among some forty virtuous Bostonian reformers—socialistic vegetarians, Ransom thinks, who would give the ballot to women and rob men of their drink. Ransom realizes with some disgust that he is in the citadel of his enemies—Boston, "city of reform," "the Puritan city," cradle of abolitionism—the people who destroyed the South, his home-land.

The opening sections of *The Bostonians* created something of an uproar in the Massachusetts capital when they were serialized in the *Century* in 1886, for James had modeled Birdseye on Nathaniel Hawthorne's elderly sister, Elizabeth Peabody, a widely admired local idealist about whom many of the Puritan city's "social leaders" would have shared Olive Chancellor's view: "She was heroic; she was sublime; the whole moral history of Boston was reflected in her displaced spectacles." James, on the other hand, draws a portrait of the lady that would have been quite acceptable to Basil Ransom. Here is James, again in his own voice, on Boston's Miss Birdseye:

> She belonged to the Short-Skirts League, as a matter of course; for she belonged to any and every league that had been founded for almost any purpose whatever. This did not prevent her being a confused, entangled, inconsequent, discursive old woman, whose charity began at home and ended nowhere, whose credulity kept pace with it, and who knew less about her fellow-creatures, if possible, after fifty years of humanity zeal, than on the day she had gone into the field to testify against the iniquity of most arrangements. . . . Since the Civil War much of her occupation was gone; for before that her best hours had been spent in fancying that she was helping some Southern slave to escape. It would have been a nice question whether, in her heart of hearts, for the sake of this excitement, she did not some-times wish the blacks back in bondage.

A few pages later James calls Birdseye a "poor little humanitary hack."

Much as, in recent U.S. history, high-minded idealists went from the civil rights movement in the South, to the antiwar movement during the Vietnam conflict, to environmentalism, to—after some lay fallow for a bit—the quasi-pacifist "peace" movement, so did the high-minded Bostonians of over a century ago move from one noble cause to another. After abolitionism had achieved its aim, the high-minded of that earlier period went, approximately simultaneously, into female suffrage, prohibitionism, and spiritualism—mediums, ectoplasm, seances, and all that—at the time (unlike now) considered intellectually quite respectable, even avant-garde. (A comic echo of this anti-rational component among those wishing to "do something for the human race" occurred in a young woman of my acquaintance. Having fought on the barricades of freedom for "peace" in Vietnam, waving a Vietcong flag, she developed during her apolitical fallow period—when she did not know the name of the governor of her state, let alone what was happening in Southeast Asia—an obsessive interest in the occult, in parapsychology, and in Uri Geller, the Israeli charlatan who could stop clocks and bend nails by magic. A new cause having appeared, she is now at the forefront of the movement for nuclear disarmament.)

For Olive Chancellor, of course, the cause for which she was destined was feminism:

> Yes, she would do something, Olive Chancellor said to herself; she would do something to brighten the darkness of that dreadful image that was always before her, and against which it seemed to her at times that she had been born to lead a crusade—the image of the unhappiness of women. The unhappiness of women! The voice of their silent suffering was always in her ears, the ocean of tears that they had shed from the beginning of time seemed to pour through her own eyes. Ages of oppression had rolled over them; uncounted millions had lived only to be tortured, to be crucified. They were her sisters, they were her own, and the day of their delivery had dawned. This was the only sacred cause; this was the great, the just revolution. It must triumph, it must sweep everything before it; it must exact from the other, the brutal, bloodstained ravening race, the last particle of expiation! It would be the greatest change the world had seen: it would be a new era for the human family, and the names of those who had helped to show the way and lead the squadrons would be the brightest in the tables of fame.

Olive Chancellor's principal obstacle in all this was "Charlie." For Boston's shop girls—with whom Olive for some reason had the most inordinate difficulty establishing a relationship—

always ended up being odiously mixed up with Charles. Charlie was a young man in a white overcoat and a paper collar; it was for him, in the last analysis, that they cared much the most. They cared far more about Charlie than about the ballot. . . .

The star performer of the soirée at Miss Birdseye's is beautiful, young, fresh, delightful Verena Tarrant, an "inspirational speaker" and the third element in the novel's central triad. Her mother is of "good abolitionist stock," and her father, a combination faith healer and "mesmerist," puts Verena into a trance before the assembled company until she makes contact with a "voice." One is given to understand that Verena hears different kinds of voices, depending on the section of the country she is in and the audience, but here in Boston before a feminist group, lo, the voice she hears is feminist. Verena, sitting, her eyes closed, mumbles incoherently at first, then rises and opens her eyes, whose shining softness makes up half the effect of her "inspirational" discourse.

Her talk is "full of schoolgirl phrases, of patches of remembered eloquence, of childish lapses of logic, of flights of fancy which might indeed have had success at Topeka." She speaks first of the dreadful misery of mankind:

Poverty, and ignorance, and crime; disease, and wickedness, and wars! Wars, always more wars, and always more and more. Blood, blood—the world is drenched with blood! . . . The cruelty—the cruelty; there is so much, so much! Why shouldn't tenderness come in?

After which the "voice" explains how the tenderness of women will change the world:

I am only a girl, a simple American girl, and of course I haven't seen much. . . . But there are some things I feel. . . . It is what the great sisterhood of women might do if they should all join hands, and lift up their voices above the brutal uproar of the world . . . the sound of our lips would become the voice of universal peace!

As it happens, both Basil Ransom and Olive Chancellor are quite taken with Verena. Ransom finds every word she has spoken sheer drivel, "inanities," "trash," but feels he has witnessed an absolutely charming performance. If on completion of her speech Verena had brought out castanets and a tambourine and begun to dance, he wouldn't have been in the least surprised. Olive, by contrast, has drunk in every word as if it were incandescent truth. Utterly smitten, she believes she has found at last the leader who will inspire the invincible battalions of women in the final victory of tenderness, peace, and love.

Once one has the three main characters of *The Bostonians* fixed in one's head, the plot of the novel is simple. It is the battle between Olive Chancellor and her cousin Basil Ransom for the possession of Verena. It goes right down to the wire. A defeated but still virile South against goody-goody Boston. Conservatism against reform. A struggling poor man against a rich idealist. Male against female. Sex against virginity. Heterosexuality against lesbianism (sublimated). And Ransom wins going away.

There are people willing to fight to the death at the suggestion that Olive Chancellor is a lesbian, and they don't much like such expressions as "sublimated lesbian" either. Although perfectly aware that sexless "New England marriages" (also known as "Boston marriages") between women were a commonplace in James's day (this before Shere Hite's legions demanded the "Big O" as their constitutional right), I am quite prepared to accept Louis Auchincloss's succinct formulation: "Olive is a classic example of a 'sublimated' invert; her sexual drive has been converted into a hatred of men and a lust for power."

The Bostonians occupies a special place in the Jamesian canon. It is his most American novel. Almost all his other major works are set in Europe, and although most contain American characters, they have as their great theme the contrasts between American and European societies. We must remember that James, for his period, was a very cosmopolitan American. Although he lived his first twelve years in New York, his later school years were spent largely in French-speaking Switzerland and he spoke and wrote perfect French. He knew Paris well—

forming friendships with Flaubert, Zola, and Turgenev—not to mention London, where he eventually settled.

But in between his school years and his final return to Europe, he had spent five impressionable years in Boston and Cambridge (from twenty-one to twenty-six), and had aspired since boyhood to write what he himself called the "great American novel." While still young, he had underlined in his copy of *The Correspondence of Thomas Carlyle and Ralph Waldo Emerson* a line by Emerson: "We are a little wild here with numberless projects of social reform." In 1883 James wrote in his notebooks: "I wished to write a very American tale, a tale very characteristic of our social condition, and I asked myself what was the most salient and peculiar point in our social life. The answer was: the situation of women . . . the agitation on their behalf." So those were the themes: reform and feminism. And the result was *The Bostonians*.

But the novel is unusual for James in respects other than its concentration on Americana. As Lionel Trilling has pointed out, it contains by far the most social (and sociological) observation of any of his works. Departing from the style of his other great novels, James fills *The Bostonians* with pages of minute description, and also unusual for him, he is not content with describing, but also "editorializes," giving the reader again and again his own judgment of the character in question. It takes James nine chapters to get through the book's first evening, and twelve— almost a quarter of the novel—to get through the first twenty-four hours.

The Bostonians ran to over twice James's planned and contracted-for length in serialization, for none of which extra work he received a penny. He was plainly obsessed with the material, for there can be no question that he harbored a deep-seated animus against Boston for its moralism, its preachiness, and, yes, its feminization. With his cosmopolitan standard of comparison (which most Americans lacked), James did not at all subscribe to the Boston feminists' view of women as tender, weak, and pitiable. To the contrary, *The Bostonians* alone is strong evidence that he found the essential traits of the American woman above all to be (I quote his biographer Leon Edel) "her assertiveness, her pushing, ruling, dominating mastery of men and children," and even (Edel) "her threat to American life."

It is noteworthy, although not surprising, that *The Bostonians* is probably the wittiest of James's novels, mockery being the means by which James chose to deal with what, as he proceeded with his planning, he found a thoroughly unattractive subject. More unexpected, perhaps, is the fact that *The Bostonians* is the most openly sexual of his works, with its story of blatant sexual rivalry and highly interesting, to say the least, kissings and tremblings between Olive and Verena ("She came to her slowly, took her arms and held her long—giving her a silent kiss").

The book, when it appeared, was greeted with marked hostility. Boston, understandably, was decidedly chilly. Even Mark Twain swore that he would rather be condemned to John Bunyan's heaven than read it. For whatever reason, the book sent most American critics into a rage, perhaps because, as James knew perfectly well, over the preceding generation the U.S. reading public had become overwhelmingly dominated by women. The book offered women of the period no conventional happy ending; nor is a single one of the major female characters portrayed attractively. Olive Chancellor is a man-hating hysteric. Verena is a charming ninny. Adeline, Olive's sister, is a scheming minx. Miss Birdseye is a moralistic old fool. Verena's mother is a vulgar sycophant.

In short, *The Bostonians* (like James's *The Princess Casamassima*, published later the same year) was a disaster in its own time and caused a serious decline in James's reputation and market. Scribner's, in consequence, prevailed upon James to omit *The Bostonians* from his 1907 collected edition, in which each of the published novels was accompanied by a preface written by the author himself. James later regretted the omission, feeling the novel had never received its due and saying in 1915, the last year of his life, "I should have liked to write that preface." With the passage of time, his judgment seems to have been vindicated. F. R. Leavis, in *The Great Tradition*, wrote that *The Bostonians* and James's *The Portrait of a Lady* were quite simply "the two most brilliant novels in the language."

By a curious coincidence of fate, shortly before James began planning *The Bostonian*, his mother died, and he wrote of her in his notebook: "She was our life, she was the house, she was the keystone of the arch. She held us all together, and without her we are scattered reeds." And farther on:

It was the perfect mother's life—the life of a perfect wife. To bring her children into the world—to expend herself, for years, for their happiness and welfare—then, when they had reached a full maturity and were absorbed in the world and their own interests—to lay herself down in her ebbing strength and yield up her pure soul to the celestial power that had given her this divine commission.

As can be seen, this is somewhat at variance with Olive Chancellor's view of the mission of womankind upon this earth. But the congruence of James's views with those of Basil Ransom, on this point and others, is startling. James, in unadorned fact (worth stressing in the present age when the general assumption of the semi-educated is that artists are automatically "on the Left"), was an utter Tory.

Prevented by an injury from serving in the Civil War, James deeply envied those who had. His brother William's closest friend, Oliver Wendell Holmes, Jr.—the same man who, appointed to the U.S. Supreme Court by Theodore Roosevelt, remained on the bench long enough to become a hero of Theodore's cousin Franklin—was wounded and almost killed at Antietam, and considered until his dying day that having fought and faced death with the Union forces was the most exalting experience of his life. "Now, at least," said Holmes, "and perhaps as long as man dwells upon the globe, his destiny is battle, and he has to take the chances of war." William James himself wrote:

Marital virtues must be the enduring cement; intrepidity, contempt of softness, surrender of private interest, obedience to command, must still remain the rock upon which states are built—unless, indeed, we wish for dangerous reactions against commonwealths fit only for contempt, and liable to invite attack whenever a center of crystallization for military-minded enterprise gets formed anywhere in their neighborhood.

When it is remembered that Henry James renounced his American citizenship because the United States did not instantly enter World War I in 1914 on the side of the Allies, it is not difficult to surmise that a further reason for his sharing Basil Ransom's view that the whole cause of women's suffrage was essentially specious was (in Louis Auchincloss's words) that it tended to "dilute the masculinity of a great nation."

James was somewhat dissatisfied with his portrayal of Basil Ransom, since, as he admitted, he did not really know the South. To which my comment is that Ransom might be even truer than James realized. I myself have seen Southerners (military men, I confess) brooding almost a century after the event on why Longstreet delayed his charge at Gettysburgy—thereby costing Lee the battle. I have seen Southern tempers flare at the suggestion that the South used conscription, since the men of the Confederacy fought, uncoerced, for "honor and duty." I have even heard Southerners, in a mood not entirely jocular, sing the old Confederate folk song which begins, "In eighteen hundred and sixty-one/ Skoogaw, says I/ In eighteen hundred and sixty-one/ Skoogaw, says I/ In eighteen hundred and sixty-one/ *We beat the Yankees at Bull Run. . . .*" I would suggest that no one who fails to comprehend the sentiment behind these lines can fully understand *The Bostonians*, for the novel's victor, after all, is Basil Ransom.

Well, there was a second battle of Bull Run, which the South also won, and now we have upon us the second battle of *The Bostonians*, which—in a twist—is won, at least morally, by Olive Chancellor. For feminism today stalks the land, in case you hadn't noticed, and perhaps feminization as well, pretty much as James feared. And they might well be with us for a long time.

In the present circumstances, why would an eminent producer-director-writer team (Ismail Merchant, James Ivory, and Ruth Prawer Jhabvala), with a long line of distinguished films escaping the platitudes and hackneyed turns of Hollywood, choose to run the risk of making a motion picture of *The Bostonians* which, in addition to being one of the most brilliant novels in the language, is also one of the most anti-feminist? Ismail Merchant is of course an Indian. Ivory, though a native Californian, has spent many years in India and done much good work there. Jhabvala, although German-Jewish-English by birth and upbringing, married one of India's leading architects and lived in India continuously for twenty-three years ("I loved everything there . . . even the beggars, the poverty. . . ."). In recent years her fiction has been published frequently in the *New Yorker*, she has won Britain's Booker Prize, and in America the MacArthur Foundation's quarter-million-dollar, tax-free "genius" award. Perhaps what we are getting here is an Indian view of Henry James. The team, in any case, has solved the problem of how to make a movie out of such an anti-feminist book by turning *The Bostonians* on its head. How they did it I shall explain. Watch closely.

First, the minor characters. It will be remembered that James called Miss Birdseye "a poor little humanitary hack." Although she is later granted a dignified death, this is perhaps the most insulting description of any character in the whole book. But in the movie, behold, Miss Birdseye (well played by Jessica Tandy) has become simply a sweet, kind old lady. Do not look for the crusading zeal or the idiotic credulity. They are not there any more.

Then there is Doctor Prance (Linda Hunt, who won an Academy Award for her performance in *The Year of Living Dangerously*), a character I have not yet described. In the novel, she is a hard-bitten little woman doctor entirely out of sympathy with the feminist movement ("I don't want anyone to tell *me* what a lady can do!"). With obvious approval, James writes of her that she had "as many rights as she had time for. It was certain that whatever might become of the movement at large, Doctor Prance's own little revolution was a success." In the movie, Doctor Prance's hard, critical edge is removed as if by surgery. Not a single one of her character-defining lines of dialogue remains, nor anything to substantiate James's commentary. And she, too, is played—completely against character—with a dulcet gentility.

But it is on the novel's central triad that the sense of the story depends. Madeleine Potter as Verena Tarrant, I confess, is faithful to the book, certainly in spirit. In the novel she is a charming nincompoop, and in the film she is certainly a nincompoop. Charm is one of those subjective qualities that I will leave to the viewer to decide for himself. I, personally, could not bear the woman.

Basil Ransom, as played by Christopher Reeve, the film's biggest star, is another matter. Now I would never hold having played Superman against an actor. In fact, I found Reeve quite engaging in *Deathtrap*. But in *The Bostonians* he seems not to have the faintest clue what his character is about. He plays a "romantic lead," a nice young man with a Southern accent, and that's about it. British theater people often say that American actors generally cannot do "period" roles—presumably because they have little sense of the past. They are quintessentially modern. But Reeve's problems go further than this. Basil Ransom is in the stronghold of his enemies, the "reformers." We do not see this in Reeve's performance. Ransom has the most bitter contempt for their values. We do not see this, either.

One of the sillier things that producers do in promoting a new film is to have the leading actors (no doubt the best-known figures to the public) "explain" the movie. We have therefore been apprised by the press that Reeve feels that, after the end of James's *The Bostonians*, Basil Ransom and Verena live a life "a lot like" that of Tom Hayden and Jane Fonda. As it happens, Henry James makes clear again and again that, if Ransom wins Verena, he will insist she give up this public life on the lecture platform (or the stage). She is headed for the kitchen and the nursery. Furthermore, Ransom's intensely conservative view of the relations between men and women would forbid his allowing himself to live off his wife's earnings. I submit that there could be nothing more radically wrong than playing Ransom and Verena as if they were about to turn into Hayden and Jane Fonda.

The most interesting distortions of James's work, however,

are presented by Vanessa Redgrave's performance as Olive Chancellor. I must make perfectly clear that Redgrave's performance is quite remarkable, filled with sudden surges of emotion and moments of sublime awkwardness. But is it Olive? Even as ardent a devotee of Olive as F. W. Dupee admits that James himself feels not the slightest sympathy for her. Consider, for example, the description James gives of Olive as she refuses to disclose Verena's whereabouts to Ransom, thinking she has thus gotten rid of him: "Her enjoyment of the situation becoming acute, there broke from her lips a shrill, unfamiliar, troubled sound, which performed the office of a laugh, a laugh of triumph. . . ." In the film, by comparison, Vanessa Redgrave gives us only a look of great dignity, the look of a noble spirit. And in general Redgrave's performance is nothing but warmth and sympathy. Poor Olive! Poor heartsick sublimated lesbian! Poor early feminist, who cast her brave light upon the path we all must follow! Poor lamb! Redgrave, in fact, announced in a television interview her delight at the opportunity of playing such a sympathetic character.

But the most shocking thing the adapters of a classic work can do is to change the ending, a practice infrequently resorted to even by the uncouth Hollywood mastodons of the thirties. It is something one would never expect of the Merchant-Ivory-Jhabvala team. But feminism, some say, is the most pervasive force in our society, and the makers of *The Bostonians* dared not affront it.

The last scene of the novel, as of the film, is set in the Boston Music Hall (a real place, which gave way in time to Gilchrist's department store). Ransom swoops down on his prey backstage in the dressing room just before she is to go on stage to deliver an inspirational speech on the position of women. Verena's knees turn to water. Her will dissolves. And, on the last page, Ransom carries her off for good. The novel's celebrated closing lines read:

"Ah, now I am glad!" said Verena, when they reached the street. But though she was glad, he presently discovered that, beneath her hood, she was in tears. It is to be feared that with the union, so far from brilliant, into which she was about to enter, these were not the last she was destined to shed.

I think it would be a mistake to read tragedy into these lines, as do some. I feel they mean merely that, with Ransom's less than "brilliant" prospects, and their different temperaments, the marriage will be a difficult one for Verena. But there is no debate about Olive Chancellor's end. James makes it plain in the novel that, if Olive were to lose Verena to her cousin Basil Ransom, she would be utterly crushed and humiliated and would never recover. And in the event nothing mitigates her defeat. Having explained earlier, "I can't speak . . . I have no self-possession, no eloquence; I can't put three words together," Olive is last seen in the novel rushing toward the stage to tell the restive audience that Verena will not appear, looking as if she were "offering herself to be trampled to death and torn to pieces." So ends the novel.

It was with some surprise, therefore, that I saw at the end of the movie Olive Chancellor, unconquered, appear on the speaker's platform of the Boston Music Hall and deliver a rousing feminist speech. I do not know whether Ruth Jhabvala wrote this speech, or Vanessa Redgrave, or perhaps Redgrave's friend, Jane Fonda. It is not, in any case, in the novel:

> What I want to say to you is that when there is a great cause the individual is of no account. You've come to hear not the voice of one individual, however sweet, however harmonious, but the cry of all women, past, present, and future. For, like the great William Lloyd Garrison said in his fight against slavery, I say we will be as harsh as truth, as uncompromising as justice. Of this subject we will not think or speak or write with moderation. We will not excuse! We will not equivocate! We will not retreat a single inch! And we will be heard!

As you might expect, at a recent evening showing in New York, feminist rowdies in the audience booed Basil Ransom when he carried off Verena, and cheered Olive Chancellor at the end of her tub-thumper, as the credits rolled. For me it was as if, at the end of a production of *Othello*, Iago were to step to the front of the stage and announce that he has a very good explanation for everything, proclaim himself the hero, and call for a Boola Boola for the team.

9

The Clint Eastwood Phenomenon: How He Became the World's Favorite Movie Star

IT STARTS WITH a vulgar case of armed robbery. Three thugs break into a lunch counter, where, to their misfortune, Dirty Harry Callahan is in the habit of taking his absent-minded snacks. Tipped off, Callahan enters the coffee shop, is fired at, and returns the fire, putting two of the thugs permanently out of action. But a third thug is still on the loose, and grabs a waitress as hostage. Police sirens are beginning to wail outside, and the thug knows that his one chance of escaping is to demand a getaway car and safe passage, keeping the waitress as his cherished hostage. His only problem is Detective Harry Callahan. The nervous thug clutches the waitress to him tightly, his pistol against her head. At a shot from the police he will kill his hostage, but not, of course, if a shot from the police blows his head off first. Carefully, Callahan raises his .44 Magnum until he has the criminal's eyes in his sights. The thug is agitated. The waitress, is understandably, terrified. Callahan is suffused with a deadly calm. "Go ahead," he says to the thug, who is still considering whether to attempt a getaway. "Make my day." The criminal's nerve slackens and he throws his weapon to the floor. It is over.

In one form or another, this scene is repeated several times in Clint Eastwood's *Dirty Harry* series: *Dirty Harry*, *Magnum Force*, *The Enforcer*, and *Sudden Impact*, from which the above episode is taken. In every one of the scenes there is a criminal who has killed, attempted to kill, or is threatening to kill innocent people. In every one Eastwood, who plays a police detective in San Francisco, places his life on the line. In every one, there is the sardonic, icy challenge: "Try me." "Do you feel lucky?" "Make my day." Usually the criminal loses his nerve and surrenders. If not, Callahan blows his head to bits. For dealing with murderers, real or potential, in defense of innocent people, and acting entirely within the rules, Harry Callahan does not hesitate to kill. One might almost suspect he enjoys it. One can see why Clint Eastwood, the world's biggest and most highly paid movie star for some fifteen years, is not a particular favorite of the American Civil Liberties Union.

His ethic is not different from that of a soldier. Volunteer or conscript, the infantryman answers his country's call. His life is placed in peril. At the orders of his captain, or in accordance with the ordinary rules of engagement, he kills the enemy, feeling no qualms—particularly if the enemy has been threatening to kill him or his comrades. It is the law of war, and also common sense. As for the heartlessness, even gratification, that the Clint Eastwood character demonstrates in destroying the social vermin who, he obviously feels, are themselves destroying the fabric of our society, I can only quote a French official's comments on the special anti-riot force which in 1968 played a key role in containing the social turbulence that was thought to threaten the French Republic: "Well," he smiled. "You have to find the right man for the job." Harry Callahan, one feels, is the right man for the job.

But he is not the right man for the job as it is defined by the ACLU, which, starting from the admirable goal of defending civil liberties, now seems more concerned to protect the rights of suspected criminals (often confessed criminals) than the rights of law-abiding citizens. A friend of mine, who happens to be a former member of the National Security Council, has characterized this position as "the domestic equivalent of 'Better Red than Dead.' " My own view is that the constant hedging-in of the power of the police to accomplish their mission, and of public prosecutors to obtain convictions, is worse than either "Better Red than Dead" or pure pacifism, both of which are rationally defensible positions for those who are willing to accept servitude or who actually desire a Marxist-Leninist regime. (The true pacifist, moreover, might well be prepared to sacrifice his own life, and that of his wife and children, rather than commit the, to him, monstrosity of taking the life of another human being no matter how bloodthirsty.) But my friend was basically correct. There is a link between the extraordinary reluctance of many on the Left to use U.S. military power anywhere in the world, even in self-defense, and the efforts of many liberals at home to inhibit the application of harsh penalties against even confessed criminals. Both groups (and they are often the same people) shrink from the use of force, and this shrinking, on a national scale, might well place in question the nation's ability to survive under its present institutions.

Clint Eastwood, to judge by his films, has never had the slightest doubt as to the legitimacy of the use of force in the service of justice, even rudimentary justice, and he has certainly had none whatever when its use is necessary to assure survival. This attitude has earned him, among some movie reviewers, a reaction that I think it only fair to call hatred. But the animosity of critics, often fatal in our times, has not stopped Clint Eastwood from becoming far and away America's leading movie star—indeed, far and away the leading movie star of the entire world. The critics have their darlings, like Meryl Streep and Woody Allen, no movie starring either of whom has yet to break into the big money. But far aloft looms Eastwood. Eastwood is number one.

Every year thousands of the nation's theater owners vote for the most popular movie star. Not only did Eastwood top the list for 1983 but he is the only living star to have made the top ten a full sixteen times—bringing him even with Clark Gable, and snapping at the heels of Gary Cooper. The only member of the Great Dead still out in front is the Duke himself, John Wayne, who, when once asked to guess who would succeed him, answered with his laconic smile, "Eastwood . . . my only logical successor." As for money, after *Every Which Way But Loose* (1978), a film Eastwood said ironically he had made for "the bare-knuckle subculture," he walked away with an estimated

$15 million, making him at the time the world's highest paid actor.

With the loss of the giant mass audience to television, and with both TV and Broadway now considered by almost universal accord to be dross, the cinema has been forced almost willy-nilly into becoming the "class act" of the popular entertainment world. Its audience, compared with that of its competitors, is young, affluent, and educated, centering roughly on the university, pre-university, and post-university sectors of the population. Yet, true though this may be for the bulk of films produced by Hollywood, it is obviously not true for the films of Sylvester Stallone and Clint Eastwood.

Everyone in the movie industry knows that Eastwood and Burt Reynolds have a "regional" appeal—so-so at best in New York (where the critical community is centered), but colossal draws in the West and South. My own observations of the crowds that turn out to see a new Eastwood movie in small industrial or agricultural towns near liberal-arts colleges, compared with those that turn out in the same towns to see a new film with Jane Fonda, lead me to think that there are virtually two nations, each easily recognizable by manners and speech. Jane Fonda draws the "university" crowd. Eastwood draws the skilled industrial workers, farmers, men who if they no longer work with their hands come from a different America from the Vassar that produced Jane Fonda and Meryl Streep. Another devoted bloc of Eastwood supporters—a fact not widely realized outside the movie industry—is American blacks. Perhaps one reason for this is that blacks are the first to suffer from increased inner-city crime, and they (if not all their leaders) tend to have extremely severe law-and-order attitudes.

What you see in Clint Eastwood is pretty much what you get. You would think someone named Clint Eastwood would be named something like Clinton Eastwood, and that's exactly what his name is: Clinton Eastwood, Jr. His genealogy is also not far off the mark: English, Scottish, Irish, Dutch, a close approximation of an amalgam of this country's original stock. Born in San Francisco in 1931 in extremely modest circumstances, Eastwood was a child of the Depression. His father,

Clinton, Sr., could not find steady work and traveled from town to town, holding a series of temporary jobs, taking his wife and little son and daughter with him. Eastwood estimates that they moved so often that in his first ten years of schooling he must have attended ten different schools, making him something of a loner, a wanderer, another throwback to an older America when the country was filled with men roaming the land, looking for work and a place to build a new life. Finally his father found permanent employment in Oakland, California, and Eastwood attended Oakland Technical High School.

Eastwood's early relationship with his family offers a simple clue to his attitudes toward life and toward his country. He once said in an interview, "My father always kept telling me, you don't get something for nothing, and although I rebelled, I never rebelled against that. . . . I always got along great with my parents." And also: "I think my parents and my grandmother— she was quite a person, very self-sufficient, lived by herself on a mountaintop—probably had more to do with my turning out the way I am than any educational process. I may have gone through. . . . I was lucky to have them."

All his life Eastwood has worked. He has cut timber, baled hay, fought forest fires, labored more than a year as a lumberjack in Oregon. He has worked a blast furnace for the Bethlehem Steel Company in Texas, worked for Boeing in Seattle. Drafted into the army, he managed to work part-time as a stevedore. When the Korean war broke out, Eastwood was teaching other young soldiers how to swim. "My name just didn't come up," he says. In a fluke, he was the only man in his outfit not shipped to Korea. But he still managed to crash in a U.S. Navy bomber off the California coast, swimming for miles to save his life. So he had known danger.

After the army, Eastwood enrolled in Los Angeles City College in business administration, earning his way in an ever-lengthening list of spectacularly non-upwardly mobile jobs: gas-station attendant, janitor, digging foundations for swimming pools. He had been nagged for years by friends to make a try at acting in movies, and he finally went to Universal Pictures, asked for an appointment, took a test, cold, and to his surprise was offered a job as a "contract player"—at $75 a week. His first part was a minor role in *Revenge of the Creature*. He was soon promoted to $100 a week, but, in time, Universal decided Clint Eastwood just didn't have what it takes and dropped him. By 1958 he was back to digging swimming pools.

Like politicians, actors need to be lucky, and later in the same year, by sheer chance, Eastwood caught the eye of an executive of CBS-TV while having lunch with an employee of the company's story department. The random encounter led to the offer of a leading role in the network's upcoming Western series *Rawhide*, an endless cattle drive suggested by Howard Hawks's 1948 classic Western, *Red River*, starring John Wayne and Montgomery Clift. Oddly, in view of his subsequent career, but logically in view of his age—still only twenty-seven—Eastwood was not given the John Wayne role but that of Montgomery Clift, the younger man, a part he has described as "sheepish." *Rawhide* became one of the most successful series in the history of television, running for a full nine years and syndicated throughout the world.

Most television stars are born, flourish, and return to dust without ever having made it to the Elysian Fields of "the movies." This would probably have been the lot of Clint Eastwood if not for one of the more bizarre international cushion shots in the history of the world cinema.

First, it should be known that Akira Kurosawa, almost universally held to be the greatest film director in Japanese history (*Rashomon*, *The Seven Samurai*), is a great fan of American Westerns. This is not as eccentric as it sounds. A staple of Japanese movies for decades was the so-called *chambara* film (the word is an onomatopoeic rendition in Japanese of the clinking-together of swords), action movies set during the endless civil wars of the two-century Tokugawa Shogunate. Although the chambara film is already a close equivalent to the U.S. Western, this was not enough for Kurosawa. He decided to make a chambara movie following the standard story line of the American genre. The result was his masterful *Yojimbo*.

Next, an obscure but not untalented *Italian* director named Sergio Leone, seeing *Yojimbo*, determined to make an "American" adaptation of this Japanese adaptation of an American Western. Leone had also been watching *Rawhide* on Italian television. He liked Clint Eastwood's looks, and for $15,000 he had a deal. During the "hiatus" (off-season) from *Rawhide*, Eastwood turned up in Almeria, Spain, found he was the only man on the set speaking English, somehow or other finished a film he was told was to be named *The Magnificent Stranger*, and returned to California and *Rawhide*.

He had kept himself entertained in the acting, however. Tired of the engaging, ingratiating character he played in *Rawhide*, which had made him the idol of American teenagers, he went all the way in the other direction. In *The Magnificent Stranger* the Man With No Name, self-possessed, cold-eyed, kills a lot of people and never flinches once. They are all very bad people, of course, so there is no need to feel sorry for them. But the Man With No Name's hand never trembles. Uncertainty never clouds his brow. Eastwood, who felt the character was far too ruthless for American audiences, returned from Spain certain that the Leone film would never be shown in America. But he had made film history. He had hit the mother lode.

Back in Los Angeles, months after his return, Eastwood was browsing through *Variety* and noticed that Italy was aboil with plans for more Westerns after the spectacular success of a film called *A Fistful of Dollars*. The title meant nothing to him. It was only when he saw a second story, that the film sweeping Europe *starred Clint Eastwood*, that he realized what had happened. The next year he was back making the second of what were to become known as "spaghetti Westerns," *For a Few Dollars More*. And the year after that, in 1966, he made the third and last of the Leone-Eastwood collaborations, *The Good, the Bad, and the Ugly*.

Each film was better directed and brought in more money than its predecessor, making Eastwood one of the world's highly paid actors. The world, apparently, still loved Westerns, that quintessential piece of U.S. folklore (or mythology, if you will). It loved the action, the blood-and-guts. It loved the directing. And it certainly loved Clint Eastwood. It loved his steely confidence, his self-control, his fearlessness, his assurance that he would win. For if you're winning, people join you. If you lose confidence in yourself, they fall away. It is the way of the world.

In the United States, however, in the mid-sixties, certain highly vocal elements of the population had not only lost confidence in America, they hated it. They accused it of genocide, oppression, official racism, waging unprovoked war against harmless Third World people. They spelled America with a "k" as if it were Nazi Germany reborn. As of the end of 1966, not a single American movie distributor was willing to take a chance on the hottest property in world show business—a native-born American starring in a native American genre. Then in 1967 United Artists took the plunge, and for a modest figure picked up the U.S. distribution rights for the Eastwood-Leone trilogy. It turned out to be one of the best investments the company ever made. Released in chronological order beginning in early 1967, the films received the expected disastrous reviews, but *A Fistful of Dollars* was one of the company's biggest moneymakers for years. *For a Few Dollars More*, released later the same season, made even more money. By the time *The Good, the Bad, and the Ugly* opened in early 1968—the year, interestingly, of the Tet offensive in Vietnam—crowds for the Eastwood film were vast.

It has often been said that the recent spectacular upsurge of the so-called women's "gothic" novel is a reaction against the new feminism, and I think the point could easily be made that the meteoric rise of Clint Eastwood was a reaction against the radicalism of the sixties. Not that there weren't heavy thinkers around who did their best to get things upside-down. Two film historians, writing from the perspective of the "unalleviated pessimism" of the seventies, explained the Eastwood phenomenon as an expression of "revolutionary violence," going so far as to say that the Eastwood character was "Guevara without the encumbrances." This is on a level of silliness with claiming that the Lone Ranger was "Lenin without the encumbrances." Whatever the explanation, before long *Life* magazine, in its earlier, grander incarnation, ran a cover story with the astonished headline: "The World's Favorite Movie Star Is—No Kidding—Clint Eastwood!"

In the four years after his return to Hollywood as an international star, Eastwood made a mixed bag of eight movies with no clear-cut polemical bent but conventional enough in their morality and patriotism: three Westerns, two World War II films, and a "cop" movie. The one for which he got greater critical praise than he had ever received before in his life was the "Hitchcockian" *Play Misty for Me*, which he directed himself. In a plot whose initial stages seem to have been suggested by Nathanael West's *Miss Lonelyhearts*, Eastwood plays the most popular disc jockey in the Carmel-Monterey area in California. He attracts the passionate attentions of a very forward woman who gradually reveals herself to be hysterically jealous, psychotic, and, ultimately, murderous. In the film's final scene, with her trying to kill him, he lands a bone-crushing punch to her face, knocking her through the windows, over the balcony, and down into the ocean below. It is all in justifiable self-defense, but one doubts that *Play Misty for Me* is Gloria Steinem's favorite movie.

In film after film, with occasional dips and then "corrections," as with stock-market charts, Clint Eastwood kept moving steadily higher and higher. Several changes also occurred during this period in the way Eastwood worked and led his life. First of all, he left Hollywood and built himself a home on the outskirts of Carmel, some ninety miles from where he was born in San Francisco. He is not a Hollywood-type person and is never, or almost never, seen at gatherings of Hollywood's gilded set. He does not go with the herd. Second, he organized his own production company called Malpaso Productions (after a creek crossing his property in Carmel). "My theory was that I could foul up my career just as well as anyone could foul it up for me, so why not try it?" he said. And also, "I've got a six-pack under my arm, and a few pieces of paper and a couple of pencils, and I'm in business. What the hell, I can work in a closet." Eastwood seems to have no love of show and not a speck of Hollywood megalomania. He knows the movie business well, however, and all his productions come in under schedule and under budget.

In 1973, for reasons of his own, Eastwood decided to make

High Plains Drifter, such an obvious reprise of the themes of his collaborations with Sergio Leone that one is almost tempted to think he wanted to give the "official" Eastwood version of the trilogy. This time, Eastwood directed the picture himself, and his screenwriter was the celebrated Ernest Tidyman, who had recently won an Academy Award for his screenplay for the hugely successful *The French Connection*. But *High Plains Drifter* also has similarities of structure with *High Noon*, one of the greatest of the classic Westerns, directed by Fred Zinnemann and acted by Gary Cooper almost exactly twenty years before.

In *High Noon*, frightened townspeople approach their sheriff (Cooper) with the alarming news that a gang of outlaws is heading for the town with the intention of taking it over. The sheriff prepares a defense, but at the last minute finds that not a single other man has the courage to stand with him against the bandits. All alone he guns them down, one by one, but then, out of contempt for the cowardly townspeople, unpins his sheriff's badge and throws it in the dust.

In *High Plains Drifter*, the beginning is Leone-esque. The Stranger (Eastwood), as the Man With No Name is known in some of the Leone films, rides into an isolated town in the Southwest some time in the 1870s. The only clue we have to the Stranger's identity is nightmares he has as he sleeps in the town hotel. In the nightmares we see a helpless man being whipped to death by shrouded hoodlums as a terrified citizenry stands by, too cowardly to help. By day, the general plot of *High Plains Drifter* proceeds for a time almost identically with *High Noon*.

A gang of outlaws is on its way to take over the town. Since there is no sheriff the terrified citizens plead with the Stranger to save them. They are a gang of sniveling cowards, however, and not a man jack among them can be induced to help. Here slight surrealistic and sometimes supernatural notes begin to appear. The Stranger (Eastwood) agrees to save the town, but makes the residents repaint it bright red and rename it "Hell," after which he disappears. The outlaws arrive and start to kill and loot and burn, but where is the Stranger? It is only when they begin to put the town to the torch that he reappears and wipes out the marauding outlaws to the last man. Now suddenly the townspeople have a mysterious vision of the scene that has haunted the Stranger's nights: it is of their former sheriff, being whipped to death by these same outlaws while they stood by, afraid to save him. "But who are you?" one of the citizens timidly asks the Stranger who has saved their town, perhaps, but not before allowing a very considerable amount of mayhem and destruction. "You know who I am," answers the Stranger calmly, and rides out of town as mysteriously as he came.

Now I, personally, have no idea who Clint Eastwood's mysterious Stranger is, whether he is the dead sheriff's brother, or his ghost, or perhaps an avenging angel. But I have no difficulty whatever in reading the morality of the tale, or understanding why the Stranger has the town painted red and renamed "Hell." What some of Eastwood's elite critics have difficulty grasping is that in his canon, cowardice is a punishable offense. The idea has become so pervasive among our educated classes that the proper stance for facing the world should be one of accommodating sensitivity that Eastwood's contrary view—that the proper stance should be one of bravery—marks him as some kind of barbarian. I suspect this is one of the reasons many people cannot bear him—although his attitudes were almost certainly shared by Gary Cooper and most of the team that made *High Noon*.

But the difference between the elite reactions to *High Noon* and *High Plains Drifter* is a lugubrious comment on some of the changes that came over America from 1952 to 1973. From many points of view, the stories are identical. Both the Gary Cooper character and the Clint Eastwood character look with bitter contempt on townspeople not brave enough to fight in their own defense. The Gary Cooper character throws his sheriff's star in the dust, leaves town in utter distain—and admittedly lets it go at that. But his story, after all, has started from scratch. In the Eastwood story, there is a score to settle. A man has been beaten to death while cowards stood by, afraid to help him. The Lord is trampling out the vintage where the grapes of wrath are stored.

Careful readers of Norman Mailer—and those who do not expect his instincts to accord with his professed politics—will not be entirely surprised to learn that he is an ardent fan of Clint Eastwood. Mailer's favorite films seem to be the Westerns that Eastwood made in the United States in the seventies and eighties, and the movie with which he leads his list is *High Plains Drifter*. These films, says Mailer, "come out of the old, wild, hard, dry, sad, sour redneck wisdom of small-town life in the Southwest. All of Eastwood's knowledge is in them, a sardonic, unsentimental set of values that is equal to art for it would grapple with the roots of life itself." Mailer goes even farther, quoting a speech of the Eastwood character in a later Western, *The Outlaw Josey Wales*. "When things get bad," says the character played by Eastwood, "and it looks like you're not going to make it, then you got to get mean. I mean plain plumbdog mean, because if you lose your head then, you neither live nor win. That's just the way it is." This carries the moral to an even grimmer point than in *High Plains Drifter*. We are no longer concerned here with bravery, or the punishment of cowardice, but simple, back-to-the-wall survival. It is them or you. Live or die.

Eastwood was making these later Westerns alternately with his *Dirty Harry* series, police stories set in present-day San Francisco. And with each film, whether detective or Western, the Eastwood audience—irresistibly, it would seem—continued to grow and grow. The detective series and the Westerns were strongly linked morally, but it is perhaps no puzzle that the "unsentimental sense of values" Norman Mailer so admired in the mythic and even present-day small-town West he found totally inapplicable in modern San Francisco. The *Dirty Harry* series, Mailer decided, was made to "satisfy producers." (What producers? The late Louis B. Mayer? Hollywood doesn't work that way anymore. Clint Eastwood is his own producer.) For when you try to do justice and pursue criminals in a great, modern U.S. city you come up against the American Civil Liberties Union and other such groups.

It seems as if any American with even the mildest interest in public affairs must be able to recite the Miranda warning in his sleep by now (and the young probably think it was written in the Bill of Rights), but it dates from only 1966 and the famous

Miranda decision of the Warren Court—historically a mere blink of the eye. What is not often recalled is that, even in the ultra-liberal Supreme Court of Chief Justice Earl Warren, the decision on *Miranda* was only five to four. Still, over a mere five years, from *Mapp* in 1961 through *Miranda* in 1966, the Warren Court radically altered the relationship of the police and prosecutor to the criminal suspect, and entirely to the advantage of the latter. This, at a time when the authority of family, church, and school were all declining drastically, narcotics were introducing into our society disruptions of which we are not yet able to take the full measure, and crime rates were rising alarmingly.

The Miranda warning, recited by the approaching officer at the time of arrest, assures the suspect that he has "the right to remain silent and refuse to answer questions," and "the right to consult an attorney before speaking to the police and to have an attorney present during any questioning now or in the future. . . ." Then there is the "exclusionary rule," according to which any evidence—corpses, murder weapons, whatever—gathered at variance with the strictest constitutional proprieties is "tainted" and inadmissible in court even when the police have acted in perfectly good faith, sometimes even under instructions from a judge. So people who have committed revolting crimes—which no one questions for a moment—are now walking the streets, or have been clogging the judicial system with appeals for as much as fifteen years.

The country is in a ferment over the "exclusionary rule," and public disgust with crime has reached a high level. [This essay, written early in 1984, preceded by many years recent decisions by the Supreme Court changing judicial doctrine on criminal law.] My own feeling is that the American people, in a popular vote, with that "unsentimental sense of values" we have heard so praised, would have expunged or radically modified the exclusionary rule long ago—at least as long ago as 1971, when Clint Eastwood made the first *Dirty Harry* movie, which came close to tripling the success of any Eastwood vehicle to date. Clearly, he hit a nerve.

Kent State had been in 1970. The campuses were alive with peace demonstrations. Students carried the Vietcong flag, called their own country fascist. Policemen were known as pigs. But Clint Eastwood and director Don Siegel thought that there was another America out there and Warner Brothers, which put up the money, agreed with them. Judging by the forty-nine states that went for Nixon in 1972 and the success of their film, they were right.

The scene is San Francisco. "Dirty" Harry Callahan (Eastwood) is a police inspector known, in these immediate post-*Miranda* years, as a little hard to keep leashed. A psychopath announces that he has buried a fourteen-year-old girl alive and will let her suffocate to death unless he is paid $200,000 within hours. In a first encounter both Callahan and the psychopath, who calls himself Scorpio, are wounded, but Callahan continues in hot pursuit. Discovering that Scorpio is the groundskeeper at a football stadium, and thinking the buried girl has only minutes to live, Callahan (with no warrant) blasts through the grounds-keeper's quarters and finally runs him to earth in the middle of the football field. Still thinking the girl's life is at stake and that every minute counts, he brutalizes the extortionist until Scorpio reveals where he has buried the girl. Police rush to the spot and lift her up out of the ground. She is dead. But is Scorpio charged with murder? Kidnapping? Extortion? Or any of a dozen other felonies? No, because every single piece of evidence against him is tainted. Callahan has entered his quarters without a warrant, failed to read him the Miranda warning, violated his rights under at least the Fourth, Fifth, and Sixth Amendments. Scorpio "walks."

Callahan predicts that Scorpio will strike again, and he does. This time he hijacks a school bus filled with terrified children and demands both ransom money and an escape plane. Against orders, Callahan goes after Scorpio on his own, leaps onto the roof of the bus from a bridge (Eastwood does his own stunts), and, finally, it is the two of them by the waters of the bay. There has been gunplay, Scorpio has attempted to hold a young boy as hostage, gun to his head, but Callahan has freed the boy, wounding Scorpio. At last, there is one of those trademark Dirty

Harry moments of truth. Scorpio is about to reach for his pistol from where he lies sprawled on the dock. Callahan seems to have fired all the bullets in his .44 Magnum. "Been counting the rounds, punk?" asks Callahan icily. "Maybe I'm empty. The question is: do you feel lucky?" After an agonizing moment of hesitation, Scorpio reaches for his weapon, and Callahan blows him to kingdom come. As a last touch (another note from *High Noon*), Callahan slides his police inspector's badge out of his wallet in disgust and scales it out over the bay.

The film caused an uproar. It is unquestionably contrived. It is juvenile. It is popular entertainment. But if the plot of the film were to be reproduced in real life, it is hard to imagine that more than 1 percent of the American population would consider Harry Callahan, fighting desperately to save a girl's life, a contemptible person, or would consider the freeing of Scorpio, whose civil rights have been violated, a triumph of justice. True, this 1 percent was well represented among those who wrote about *Dirty Harry*. Eastwood was called a brute, a fascist, and worse. But he had his defenders, too, and it was curious how those sympathetic with the film in general tended to like Eastwood's acting, while those who hated the film thought he was the worst performer who had ever stepped in front of a movie camera.

I, personally, think Eastwood is considerably underrated as an actor. He is not Robert Duvall, or Robert de Niro, or Dustin Hoffman. He operates within a narrow range. But it is no narrower than the ranges of Gary Cooper or John Wayne. Humphrey Bogart—to cite another demigod from the past— worked within an extremely narrow range. Eastwood is 6-feet-4, all bone and muscle, and it is admittedly not every man who has the looks of a Clint Eastwood. But even with these physical qualifications, it is insufficiently appreciated how difficult it is to be a convincing Dirty Harry. Precious few of Hollywood's leading men could do it. Eastwood looks right, walks right. He is never self-conscious. He uses no profane display of mannerisms, but this makes the part harder, not easier. It seems he belongs there and that if you violated his sense of the ethical order of society, with no hysteria or loss of contact with his moral center he could calmly kill you. The ultimate test, you might say.

I do not have quite so high an opinion of Eastwood's directing. He is a competent director, perfectly adequate professionally, but his most skillfully made films have been directed by other men, such as long-time crony Don Siegel (still perhaps best known for his original version of *Invasion of the Body Snatchers*) and Michael Cimino (*The Deer Hunter*), to whom Eastwood gave his first chance to direct in *Thunderbird and Lightfoot*. In addition to Cimino and Tidyman (*The French Connection*), Eastwood has used as screenwriter such a self-declared Hollywood right-winger as the flamboyant John Milius (who went on to direct *Conan the Barbarian*). Eastwood fired director Philip Kaufman from the set of *The Outlaw Josey Wales* (1976) after one week's shooting, thereby perhaps saving that highly successful Western from the havoc which I am convinced Kaufman wrecked upon Tom Wolfe's wonderful *The Right Stuff*. But Eastwood's greatest shortcoming as a director is his casting and handling of actors. Locked within the stoic self-possession of his characters, from the Man With No Name to Dirty Harry—a self-possession that absorbs substantial psychic energy—Eastwood seems rather insensitive to other actors' performances, although he did have the acumen to team up with Robert Duvall in *Joe Kidd*.

In 1978 Eastwood walked straight into another one of his lucky flukes. *Every Which Way But Loose* was his first "bare-knuckle subculture" film, but it also had broad comic elements, with an orangutan as co-star, also Ruth Gordon. But the main cause of concern was that Warner Brothers, the distributor, was spending most of its promotion money that season on its $30-million spectacular, *Superman*, on which the studio's life depended. Malpaso and Warners devised a strategy, however. That Eastwood was king in the South and West was established. But in the cities of those regions, heavy advertising budgets had already been committed for *Superman*. The answer was to open the Eastwood film first in *small towns* in the South and West, sometimes in back-country areas. The result was the most successful Eastwood ever. It finished the year second only to

Superman, and ahead of *Rocky II* (which itself had bettered *Rocky*).

Meanwhile, Eastwood has gone on intermittently with his *Dirty Harry* series, which has now reached its fourth film, *Sudden Impact*. In *Magnum Force* (1973), he attempted to disarm his liberal critics: the villains are a band of young policemen who assassinate murderers and criminals escaping punishment through the laxity of the laws. "There are things wrong with the system," says Callahan angrily, but he stops a long way short of condoning extra-legal groups exercising retribution under no authority but their own. In *The Enforcer* (1976), he attempted to placate feminist critics by having his police partner a woman (Tyne Daly), assigned to act as his "watchdog." As it happens, she is the only woman Callahan ever falls deeply in love with. Unfortunately—if conveniently—she dies.

In the opening episode of *Sudden Impact*, released in the Christmas season of 1983, Callahan is wrestling again with the exclusionary rule. He has arrested a criminal. No one questions either the man's guilt or Callahan's good faith in acquiring evidence. But there is a slip somewhere. The evidence is tainted. The judge reprimands Callahan scathingly in court. And the criminal walks. But the main action of *Sudden Impact* is about a woman who has been the victim of a gang rape, of which the perpetrators have all been found innocent through perjured testimony. The woman (Sondra Locke) sets about taking justice into her own hands, and when finally caught by Callahan, after the usual firefights with thugs and hieratic shots on misty streets, she is pityingly let go.

For the theme that hangs over all the *Dirty Harry* movies, and perhaps to a lesser extent all of Eastwood's career, is vigilante justice. It is a theme deep in American culture, literature, films, and popular fiction: a man alone in a corrupt world, the lawless West, or the jungle of cities. The sinister twist in the *Dirty Harry* series is that what has corrupted justice in our time, and made it so hard to obtain, is a kind of liberalism gone mad. Thus: Dirty Harry.

But Christmas offered an interesting development. Throughout the nation at large, *Sudden Impact* had the strongest opening of any Eastwood film ever. In New York City, moreover, which to say the least is not Clint Eastwood country, *Sudden Impact* went off like dynamite. Eastwood, who almost never grants interviews, denies that his films are the least bit political.

In his private life, Eastwood financed the mission of Bo Gritz, a decorated Vietnam war veteran, in his recent armed attempt to recover U.S. MIA's in Laos. Perhaps Eastwood's patriotism, his belief in the legitimacy of force, and his determination to see predators punished are so deeply ingrained that he doesn't even think of them as political. Perhaps he thinks such fundamental assumptions should be beyond the realm of political debate. And the man might have a point.

10

Treason Chic: Britain Acclaims Its Traitors

TREASON IS IN STYLE. At least British treason. Or at least British treason when it is committed by Englishmen with posh accents wearing old Etonian ties. There is something poignant, and nostalgic, and bittersweet about it—to the point where all three of the leading British film imports into the United States in the closing months of 1984 have wildly romanticized fictional creations suggested by the lives of Guy Burgess, Donald Maclean, and Kim Philby, Britain's three most famous, and infamous, traitors of the last half-century. And cultural despair is all in style, British cultural despair, that is, and even British cultural despair transposed, as in John le Carré's *The Little Drummer Girl*, which Hollywood has just turned into a big-budget movie starring Diane Keaton.

Some twenty years ago I noticed in West Germany a cover line on a magazine which read, *Warum Kulturpessimismus?* ("Why Cultural Pessimism?"). Since that time, of course, the German intellectual classes have moved to the Left. The French—apparently always odd men out—have moved to the Right. America has moved first one way and then the other. British intellectuals and semi-intellectuals, curiously enough, have moved in the same direction as the Germans. With no Vietnam war and no Watergate, large sections of British elite opinion have lost contact with the mass of the population as thoroughly as any U.S. McGovernite. (During the Falklands war fair numbers of self-styled British intellectual "leaders" were

185

wandering about in bafflement saying, "Who *are* all these patriotic people?")

The British cinema, nothing if not modish, reflects accurately the attitudes of the United Kingdom's own Yuppies and pre-Yuppies—a very close sociological equivalent of America's movie audience. But whereas America's radical-Left filmmakers content themselves with movies implying that the Rosenbergs were innocent, or that the Sandinistas in Nicaragua are splendid fellows—and even these fail miserably at the box office—Britain's movie industry has produced a quite remarkable genre, a special subdivision of cultural despair that I can only call Treason Chic. Who would have anticipated that any fragment of British opinion would ever bathe in the roseate glow of fond memory some of Britain's most heinous traitors, men who joined the enemy and placed their country in mortal danger, and one of whom (Guy Burgess) may have been responsible for the deaths of thousands of American soldiers in Korea? But it has come to pass.

The first example of Britain's new Treason Chic is *Another Country*. Inspired quite openly by the life of Guy Burgess, the film is essentially an ode to the beauties of homosexuality accompanied by a self-pitying lament over some minor disappointment suffered by the Burgess character at public school. If the film means anything at all, it means that any country beastly enough to inconvenience its homosexuals rather deserves to be betrayed, and that Burgess's behavior in becoming a Soviet agent and eventually defecting to Moscow was not only comprehensible but in the last analysis justified.

I had no idea when I saw *Another Country* that it was to begin a whole new style, but before many weeks had passed we received from Britain *The Jigsaw Man*, starring Laurence Olivier and Michael Caine. If *Another Country* is an "artistic" film (whose claim to quality rests heavily on its *Town and Country*-style photography). *The Jigsaw Man* is a "big" movie, an action thriller. But it, too, has its celebrated traitor, in this case patterned plainly on Kim Philby. The story begins in Moscow, where we meet an elderly British defector (and former Soviet agent in his own country), played by an actor of appropriate age with Michael Caine's voice (dubbed). The Kremlin is about to send him back to Britain on a thrilling mission and in order to escape detection he is given plastic surgery. To the amazement of one and all, the character emerges from surgery looking like Michael Caine at his true age.

The plot is trashy, as is usual in this sort of film, and really not worth recounting in detail except for two turns. Shortly after returning to England, the Philby character (Caine) encounters the head of British intelligence (MI-5), played by Olivier, who does not at first recognize him, due to the surgery and a Russian accent. But when he finally does, they greet each other like old comrades in arms. The reaction of the director of MI-5 at discovering his antagonist's true identity is, more or less, "Oh, you devil! You rascal! You scamp!" This for a man who has committed high treason.

But Caine-Philby is not really a bad fellow, you see. In fact, suspecting that his Kremlin masters plan to "terminate" him once he gives them the list of Soviet-British double agents he has come for, he decides to double-cross *them* and sell the list to the highest bidder, escaping afterward with the loot to Switzerland. Since the head of MI-5 is onto his game, Caine-Philby offers to cut him in on the deal. They will *both* sell the list to the highest bidder, *both* escape to Switzerland. The movie ends with the two men laughing riotously, clearly in accord. They are both rascals, it turns out, both scamps.

Americans who do not specialize in these matters may not know that the director of MI-5 during the crucial years was a man named Sir Roger Hollis, who, as it happens, fell under heavy suspicion of being a Soviet agent himself, the mole of moles. Sir Roger—elusive as ever—has since died, but many who knew him best in MI-5 are convinced of his guilt, a fact which no doubt suggested the Olivier character in *The Jigsaw Man*. It is almost impossible to imagine this story transposed to an American setting. Alger Hiss as, first, a Soviet agent, and, further, a *lovable* Soviet agent? Although *The Jigsaw Man* is pretty small beer as films go these days, it must be admitted that, even in an "entertainment" movie, the lovable traitor is a novelty, perhaps even a historic novelty.

The third of these Treason-Chic movies is *An Englishman Abroad*, directed by one of Britain's most gifted filmmakers, John Schlesinger (*Darling, Midnight Cowboy*), and starring Alan Bates. Skillful, witty, well acted, well written (by Alan Bennett), it has come to America as a television movie on PBS's Great Performances series, but is a far superior piece of work to either of the two earlier films.

An Englishman Abroad tells us, once again, the story, or part of the story, of Guy Burgess—who is decidedly the figure most beloved by the Treason-Chic set. This time, although the film's authors admit to having concocted "imaginary incidents," the Guy Burgess character is called, in all simplicity, Guy Burgess.

It seems that sometime in 1958 a young Australian actress named Coral Browne went with the Old Vic to Moscow, where—pure chance—she encountered Burgess, who had defected to the Soviet Union seven years before. Burgess, always something of a *canaille*, came bursting into her dressing room unannounced and threw up three times in her washbowl. But he had "bags of charm," reported Browne, and I confess that if Burgess succeeded in captivating her while intermittently vomiting in her washbowl he must have been charming indeed. Burgess (a flaming homosexual) invited Browne to lunch, which turned out to be a squalid affair in his grubby little Moscow flat. Burgess sailed through it with superb aplomb, as if he were in the Reform Club in London's West End or even Buckingham Palace. The brazen Burgess had an objective, however. He could not bear Soviet clothing, and had Browne measure him for some new suits from his old Savile Row tailor.

Some twenty-five years after the event, Coral Browne told this story to author Bennett, who determined to write it as a screenplay. The result is *An Englishman Abroad*. Since the age of the actress is immaterial to the plot, Browne plays herself in the movie, although the years have promoted her to Gertrude in *Hamlet* (possibly from Ophelia).

The film has an unusually ironic beginning. While a huge poster portrait of Joseph Stalin fills the screen, we hear a tinny, English rendition of the American Tin Pan Alley favorite, "Who—stole my heart away? Who—makes me dream all day?"

Since by 1958 all the portraits of Stalin were down in Moscow (and his mummy was soon to be yanked unceremoniously from its resting place beside that of Lenin on Red Square), the juxtaposition of Stalin and the supremely silly "Who Stole My Heart Away?" is thematic, plainly symbolizing the romantic shallowness of most Western Communists' understanding of the Soviet state.

In the movie, Stalin's portrait is succeeded on the screen by those of Marx, Engels, and Lenin ("Dreams I know will never come true. Who—stole my heart away?"), these last three mounted on the front of a Moscow theater. Within, the Old Vic company performs *Hamlet*, Coral Browne playing Gertrude, while in the house sits Guy Burgess, gradually growing queasy with drink, and our story is under way.

Alan Bates's Burgess is a true virtuoso performance, one of the finest I have ever seen from him. His cleverness, unscrupulousness, rudeness, wit—all with the impeccable accent and demeanor of the well-born Englishman of the period—have an uncannily authentic ring. "I'm sure I'm not the first person to remark on your pronounced resemblance to the late Ernest Bevin," he tells the *babushka* guarding the stage door. "You could be sisters." At lunch he brightly pumps Browne for London gossip: "Do you see Harold Nicolson? . . . What about Cyril Connolly? Auden, do you know him? Pope-Hennessy? . . . Do you know Auden?" "You asked me. No," answers Browne, who evidently knows no one worth knowing.

Coral Browne herself seems far from sympathetic toward Communism, although, given the fact that Khrushchev's "secret" speech to the twentieth Congress of the Soviet Communist party had revealed to the world two years earlier the true nature of the Stalinist state, her condemnation is somewhat superficial. "If this is Communism I don't like it because it's *dull*! The poor things look so tired," she says. "Some people think Australia's dull. . . . And look at *Leeds*!" At one point she tells Burgess, "I'm only an actress, not a bright lady by your standards." And we can believe it.

As for Burgess, Alan Bates's brilliant, highly entertaining character portrayal never seemed to me to jar with the Stalin-

Stole-My-Heart-Away theme. I am perfectly willing to concede that Burgess was a charming, outrageous scalawag—which wouldn't have deterred me in the least from wishing him hanged if he'd been seized in time.

But imagine my surprise at the manner in which the story unfolds after Browne's return to London. She goes first to Burgess's tailor and is received with courtesy, sympathy, and discretion. "How is Mr. Burgess? . . . He was one of our more colorful customers. Too little color in our drab lives these days," says the shop assistant. "Mum's the word," cautions Browne. The assistant replies, "Mum is always the word here. Moscow or Maidenhead, mum is always the word."

So far, so good. But then Browne receives a letter from Burgess asking her to order some pajamas from his old haberdasher. Here things do not go smoothly, the assistant informing her politely that Mr. Burgess's account is closed. "The gentleman is a traitor, Madame." At this point Browne's voice rises into the fishwife range, causing other customers' heads to turn. "Suppose someone commits adultery in your precious pajamas. . . . What happens when he orders his next pair of jim-jams? Is it sorry, no can do?" she shrills. (The equation of adultery with treason is interesting.) "Jesus Christ, you were happy to satisfy this man when he was one of the most notorious buggers in London! . . . But he was in the Foreign Office then! [screeching now] It's pricks like you that make me understand why he went!"

Come again? as Coral Browne might say. It's because of people who know a traitor for a traitor that Guy Burgess became a traitor? And this is the film's climactic, epiphanic moment, followed only by a sequence in which Burgess struts about Moscow among the ill-dressed Russians in his new Savile Row suit to the tune of the famous Gilbert and Sullivan ditty, "For He Is an Englishman" ("But in spite of all temptations/To belong to other nations/He remains an Englishman/He remains an Englishman")—which in context seems to say fondly that an English gentleman is still an English gentleman even if he does commit treason. This implies exactly the indulgence that so enraged Britain at the time of the great defections: that members of the

British upper class were more loyal to each other than they were to their country.

A sixth sense tells me that the scene in the haberdasher's did not take place, that it is one of those "imaginary incidents" about which the film's titles have the decency to warn us. I do not believe that an Old Vic actress would have screeched out the word "prick" in a fashionable Bond Street haberdashery in the fifties—particularly since, in that decade, the word was still largely an Americanism. I also do not believe that a person would have mounted a screaming public defense of a British traitor in that period. In 1958 British troops had been (successfully) fighting a Communist insurgency in Malaya for a full decade under both Labor and Conservative governments, and the patriotism of World War II was still very much alive.

In the thirties, it is worth recalling, the greatest of British music-hall entertainers was Gracie Fields, beloved, especially by Britain's working classes, as "Our Gracie." When the Luftwaffe bombs began to fall, however, Fields, not even volunteering to entertain the troops, fled to America. The war over and the victory won, she returned to England and opened a new show at one of London's largest music halls—to an empty house. She had abandoned her countrymen in their hour of need and they wouldn't take her back. Her career was over. If feelings were this violent in 1945 about a mere entertainer, one can imagine the intensity of popular outrage when only six years later blaring London headlines announced that Guy Burgess and Donald Maclean, two pampered children of Britain's upper class, were Soviet agents and had defected to Moscow.

So *An Englishman Abroad*, produced by the BBC, tells us little about Britain of the fifties but a great deal about Britain today, where treason seems to have been reduced to the level of a minor misdemeanor, entirely forgivable as an upper-class peccadillo—at least if committed by a gentleman with verve and the right sort of tailor. There is even something saucy and fetching about it, something rather stylish and U, as Nancy Mitford might say. An Englishman who betrayed his country used to be "the vilest creature known to man." But no more, apparently. No more.

John le Carré (real name David Cornwell) has not concerned himself with treason in particular. He has made a career of writing spy thrillers denigrating Western intelligence services. When his *The Spy Who Came in from the Cold* appeared in 1963 (with a rapturous blurb from Graham Greene), the top of the line in spy fiction was Ian Fleming, whose James Bond series was the purest fluff. Le Carré provided a sharp contrast. In Fleming, intelligence "agents" wear evening clothes, drink champagne, gamble at elegant casinos, drive expensive cars. In le Carré, shabby men in seedy offices do demeaning work for squalid ends. Le Carré's prose was, and has remained, lumpy, his dialogue leaden, his plots implausible, and his characters impossible, but a man who takes a gloomy view of the world recommends himself as a serious thinker, and le Carré was widely felt to have brought a kind of higher realism to espionage fiction. Long before the U.S. Congress began to impose legal limits on the operations of the Central Intelligence Agency, le Carré familiarized the reading public with the notion that Western intelligence services—the American even more than the British—were engaged in enterprises of a squalor and sordidness at least equal to those of the Soviet Union. (An element of perversity appears when we consider that le Carré has stated in conversation that he is a "frustrated British imperialist," which seems to imply that envy and a twisted despair play roles here, too.)

In *The Little Drummer Girl* le Carré pulls out all the stops. Whereas his earlier espionage thrillers had concerned the British intelligence services, a community of which he was an alumnus, *The Little Drummer Girl* deals with the Israeli and Palestinian Arab services, organizations he could have known about only through reading and hearsay and which he consequently described exactly as they existed in his imagination. This turned out to be at least a partial mistake. Deprived of le Carré's seeming authority when writing about British intelligence, *The Little Drummer Girl* had to stand on its own two feet as a work of literature, and the British press—at least the more or less conservative organs of the British press—gave it a long overdue slamming. While in America *Time* magazine saw fit to devote a major story to le Carré, in Britain the *Times Literary Supplement* called the book kitsch, the London *Times* compared it with the work of pop adventure writer Mary Stewart, and the *Daily Telegraph* described it brutally as "a failure," adding that le Carré "takes himself . . . much too seriously."

The central character in the film, on whom everything turns, is one of the most absurd in recent memory: "Charlie" (Diane Keaton), a London actress and PLO groupie. One would think that an actress with the approximate politics of Vanessa Redgrave would make a rather poor prospect for recruitment by Israel's Mossad, but those Zionist devils go after her nonetheless. Their stratagem is bewitching. A secret PLO operative gives a talk to a group of sympathizers in Nottingham, England. Charlie, who seems to make a habit of this sort of thing, feels her heart bleed, her knees turn to water; but the Palestinian, wearing a ski mask and a bright red blazer, slips off into the night. Several cranks of the plot later, Charlie, now in Athens, spies a man of Middle Eastern appearance wearing a bright red blazer. Knowing that any man in a red blazer must be "her" Palestinian, she makes rather bold advances, tugging him, as it were, toward the nearest bed.

But our Palestinian is a straight arrow and, after a bit of the Parthenon by moonlight, takes her to meet his comrades, led by Kurtz (Klaus Kinski). And darned if the whole pack of them don't turn out to be Israelis. Kurtz is an Israeli. Joseph, the man in the red blazer, is an Israeli. Even the "Palestinian" in Nottingham was an Israeli. But they have doped out our heroine by means of some rough-and-ready psychology: poor, lonely, sexually promiscuous Charlie, what she really wants is a "family." They offer her this family and, *bam*, Charlie throws in her lot with the Jewish people.

The Mossad operations group trusts this new recruit so completely that, as her first mission, she is sent to penetrate the Palestinian terror network and lead the Israelis to the master terrorist of them all, Khalil (French actor Sami Frey). Charlie accomplishes this in about forty-five shakes of a lamb's tail (tedious plot and counter-plot), the only problem being that she now falls in love with Khalil and sleeps with him, too. Khalil,

Joseph, Joseph, Khalil. What's a poor girl looking for a family to do? First she falls in love with Joseph because she thinks he's a Palestinian. Then he turns into an Israeli, but it's okay because he's got a family. Then she falls in love with Khalil because the Palestinians have a family, too, and also he's cute. But it's all so senseless! And Charlie feels it is true tragedy when the Israelis blow Khalil away.

But she is not alone! Romance is not dead! Joseph defects! Back in England, rehearsing a play, a broken woman, Charlie casts her eye to the back of the empty theater, and there is Joseph. "I don't know the difference between right and wrong any more," he says portentously, to which Diane Keaton replies, with the magnificent silliness of an actress far, far beyond her depth, "I'm dead, Jose. You killed me, remember?" After which deep closing line, the two of them walk off into the gloaming.

Compared with the book, the film seems fairly muted on the issue of where justice lies as between Israel and the PLO. Many a moviegoer, not dwelling overlong on the meaning of Joseph's not knowing the difference between right and wrong any more, may not take in the fact that he has deserted both the Mossad and his country, something that is made quite explicit in the book. Le Carré's own official comment on *The Little Drummer Girl* is that it is saying, "A pox on both your houses." This, however, is nonsense, and in the same logical category as crying, "A pox on all nuclear weapons!" while calling on only the West to disarm.

Moreover, to confine myself to the movie, Klaus Kinski—although an actor of some power—has never played a sympathetic role in his life, nor does he here as Kurtz. Sami Frey (Brigitte Bardot's ex-fiancé) is a matinée idol, and charming. The Israelis conform fairly closely to the Nazi model (the name "Kurtz" hardly spoiling that impression) and many of the Palestinians, among them Khalil, seem quite idealistic. Both sides are violent, but we *see* the Israelis' victims. There is no doubt about it, Warner Brothers has made America's first forthrightly anti-Israel movie. It is dropping like a stone all over the country, a complete fiasco.

This leaves me with the problem of America's movie critics,

who, with the honorable exceptions of the *New York Times* and *Time*, are in the odd position of having fallen into raptures over a film that is both bad and a failure. It has been widely reported that American journalists are substantially to the left of the American people: I submit that American film critics are, in their ecstatic way, far to the left of other U.S. journalists. I have before me a full-page advertisement for *The Little Drummer Girl*, consisting largely of eulogistic quotes from eleven major reviewers. It is perhaps no surprise that *Newsweek*'s reviewer should have found the film "the most riveting movie of the year," or that the reviewer for the *Village Voice* should have found it "tense and provocative." But the critic for Rupert Murdoch's *New York Post*, a paper hardly guilty of indulgence toward the Left, or of being anti-Israel, also thought it was "gripping and powerful, riveting entertainment," while the critic of the *Daily News* (which endorsed Ronald Reagan for president) felt it was "thrilling, involving, brilliantly done. . . . I was riveted to the screen from beginning to end."

But the most bizarre review of all appeared in the pages of the *Wall Street Journal*, a newspaper whose editorial pages are dedicated unswervingly to the advocacy of traditional, patriotic pro-Western positions. Israel probably has no more influential friend in the U.S. press than the *Wall Street Journal*. Yet the newspaper seems to resist tenaciously the notion that art in our age has become heavily politicized, feeling, I suppose, that it is "only entertainment." In any event, the paper's movie reviewer, Julie Salamon, wrote one of the most laudatory notices of *The Little Drummer Girl* in the entire country. At the end of a piece which affirms that John le Carré's novel stirred up controversy because it treated Palestinians and Israelis "more or less with an even hand" (the book's anti-Israel bias is naked), and which describes Klaus Kinski as playing Kurtz with a "frighteningly gentle cruelty," Salamon writes:

> We see brutality, kindness, and fanaticism in both camps and are left with the message that this war is senseless and hopeless. This is certainly no great revelation, but it is enough to sustain a spy story where everything else works

well. In *The Little Drummer Girl*, everything else works very well indeed.

The movie, as I have said, shows us fanaticism and brutality almost entirely on the Israeli side, while kindness seems to be a Palestinian monopoly—with the exception of only one Israeli, Joseph, who in the end defects. But, more important, the war between Palestinian and Israeli intelligence services is in actual fact not "senseless," any more than the contest between the United States and the USSR is "senseless," and anyone who thinks it is should have an enforced course of reading in Clausewitz. Perhaps Salamon has lost exactly what John le Carré has lost, a sense of the moral worth of our civilization—and that of Israel, so much a part of ours. But if that is true of a reviewer, what are we to make of American editors who publish such reviews but who have not for a moment forgotten the moral worth of our civilization?

A residual hangover from the days when we dominated a new continent unchallenged, plus a certain strain of philistinism, may make it hard for many Americans to recognize that contemporary culture is utterly permeated with ideology. Yves Montand, a French entertainer whose spectacular break with the Communist Left has prompted wild if good-hearted speculation that he might become a new Ronald Reagan, once told me that he had never read a word of Karl Marx, but had been converted to Marxism by seeing Sergei Eisenstein's Soviet film classic, *The Battleship Potemkin*. Our opponents consider culture a battleground like any other. Yves Montand knows this. Shouldn't we?

11

Eddie Murphy in Post-Racist America

IF THE WORLD OF entertainment is any guide, something of note is happening on the American racial scene. In the early months of 1985, three events occurred, each in a distinct entertainment medium. The names of these events are: (1) Michael Jackson, (2) Bill Cosby, and (3) Eddie Murphy.

In popular music, someone is always on top. There is always a number one, and a number two. But in the memory of Americans alive today, there have been at most three super-super-super star singers or groups, of the kind that makes girls faint and drives crowds hysterical. Over the years, Frank Sinatra, Elvis Presley, and the Beatles stand out, strange, giant monuments thrown up by the *Zeitgeist*, and all white. A fourth name has now been added to this august list: Michael Jackson. No black entertainer has ever drawn such huge and feverish mobs (and white mobs) as did Michael Jackson during his "Victory Tour" of the United States in the summer of 1984.

In September of the same year, NBC brought veteran comic Bill Cosby back in a new TV comedy series slotted for 8 P.M. on Thursday nights. It was a "black" series, but with a twist—it was about an upper-middle-class black family (Cosby an obstetrician, his wife a lawyer), which is to say, the comic stereotypes in it had nothing to do with race. It was about an American family that just happened to be black. Nothing in plot or situation depended on being black in a white society. *The Cosby Show* shot to the top of the ratings list—number one—and, some five months later, it has never been out of the week's top ten.

But perhaps the most dazzling rise of all has been that of a twenty-three-year-old black from Long Island named Eddie Murphy. A member of the third generation of performers on NBC-TV's *Saturday Night Live* (Bill Murray, Chevy Chase, John Belushi, Dan Aykroyd, and Gilda Radner had all come out of the first), Murphy made his first two movies in 1983, *48 Hours* and *Trading Places*. Both ended up among the ten biggest money-makers of the year. But Murphy was still suspected of being a mere novelty, possibly just a flash in the pan, especially after the failure of his next film, *Best Defense*. The entry of his fourth movie, *Beverly Hills Cop*, into the lists for the big Christmas competition of 1984 was attended with much curiosity, particularly since Murphy was playing a role once intended for Sylvester Stallone.

The film took off with such velocity as to leave Hollywood somewhat stunned. At the close of the Christmas-New Year's holiday season (for the movie industry the year's second most important after summer), *Beverly Hills Cop* not only led the field, it had brought in three times as much money as its closest competitor (*2010*), while in third position was a film starring both Clint Eastwood and Burt Reynolds. In 1984, Hollywood's aggregate domestic box-office returns crossed the $4 billion line for the first time, a result which had been anticipated by *Variety* months before. "But nobody knew at the time," reported the trade journal, "that Eddie Murphy would almost single-handedly be pulling the year's final tally" to an all-time record.

It had never happened before. No one knew how long it would last. No black actor before had ever come within a country mile. But after years of laments over the dearth of roles for black actors and actresses, suddenly, out of the blue, young Eddie Murphy was the biggest star in Hollywood.

How did such an extraordinary thing happen? Talk of "crossover appeal" ("black" entertainment which appeals to white audiences as well as black) seems somehow out of date. Eddie Murphy's audience does not just include whites; it is overwhelmingly white. He lives, and excels, entirely in what would once have been considered exclusively a white man's world. His home is in Alpine, New Jersey. His idol is Elvis Presley. He is patterning his career on that of Bob Hope—whose cheeky confidence his own style recalls in an eerie way.

Nor does Eddie Murphy interpret "black experience," except to a minor degree. He interprets American experience. If he did not, the whole thing, simply, would not have happened. He has freed himself entirely from the Dick Gregory tradition of playing to white guilt. The fact that, for almost a generation, black satirists attacking American racism have been able to count on the instant sympathy of white audiences all over the country leads one to think that the racist America of pure liberal doctrine has not existed for many years now, and is, indeed, a piece of liberal mythology. Eddie Murphy, in any event, will have none of it. Actually, much of his material is devoted to satirizing, not racism, but liberal stereotypes about racism, and there is no better example of this than the show Murphy gave just before Christmas 1984 when he returned as honored guest-host to the television program of which he is an alumnus, *Saturday Night Live*.

Murphy's hallmark is a kind of sassy self-assurance, strangely without malice. He gets off the most biting lines in a sunny manner which magically neutralizes any suspicion that he himself is malicious. But cheeky, he is. Greeting the audience on the Christmas show, he explains that he swore he would never do *Saturday Night Live* again because "the show is *terrible!*" [Hilarious laughter] "I did *48 Hours* and *Trading Places* and I felt like I was an *actor* now. It was like—*Saturday Night Live? Huh!*" Unfortunately, he says, he soon made another movie called *Best Defense*, which failed dismally:

> It turned out to be the worst movie ever done in the history of anything and, all of a sudden, I wasn't that hot no more, so I called up the producer of *Saturday Night Live* and I go, "You still got my dressing room?" . . . So I signed the contract for the Christmas show, and while I was waiting for Christmas to come, sitting in the house, all by myself, somebody brought a script for a movie called *Beverly Hills Cop*. [Sustained applause and cheering] *Beverly Hills Cop* is a hit! All of a sudden I'm an actor again! But it's too late to pull out! . . . Now listen. Not everything on this show is

hysterical. They lied to you. You're going to see some things that suck. I want you to be prepared for that.

As can be seen, Murphy's material contains a strong strain of veracity. At this point in his opening monologue, in any case, Murphy, in a smooth transition, adopts the solemn manner of a person about to make an appeal for victims of cerebral palsy. "Now before we get onto the funny stuff," he says, "I want you to see something that I take very seriously. I want you to watch something. Watch this." After a dissolve, Murphy is back, speaking with the utmost gravity:

A lot of people talk about racial prejudice. And some people have gone so far as to say that actually there are two Americas, one black and one white. [Sternly] But talk is cheap. So I decided to look at the problem myself, first hand, to go underground, and actually *experience* America [he drops his voice] as a white man.

Da da! trumpets blare portentously. "I hired the best makeup people in the business," Murphy continues, maintaining dramatic intensity. "If I was going to pass as a white man, everything had to be *perfect*." We watch as Murphy is transformed into a rather plausible, pink-faced white man. He studied for this role very carefully, the actor explains, watching the television serial *Dynasty* ("See? See how they walk? I got to remember to keep my butt real tight") and reading Hallmark greeting cards ("You always mean lots more to me, than you could ever guess. For you have done so much to fill, my life with happiness"). At last he is ready!

As the audience screams with laughter, Eddie Murphy begins his life "underground" as a white man. The first thing he discovers, when he tries to buy a newspaper, is that white people don't have to pay for things like black people. *For white people, everything is free!* Riding a bus, he makes another startling discovery. On the bus there is only one other black man, and when he gets off at 45th Street, the conductor, thinking there are no more blacks aboard, turns on dance-band music and the passengers begin to dance and party, turning the bus into a kind of mobile Club Med resort. *So this is the way white people really live!* Murphy intones: "The problem was much more serious than I had ever imagined."

His next experience as a white man is borrowing money from a bank. He is first received by a black loan officer, who points out regretfully that "Mr. White," although he wants to borrow $50,000, has no collateral, no credit, and even no ID. But the bank manager, seeing that the client is a *white man*, sends the loan officer off and grants the loan with no "formalities." Murphy, catching on now to the way things are done in the white world, joins in the bank manager's laughter and, referring to the departed black loan officer, giggles, "What a silly nee-grow!"

As the sketch closes, Murphy, black again, asks, "So what did I learn from all this?" And then, as *My Country, 'Tis of Thee* swells in the background, he concludes solemnly, "Well, I learned that we still have a *very* long way to go in this country before *all* men are *truly* equal. But I'll tell you something. I've got a lot of friends. And we've got a lot of makeup."

This sketch would not seem to need much interpretation. But Eddie Murphy does not let up. In the next sketch he plays the South African bishop, Desmond Tutu, winner of the 1984 Nobel Peace Prize, on a U.S. television talk show where he is upstaged by another guest, Boston College's star quarterback Doug Flutie, winner of football's Heisman Trophy. As Flutie is explaining his "Hail Mary" pass, wherein he drops back, closes his eyes, and prays "Hail Mary, full of grace, let this ball fall into the hands of your humble servant, the wide receiver, amen" (Boston College is a Jesuit school), Murphy/Tutu fidgets clumsily with the Heisman Trophy. Finally he breaks off the arm, which draws down the wrath of the talk-show host: "You fix it! Do it! Quickly! Okay?" "But I didn't break it on purpose!" cries the woebegone Murphy/Tutu in a South African accent. "And what about that stuff on your hair? What is that?" demands the host irritably. "That's just Carefree Curl," pleads Murphy. "It just makes it curlier." When Murphy tries to bandage the broken arm with the ribbon from his Nobel Prize (Murphy, joyously: "It is a unifying symbol of our commitment to fighting racism all over the world!''), the host says wearily, ''Well, that's real nice, Tutu.'' And when the bishop's good-hearted but clumsy attempts to repair the trophy finally destroy it utterly, the host turns to Flutie, obviously the show's real star, and says, ''Thanks for coming, Doug! . . . And . . . uh . . . yuh, Tutu, if you win anything else, come back, okay?''

But if Murphy's treatment of Bishop Tutu is disrespectful, the working over he gives a (fictitious) Black Studies professor named Shebaz K. Morton during the program's ''Black History Minute'' is merciless. At the opening of the Black History Minute, Murphy appears as Morton, glaring censoriously at the audience. This in itself brings a laugh. ''I don't see what's so funny!'' snaps Murphy, which brings even more laughter. When he fluffs a word, Murphy barks, ''So I messed up. *Shut up!* You're not going to make me smile!'' He then proceeds to tell the story of George Washington Carver, with a few modifications.

Now, George Washington Carver, needless to say, is a truly sacrosanct American figure. Born a slave, he became one of the country's first educated black men and made important contributions in the field of agricultural chemistry, teaching soil improvement and diversification of crops and finding hundreds of new uses for the peanut, the soybean, and the sweet potato, thus stimulating substantially the agricultural productivity of the South. In Murphy's satire, however, the object is not George Washington Carver himself but the gross distortions introduced by the teaching of ''black history.''

One night (Murphy begins in his persona of Shebaz K. Morton), Doctor Carver was having a few friends over for dinner, and one of them said, ''Excuse me, George, what's that you're putting on your bread?'' It turns out that it is nothing less than a butter substitute made from peanuts, the recipe for which Carver gives two of his guests, ''Skippy'' Williamson and ''Jif'' Armstrong, preferring himself to work on a method for compressing peanuts into phonograph needles. Thereupon Skippy and Jif, both white men, *steal* Carver's recipe, patent it, and reap untold fortunes, leaving Carver to die penniless and insane, still trying to play a phonograph record with a peanut. Thus our

Black History Minute. (The real Carver died sane, wealthy, and widely admired, founding at his death a research foundation at the Tuskegee Institute.)

Beverly Hills Cop is a fairly conventional *film policier*, which without Murphy's star performance would certainly not be one for the history books, although it also has a talented young director, Martin Brest. Murphy plays Foley, a Detroit police detective whose best friend is murdered early in the movie. The trail leads Foley, on leave, to Beverly Hills, where the police procedures provide some comic contrast with those of Detroit. (The politeness of the police of the whole Los Angeles area must be somewhat incredible to anyone accustomed only to the inner-city police of the great metropolises of the East.) Foley, after scenes of high adventure, breaks open an international crime ring and avenges the death of his friend.

If this role had been accepted by Sylvester Stallone, an actor not without talent, the result would no doubt have been a straight action movie with vengeance as its driving force. With Eddie Murphy in the role it became what is known in the trade as an "action comedy." But the outline of the plot has remained quite unchanged, and almost no alterations at all were made to accommodate the fact that Murphy is black. He is simply a Detroit cop. In only one scene is there even any mention of race, when with no reservation Murphy bluffs his way into one of Beverly Hills's top hotels by raising his voice and charging the hotel with discriminating against him because he is a "Negro." (It is not discriminating, and both he and the audience know this full well.)

What the authors of the film have done is simply to ornament the basic story line with a number of occasions where Murphy can display his glib, sunny, comic talents. In one of this best scenes, he impersonates a federal-government inspector in order to intimidate a whole warehouse full of the chief villain's private security guards. One of Murphy's principal stocks in trade, in fact, is brassy, fast-talking impersonations in which he assumes another identity in order to get past some obstacle. In this one film alone he impersonates a government inspector, a correspondent for *Rolling Stone*, a street black involved in the cocaine trade, and a homosexual lover of the villain. The fact that in most of these cases Murphy is a black man outwitting and getting the better of white men might add a certain something to the scene for some viewers, but perhaps not that much. Heroes have a way of being smarter, stronger, or more courageous than their adversaries in any case. That's what a hero is.

So here we have young Eddie Murphy, the first black star to make it to the very, very top in Hollywood—and I mean $25 million for a six-picture deal. His father was a policeman. His stepfather is a plant foreman. Eddie Murphy does not take drugs. He does not drink. He even goes light on caffeine, preferring herbal tea. He wears a small gold crucifix around his neck. Murphy offers a sharp contrast to the other outstanding black movie comic today, Richard Pryor, who almost burned himself to death a few years ago while freebasing cocaine and whose whole comic persona is based on the stereotype of the feckless, improvident, black wastrel—be he junky, wino, pimp, or just general lowlife.

The differences between the two men, both extremely gifted, might be partly generational. When Martin Luther King, Jr., was assassinated, Richard Pryor was twenty-seven, Eddie Murphy was six. In Richard Pryor's impressionable years, Governor George Wallace of Alabama was one of the country's leading racists. In Eddie Murphy's, Wallace had become the black man's friend, winning massive black support when he reentered politics. There are no longer prominent men in the United States like the old Governor Wallace. Eddie Murphy did not need to read about this in a sociology text; he has just been keeping his eyes open.

Conquest of the supreme heights by a black entertainer—let alone a hat trick, three in the same season—is unprecedented. Murphy, Cosby, and Michael Jackson might be the first black superstars of post-racist America.

12

The 'Auteur' Cult: Truffaut and What France's Nouvelle Vague Was All About

W HO IS THE author of a movie? What is an "auteur," anyway? What was in the mind of the late François Truffaut and his friends when they thrust this idea upon the world some thirty years ago? The concept has certainly served its purpose as far as the Truffaut circle is concerned, in that it contributed effectively to establishing its members as France's leading and most talked-about film directors. But the notion, at best hazily grasped in America, has led to something of an auteur cult, which bids fair to be with us for some time.

The French origins of the auteur concept are not lost in the mists of history. It was launched in the 1950s by a French journal, *Cahiers du Cinéma*, to which Truffaut himself contributed, as well as Eric Rohmer, Jean-Luc Godard, Claude Chabrol, and Jacques Rivette—all of them now better known as directors than as critics. [In the 1960s, the present author was also a contributor, as well an actor in Jean-Luc Godard's *Pierrot le Fou*.]

As is clear from an anthology drawn from the early years of the journal (*Cahiers du Cinéma: The 1950s, Neo-Realism, Hollywood, New Wave*, edited by Jim Hillier), the opinions of the Cahiers critics were rather bizarre. Truffaut considered Nicholas Ray's *Johnny Guitar* with Joan Crawford a "triumph." Anyone who rejects this movie, he wrote in his impassioned style of the period, "will never recognize inspiration, poetic intuition, or . . .

205

an idea, a good film, or even cinema itself." He thought Frank Tashlin's *The Girl Can't Help It* with Jayne Mansfield was "more than a good film, more than a funny film . . . it is a kind of masterpiece of the genre." Of Jean Seberg's performance in Otto Preminger's *Bonjour Tristesse*, Truffaut wrote, "Everything is perfect; this kind of sex appeal hasn't been seen on the screen." And Truffaut's Cahiers colleagues had equally curious views.

How could a gang of young Frenchmen with such peculiar tastes launch upon the world such an influential concept? That so many of them shortly became successful filmmakers was no doubt the decisive factor. But there was also another factor at work.

France protects artistic achievement as perhaps no other country in the world. By the exercise of the so-called *droit moral* (literally "moral law"), artists of all kinds retain artistic control over the art they produce. An art dealer cannot modify a Picasso he owns in order to increase what he thinks will be its salability—this seems reasonable enough. But a French movie producer can no more alter a film he has financed than an art dealer can alter his Picasso. The producer can distribute the film, exhibit it, perhaps make a fortune from it, but he is powerless to modify it. He can starve his director for cash during the making of the movie. He can threaten never to employ him again. He can shout. He can scream. But even though he owns the film, he cannot tamper with it in any way. The director is the film's creator, its author. The state protects his art as a thing of utmost value. This is no "theory." This is the law.

Indeed, Truffaut and his friends never enunciated any such thing as an "auteur theory." Misunderstandings of the French notion were due in some measure to mistranslation. What the Cahiers critics were calling for in plain French was, after all, *une politique des auteurs*, which means "an author policy." As was only reasonable from their national experience, these critics felt that everyone already knew that legally the director was the author of a movie. At least this was known by all Frenchmen—and these were the people they were addressing.

Unfortunately, the Cahiers critics claimed, France was cursed with a generation of filmmakers who failed to exercise their prerogative as creators of this new art, remaining subservient to the country's literary class. The Cahiers group particularly hated both Claude Autant-Lara, who had recently done an excellent film adaptation of Raymond Radiguet's renowned *The Devil in the Flesh*, and Jean Delannoy, who had directed an equally skillful version of André Gide's *Symphonie Pastorale*.

But the group disliked France's reigning quality directors even when they worked from original screenplays. Truffaut proclaimed in a celebrated 1954 essay, "A Certain Tendency of the French Cinema," that French movies were dominated by seven or eight leading screenwriters. And it was these screenwriters, he said, who were the instrument of subservience to the French literary class and its morbid values. The art of the cinema, said Truffaut and the other Cahiers critics, lay in the actual filming, not the story—as Hollywood, according to them, knew so well. Hollywood, wrote Eric Rohmer, was to the cinema what Florence was to Italian painting of the Quattrocento.

The Cahiers critics were not completely uninformed about the functioning of the classical studio system in Hollywood. They knew, roughly, that a director was handed a screenplay from his studio's story department which he was unable to change substantially. They knew that once he had shot a scene—much of it, in the American style, all the way through from a variety of angles and distances—the whole mass of developed film was then turned over to the studio's editing department and that, for all practical purposes, the director might never see it again.

Knowledge of film theory might have indicated that these new critics should give at least the editor as well as the director credit for the "filmic" qualities of the end product, but the Cahiers critics were single-minded. Ignoring the editor—who was a subordinate figure in France—they maintained it was the Hollywood director's choice of "shots," his angles, his framing, his lighting, his placing of actors and properties on the set, his ordering of movement, that constituted the essence of film. And if the director (even without the support of a droit moral) could impose on these variables his personality, and even better express a world view, he qualified as a true "author." Truffaut,

Rohmer, Godard, and the other young Cahiers critics complained that most contemporary French directors thought the essence of a movie was the story. The directors were not only wrong, these critics said, they were witlessly forfeiting their opportunity to become masters of a new art.

The virulence of the Cahiers critics' attack on the Paris movie establishment of the time can only be understood as proceeding from a deep-seated cluster of envies. First, as is now widely acknowledged in France, the Cahiers critics were all desperate to direct films themselves, and almost any argument that came to hand to discredit their seniors was welcome. Also, as movie addicts since childhood, and actually preferring film to literature, they strongly resented the traditional prestige accorded in France to letters as well as to the other older arts. They wanted film, their favorite art, to have its Tolstoy, its Mozart, its Michelangelo.

Moreover, they were in burning revolt—and this is of extreme importance—not only against the prestige of letters in France but against the prevailing values of fashionable Left Bank literature: its negativism, its pessimism, its Marxism. It is this aspect of Cahiers criticism and, later, of the New Wave films the Cahiers critics made when they became directors, that has effectively eluded most foreign observers. But Jim Hillier, a British scholar, notes it carefully in an excellent introduction to the Cahiers anthology. He quotes an American critic, John Hess, as saying that for the Cahiers group an auteur in the last analysis was a film director who expressed an optimistic image of human potentialities: "By reaching out emotionally and spiritually to other human beings and/or to God, one could transcend the isolation imposed on one by a corrupt world."

In his later years Truffaut admitted to me that he and his friends had greatly overplayed the "filmic" side of movie authorship; the story counted a great deal. The simple fact was that the Cahiers critics actually preferred the hopeful little plots of Hollywood B movies with their scorned happy endings to the *noir, maudit* pessimism so in vogue among French literary intellectuals. Nor was this a case of the high using the low in order to cudgel the middle. Truffaut, for one, was working-class, a high-school dropout with genuinely popular taste, fiercely resentful of the values the contemporary high culture wanted to impose on him.

Intermittently, in fact, he said as much, as in "A Certain Tendency of the French Cinema." In a scathing attack on France's two leading screenwriters of the period, Jean Aurenche and Pierre Bost, he heatedly accuses them of introducing "anti-militarist," "anti-bourgeois," and "blasphemous" elements into their adaptation of Radiguet's *The Devil in the Flesh* and cites no fewer than five screenplays in which they are guilty of blasphemy. He accuses another celebrated screenwriter, too, of blasphemy, and charges actor-director Marcello Pagliero—"the Sartre of the cinema"—with using dirty language. He cites with apparent low regard film examples of both homosexuality and "semi-pornography."

Truffaut comes right out with it. Modern literature, he says in strong disapproval, is half-Bovary, half-Kafka. In consequence, "Not a film is shot in France any more in which the authors don't think they're redoing *Madame Bovary*." The dominant characteristic of the period's ruling school of French cinema, he asserts, is its "anti-bourgeois" bias, a bias not shared by France's common people. In time audiences will understand, Truffaut writes earnestly, that the abject family shown by the French cinema is their family, that the thwarted religion is their religion. They will have little reason to feel gratitude, he says, toward a French cinema which has gone to such pains to show them life "as seen from a fourth-floor apartment overlooking Saint-Germain-des Près." Truffaut is referring to the residence of Jean-Paul Sartre, notorious for his infatuation with the far Left.

If these remarks have a conservative cast (to say the least), they are part and parcel of Truffaut's orientation in the French intellectual life of the 1950s, his formative years. France at the time had a powerful and aggressive Communist party, the country's largest, which won a full quarter of the popular vote at election time and was far stronger in the intellectual and artistic communities. The French movie world, as so much else, was sharply divided, Paris's two leading film societies being the

Communist-run *Ciné-Club Universitaire* and the anti-Communist (or at minimum scrupulously non-Communist) *Ciné-Club du Quartier Latin*. Truffaut, like Eric Rohmer (*My Night at Maude's, Claire's Knee*) and most of the other Cahiers people including their spiritual leader, film historian André Bazin, were affiliated, naturally, with the *Ciné-Club du Quartier Latin*. Director Claude Chabrol recalls a meeting when the future leaders of the *nouvelle vague* were gathered in one of their homes listening to a "murky" speech by Eric Rohmer, of which all he can remember is the impassioned conclusion: "We must vote for Pinay!" Since Antoine Pinay was a classical-conservative French premier and finance minister, it was the equivalent of a gang of American artistic hotheads gathered to support Robert Taft or even Barry Goldwater. The political atmosphere of French artistic life in Truffaut's early years has escaped most foreign observers entirely, but Truffaut formed and expressed his basic alignments in this period. Nor did he ever change.

The case could be made that Truffaut was "apolitical," in the sense that he did not wake up every morning worrying about the state of the body politic. He lived for movies. But there are apolitical people alienated from their society and others who accord it their unstated but nonetheless powerful allegiance. Given the opinions expressed by Truffaut in the essay quoted above, it was not hard for General de Gaulle or his culture minister, André Malraux, to grasp that France had produced in Truffaut and the Cahiers group a school of filmmakers whose conservatism, both cultural and political, was profound. Once de Gaulle returned to power in 1958, Malraux did everything in his power to push them to the fore. Jean-Luc Godard later careened off to the radical Left for some years, but by and large the Gaullists had taken the Cahiers group's true measure. During the eight years of France's Algerian war, for example, a national trauma comparable in some ways to America's war in Vietnam, *Cahiers du Cinéma* never published one word against it.

It was not to be expected that an aesthetic doctrine conceived under such special circumstances as the *politique des auteurs* could be exported intact. Yet there is some irony in the fact that

Hollywood—a source of such inspiration to a group of young Frenchmen engaged some three decades ago in a populist rebellion against their country's intellectual elite—should have received back in the "auteur theory" a highly elitist doctrine.

For if the circumstances and basic thrust of French auteurism were hardly understood at all in America, the notion that the director of a film was a person of enormous importance was grasped quite readily.

It was not ever thus. F. Scott Fitzgerald, who did his time in Hollywood, considered directors "glorified cameramen," and James Cagney, who saw them from another angle, called them "pedestrian workmen, mechanics," some of whom "couldn't direct you to a cheap delicatessen."

For the general American public, meanwhile, most film directors had been simply invisible. On January 1, 1940, the *New York Times* reviewed a new movie of Victor Hugo's *Hunchback of Notre Dame*, starring Charles Laughton, without once mentioning the director's name. The director, William Dieterle, was well known, highly paid, and had made any number of major films, including *Juarez*, with Bette Davis and Paul Muni, and *The Life of Emile Zola* and *The Story of Louis Pasteur*, both also with Paul Muni—this in a period when biographical pictures were among Hollywood's most prestigious products. But Dieterle's artistic contribution as director was not considered worth mentioning. It was not, as it were, a "Dieterle" movie, it was a Charles Laughton movie, or perhaps even a Victor Hugo movie.

Giant newspaper advertisements for films in those days rarely featured the name of the director. Well into the 1950s, the reviewers for the *New York Times* often failed to mention the director or cited him in a perfunctory manner, whether he was Raoul Walsh, David Lean, or Akira Kurosawa. As late as the early 1960s when the American director Martin Ritt arrived in France, he was dazzled at the status that being a director gave him there. "In America even a director's *mother* doesn't know what he does for a living," exclaimed the man who was to film *Hud* and *Norma Rae* and had already directed *Edge of the City.* "But here!" he exclaimed. "What a country! Look! My name! *Big print!*"

By the time the new French idea came along, things had changed in Hollywood, of course. The studio system had broken down, and it almost seemed as if Hollywood was positively waiting for auteurism in its American incarnation—which often consisted mainly of surrounding the director with a previously nonexistent nimbus of glory and giving him credit for great powers, some real, some not.

The "auteur theory" arrived, moreover, at a time when the American cinema was vastly increasing its prestige as an art and people wanted to personalize these new artistic achievements, if sometimes speciously, by singling out their creators. Hollywood directors, although they still rarely had the "final cut," had indeed expanded their authority: they usually supervised their film's editing and contributed to many aspects of the film's production from which they had previously been excluded. And now they had this new notion, fresh from France, in accordance with which—as it now came to be said—the movies were truly "a director's medium."

But the new notion produced an unrealistically inflated idea of the director's authority. When Bill Conti, composer of the scores of the *Rocky* series, was called in to do a fresh score for *The Seduction of Joe Tynan*, the first movie written by and starring Alan Alda, he thought he had best deal prudently with the film's director and presumptive auteur, Jerry Schatzberg. What had Schatzberg disliked about the first attempt at a score? he asked. "Oh, I liked it fine," Conti reports the director as saying. "Alan didn't like it." "Then what am I doing talking to you for?" the musician replied somewhat bluntly. "Let me see Alan."

For contrary to the popular understanding of this new "auteur theory"—and it being Hollywood, not Paris—Jerry Schatzberg, the director, was not the lord of all he beheld on the set of *The Seduction of Joe Tynan*. Most of the key decisions were made by Alan Alda. And two years later, when it came time to film the second movie Alda had written, *The Four Seasons*, he significantly decided to carry the process a step further and direct it himself, which he did successfully, a practice he has continued.

Nowadays, Clint Eastwood also directs most of his own movies. Sylvester Stallone, who recently brought forth *Rocky IV*, took over the direction of the *Rocky* series from the second film on. Two years ago Barbra Streisand directed her own hit movie, *Yentl*. Woody Allen has directed his films for many years, rain or shine, a real auteur. Robert Redford, although he has yet to direct a movie in which he plays the lead, maintains close control when he is simply acting. A screenwriter who wrote one of the recent pictures in which Redford was merely the leading man had little to do with the movie's prospective director while the film was in development. "But I went to see Redford with the new pages every day," he says. A roughly comparable story is told by a screenwriter developing a screenplay for Sean Connery.

The basic pattern is plain. In today's Hollywood, a place of essentially independent productions, the "power player" on a movie set is the person *in whose name the money has been raised*. This is usually a leading actor or actress, who occasionally also directs. It is often a powerful, creative producer. And only now and then is it a glamor director. Hollywood skeptics claim, in fact, that the larger the number of people who recognize the director's name, the greater are a film's chances of failure. Michael Cimino went straight from *The Deerhunter* to *Heaven's Gate*, and Francis Ford Coppola followed *The Godfather* and *Apocalypse Now* with *One From the Heart* and *Rumble Fish*.

Naturally, hundreds of important artistic decisions on a movie are made by people other than the "power player," but many of the most conspicuous things about a film are still decided by the man who "calls the shots," and who that man is to be is sometimes the occasion for fierce struggles. Some months ago an interesting Hollywood battle royal took place between the star Jack Nicholson and Robert Towne, the celebrated screenwriter of Roman Polanski's *Chinatown*, now risen to the rank of director and presumably a new auteur. Deep into preparation for the highly touted *The Two Jakes*, sharp differences appeared. Nicholson and Towne fought bitterly. The issues were not resolved. As things now stand, *The Two Jakes* not only has no auteur, but there will be no picture. [The film has since been completed under Nicholson's direction.]

In a knock-down-drag-out battle between a director and a major star, once a film is before the cameras, it is almost always the star who wins. During the much-trumpeted bringing together of Marlon Brando and Jack Nicholson in Arthur Penn's *The Missouri Breaks* some years ago, Brando wanted to play a scene in "drag"—i.e., dressed as a woman. Penn hated the idea. Brando had his way, however. For directors can be dismissed in mid-production. It has happened. But with the movie half-finished, if Marlon Brando had left the film, all his scenes would have needed to be reshot. It would have cost the production millions. This is why high-prestige directors often avoid using stars of the first rank in their pictures. Even celebrated directors know, if it comes to a donnybrook, that they are likely to lose.

Indeed, directors usually lost battles with major stars even when the director is producing the movie himself. There must have been moments when Francis Ford Coppola cursed the day he ever cast the notorious Marlon Brando in what amounted to little more than a cameo role as Colonel Kurtz in his *Apocalypse Now*. There they sat, wet, marooned in the jungles of the Philippines, wiped out once already by a typhoon, down millions and millions of dollars, but if Brando didn't like the way Coppola was planning to do a scene, he'd sulk in his tent. And, say what you will about Hollywood, it is hard to cut Mr. Kurtz out of even a loose adaptation of *Heart of Darkness*.

All of which has led much of Hollywood to feel that these days American directors—reversing their historical obscurity—are often credited with powers they simply do not possess and that all the attention paid them in the press and in film schools has given the public an exaggerated notion of their control over the finished product.

Critics of the director-as-auteur principle fall into different schools, of which screenwriters—once called by a studio wag "a necessary evil"—are probably the most vociferous. "In the beginning was the word!" they go about crying, although they also tell stories making fun of themselves, such as the joke about the new actress so ignorant in the ways of Hollywood that, wanting a role in a new movie, she slept with the writer. Film writers won a prestige victory some years ago, however, when *Time* magazine, at the head of each movie review, began listing first the director and then the screenwriter, almost as co-authors.

There is merit in this approach, as some of the most distinguished and harmonious films in cinema history have been made by writer-director teams. All the great Vittorio de Sica films at the height of Italy's post-World War II neorealism were scripted by the Italian novelist Cesare Zavattini, and all the imposing run of Marcel Carné films in the late 1930s and 1940s (*Quai des Brumes*, *Le Jour se lève*, *Children of Paradise*) were scripted by the French poet Jacques Prévert. De Sica before and after Zavattini, and Carné before and after Prévert, were simply not the same.

The writers' case in its fully developed form holds that John Ford's *The Grapes of Wrath* and Howard Hawks's *Of Mice and Men*—movies by two different directors but both based on works by John Steinbeck—have more in common than *The Grapes of Wrath* and some other film by John Ford, say, *The Quiet Man*. This position—absolute heresy for a pure auteur-ist—is far from absurd, and the history of sound cinema over the more than four decades since *The Grapes of Wrath* is strewn with persuasive examples.

The director-writer rivalry is agreeably absent, of course, in the case of such directors as Federico Fellini and Ingmar Bergman, who either script or co-script all their own screenplays, thereby attaining an uncommon degree of artistic unity. A young member of this privileged group is Hungary's Istvan Szabo (*Mephisto*; *Colonel Redl*), who, a director-writer himself, astonished readers of the *New York Times* during a New York Film Festival by his blatantly pro-writer stance. There's nothing a director needs to know about moviemaking, he said in an interview (conducted by the present author), "that couldn't be learned by an intelligent high-school graduate in two weeks." Really to shape a film, he felt, it was absolutely necessary for a director either to write or to co-write the screenplay himself.

Unfortunately it is not every director who, like Fellini, Bergman, or Szabo, has the talent required to write his own screen-plays. One of the most pernicious effects of the misinterpreted French "auteur theory" in America has been that it has given certain highly praised directors such as Francis Ford Coppola and Michael Cimino, cited earlier—both possessors of dazzling directorial skills—the notion that, since directing was all that really counted, they could trust themselves to carry out such a subsidiary activity as writing the story. Curiously enough, both Coppola and Cimino have delivered workmanlike screenplays when writing under other people's direction, but when they turn to writing scripts for their own films they are seized by a certain hysteria, a kind of *folie des grandeurs*.

They would do well to take a page from the book of one of France's leading directors, Louis Malle, now mainly resident in the United States. Although Malle has not had the best of luck in choosing American stories, he is the first to admit that two of his greatest French films, *Le Feu Follet* ("The Fire Within") and *Lacombe Lucien*, owe much of their excellence to the quality of the writing. *Le Feu Follet* is based very closely on a French novel of the same name by Drieu la Rochelle, who (although a fascist) was a quite brilliant writer. *Lacombe Lucien* was written expressly for Malle by a perhaps equally brilliant young French novelist named Patrick Modiano. But this "splitting of the credit" runs counter to certain Hollywood directors' urge to increase their personal glory—to which American critics have accommodated themselves. Sydney Pollack, a highly skilled director of films as varied as *Tootsie* and *Out of Africa*, but who regularly subordinates himself to his "material," is simply not as glamorous to today's critics as Francis Ford Coppola with all his fiascos.

But writers are not the only ones cast in the shadow by the director cult. The film editor, now virtually the forgotten man of filmmaking, has declined greatly in public awareness since his glory days in the Soviet Union when Sergei Eisenstein declared that editing—more than story and even shooting—was the true heart of cinema. Since a movie's editor is the artisan whose work is most difficult to distinguish from that of the director himself, "an inevitable tension infects the director-editor relationship," writes Ralph Rosenblum, editor of Woody Allen's *Annie Hall* and many other major films. "Directors never give special mention to their editors when they lope up to receive their Oscar," he writes in his excellent book on editing (*When the Shooting Stops . . . the Cutting Begins*), "lest an overeager critic surmise that the film has been in trouble and was saved by heavy editorial doctoring."

Another distinguished editor, Tom Priestly (*This Sporting Life*; *Marat/Sade*; *Deliverance*), says: "We editors know that we cannot really judge each other's work without knowing the original material. Many a lousy film has been brilliantly edited, and many a brilliant film has been just competently put together."

There are nonetheless movies known in the industry to have been "made in the cutting room," though awareness of this does not seem strong enough in the outside world to prevent most film critics, in the present flowering of the director cult, from quite routinely thinking directors responsible for everything. Pauline Kael of the *New Yorker*, at the appearance of *The Night They Raided Minsky's*, wrote: "Director William Friedkin proves his sense of cinema again by remarkable intersplicing of newsreels and striking use of black and white fade-ins to color." The intersplicing and fade-ins were done many months after Friedkin had left the picture.

Top Hollywood producers or producer teams have so much real power, and make so much money, that they are not often heard sobbing at the Bel Air Hotel about being unrecognized auteurs. But the degree of control over both story and shooting exercised by such teams as Zanuck-Brown (since *Jaws*) and Chartoff and Winkler (since *Rocky*) is considerable.

Two other producers who illustrate the immense influence producers can have on the artistic qualities of a movie are Irwin Allen, on the popular level, and, in the younger generation, Britain's David Puttnam. In the 1970s American cinema was all agog at something caller the "disaster movie." Irwin Allen, who made *The Towering Inferno* and *The Poseidon Adventure*, was the acknowledged champion of the genre and, having seen him at work, I am prepared to give him full credit as his movies' auteur. Allen drew very well—like a professional draftsman. On an artist's sketch pad, he would draw up the plan of shot after shot. Here: the machinery. Here: the flames. Here: Paul Newman. Here: the camera. Innumerable writers came and went showing him dialogue changes for future sequences. The director—talented, to judge by his other work—was plainly reduced to chief executive officer when he worked for Irwin Allen.

David Puttnam's artistic contribution, although crucial, is of a different color, consisting essentially of the inception of the project, its general shaping, and the dynamism to pull it all together and carry it through. Puttnam made his first big appearance on the American scene with *Chariots of Fire*, directed by Hugh Hudson, which tells of the victories of two British runners at the Olympic Games in the 1920s. He followed this with another great success with no stars: Sydney Schanberg's story *The Killing Fields*, set against the Khmer Rouge massacre in Cambodia. Puttnam entrusted this politically loaded screenplay to a young English television director named Roland Joffé, who has been called by people who don't share his politics "a Marxist woolly head." But those who take celebrating victories in sport as a sign of reborn cultural assertiveness might want to give the matter further thought, as both *Chariots of Fire* and *The Killing Fields* were brainchildren of the same David Puttnam.

In the late 1960s, unsurprisingly, a challenge to the auteur principle appeared from the collectivist Left. The most famous of the cinema collectives of the period was probably the so-called "Dziga Vertov Group" (after an innovative director from early Soviet cinema), the best-known member of which was France's Jean-Luc Godard, appearing in one of his several incarnations. Having been present at the creation, as it were, Godard no doubt found it fitting to celebrate the "death" of the auteur. All members of the Dziga Vertov Group, it was claimed, were paid equally. Every shot was discussed by all. "It's an attempt to smash the usual dictatorship of the director," explained Godard, "to try to make no hierarchy." If the Dziga Vertov Group produced anything of artistic value, it is not widely known. Before long Godard, not notorious for his stability, abandoned the endeavor, which was a violation of the French droit moral in any case. (Actually Godard is Swiss.) In his newest phase he acknowledges what he calls (in English) a "move" toward religion in his *Hail, Mary*, a controversial retelling of the Virgin Birth in modern dress, with the Virgin Mary working in a gas station in Switzerland.

The conclusion of the American "auteur" debate is less clear-cut than some would like. A movie is, after all, a kind of team effort, but with leadership of the pack—in the United States—varying from one film to another. The cinema obviously is a prodigious "director's medium" compared to the theater, but not all directors exploit the full possibilities of the medium or exercise genuine directorial primacy. Control of the story line, furthermore, is much more important than people who approach films from the "visual" side often think.

There are problems of "authorship," meanwhile, which in some cases may never be solved. Most critics think John Huston's *The Asphalt Jungle* is a brilliantly directed movie, but the late Trevor Howard, who had a frustrating experience with Huston on another film, refuses to give him any credit for it all. "Wonderful actors," he says. "A wonderful cameraman. A wonderful story. A wonderful editor. Huston didn't even need to come out on the set."

By the time of his death in 1985 François Truffaut was more esteemed, and certainly more loved, than even those directors he had so envied as a young man. And the paradox is that he is not remembered at all for the "filmic" qualities of his work. He never attained the technical virtuosity of which he was in such awe. No feats of dazzling, masterly cinema artistry are attached to his name. His best films, like his first, *The 400 Blows*, are quite simple. "Children and women are my best subjects," he said with some wryness late in his life, and he is admired, in contradiction to some of his most passionately held principles, for his characteristic stories: a little naive, some of them a little sentimental, simple, hopeful.

Truffaut tried his hand at various other types of films, frequently with indifferent success. He made movies about *crimes passionels*, the best of which was *The Soft Skin*. He made movies that the French call *série noire* after a famous publisher's collection of crime fiction (*Shoot the Piano Player*). He made several pictures about love and passion (*The Story of Adèle H, Jules and Jim*). His most spectacular failures were a Ray Bradbury film he directed in English called *Fahrenheit 451* and a movie inspired by Henry James called *The Green Room*, which was such a catastrophe that United Artists decided to close its French production office, which had been responsible for the picture.

Most of the above films—some acceptable but not really recognizable as the work of Truffaut—ranged from nondescript to bad to really terrible, and if he had made only them he would have left no mark on the cinema at all. But they are not what people mean by a "Truffaut movie."

Real "Truffaut movies" are a particular series of films he made about children or young adults, most of the stories autobiographical or with strong autobiographical overtones: *The 400 Blows*; the "France" episode in *Love at Twenty*; *Stolen Kisses*; *Bed and Board*; *The Wild Child*; *Small Change*; and *Day For Night*, known in French by the highly evocative title (for the French) *La Nuit Américaine* ("American Night"), a movie about the making of a movie in which Truffaut plays a director who is hard of hearing, as he was himself. People often feel quite touched by these films. In a mysterious way they feel that they know the man who made them, and that he is telling them something about human beings like themselves.

Truffaut had a miserable childhood. His hearing was bad. In his teens he worked as a welder, and not a good one, and he prized things that many people took for granted. He never had the cushion of security that allowed him to toy with despair as with a stylish luxury. As a child he took refuge in films, but he simply could not abide a cinema that told him, in accordance with the modish ideas of the Marxianized French elite culture of his early years, that the world was a rotten place, evil, doomed, that French society was unjust and repressive. A world of decay and darkness would not be a world in which François Truffaut would have wanted to live, and he simply wouldn't have it. Truffaut's personal, characteristic movies often contain sadness,

the disappointments and loneliness of youth, but, on examination, they are always about hope.

As for "auteurism" in its period sense, it is now so completely
forgotten in France that at Truffaut's death it was hardly mentioned. Only America concerns itself with such questions now.
In France you cannot even get an argument going. Auteurism,
for the French, is something that happened a long time ago.

Quick Takes

1

Writing Under a Dark Spell: George Orwell's 1984

H AVE THE MAKERS of the film *1984* succeeded in transposing into cinematic form the sterling originality of one of the twentieth century's most famous novels?

The book's skeleton is there. Winston Smith (John Hurt), the movie's protagonist, lives a squalid life in a grimy, greenish-gray, unrecognizable London of the future. (The novel was published in 1949.) Faucets drip, elevators don't work, windows are broken. There is a shortage of razor blades. Smith himself is scrawny, sallow-skinned, dressed in an ill-fitting jumpsuit of Peking blue. He has a wretched little apartment in a block where discolored paint peels off the walls and corridors are filled with litter.

The opening scene is a kind of rally in which perhaps a thousand people, men and women, all dressed like Smith, are being shown a propaganda movie. A banner marked INGSOC (English Socialism) first appears on the screen, then a series of battle newsreels. People alternately scream with rage and cheer madly, all in a peculiarly mechanical, arbitrary way. At high points they stand and, clenching both fists, cross their wrists with arms extended in what seems a combination of the Communist and Fascist salutes. They appear completely mindless.

That night, in his little flat, Smith pulls a chair into an odd angle of the room in order to conceal himself from the television screen (camera) that observes his every move. He produces a diary and writes in it the mysterious words: "To the future or to

225

the past, to a time when thought is free, from the age of Big Brother . . . from a dead man. Greetings.''

The next day, we find Smith at work in a tiny cubicle in a vast prison-like government building. Pieces of paper arrive at his desk via pneumatic tube. He seems to be modifying old newspapers, cutting out parts, rewriting others. Items which he clips out he throws into an incinerator beside his desk.

We sense, somehow, that Smith is dissatisfied with this life. What can he do to brighten it up? He begins a sexual affair with a promiscuous, attractive young co-worker, carried on by stealth because the regime is highly puritanical. But the "Thought Police" keep tabs on everyone and the two are soon arrested and Smith is interrogated by the very quintessence of "INGSOC," O'Brien (played by Richard Burton). Smith is tortured and broken, finally surrendering his life and even his mind to INGSOC and Big Brother.

Little in the film, unfortunately, makes clear that the huge government building where Smith works is Orwell's fabled "Ministry of Truth," and that Smith's job is literally re-writing history. Nor is there anything at all to indicate that the incinerator next to Smith's desk represents Orwell's mythic "memory hole" into which all record of certain events, perfectly true but now inconvenient, disappear forever.

What is missing in the movie, simply, are Orwell's brilliant essays in the novel on "Newspeak," "double-think," "INGSOC." Or on the ingeniously devised Goldstein, the regime's Antichrist on whom everything that goes wrong is blamed—Goldstein playing Trotsky, in short, to Big Brother's Stalin. (Trotsky's real name was Bronstein). Orwell was not a major literary novelist or teller of tales and his towering strength lay in his essays and memoirs: *Homage to Catalonia*, *Down and Out in Paris and London*, "A Hanging," and "Shooting an Elephant."

The world of Orwell's *1984* is divided into three social classes: Proles (animal-like proletarians), Outer Party (Smith), and Inner Party (O'Brien). It is also divided into three countries—Oceania, Eurasia, and Eastasia—which are in a vacillating state of war with one another because, since the age of opulence would otherwise have arrived for everyone, this is necessary in order to preserve material differences between the classes and to keep the Inner Party in power.

But all this discourse, despite writer-director Michael Radford's evident intelligence, is probably impossible to dramatize. The novel's most celebrated lines are INGSOC's ominous maxim: "Who controls the past, controls the future. Who controls the present, controls the past." But Radford was unable to work even this into the dialogue, and it serves as the movie's epigraph.

What is also missing in the film, inevitably, is a sense of the historical moment when the novel appeared. For few books in history can have been published at a more auspicious moment for its purposes than *1984*. There was the blockade of Berlin, the Prague coup, the explosion of the first Soviet atomic bomb, the Communist victory in China, the attack in Korea. The onset of the Cold War created a voracious appetite in the West for works explaining "the Communist mind." For a decade or more, *1984* became almost the definitive popular work on the subject.

Any number of pundits have claimed that *1984* is a warning to America today, that with our computers and polygraphs and electronic surveillance systems *1984* is almost upon us. But the most cursory study of Orwell's life, journals, letters, essays, and even of *1984* itself (which contains scores of roadsigns) reveals that Orwell was possessed of the most bitter hatred of the Soviet Union and Communism, a system which in his time at least aspired to total control over its citizens. It was the totalitarian lust to control men's minds that so alarmed Orwell, not simple information-retrieval systems.

It seems almost forgotten now that Orwell wrote under the dark spell of the famed Moscow trials (1936 to 1938), trials in which one eminent Soviet leader after another confessed to crimes which they not only had not committed, but which defied plausibility. Orwell, although never a Communist, was a radical leftist who fought in the Spanish Civil War in the brigades of Spain's Anarchist-Syndicalists, a decidedly revolutionary faction. He was both fascinated and horrified by what was happening in Moscow. How could revolutionaries of such strength and dedication have committed such incredible crimes?

Now Orwell had never lived in a totalitarian state. He had seen first hand Communist ruthlessness in Spain, but what a Communist regime would do to prepare eminent "deviationists" for a show trial he had to infer from outside the totalitarian world and from glimpses of the totalitarian mentality—which thirsted not only to penetrate all branches of society and to repress all dissent, but to crush "the revolt within the skull."

Anyone watching even the film *1984* must realize that he is seeing a nightmare vision. At the end of *1984*—both novel and movie—Winston Smith not only accepts his death as a sacrifice for the Party but welcomes it ardently, having lost all sense of his own identity. The novel's last lines:

> He was in the public dock, confessing everything, implicating everybody. He was walking down the white-tiled corridor, with the feeling of walking in sunlight, and an armed guard at his back. The long-hoped-for bullet was entering his brain. . . . But it was all right, everything was all right, the struggle was finished. He had won the victory over himself. He loved Big Brother.

Orwell's vision was simply monstrous. Extrapolating from his experiences in Spain and from what he had learned in England of Soviet behavior, Orwell feared that a Communist system that attained world dominion and went to its logical limits might seek to destroy memory, the meaning of language, independent thought, individuality—everything that makes a human being a human being. The world would be populated with mindless robots.

As it happens, this nightmare vision has remained merely that. We now know that in the Communist show trials throughout the Soviet bloc the accused "confessed" far more banally, through fear of torture or of retaliation against their friends and family. Some were tricked, thinking that if they "confessed" they would even be spared. Former Comintern chief Grigori Zinoviev, having made an elaborate and ostentatious confession during the most celebrated of the Moscow trials, took it all back as he stood before Stalin's executioners and cried out that "fascists" were in power in Moscow.

But Orwell's vision has aborted in a way that is more significant and almost reassuring. Some of the results are now in from the two most tightly controlled major societies of modern history, Stalin's Russia and Mao's China—both of which were able to sustain maximum ferocity, interestingly, for just about two-and-a-half decades. In neither case, and despite the most violent efforts, was the regime able to come anywhere near "destroying memory." Documents now abound which seem to prove, at least over this time span, that the consciousness of a people cannot be annihilated.

Many witnesses have now had the occasion to observe both the Soviet Union and China during periods in which "thought control" has been in sharp regression. These witnesses testify that people were terrified into silence by Stalin in the USSR and by Mao and the Red Guards in China, but that their memory and identity were not destroyed. The value of Orwell's *1984*, it appears, was not as prophecy but as a teaching model: on the tendencies implicit in totalitarian tyranny.

Orwell is famous, of course, from the Spanish Civil War onwards, for having "penetrated the Communist mind." But (and this is logical in some ways but extremely bizarre in others) for a time he had difficulty in picturing Nazi Germany as a comparable evil. His own direct experience had been with Communism, not Nazism, and on return to Britain from Spain, sensing the approach of war between the western democracies and Hitler, he was furiously opposed, planning, when war broke out, to go into the antiwar underground, a positive British Weatherperson.

It was only when war actually started in September 1939 that he came to his senses, an awakening certainly made easier for him by the fact that Germany was now allied with the hated Soviet Union. He preserved a stunned silence for several months, but—when next heard from—he had already volunteered to fight for his country. Rejected by the Army because of his tubercular condition, he joined the Home Guard.

One of Orwell's most extraordinary essays is his brilliant

analysis of Kipling, in which he says that a writer can never be fully responsible unless he identifies at least partially with authority—with those who bear the grave weight of command. And yet it took the bugle call and the roll of drums and the news that his country and the other Western democracies were fighting for their lives to make George Orwell realize where his deepest duty lay. It was the biggest lesson, but he had learned it at last. When the enemy shifted from Nazi Germany to the Soviet Union he was ready.

Anyone tempted to play the game called "If George Orwell Were Alive Today . . ." and who thinks the writer might have become a neutralist at a substantial distance from both superpowers, might do well to read his article "Defense of Comrade Zilliacus," published in 1948, the year of the Berlin blockade and two years before his death. He says therein:

> Surely, if one is going to write about foreign policy at all, there is one question that should be answered plainly. It is: "If you *had* to choose between Russia and America, which would you choose?" In spite of all the fashionable chatter of the moment, everyone knows in his heart that we should choose America.

Much earlier, he had expressed his disdain for fashionable anti-American chatter in London leftist intellectual circles. Two million American soldiers were in Britain in 1944 in massive preparation for the invasion of the European Continent, controlled by Hitler, when Orwell heard an English intellectual remark that they were doubtless there to put down a workers' rising. Orwell remarked sardonically that every taxi driver in London knew the Americans were there to invade the Continent. You had to be an intellectual to think they'd come to repress a workers' rising.

Note: The above article, in the *New York Times*, was almost alone in the United States in saying that Orwell's clear antipathy in *1984* was to Communism as practiced in his time in the Soviet

Union. Almost all other writers—and there were hundreds in the eponymous year 1984—maintained that, with our computers and surveillance systems, what Orwell dreaded had now come to pass here, in the West, in America. All this disappeared in a flash at the time of the massacre at Tiananmen Square in Beijing. With Chinese authorities blaring absurdities that absolutely no one in the West believed, with lurid charges and forced, abject "confessions," the American media suddenly, miraculously, rediscovered *1984*'s true meaning. As for the movie version of *1984*, it did very poorly commercially in the United States. In France, on the other hand, where there is a substantial audience for openly ideological films, it was a smash hit, one of the year's big money-makers.

2

The Serene Republic of Letters: The PEN Club

I DIDN'T MEAN TO do it but it all happened Sunday. They made me a superior sort of person and the world will never look the same to me again. They co-opted me.

There had been this tremendous advance brouhaha about the Forty-eighth International PEN Congress in New York, the greatest international gathering of writers the world has ever seen. Omar Cabezas, chief of political direction at the Nicaraguan Interior Ministry, is here (he must have written a book), as well as his compatriot, someone told me, Sandinista poet Nora Astorga, the idealistic beauty who lured that wicked Somozista general into her bedroom, where her Sandinista friends cut off his penis and testicles and stuffed them in his mouth, which pushed her stock as a poet way, way up. You can take my word for it. [Astorga, appointed Nicaraguan ambassador to the United Nations, has since died.]

My friend Yevgeny Yevtushenko from the Soviet Union was supposed to come, and would no doubt have made his speech about "writers speaking across international boundaries." But they wouldn't let him out of Moscow, I don't know why, so the writers-across-boundaries speech was made by American PEN's president, Norman Mailer.

Margaret Randall, who renounced her American citizenship and served in the Cuban militia, is here. Actually I never heard of her as a writer but she called America a "monster country" and said it "posed the greatest danger to mankind in the world today," so she seems qualified for the literary life. American

233

PEN is co-plaintiff in Randall's lawsuit seeking permanent residency status in the United States. [Her American citizenship has since been restored.]

We had a speech yesterday from Director General Amadour Mahtar M'Bow of UNESCO, from which the United States and Britain withdrew because it was a crummy outfit. And the corridors here are thick with Palestinians and correct-thinking South Africans, and the National Endowment for the Arts kicked in $40,000, so you know everything's on the up and up.

Actually there are people here who never killed anybody, and maybe a dozen who never even said America was a danger to mankind: three Nobel Prize winners, Claude Simon of France and Czeslaw Milosz of the United States (by way of Poland), also Günther Grass of West Germany, Nadine Gordimer of South Africa, Kobo Abe of Japan, Mario Vargas Llosa of Peru, and, to be fair, Amos Oz of Israel and a man Fidel Castro kept under house arrest for nine years, Heberto Padilla.

From the United States we have everybody from E. L. Doctorow to Kurt Vonnegut. And in case you don't think that's a very great distance, we have John Updike. And if that's still not great enough, we have our own Nobel Prize winner Saul Bellow.

The only trouble was that there were no more press seats. But a very nice fellow named Phil Bolla from PEN said, My God, I was a distinguished novelist, why didn't I just join PEN, which stands for "Poets, Essayists, and Novelists." Well, it had never occurred to me, I said. I didn't think they wanted people like me. But he said, hell, yes, I could just get one of my friends, Bill Buckley or Tom Wolfe, to sponsor me. But it turned out Wolfe didn't belong and Buckley had just resigned over a question of principle. I had no sponsors. But PEN called back and said the admissions committee had just voted me in anyway. By acclamation, I guess. So there I was, a literary man. It changed my way of looking at things, I can tell you that.

The first big scene was outside the side door of the New York Public Library, where we were all waiting to get in to hear Secretary of State George Shultz pay us homage. Arthur Miller, Arthur Schlesinger, and I were shoulder to shoulder in this mob of about 400 people, who were pushing and shoving, back and forth, and it gave me a real left-wing feeling. I felt like shouting, "Power to the people!" except that it's gone out of style, which is unfortunate. Because Miller, Schlesinger, and I were the people, you see. And J. K. Galbraith wasn't far off. The Left is on the side of the people! Everybody knows that. We were the people.

Then whoosh! Suddenly we went through this Venturi tube and we were all inside, strolling casually within the hallowed halls, with erudition all about us in the library's high-ceilinged main reading room. I walked up to the podium and plunked myself down right in front and found myself in the middle of a very distinguished group of people, well dressed, well groomed, good schools, good accents. This was when I underwent my personality transformation. This is the interesting part.

Now you've got to understand that I think of myself as a small "d" democrat. The only kind of conservative I am is a street corner conservative. Or, if you want liberal, I'm a paleo-liberal, like before liberalism went to the dogs. I'm a practicing equalitarian.

So you'll realize that this transformation that came over me was little short of magical. On the wings of literature I could feel myself being transported to a higher sphere. As we waited for the secretary of state, there was quite a bit of "Barbara! How well you're looking, my dear!" And there is no doubt that the 600 of us gathered in the library were a posh lot. But the real secret, while being Left and consequently heart and soul with the people—which had been indelibly imprinted on my mind in the mob scene outside the library door—was that at the same time we were decidedly superior to most people one met.

Now I can see what you're thinking. If we were so close to the people, and Ronald Reagan swept the people, how come maybe only five or six out of the 600 in that room had voted for him? And how come he seemed to enjoy a reputation in our crowd only a few notches above Adolf Hitler?

Well, I can see you're forgetting about the Third World, which is very big on the literary political agenda these days, as you probably haven't even noticed. And I'll bet you're forgetting about white guilt, or Anglo guilt if you're from the Southwest.

What's more, you're probably so ignorant you don't even know Kurt Vonnegut says literary people are actually the "conscience of the universe." That's our real constituency, you know, out there on Mars or Neptune or someplace. And if American society succumbs for one reason or another, that's where we're going to go to live, on Mars. Me and Kurt.

It pains me to point out to you, furthermore, that we submitted a petition to George Shultz, signed with sixty-six glittering names, telling him how "inappropriate" we felt his appearance was here Sunday night. The administration he represents has done nothing "at home or abroad" to further freedom of expression, it said. Lord knows, you have only to look around you to see how little freedom of expression we have in this country. This administration, moreover, supports a lot of bad people and, in the past, has gone so far as to exclude writers from the United States under the McCarran-Walter Act. How many times do we have to tell you to repeal that thing? We're really about out of patience.

I think Norman Mailer, our president, is a little two-faced. First he tells us that two-thirds to three-quarters of us oppose the administration. Then he says all of us oppose it. Then he gets irritated and declares he's not going to be "pussy-whipped"! Then he says he didn't say it. Then he tells us he invited Shultz "to establish our credibility with the media," by which I suppose he had in view that front-page story in the *New York Times* the next day. But if he thinks a single person in that room cares a fig about what they write about us in that bastion of conservatism, he really is pathetic.

Shultz, by comparison, I considered rather refreshing. He was appropriately humble. He seemed to have some notion of our true worth. The acoustics in that place are terrible but I caught snatches. He said appreciatively that Mailer's invitation to him was "another shining example of that charitable spirit for which New York literary circles have long been famous," which raised a few eyebrows. But then he told us: that literature was "the king of the humanities"; that he considered us "of primary importance for the entire range of thought, culture, and human existence"; that the writer was "at the heart of freedom" and "the creator of freedom"; that we could "illuminate" and "change" the world; and that the power of the writer was "awesome." All true enough, humdrum stuff, really, but it takes a decent man like George Shultz to know his limitations. He's only an economist, you know.

From Shultz on, I must tell you frankly, the congress was all downhill. I don't know whether it was that two-faced Mailer, or whether there was a conspiracy, or if it was the winds of change, but we had these serious panels like "Alienation and the State," parts 1 and 2, and "How Does the State Imagine?" also in two parts. And there were a few crypto-conservatives, sometimes two or three. I really have no idea where these people come from.

Even our old lions haven't roared the way they used to. Gay Talese asked Günther Grass some questions clustered reasonably around George Shultz and Adolf Hitler, but Grass refused to answer questions which mentioned Shultz and Hitler in the same breath. Daniel Ortega's wife asked about the American policy of genocide in Nicaragua, but Robert Hughes said this was a grotesque misuse of the word "genocide."

I knew something was wrong from the moment that Japan's Kobo Abe said that on the day Japan sank the U.S. Pacific Fleet at Pearl Harbor, he was on his way to the library, and whether or not the library would have the book he wanted by Dostoyevsky seemed more important to him than the war. Now he obviously said this to cater to the vulgar popular conception that writers are foolish people, whereas anyone with a brain knows that if writers had been in charge, Japan would never have attacked Pearl Harbor, and that if writers had been running things in Washington we would have surrendered immediately, or found some other intelligent solution to avoid the ridiculousness of war.

Then that Mario Vargas Llosa from Peru said that the state and literature had separate functions, and that they must remain separate, which seemed to imply in a sneaky way that writers had no business setting up shop as arbiters of politics, which really was insufferable. He also said that Shultz seemed to be the only live subject at the congress, the only one to arouse passion. Because it's been Shultz! Shultz! Shultz! Should we have let him come? Yes! No! And Vargas Llosa said writers should not feel superior, because pure imagination becomes passion, and life becomes impossible.

Mailer came to the podium again, the hypocrite, and said that Shultz had surprised him by the "liberality" of his views, and joined Grass in recommending that writers go in for "hellish laughter."

Grass was really on the right side, of course, complaining quite rightly that politicians didn't listen to us and urging writers to become anarchists again. But then that swine of a Vargas Llosa warned that artists' dreams can contaminate people as well as uplift them. Nadine Gordimer charged the state with manipulating people, and Vargas Llosa came back that after all writers manipulated readers, and that writers could be terrible people themselves.

John Updike made a speech calling for smaller government and no state grants for artists, sounding like a positive Republican.

But the chief swine was really Amos Oz of Israel. He said he could never understand—while writers at their desks had so much insight—how they could turn into such idiots when they signed petitions and the like. A writer's minimal job, he said, was to differentiate between almost-decent states, bad states, and lethal states.

Oz told this story about an environmentalist demonstration he'd seen in Vienna, with demonstrators surrounded by masses of little pigs and carrying placards, "Jesus loved them, too." Yet a lot of the demonstrators, he said, looked like people capable of shooting hostages on the hour until you promised to save their pigs. "We must not ascribe demonic attributes to the state, and angelic attributes to ourselves!" he proclaimed. And the worst thing about Oz was that for a cheap trick like that he got a great burst of applause.

Here I had been elevated to the superior status of man of letters, and that contemptible Oz made it all turn to ashes in my mouth. Ashes.

3

Are Writers Crazy? A Literary Notebook

ME AND MY PAL Pierre Elliott Trudeau, fellow citizens of the Republic of Letters, were sitting there, brooding about it all, thinking deep thoughts about this week-long PEN Club International Congress which was now drawing to a close. It had attracted many of the world's most famous writers. Were writers crazy? Did they live in the real world? Did they have any brains?

It would be nice to be able to say we were sitting on the terrace of the Sky Garden of the St. Moritz on Central Park, with the lights of Manhattan shining down below, because in a way that's how writers see the world, from an exalted position, from way up. But in actual fact we were sitting somewhere in the second basement, which is where they should put writers when they're bad.

That morning Trudeau and two other former political leaders, Brun Kreisky of Austria and George McGovern of the United States, had debated "The Imagination of the State" with one of America's goofiest fiction writers, Kurt Vonnegut; one of its most discredited historians (although still in high repute on the Left), Frances FitzGerald; a distinguished Italian novelist and filmmaker, Mario Soldati; and the Peruvian novelist who, on panel after panel, had displayed great eloquence in defending free societies against coercive utopias of the Left as well as of the Right, that champion of the West—Mario Vargas Llosa.

"Vargas missed a great career in politics," said Trudeau. "He could have been president of his country." [Note: In 1990 Vargas run for the presidency of Peru and lost.]

239

What was I doing passing myself off as a Canadian? Well, Margaret Atwood, head of Canadian PEN, heard me go off in a blaze of French at some point, spotted the Canadian name, and adopted me. Needless to say, Trudeau hadn't been fooled for a minute, since my French doesn't sound Canadian. But blood might be thicker than ink, who knows, or maybe Margaret Atwood was right when she said, fondly, that I was a chameleon. So there I was, a Canadian.

So I said to my buddy Trudeau that there had been a definite effort during the conference to become more respectable, an outreach program toward sanity. Writers of fiction and poetry— which is what we're talking about here, the Frances FitzGeralds and Arthur Schlesingers being drawn in by doctrinal affinity— were so utopian-leftist compared to the ordinary range of American politics that they'd become a joke and were afraid of losing their influence. Trudeau was gracious, with very good manners, and it was only when he said later, "Look how the United States behaved toward Castro," suggesting, as it were, that we'd "driven Castro into the arms of the Russians," that I knew that what I'd been hearing about him all these years was true, that his real politics were much further to the Left than those he practiced as prime minister of Canada.

The Beat poet Allen Ginsberg came by with this petition. The nice thing about being a pal of an ex–prime minister is that you just sit there and all the celebrities come to you. "Richard!" he says. "Allen!" I say, although the last time I saw him he was a Hindu, but he'd really cleaned himself up, showered, coat and tie, underarm deodorant, too, I bet. He hadn't cleaned up his petition though. *U.S. Out of Central America!* The Sandinista "hyper-militarization" and Nicaraguan "constriction of civil liberties" were all the fault of the "blood battle" sponsored by the U.S. Language like that.

"How many signatures have you got, Allen?" I asked. He said 137, and they were all there, including most of the stars of the conference. Ginsberg, honorable to his fingertips, was also carrying around Vargas Llosa's petition, expressing disapproval of both U.S. *and Soviet* intervention in Central America. It had two signatures.

Trudeau explained that as a politician he really couldn't go around signing petitions, but Vargas's petition was certainly the more "judicious." On the other hand, it was ineffectual.

Since the Soviet Union and Cuba weren't about to pull out of Nicaragua, I asked Trudeau—everything was in English now— what course he thought Vargas would recommend? "I think he'd support the Contras," said Trudeau. Which shows you what an unusual figure Mario Vargas Llosa was at a writers' conference.

And yet two votes for Vargas and 137 for Ginsberg-Vonnegut-Doctorow-Grass and company was perhaps not the whole story. Because Vargas had no party workers, whereas the anti-U.S. team had many and controlled the conference. Despite which, Vargas received tremendous applause when he denounced "Gulag Communism" and flailed writers who, struggling to overthrow a military dictatorship, were also deliberately promoting the advent of Marxism-Leninism. On the last day, Vargas got the most sustained ovation of the conference. I clocked it. Bravos and everything.

If Vargas had had party workers, would his petition have gotten 50 signatures, 100, 150? Or did he get the ovation because he was a brilliant speaker and handsome? Israel's Amos Oz, who also provoked a great burst of applause when he ridiculed writers for ascribing "demonic" qualities to the state and "angelic" qualities to themselves, is also handsome. I overheard at least four debates among female delegates as to who was the most handsome and magnetic writer at the conference, and the vote seemed to be first Vargas, then Oz. One, two. So charisma might not be everything, but it counts. Pass it along.

The week-long congress had its high points and its low points. The ad hoc news conference called by Arthur Miller and Vassily Aksyonov to denounce the Soviet Union for holding eighty-nine imprisoned writers was startling, with Arthur Miller appearing in an unaccustomed role as severe critic of the USSR. All American writers at the conference—particularly the giddiest— made a point of announcing firmly that they realized they were living in the freest country "on the face of the globe." Had sanity returned to the American literary class? Or was it a new

dodge, to "establish credibility," like the invitation to the secretary of the state to address the opening session?

Susan Sontag and I kissed and made up. Well, almost. I mean
we really kissed and almost made up. She said, first from the
platform, that a private notion of utopia was internally necessary
for her to write, but she'd never dream of supporting attempts
to coerce people in the establishment of a "public" utopia.
She'd been smiling at me apprehensively from the platform all
during the symposium, so, having treated her with some severity
in a story for the *New Republic*, I told her afterward that in her
present mode, I offered her my "qualified support." She shook
my hand—gratefully, it seemed to me. "You're really something," she said. What she meant by this, I know not.

A low point of the conference was the hijacking of the congress and the press by a gang of feminist Neanderthals led by
Betty Friedan for perhaps a day and a half to the disgust of
almost all the foreign visitors. Under 20 percent of the panelists
were women! they shouted, with Betty Friedan (in her fantasy
life, I'm sure, head of some longshoremen's union) bellowing
that if they didn't get satisfaction at the closing session, they
would seize the speaker's platform "bodily." It didn't happen,
alas. I would love to have seen Friedan and the white-haired,
corpulent Norman Mailer in a punch-out.

Gay Talese pointed out tartly that half of American PEN's
vice presidents were women, and half of the congress's planning
committee were women, including Susan Sontag. Yet Susan had
just signed the feminist protest petition. "What's Susan doing?"
asked Talese. "Protesting against herself?"

But the lowest of the low points was Günther Grass, who
years ago wrote *The Tin Drum*, but not much of importance
since. An intimate of former German Socialist Chancellor Willy
Brandt, he has followed Brandt off leftward into the Elysian
Fields. Outraged by all these condemnations of the Soviet
Union, Grass, speaking from the floor on the next-to-last day,
roared: "Is capitalism better than Gulag Communism? I don't
think so!" My friend Walter Goodman of the *New York Times*
and I, sitting side by side, had it word for word, both in our
notes and on our tape recorders.

I caught Grass afterward at a reception and asked for a comment. "I didn't say it!" he cried angrily. "Goodman is lying!" (Goodman had reported the statement in the *New York Times.*) A literary lady, coming to the defense of the world of letters and to belittle Goodman, put in, "What do you expect of a neo-conservative?" Grass asked, "What is neo-conservative?" "Never mind that," I said. "Mr. Grass, Mr. Goodman is not lying. If you'd like to hear your own voice saying those words, I'll play them for you on my tape recorder, which I have right here." "No!" declared Grass. "I didn't say it!" He was surrounded now by a dozen reporters, all with tape recorders and notebooks. But, not exactly to my surprise, I could never induce him to listen to the playback.

Grass was forthright about Latin America. Anything bad that happened in Nicaragua, or even Cuba, was the fault of the United States, a very wicked country indeed. So if American PEN has a new line on the United States, the "freest country on the face of the globe," it doesn't seem to have been communicated to Günther Grass in West Germany.

Little happened during the PEN Congress, in sum, to shake my long-held conviction that, with rare exceptions, the literary class parted company with representative democracy a long time ago. Imaginative writers are usually ecstatics, giddy with arrogance, dying of an envious desire to direct affairs of state, convinced that if it were only up to people like themselves all the world's problems could be solved quite speedily. Now and then what Solzhenitsyn called the "iron crowbar of events" will beat some sense into them, but their grip on reality is very intermittent.

When Bruno Kreisky said that, thanks to him, French soldiers and Libyan soldiers were no longer dying in Chad, I heard voices behind me saying, "Where's Chad?" And it occurred to me that perhaps Poets, Essayists, and Novelists (for which PEN is an acronym) should not take upon themselves the task of advising governments on affairs of national policy.

One of the conference's disappointments was the signature of Israel's Amos Oz—despite his warning about writers turning into such "idiots" when signing petitions—on the petition urging an end to United States interference in Central America. Oz added a caveat, of course, right beside his signature: "with a protest over Sandinista support of Arab terrorism."

Which is to say that, as an Israeli, Arab terrorism is real for Amos Oz, but Marxist-Leninist terror in Nicaragua, for example, or Marxist-Leninist terror in El Salvador, is quite evidently make-believe. Beaten about the head and shoulders by the iron crowbar of events in Israel, Amos Oz has some sense when it comes to the Middle East. Reality there has a harsh, bitter taste. But in Latin America he lets his literary fancy roam.

Unkindly, I taxed him with this personally at a party. Perhaps the United States should stop interfering in the Middle East as well, I suggested. Perhaps it should halt all aid to Israel. But Oz fled. I did not get an answer. And was not surprised.

4

African Dreaming: Alice Walker's The Color Purple

I HAVE FOUND THE perfect place. Not the Garden of Eden perhaps. Not Arcadia. But as close as we are going to get to it on this earth. Africa. Or, at least, the Africa that emerges from Alice Walker's prize-winning novel, *The Color Purple*. For despite the breadth, and scope, and depth of Steven Spielberg's film version of the book, which a lot of people think is the best thing to happen to American blacks since Harriet Beecher Stowe wrote *Uncle Tom's Cabin*, a movie simply cannot do credit to the wealth of knowledge and sometimes plain no-nonsense information contained in a written work.

Now the Lord alone knows—or perhaps I should say Nature, "she" alone knows (in Walkerese)—the commercial destiny in store for this big-budget Spielberg–Whoopi Goldberg production. It is known, of course, that Alice Walker is not a universal favorite among blacks. She hates black men with a passion, an antipathy black men return with some stoniness. Black women don't always like her much either. A black woman said recently she was "tired of being beat over the head with this women's lib stuff, this whole black woman/black man, 'Lord have mercy on us po' sisters.' " And it fell to a sensitive white woman, a core admirer, to confess that, once she'd gotten through *The Color Purple*'s first depressing chapters, the book was "so uplifting and *true* it made me cry."

Which is to say that this sensitive white woman was obviously not black, nor was she raised poor in rural Georgia before the

First World War, nor was she raped by her father when she was thirteen, nor did she bear him two incestuous children, nor was she later abused by her husband, nor did she become a lesbian, but that the book was so uplifting she could somehow *feel* it was true.

Alice Walker has hatred to spare, and some slurps over onto white men, and even, in a half-hearted way, onto white women. So her real fans are pretty much limited to white tearers-of-hair and renders-of-garments. But Spielberg has made so many zillion dollars from movies even his best friends wouldn't claim had anything to do with real life, and he's spending so much money advertising this new *Purple* flick, which is suddenly going to tell everyone Great Truths, that we're probably not going to know for a few weeks whether the Great American Public is swallowing it or not. [It swallowed it.]

The Color Purple is what is called an "epistolary" novel, which is to say it's made up of letters, in this case between the novel's heroine, Celie, who gets raped by her father and beaten by her husband and ends up a lesbian, and her younger sister Nettie. Things get pretty sticky when Nettie moves in with her married sister, Celie, and Celie's husband, Albert. So Nettie runs away and the next thing you know she's a missionary in Africa.

The first miracle in this story is the improvement in Nettie's prose style as soon as she gets away from home. Celie, of course, writes in Black English, which, for all I know, they're teaching at Princeton these days. *We fall on each other neck. She be my age but they married.* But Nettie hasn't been away from home a week and already she's saying things like "I dare not" and "I dread parting from them." And by the time love with a kind and gentle man comes to Nettie, she's writing, "I was transported by ecstasy in Samuel's arms . . . I love his dear eyes in which the vulnerability and beauty of his soul can be plainly read." In the end it came to me that the book's title, *The Color Purple*, was in honor of Nettie's prose.

But the real, world-class miracle in the book is Africa, the Africa that emerges from Nettie's letters home. Now I realize that the Back-to-Africa movement isn't very popular among American blacks. Stokely Carmichael and a few of his friends tried it for a while, but it didn't last. The late Huey Newton even tried Back-to-Cuba (where Alice Walker interviewed him reverently), but only stuck it out three years. Even the 15,000 or so "Free Negroes" who were sent off to Liberia beginning in 1822 went begrudgingly, they say, even though they now run Liberia. God knows, it's hard enough to get Jews to go to Israel, which their religion calls on them to do, I think, but American blacks won't go back to Africa, period. Now is this plain horse sense, or does Alice Walker know something about Africa nobody else knows?

Toward the end of *The Color Purple*, which is somewhere in the 1930s, Celie twice has dealings with the U.S. "Defense Department." But since at that time the Defense Department didn't exist, you start to wonder, does Alice Walker's Africa exist? Also, when Nettie passes through Liberia on her way out to Africa in about 1910, the Liberian president is named Tubman. But since William Tubman's big years were in the 1950s (and even 1960s), this is like getting Dwight Eisenhower mixed up with William Howard Taft. Or perhaps Woodrow Wilson. Picture the 1916 election with an amalgamated Eisenhower-Wilson platform. *We like Ike! He kept us out of war!*

The Color Purple contains what Eddie Murphy calls a "Black History Minute," a bit of encapsulated African history. Africans, we learn, once had a higher civilization than Europe but for several centuries fell on hard times, the fault of "the English." Millions of Africans were sold into slavery (by other Africans, incidentally), as a result of which those remaining in Africa don't know how to read and write any more. But despite the depredations of colonialists, they possess a culture and contact with nature that white people will never match.

Nettie spends thirty years with a coastal tribe called the Olinka, so she must know them pretty well. They worship the holy roof leaf, apparently a high-class religion. Although Nettie has come to Africa to preach Christianity, she finds this roof

leaf religion absolutely first rate—as, indeed, she finds everything else about the Olinka. "We know a roof leaf is not Jesus
Christ," she writes her sister, "but in its own humble way, is it
not God?"

Nettie spends no time at all evangelizing but seems to regard
her mission in Africa as a combination of social work and deep
learning experience. Unlike those uppity Americo-Liberians,
who are more American than Americans, Nettie's missionaries,
in the arms of whose wonderfully vulnerable leader she finds
ecstasy, drink deep of the Olinka culture (this in 1910). They
savor the wonderful friendships among the Olinka women. The
missionary's children "love the open feeling of the village, and
love living in huts. They are excited by the hunting expertise of
the men and the self-sufficiency of the women in raising their
crops." The Christian missionary's boy scars his cheeks like the
male Olinka.

The Olinka scarify their children's cheeks as a mark of their
tribe, and have puberty rites for both boys and girls (although
only Steven Spielberg introduces coeducational puberty rites,
doubtless the influence of Reform Judaism on Africa). And when
occasionally the Olinka do something a little disgusting, Nettie
reflects, "But the white man has taken everything else!" So she
views these disgusting things they do as a sign of tribal vigor,
which is great.

On the other hand, perhaps the most wonderful thing about
Africa is that tribes don't count at all. Not too far from Nettie's
mission, apparently, there's a deep rift in the earth where are
gathered a thousand people from dozens of African tribes, all
united to free Africa! There is a school (what language?). A
temple (what religion?). An infirmary (what kind of doctors?).
"Male and female warriors" go on sabotage raids against white
plantations, all united in a common goal, "the uplift of black
people everywhere." Reading the book, I wondered—with fifty
African states having attained independence at least twenty-five
years ago and African culture now doubtless in full bloom—
what Alice Walker is doing living surrounded by all those
degenerate white people in northern California (with homes both
in the country and in San Francisco).

Imagine my shock, furthermore, when on consulting every reference book on Africa I could find no entry under "Olinka." Since it's a Slavic diminutive for "Olga," it's been suggested that Alice Walker might have picked it up at the Soviet-sponsored World Youth Peace Festival in Helsinki which she attended with Angela Davis, recently candidate for vice-president of the U.S. Communist Party. But maps produced a further shock. Although Nettie is peculiarly vague about just which British colony her Olinka inhabit, as we work down the African coast from Liberia we have only Ghana and Nigeria. I'll give Nettie a break and bypass Ghana, Kwame Nkrumah, and all that mess, leaving us oil-rich Nigeria.

Well, Nigeria has about 250 tribes, including four really big ones: Hausa, Fulani, Yoruba, and Ibo. The smaller ones are the Kanwri, Nupe, Tiv, Edo, Ijaw . . . (I could go on, but you will not find Olinka). Some 50 percent of Nigerians are Moslem, 35 percent Christian, the rest pagan, but, amazingly, no roof leaf.

Since independence in 1960, Nigeria has had an interesting history. The early years were marked by bitter conflict, which culminated in 1966 in two military coups d'état, the first by Ibo army officers, the second by Hausa army officers. In September Hausa tribesmen began massacring Ibo in the north, whereupon Ibo in the south seceded to form the temporarily independent state of Biafra. The two sides then fought a bloody, three-year civil war which left one million dead, all blacks killed by other blacks. Now where, you might ask, is that wonderful gathering place filled with Alice Walker's happy Africans, united for the uplift of black people everywhere? The answer might explain why Alice Walker is living in California.

A difference between Alice Walker and me, of course, is that I have been to Africa, many times, while I have the funny feeling she has not. It takes a lot of nerve to set a large part of a major novel in a place you've only daydreamed about. And since I don't believe a word of what Alice Walker says about Africa, why should I believe what she tells me about the woes of a black lesbian in the Georgia of 1910—a place she's never been to either, come to think of it.

Searching for the root of Alice Walker's African daydreams,

I've read her collected essays in what she calls "womanist" prose. I find she's written a passionate celebration of Fidel Castro's Cuban Revolution. She's an ardent admirer of nuclear-surrender advocate Helen Caldicott. She writes that nothing bad happens in China any more since the Communist Revolution. She published this in 1976, before the death of Mao and the fall of the Gang of Four. With 30 million Chinese dead thanks to Mao, according to his successors, and even more recent dramatic events, one wonders what Alice Walker has to say about China now.

Pondering how a sane college graduate could possibly have dreamed up a place as fanciful as Alice Walker's Africa, I came across the most curious of her "womanist" memoirs. A male cousin of hers has left white, wintry Boston to return to Atlanta and he glories, she says, in not having to see a white person from one year to the next. Alice Walker asks his wife, who seems to have been raised in Boston, how she feels about it. The wife admits Atlanta is nicer, but misses all her friends back in Boston. It hurts, she says, but you can't have everything. This fills Alice Walker with derisive scorn, and she thinks jeeringly if mysteriously, "Yes, two hundred years ago you might have tried to escape to Canada, no matter what the slaves who'd already settled there wrote you of the murderous cold."

I puzzled over this sentence quite a bit—because surely Alice Walker can't be expressing contempt for a slave's determination to be free. Surely a Canadian winter is less bad than continued servitude. Until I realized that the hot button was her relative's remark, "You can't have everything," and I saw how limited was my sense of what is possible in this world. It suddenly came to me with a dizzying surge that the slave not only had a right to freedom, *she had the right to a warm Canada.* It's that old earth-bound side of me. No imagination. I don't believe in that wonderful secret gathering place filled with happy Africans united for the uplift of black people everywhere. And I'm not out there demanding a warm Canada.

5

Hitler's Favorite Baroness: The *Dinesen-Streep* Out of Africa

ADOLF HITLER's literary taste is not taken seriously enough. Here the film version of a book by one of his favorite writers was nominated for eleven Academy Awards with the heartfelt support of Meryl Streep and Robert Redford, all the right people, and still they won't give the man his due.

Hitler was very eager in 1940 to meet Denmark's Isak Dinesen, the pen name of Karen Blixen, author of *Out of Africa*, and to induce her to autograph copies of her books. She, however, thinking perhaps that *blitzkrieg* in Poland was one thing but these victories might not go on forever, prudently caught a diplomatic cold and passed up a scheduled meeting with this devoted fan.

Not that she was harsh on Hitler in her *Letters from a Land at War*, written in Nazi Germany in 1940, the year of the fall of France, Belgium, and the Netherlands. The Nazis recalled to her the righteous ardor of the Catholic priesthood during the Church's period of greatest power. Part of *Mein Kampf* reminded her of the Koran. Regarding Hitler himself, she mused on the personality of a man who, like a magnet passing over a collection of metal fragments, "can rearrange and transform a society." At her most reflective, she concluded that the difference between the belligerence of the Nazis and that of the aristocratic Germany of Wilhelm II was one of "class." Because, say what you will about Hitler, he was vulgar.

The Baroness Blixen, you see, was not vulgar, at least not in

251

her own eyes, although a friend called her infatuation with her own title "idiotic." Karen Blixen was born just your ordinary Danish millionaire with money her family had made—horrors— in "trade." And the most galling thing of all was that she was related on another side of her family to some of the grandest noble families of Denmark—but no title. So she contracted a marriage of convenience with a Swedish baron named Bros Blixen, who, as a *digestif* to accompany the title, as it were, gave her syphilis. But Karen never complained. She declared repeatedly that getting syphilis was a quite acceptable price to pay to become a baroness.

Some people do not know how to live up to a title, of course, something of which Baroness Blixen was never accused. On trips from Africa to the capitals of Europe in the 1920s, she was followed everywhere by two little blackamoors in livery. Didn't Princess de Faucigny-Lucinge and Marquesa Casatti also have little liveried black page boys? Baroness Blixen, furthermore, had a wonderful understanding of Africans from her life in Kenya, where she learned that one must speak with them, she wrote, "as repetitively and as simply as with small children."

Ah, those grand days in Kenya in the 1910s and 1920s, with half of Debrett's Peerage quartered on grand estates, or visiting, partying, hunting, and going on safaris. For it must be realized that what are now called the "white highlands" of Kenya were not then just another African colony but, with their magnificent landscape and superb weather and dangerous game to hunt, a place which offered the high-living aristocracy of Europe the life of which the Industrial Revolution had robbed it. In Kenya, only the skin color of the serfs had changed.

Isak Dinesen's lightly fictionalized *Out of Africa* begins with the resonant sentence, "I had a farm in Africa," which was not an outright lie, of course, provided you call 6,000 acres worked by 1,200 black laborers under the control of white overseers a "farm." The Blixens had the Prince of Wales as a house guest, and more than once, and the Baroness, needless to say, was "smitten."

It was all doomed, naturally. Not just by bad management of the estate, or even by Kenya's independence and black rule (which would have seemed quite diabolical to the Baroness), but by those despicable little shopkeepers and bookkeepers and accountants and real-estate developers, white or black, who came flocking into "her" Kenya. For while the Baroness was given spasmodically to declaring her love for "the people"—by which she meant properly humble little persons who didn't have the impertinence to think of rising above their station—she was extremely consistent in never feeling anything but raging hatred for the middle classes, the social groups that usually come to dominate in democratic societies.

The Baroness, you see, was no democrat. She was a fanatic defender of a highly stratified society, of rank, privilege, class, and "blood" (nothing to bother Hitler here), and was fiercely hostile to any kind of "social leveling" which might blur class distinctions. She loved luxury, bought her crystal from Baccarat and custom-made dresses from Paris's most expensive couturier, and, in her best understanding of the aristocratic manner, left Africa with all her bills unpaid.

Now you are thinking that this Karen Blixen is different, somehow, from the warm, compassionate, democratic Karen Blixen that emerges from Meryl Streep's portrayal in the movie *Out of Africa*. You think, how dare Meryl Streep (and the film's director and screenwriter) take such liberties with a very recent historical personage, described by a number of people, moreover, as "an iceberg."

Well, a film star has to be practical, you know. And it's not as if misrepresentation of the personality and politics of Karen Blixen is the only change made in the movie. The women of America have been crying for a "woman's film," a love story, so Meryl Streep gives them a love story. As it happens, the Right Honorable Denys Finch Hattan (Robert Redford), the son of an English earl, hardly figures at all in the book. In addition to which, half the people who knew the two of them are convinced that their relationship, such as it was, remained unconsummated.

The better sort of person in Hollywood these days is a feminist, so the movie contains a heavy dash of female derring–do not in the book.

Despite the vast success of such war-hungry, blood-lust movies as *Rambo*, Hollywood's better sort is vaguely pacifist, furthermore, hence Finch Hatton's conversion into some kind of war resister. "It's not my fight," says civilian Robert Redford, a man of peace. Yet the real Finch Hatton fought all through World War I in one crack military unit after another—Somali Irregulars, East African Mounted Rifles, as General Hoskins's aide-de-camp in Mesopotamia. He was decorated for valor in combat, winning the Military Cross, the British equivalent of our Distinguished Service Cross.

Finch Hatton's great friend, Berkeley Cole, also featured in the movie as a civilian, was an officer with the Ninth Lancers even in the Boer War and fought through World War I in some of the same units as his friend. Although Sweden and Denmark were neutral in the war, Baron Blixen himself would have considered it an act of personal cowardice not to fight alongside his British comrades, and Karen's younger brother Thomas, fighting in France with a Canadian Black Watch regiment, won not only the Croix de Guerre but—a decoration few soldiers who win it live to see—the Victoria Cross.

All these people fought. They hunted, gambled, boozed, womanized. Many were snobs or rascals. But it is a very ignorant misunderstanding of their mentality and historical role not to realize that few members of this class, at this period, would fail to leap at the chance to play their part in the Great Game, which was what they sometimes called it. Hunting lions was to amuse themselves in peacetime. In war, their time had come.

But Meryl Streep and Robert Redford are against war, you see. They no doubt would have found it most unseemly to show Denys Finch Hatton, the love of Karen Blixen's life—a big-game hunter, killed in a private plane crash when flying was only for the daring—as a man who loved danger and war. The Baroness herself, as she made clear again and again, despised safety and loved danger.

You must understand that, if Meryl Streep and Robert Redford wanted to give their audience a love story it would like, they also wanted to do good, to impart wisdom. And, somehow, it always seems to be the most deceitful people who think their role is to impart Great Truth.

6

For Export Only: PBS's The Africans

A<small>RE YOU AN ADMIRER</small> of Muammar Qaddafi? Are you looking forward to a world where Africans (from Africa) will be the new "Brahmins" while Westerners are the new "Untouchables?"

Where the roles of privilege will be unabashedly "reversed"? Where Africans, taking their lead from OPEC and Qaddafi (whose terrorist bombs in airports and discotheques are perfectly reasonable) will have us over a barrel economically? Where they'll be able to ground our military and civilian aircraft by withholding their precious minerals? Where they'll squeeze us, sweat us, get back at us for what we've done to them "from slavery straight to to multinational corporations"? Where South Africa will be a black-ruled state with "convincing nuclear credentials" (shots of an atomic explosion, just a little hint)?

Were you a supporter of the Reverend Jesse Jackson in his 1984 campaign with prominent positions accorded Marxist-Leninists? Do you believe that a person of even partly African ancestry can live in America "for a thousand years" without becoming an American? In short, are you a vengeful black racist? Perhaps a masochistic white flagellant?

If so, look no further. I have found the impartial television show of your dreams, the nine-part PBS series "The Africans." You will be particularly gratified, as you thrill to the series's racist fantasies and kindergarten Marxism, to know that it was funded mostly by $1.1 million in U.S. public or public-controlled monies—meaning our old friends at the National Endowment for the Humanities, Public Broadcasting Service, and Corporation for Public Broadcasting.

Lynne Cheney, the new chairman of NEH, put up a real squawk when WETA came to her for an extra $50,000 to "promote" this wonderful series. She made them take NEH's name off the thing and read them the riot act. But how about William Bennett, later Secretary of Education but Cheney's predecessor at NEH? [Since gone on to even greater things as President Bush's drug czar.] Bennett talks a terrific game but he let some unappetizing big-ticket funding projects slip by him during his NEH dictatorship. And "The Africans," if it's his doing, is a doozer. Because I've been peeking at this whole nine-part series to see what you folks have in store.

Africa. Ah, Africa. Sounds romantic, perhaps. But it wasn't romantic as I listened to Ali A. Mazrui, professor at universities in Michigan and Nigeria and the series's monologuist, drone on in fruity tones about the "soil of Africa recoiling with a whimper" at the arrogant Europeans' arrival, about recent African history being about "steel-mill building capitalist sharks in search of their pound of flesh."

Mazrui expresses lofty contempt for the West's "law of supply and demand." If the world were run by intelligent, high-minded people like Mazrui and Colonel Mengistu of Ethiopia, they and they alone would decide how many "I love Mengistu" T-shirts were to be produced, and if people wanted more—or perhaps none—it would be just their tough luck and might even unmask them as not good Socialists.

But what stuck in my throat, even more than "the culture of violence imported by Africans from the West," was Mazrui winding up the last section of the nine-part series with the statement: "Before slave days, we were back in one huge village called Africa." [It should be noted that Mazrui was born in Kenya to a wealthy African family that made its fortune in the slave trade.]

Do tell. One huge village before the coming of Europeans. Back "before slave days." But when might that have been, pray, since in Africa slavery was endemic and nearly universal from earliest recorded history and even from African legend, along with the most promiscuous forms of violence?

Before the arrival of Europeans most African tribes were in a constant state of low-level warfare with their neighbors, to the point that any and all travelers strange to a tribe were normally assumed to be a raiding party in search of booty and slaves. One huge village?

I have encountered this fairy-tale view of Africa before, of course, in *The Color Purple* by Alice Walker, in whose Africa, mysteriously, all Africans seem to speak the same language. But, more significantly, I've encountered Mazrui's Africa in Manhattan when for a time I covered the United Nations— where in fact this Africa was created, certainly not in Africa.

To understand Mazrui's Africa, you have to accept that anything bad or even indifferent that ever happened in that continent was, is, and forever will be the fault of Europeans or Americans. "What do we have for 300 years of Western contact?" he asks in stern reproof, while never asking what they have for more than 1,000 years of contact with the Arabs, many of whom (although the Arabs certainly don't think of themselves this way) are after all fellow Africans. Arabs, the earliest and fiercest of international slave traders, are in Mazrui's series so nice they're almost black.

When Africa produced primary products and had no industry, this was the West's fault. When Africans, like Ghana's Kwame Nkrumah, went on a binge building factories and hydroelectric plants, and the plants were under-utilized and the factories filled with cobwebs, this, too, was the West's fault.

If the radio doesn't work, it's the West's fault. If the telephone doesn't work, it's the West's fault. When the freed slaves from America who founded Liberia didn't revert to African tribal ways, it was the West's fault. When Samuel Doe executed a sizeable number of those English-speaking Liberians after his 1980 Liberian coup d'état, this, too, was the West's fault—since, before the arrival of the West, Africans presumably used to tickle their adversaries with feathers until they gave up.

Nigeria was the scene of one of the bloodiest hecatombs in decades when some million Nigerians died in the Biafran revolt of the late 1960s. How did such a frightful thing happen? Well, Nigeria has these tribes, you see, the Hausa, Ibo, Yoruba, Fulani and even others. In 1960 some Ibo officers staged a military coup, but six months later Hausa officers arranged a counter-coup and, more in sorrow than in anger, the Hausa massacred large numbers of Ibo—a procedure no doubt taught them by the West.

A whole area which called itself Biafra seceded, a purely African affair, and by the time the war was over a million people lay dead. Even inspired in unseen ways by the violent West, how could such a murderous thing have happened in the benign, lovable, unified Africa presented to us by PBS? To put it simply, it could not.

But PBS's purpose is not to present a real Africa, or even a critical African view of the West, since Mazrui's Africa exists only at the U.N. and in Black Studies departments on American campuses. PBS's purpose—sometimes perhaps unconscious, often so naked even its own people must see it—is at public expense to show in a hostile light Western and American institutions. The Congress doesn't seem to have figured this out yet.

7

Virtue in an Unknown Land: *Argentina's* **Official Story**

THERE IS NOTHING like seeing a noble, idealistic movie from a far-off place like Argentina while bathing in the white milk of purest ignorance. Argentina is this emotional, moralistic never-never land, you see, a kind of thinking man's Ruritania, where evil is black as a raven's wing, and virtue shines with a heavenly light, and you'd have to be a fool not to be virtuous because it's free. And if there's any cost/benefits analysis on this virtue business, the people who made this new Argentine movie certainly aren't going to tell you. No, sir. Not them. Anyway, who knows anything about Argentina?

The film critics of New York have thrown themselves into paroxysms of praise for *The Official Story* such as I have rarely seen in my lifetime. A "shining miracle." "Riveting." "Luminous." "Glowing." "Explosive." "Incredibly moving." "Chilling." "Heart-breaking." "Exalting." "Shattering." "Compelling." "Powerful." "Astonishing." "Devastating." "An epic of the spirit." And this not just from the heavyweights of *Glamour* and *Vogue* and *Playboy*, but all the way up to the *New York Times*, which said the film "takes us to where politics meets the human heart." If you don't know anything about Argentine politics, that is, in which case your heart might get a little stony.

I must be fair. Our New York film critics do their modest best to keep up with world events. They'd seen Broadway's *Evita*, hadn't they? In which Evita Peron is shown as a kind of Argentine Helen Gurley Brown, very knowing about getting a

259

man, very eager to get to the top, and with Che Guevara, of all people, crooning from downstage left about how she "had style."

As the beginning of wisdom, just to give the critics a little clue, I would like to suggest that *The Official Story* is the present Argentine official line, and to inform the critics, just in case they might have missed it, that *Evita* is still banned by the censors in Buenos Aires. Now why would Argentine censors want to do a thing like that? I will tell you. Because *Evita* shows disrespect for Juan Peron.

Called a "Fascist" many times in the American press, Peron is still revered by many Argentines. [Witness the results of the 1989 election.] But the same Alfonsin Argentina that gave us *The Official Story* sentenced five generals and admirals to long prison sentences for their roles in the disappearance of the country's famous *desaparecidos* ("disappeared ones"). [In his 1989 election campaign, however, Alfonsin's victorious opponent promised pardons, so there is perhaps more than one side to this story.] And if now you're all confused, read on.

First, the plot of *The Official Story*. A well-to-do Buenos Aires business family: Mommy, Daddy, and an adorable adopted girl of about six. The key word here is "adopted," starting from which the filmmakers have contrived to tell a didactic tale. Because before the plot proper comes what in Hollywood they call the "back story," a terrible time following the military coup of 1976, when the military, police vigilantes, and death squads "disappeared" people all over the place, racking up a score of desaparecidos that adversaries of the new regime first put at 40,000, then 30,000, but have now reduced to 9,000. The point is that some of these disappeared people had little babies, and a number of *sub rosa* adoptions were arranged by the police for families who wanted children but couldn't have them. Our fictional happy Buenos Aires family—the filmmakers clearly suggest—got their lovely little girl, Gaby, by this morally unspeakable procedure.

The trouble with this back story—as is often the case with political back stories—is that it doesn't go back far enough. Where are the Montoneros and the *Ejercito de Liberacion del*

Pueblo ("People's Liberation Army"), those savage left-wing terrorist groups who were running wild in the last days of the government of Isabelita Peron (not to be confused with Evita Peron), assassinating someone on average every three hours, making Buenos Aires at the time the unchallenged terrorist capital of the world? For that matter, where is that incompetent clown Isabelita herself, who, with her astrologer boyfriend, had completely lost control of the country? Without a back story to the back story, the spectator of this sanctimonious movie doesn't have the foggiest idea of why the coup d'état even took place.

I have a distressing but simple truth for people who want to know something about Argentina. *Every military coup in Argentine history has had the support of the Argentine people. Peron in. Peron out. Aramburu in. Isabelita out.* The military sees that the government has failed or lost control, that disaster looms, and steps in to the cheers of the populace. It's a funny way to run a country, you might think, and it's not a way I like very much, but that's the way they run it.

And I have another home truth for the spectators wallowing in virtue at *The Official Story* (*La historia official*). In any nation facing a truly major threat to public order, civil liberties go by the board. Abraham Lincoln suspended habeas corpus during the Civil War. The British have suspended due process in Northern Ireland—where compared to the Montoneros the IRA Provos practice friendly persuasion. The trouble with suspending civil liberties, of course, is that the authorities charged with reestablishing order often go in for some gruesome excesses themselves, such as "disappearing" some 9,000 people, many Marxist-Leninist terrorists, many only suspected (like the IRA suspects languishing in prison near Belfast), some guilty of nothing more than having a face the police didn't like.

Now I am neither a defender nor detractor of Argentine honor in this matter. But it is no secret that the majority of Argentines either didn't care about the disappearances while they were going on, or, more usually, didn't want to know about them. Remember this fellow named Adolf Hitler? Remember when

U.S. troops arrived in Germany, how they couldn't find any Germans who knew about Auschwitz?

Of course, Galtieri and the other Argentine generals made the mistake of losing the war in the Falklands, and not many regimes in any country survive a defeat in war. Hitler also lost a war, if I remember correctly. And now every office worker in Buenos Aires is outraged about these "disappearances," which he didn't know about, or course, or perhaps even grieved about in his heart—while cheering the Argentine generals. The courts sentenced five flag officers to heavy prison terms? It's the right thing to do, no doubt. But I can't get rid of the feeling there's an element of scapegoating here.

As for *The Official Story*, if the critics weren't on such a cloud nine of sanctimony they might see, even judged by internal evidence, that the plot doesn't make too much sense. The adoptive mother played by Norma Aleandro, who has been festooned with acting awards, begins to suspect that there was something fishy about the way her husband procured their beloved little Gaby. So she starts lining up with parents and relatives trying desperately to get their "disappeared" children back. The peculiar part is that Aleandro is searching, and lining up, and demonstrating to *get rid of* this adopted little girl she loves so much. To my knowledge, this has absolutely never happened in conflicts over children between adoptive and biological parents. But perhaps that is why Aleandro is so wonderful.

Following vast labors, Aleandro finally presents to her husband an elderly working-class woman (played as if she were Mother Teresa) who, she says, "might" be the grandmother of their adored little Gaby. Now if he were a decent person, we are made to feel, the husband should immediately stand up, salute the Human Rights Convention, and hand over his little girl. After all, with the wickedness of the Argentine generals suddenly aperceived, wouldn't you turn over your cherished little adopted daughter instantly to some old lady who "might" be her grandmother? But the husband is not a decent person. He is a bad person. And I will tell you how I know.

I am absolutely astonished that an otherwise highly intelligent critic wrote in the *New York Times* that *The Official Story* politically "imposes no ideology or doctrine."

Really? Let's see about that. Roberto, the husband, Gaby's adopted father, is a rich man, as I have said. But he, too, has a father, who is not only a poor man but an anarchist. He has a brother, who is not only a poor man but a manual worker. They argue on camera about unprincipled wealth versus honest poverty. They re-fight the Spanish Civil War. (How's that for a non-ideological event?) The director gets his point across, as do the actors.

And if you still have doubts, I should point out that Roberto has an Argentine general and an American businessman as business partners, as well as close ties with the Argentine police. Someone who doesn't realize that this is a politically partisan movie couldn't be trusted to tell "Little Bo Peep" from *The Communist Manifesto*—if both were filmed, of course, in living color.

Note: The Official Story was made in Argentina under the radical government of Raul Alfonsin, eager to discredit its military predecessors. In one term Alfonsin's policies turned Argentina, not long ago the richest country in Latin America, into an economic disaster area. He was defeated by a landslide in the 1989 election by Peronist Carlos Menem, one of whose campaign promises was a "broad pardon" for those convicted of crimes during the *desaparecido* period. It would be loading French film director Alain Resnais a trifle heavily to hold him responsible for Argentina's economic collapse, but it is nonetheless a savory detail that Alfonsin's favorite movie was Resnais's fervently anti-American *Hiroshima, Mon Amour*, written by French novelist Marguerite Duras. Duras has openly vaunted her allegiance to the French Communist Party, which, if nothing else, does suggest a predisposition. What this tells us about Alfonsin is more shadowy, but interesting.

8

Sex and the Military Man: *Laclos's* Liaisons Dangeureuses

J AMES WEBB, HEAVILY decorated for valor as a Marine officer
in Vietnam and later Secretary of the Navy, is also a distinguished literary man. Did the enthusiastic sell-out audiences at
Broadway's prestige hit, *Les Liaisons Dangeureuses*, rally to
his support in his bitter controversy with the State Department
over security at the U.S. embassy in Moscow?

One has the right to wonder, although Choderlos de Laclos,
Liaisons's author, was also very much a military man, the only
writer in fact whose name is on Paris's renowned Arch of
Triumph, being as he was one of Napoleon's generals.

The irony is that the key to Laclos—a subject of fascination
and sulphuric controversy in France from Baudelaire and Sten-
dahl to Jeanne Moreau, who played a leading role in a French
film adaptation—is that Laclos applied to sex the unswerving
purposefulness and drive for victory of the military mind. But
sex, as you know, has become a big ha-ha. And when "sex
comedies" are enacted in English accents, this time by the
Royal Shakespeare Company, the comedy becomes exquisite.

General Choderlos de Laclos produced far more than his
celebrated epistolary novel, *Les Liaisons Dangeureuses*. He
wrote a renowned treatise on military strategy, urging total
destruction of the enemy, economic as well as military. He was
thus one of the first advocates of total war, a kind of French
General Sherman.

Not faint-hearted, as a young officer Laclos attacked the

265

strategies and principles of Louis XIV's great Marshal Vauban. Within a few decades Laclos was vindicated, his principles and famous "hollow" shell (he was an artillery officer like Napoleon) becoming standard in the French Army.

Laclos had an exciting life. As the French Revolution approached he became a ranking aide of the Duke of Orleans—who favored a constitutional monarchy, changed his name to Philippe Egalité ("Philip Equality"), and voted to send his cousin Louis XVI to the guillotine. Under the Terror, Philippe Egalité was guillotined himself. Laclos, too, was thrown in prison, escaped the guillotine twice, and finally joined the conspirators supporting Napoleon. He had nerves of steel and, for a writer, saw a lot of action. Some of this steeliness is apparent in his writing.

Whether or not *Les Liaisons Dangeureuses* is an accurate depiction of the mores of the high nobility of the *ancien régime* in France has been debated for 200 years. The book was in turn banned, burned, indexed, the subject of dark fascination, only to end up, in the twentieth century, a classic.

The novel's chief characters are the Vicomte de Valmont and the Marquise de Merteil, both young, handsome, witty, single, and in sexual matters totally unprincipled. Once lovers, they are now confidants of a sort, plotting stratagems for the seduction of various innocents. The classic French "war between the sexes" is assumed throughout.

We must remember that we are in the age of the *mariage de raison* ("arranged marriage"), a tradition that prevailed in France in the propertied class until well into the twentieth century, perhaps explaining the book's long popularity. That a duke in this period might be in love with his duchess would never cross anyone's mind. The duke could, and did, have mistresses, of course. And the duchess, often, lovers.

Laclos's singularity is that he carries loveless sexual relations to their ultimate extreme. Not only is the *mariage d'amour* unthinkable, but love between man and woman is by its very nature ludicrous and unseemly, implying a loss of self control, dignity. For Valmont, as for La Merteuil, victory in an affair of the heart is not winning the love of a member of the opposite sex and then cherishing it, but, by whatever ruse and deception necessary, bringing the "adversary" to bed. And the more difficult the odds, the more virtuous the antagonist, the greater the victory.

It was Laclos's most deeply held belief that *virtue and high morality are by themselves no match for evil*, which will always prevail. Virgins, devoted wives, the purest of the pure, all fall to Valmont and are villified, dishonored, destroyed. As one of Napoleon's generals in Italy, Laclos met the Bishop of Pavia, who, interestingly, had understood this cautionary meaning of the already famous *Liaisons*. The bishop told Laclos the book was "very moral" and should be read by everybody, particularly young girls. It was an evil world. They should not go forth into it unarmed.

What caused such a tumult in France was that, unlike the bishop, many believed that Laclos felt all too much sympathy for his patently wicked hero and heroine. Of the two, curiously, La Merteuil, the woman, is by far the more sinister, a positive female Iago—Valmont becoming virtually the instrument of her malice.

It is hard to see how much of this could get across to the giggly sell-out crowds in New York, for a more preposterous travesty of a literary classic I have never seen. This ritzy production of *Liaisons* fresh from London asks us to believe: (1) that all this sexual treachery is good fun because sexual virtue or fidelity is a big joke; and (2) that all this sexual treachery is terrible, which is why France got the Revolution.

Near the end of the last act, arbitrarily, the revolutionary French *tricolore* is unfurled and a drum starts to beat. Although *Liaisons* was written in 1779 and 1780, a full decade before the fall of the Bastille, this does not stop La Merteuil from stepping to the front of the stage with the following curtain speech, contrite, anachronistic, and absurdly out of character, a speech obviously not in Laclos: "We are already more than halfway through the eighties. Our best course is to believe in God, believe in life, and look forward to what the nineties will bring." But what, pray, *did* the nineties bring? Democracy, one is supposed to assume. But an end to sexual intrigue?

The Bastille having fallen in 1789, I will tell you exactly what the nineties brought: Robespierre and *La Terreur*, the guillotine, tumbrils rumbling through the streets, heads rolling, the Committee for Public Safety, insurrection in Vendée, massacres of helpless women and children on a massive scale. Thermidor, the revolt of Vendémiaire, the coup of 18 Fructidor, and finally 18 Brumaire, 1799, the return of order under the man of destiny, Napoleon Bonaparte.

Laclos lived through this chaotic, murderous firefight. Broadway audiences are giggling their way through *Liaisons* without the faintest notion that what it is about (a soldier's view) is the pathetic weakness of high-minded virtue, and the certainty of its destruction by the forces of evil.

Note: A successful Hollywood movie was made of *Les Liaisons Dangeureuses* and covered with honors. Most of what I have said about the stage adaptation of *Liaisons* applies to the film, which has a moralistic ending, however, perhaps influenced by the earlier French film of the novel, directed by Roger Vadim and starring Jeanne Moreau and Gérard Philippe.

9

Cry Fraud: Attenborough's Cry Freedom

WHEN THE DUKE AND THE DAUPHIN, rightful King of France, known to his friends as "Bilgewater," get pelted with tomatoes and dead cats for their Grand Shakespearean Revival (a mixture of *Hamlet* and *Macbeth*), the logical thing for them to do in Mark Twain's immortal *Huckleberry Finn* is to skedaddle out of town and float down the Mississippi on a raft with Nigger Jim and Huck, until, guileful and sassy as ever, they can set up in business again with mesmerizing, telling fortunes, and other assorted cons in a new river town where nobody knows them.

Well, that was a bygone age, you think. In today's "global village," with microwave transmission, infrared scanning, satellite dishes, and other communications marvels, such things are no longer possible. But aren't they? The global village is nowhere near as "global" as the gullible think.

Take Donald Woods, author of books that serve as a dubious basis for the supremely smug movie *Cry Freedom*, supposedly about the black South African martyr Steve Biko, but actually far more about the glamorous Donald Woods (two hours out of a three-hour film). The movie—which is why its commercial prospects are so dim—should be called "The Donald Woods Story," or "Donald Woods's Great Escape." Which bring us to the question, "Who is Donald Woods?"

Donald Woods has been called by blacks in his native South Africa as well as Englishmen in Britain, where he now lives, a

269

"self-promoter," "charlatan," and "fraud." And he has been charged with having almost entirely invented his great "friendship" with Steve Biko. Britain's Richard Attenborough, who directed and produced the new movie—with $4 million from Comrade Robert Mugabe's Zimbabwe—has "disgusted" numerous South African blacks because of his film's gross historical distortions.

But are Woods and Attenborough suing? My goodness, no. Exactly like the Duke and Dauphin of *Huckleberry Finn*, they have moved on to new territory—in this case the naive, well-meaning United States—where only a microscopic portion of the population has even dreamed of going to South Africa and where the American citizenry is, frankly, woefully uninformed.

A few precautions were in order, of course. The producers chose American actors to play both Woods and Biko (which shows the market for which the movie is intended), and went to considerable lengths to keep those familiar with South Africa from seeing the film before it opened. African journalists resident in the United States, whatever their political sympathies, were simply refused admission to screenings. Which allowed Donald Woods, certain that his interlocutors on U.S. television did not know South Africa, to say brazenly, "Have you been to South Africa lately?"

Well, yes, Mr. Woods, now that you mention it, I have. And far more recently than you. On my way to and from such romantic places as Angola, Mozambique, Zaire, and Zimbabwe, I have been to South Africa four times in the last six months. I've crawled all over Soweto, and Crossroads, and Guguletu, and KwaZulu, and the Transvaal. Whereas you haven't been there in the ten years since you made your suspense-ridden, thrilling "escape" by walking across a bridge.

When your film doesn't engage in outright lying (politely called "cinematographic license"), it's as out of date as the Trojan Wars. "Pass Laws," "Influx Control," the Anti-Miscegenation Act, the Immorality Act (forbidding sex between the races) were all rescinded years ago. South Africa's hotels, restaurants, the theaters, movie houses, buses, beaches, and swimming pools are now all integrated. [This was in 1987. There has been a modest regression since.]

The (nominally white) Hillbrow section of Johannesburg has more blacks than New York's Greenwich Village. [Still true.] White South Africans adore Eddie Murphy in the movies, Bill Cosby on television. Their favorite rock singers are Michael Jackson and Whitney Houston. One of my recent visits to South Africa was with two black American clergymen, who were stunned. The whole experience turned them against sanctions.

Soweto's latest rumbles were between "Zim-Zims" and "Wararas" (contending black groups). But who knows a Zim-Zim from a Warara in America? Eh, Mr. Woods?

One of Donald Woods's favorite techniques on U.S. television, when the shadow of his South African or British past threatens to catch up with him, is to bleat, "Nameless accusations! Nameless accusations!" Which proves what I have long maintained: that television is an improper medium for demagogues or shameless charlatans. Nameless accusations? I will give Woods some names.

Muntu Myeza is the spokesman of AZAPO, the Azanian People's Organization, linear descendant of the South Africa's "Black Consciousness" movement of which Steve Biko was one of the founders. "This is not a film about Biko," said Myeza of *Cry Freedom*. Not only does it totally misrepresent Biko's policies, "It is merely a film about Donald Woods's experiences, which if it had not been for Biko would have been mediocre." The AZAPO leadership was so incensed that it threatened to "drive the film from the screen" unless the producers included a notice in the credits pointing out that AZAPO entirely dissociates itself from the movie.

Another name: Strini Moodley, now a journalist, heavily involved in the Black Consciousness movement, and one of Steve Biko's closest companions for ten years before Moodley was sent to prison on Robben Island. Moodley declared, "We are disgusted that Attenborough should use Woods's brief acquaintance with Steve as the basis for a feature film."

Joining innumerable other former colleagues of Biko, Moodley declared it was completely out of character for the Black Consciousness leader so completely to have swallowed his principles as to form a genuine and equal friendship—no matter how brief—with a "white liberal."

For Steve Biko, said Moodley, white liberals were phoneys who pretended to have "black souls wrapped up in white skins." Biko proclaimed unambiguously that to accept white liberals like Woods as allies was (I quote) "the biggest mistake the black world ever made."

Woods, who lived in South Africa in cushioned luxury and drove a Mercedes Benz, simply published for a time a column by one of Biko's associates. According to Muntu Myeza, Strini Moodley, and many others, this was the extent of their great friendship. After Biko's death, of course, Woods went into his "I-Was-Hitler's-Barber" mode.

South Africa's "Black Consciousness" movement was, to put it in American terms, a black nationalist movement—with Steve Biko as its Stokley Carmichael, Rap Brown, or Malcom X. With Abraham Tiro, Steve Biko was the main mover of a 1972 Saso Conference resolution which proclaimed: *This country belongs to the black people and to them alone.* Otherwise put, "Whites Out."

In the present movie ("Donald Woods's Great Escape," so to speak), Steve Biko—scarcely more than a character role—is made to mouth the current African National Congress watchword, "The land belongs to all." Which sounds much nicer to Senator Ted Kennedy. This tasteful touching-up is not surprising, since the ANC had veto power over the film's screenplay. ANC leader Oliver Tambo's son was the movie's "consultant." But Muntu Myeza and Biko's old associates say this ANC line is in blatant violation of Biko's most deeply held convictions, and an attempt by the ANC to steal someone else's martyr.

So the magic of the cinema has converted Rap Brown into Martin Luther King, Jr. But Dickie Attenborough can work miracles when someone puts up the money. The Indians paid for his *Gandhi* and we got the Indian (and Soviet) "peace" line. And he has done it again.

During the June 1976 riots in Soweto, it was not white police who did the firing as shown in *Cry Freedom,* but black police.

Woods said it would have been "too confusing" to show black policemen shooting blacks. Tribalism, omnipresent in Africa, is totally absent from the movie. Moreover, the person who examines the body of Biko, who died in the hands of the police, was not Woods, as shown in the film, but a pathologist as required by South African law. Justice Minister James Kruger, in a development of great importance omitted from the film, was held responsible for the scandal and left office in disgrace. The whole affair, which was also not shown in the film, contributed to the subsequent downfall of the Vorster government.

Just a few years before Steve Biko's death, and not too many miles to the north in Zambia, the Zambian security forces slaughtered hundreds and hundreds of their own citizens when they liquidated the dissident Lumpa Church—over ten times as many people as were killed at Sharpeville. And the Lumpa Church massacres were really black on black. Black victims, black police, black government. But no Zambian justice minister was forced to resign in disgrace. Nor did any Zambian government fall.

What? You've never heard of the Lumpa Church massacres in Zambia? How strange. If some nice nonaligned country puts up the money, perhaps Sir Dickie Attenborough will make the movie. You say he won't? Well, I suppose you're right. The man has principles.

Note: Whether the American movie audience has principles or for whatever reason, *Cry Freedom* was one of the worst box-office fiascos of the season.

10

Splendor and the Beijing Party Line: Bertolucci's The Last Emperor

I WAS A LITTLE SWINE when I was Emperor of China—mean, vicious, thinking only of myself. Other people were hardly human beings. I was really rotten. Then came these saintly people called Communists under the leadership of our beloved Chairman Mao and they completely remolded me into a socialist man, caring, generous, for the first time in my life feeling love for my fellow creatures.

Beijing has even made a movie about me called *The Last Emperor,* as I'm now an ornament of the regime, proving the regenerative power of socialism working even with a little turd like me. My old palace servants say I'm as abject and servile to the Communists as I was earlier to the Chinese warlords and Japanese imperialists—whose "puppet emperor" I was in the days when they ruled Manchukuo. But don't believe them! I'm really this remolded socialist person.

I would like to point out, furthermore, that for five years at the end of World War II I was held by the Russians, receiving VIP treatment of course. But did they remould me? No! It took idealistic *Chinese* Communists to rebuild me into a socialist man. That's a little point I wouldn't want you to overlook.

Beijing has sunk $25 million into this movie. And we got a nice little Italian Communist to direct it, Bernardo Bertolucci, a member of the Italian Communist Party (stipulated in the contract). An article of faith of our leaders is that socialist man is almost a different animal from capitalist man, warlord man, landlord man, emperor man, and certainly Soviet man, but that you can remold these latter debased types. The film illustrates this deeply held faith, and I want you to consider the fact that we paid for the movie pure coincidence.

We had a nasty experience with another Italian Communist, Michelangelo Antonioni, who made a movie in China once and did us dirty because he was a Moscow-line scumbag. We launched an Anti-Antonioni Campaign against him later, along with our Anti-Confucius Campaign and our Anti-Shakespeare Campaign. Wiser now, we watched this Bertolucci like a hawk.

The new film contains substantial departures from the historical record. It even contains substantial departures from my autobiography, at which my ghostwriter and I labored so tirelessly for four years at the luxurious Fragrant Hills Hotel, eating and sipping tea while people were starving. Because I was a remolded socialist man by then, and had dinner every Chinese New Year's with Premier Chou En Lai, of whom I was a real pet. But all departures from history and autobiography are hereby authorized by me, because for a socialist man the Party, at any given time is always right.

In socialist China we've concluded, by the way, that sex is bad for you. We're a little puritanical. But since we wanted to make the movie attractive to foreigners, we allowed Bertolucci some sex scenes, particularly one in which the empress, I, and my number-two wife have sex, all three of us together. Now modesty forbids me telling of my real sex life. But I think I can repeat what is said of me: that I was homosexual, or bisexual, totally impotent with my wives, liked little girls, and had sadistic tendencies. You can see this wouldn't look good in a movie even about my pre-socialist period.

The film sequences with me and my wet nurse also somehow look like sex scenes, with my nurse beautiful and with gorgeous breasts, dressed like a rich and glamorous member of the court. Actually I was devoted to this humble woman precisely because she was poor, uneducated, and so unlike the repulsive royal family. She was a peasant girl selected for the quantity and quality of her milk, and breast fed me until I was eight. But wonderful, simple, humble person that she was, she never complained at my chewing on her nipple, and I gleaned from this selflessness on her part my first inkling of the virtue of the common people.

I must pay tribute to this Bertolucci. Even living the luxurious high life in Rome, a positive cesspool of capitalist exploitation, selfishness, and individualism, he realized that we, in socialist China, have attained a higher moral order. He nonetheless *compels* himself in the movie to show the appalling opulence and pageantry of the Manchu court, which made me the terrible person I used to be.

The biggest departures from the historical record, however, are omissions. It is now accepted in Beijing that Mao's half-baked "Great Leap Forward," the repression that followed his sneaky invitation to "Let A Hundred Flowers Bloom," and above all his murderous "Cultural Revolution," were flaming catastrophes. I mean 30 million dead (official figure), or 40 million dead (unofficial). Big numbers. It is also official now that for all the deaths, deportations, maimings, with Mao's Red Guards running rampant beating people to death in the streets, China's net economic progress for the last twenty years of Mao's life was: zero.

This was a very tricky business for me to handle in my autobiography, *From Emperor To Citizen,* published in 1964. Here I was abasing myself, atoning, remolding myself into a socialist man, and for what? Mainland China was bloody, chaotic, and starving, while Taiwan, under that devil Chiang Kai Shek, was skyrocketing, doubling its standard of living every eight years. Even poor people were rich. I figured the better part of valor for a remoulded emperor was to shut up.

With the Red Guards on the rampage, only Shirley MacLaine was safe. President Liu Shao Chi died in agony. Marshall Chuh Teh, hero of the Long March, died after repeated humiliation by Red Guards. Leader Teng Hsiao Ping's own son was thrown out of a three-story window and is now a paraplegic. Fortunately most of this happened after my pub date.

It was all officially recognized before this Bertolucci movie, of course. The present masters of the Imperial City are prudent men, however, and haven't gone in for wholesale de-Maoization for fear of delegitimizing the whole system. The film therefore contains only "hints." When I return to Beijing after my remolding I am fictitiously shown witnessing a parade where my "teacher," the man in charge of my remolding, is paraded through the streets by Red Guards with a dunce cap on his head.

I protest, am ignored. But it is only an incident. A bit of whimsy that stands for perhaps 40 million dead. You soon see me in the movie happily gardening, something I never really did. Even as a socialist man I was never good with tools and never bothered to turn off faucets, flush toilets, or anything tedious like that. I gave a lot of people a pain.

I understand film critics in foreign lands, who wouldn't know a Red Guard from a Grand Imperial High Consort, are raving about *The Last Emperor,* some calling it a marvelous "lesson in history." If the scriptwriter told them I was George Washington's grandson, I suppose they'd believe that, too. Ten years remolding in a socialist corrective labor camp would do some of them a lot of good.

11

From Russia With Angst: The Burglar

THERE IS NO HOPE. All is despair and alienation. Society has failed the individual, who is offered only bankrupt values and the meaningless shards of a dead culture, inhumane, indifferent, hypocritical. Alcoholism and drugs are rampant. Uncared-for children, with nothing to believe in, cluster in antisocial groups, delinquent.

No, not America, you dummy. Russia! The Soviet Union! And this according to the latest Soviet art film, *The Burglar,* surely one of the most innovatively gloomy artistic works to be produced in the whole history of the Soviet state.

Someone who has not suffered total immersion in Soviet culture probably finds it hard to imagine how goody-goody its movies, art, and literature have been, above all since the introduction some sixty years ago of "socialist realism" as the enforced artistic canon. Visiting Englishmen have sometimes been reminded of the combination of prudery and uplift that made up High Victorianism. Much of it had me thinking: "Early YMCA."

A modest degree of criticism of the little imperfections of Soviet life has always been allowed, but this was inevitably accompanied by strenuous exhortations to the individual to live up to what was after all a perfectly conceived system. The tone of all art and literature was relentlessly optimistic. *Glasnost* (which doesn't mean "openness" but "giving voice") is not as great a theoretical departure as the West often imagines. Al-

279

though limits have been hugely extended, *glasnost* is still purposeful. Its intention is to improve the functioning of Soviet society and the Soviet economy, to make "Soviet man" more productive.

At election time, Americans hear extensive discourses on the "American dream." But the Soviet Union, too, has a dream, of which its citizens hear their fill: a collectivist dream, as befits a collectivist state. The dream is that their society—collectively—will forge ahead, must forge ahead. The workers' paradise is coming. Onwards and upwards with Soviet man. Moscow wants its citizens to raise their *glas* (voice) usefully. Official Soviet culture has never had room for romantic brooders like Arthur Rimbaud or Herman Melville.

The Burglar, then, is a *glas* I frankly never expected to hear raised in the USSR. It's the very model of what the French understand when they call a film or novel *noir* ("black") or *maudit* ("accursed"), meaning deeply pessimistic. *The Burglar* is pessimistic about Soviet youth, Soviet culture, Soviet life, and even the Soviet future.

The movie was shot in Leningrad, Russia's grandest city, but we see nothing of the czarist capital's splendid palaces, canals, bridges, or indeed any exteriors at all, only interior squalor. We have slummy, overcrowded apartments, each lodging several families; archaic plumbing; peeling paint; waterstained walls; young Leningraders dressed in tacky imitations of Anglo-American "punk" styles with spiky dyed hair.

The film's central character, twelve-year-old Senka, is a victim of what sociologists call anomie, "a breakdown of social norms." His father is a drunken workman, his older brother, Kostya, a third-rate rock singer. (If you've never heard Russian rock, you can die happy.) His father's girlfriend washes dishes for a living and is miserable. His brother's girlfriend is a manicurist and also miserable.

All Kostya's friends are aimless Russian punks and rockers. Nowhere, anywhere in *Burglar* is there the slightest hint of "proletarian idealism" or what Kremlin ideologues used to call the "workers' state," where the individual achieves fulfilment by harmonious integration into the collectivity.

The state's attempts to integrate its citizens culturally is, in fact, ridiculed. We see a prissy schoolteacher and pitiful middle-brow dance numbers coming over Soviet black-and-white TV sets. Young Senka is shown ineptly playing the French horn in a school orchestra. The conductor is remarkably fatuous, his chest covered with World War II ribbons, which plainly no longer mean anything to the movie's young people.

Nor does *The Burglar* end on an upbeat. Depressing from the first frame, it goes even lower for the final sequence. Senka is apprehended for robbery and in a last, sustained shot is shown sitting bleakly on a symbolic pile of rubble. Is this what the future holds for Soviet youth? What are we to make of such an unrelievedly morbid Soviet film?

The Burglar is obviously a reaction to decades of compulsory social and artistic optimism. There might also be an element of artistic affectation—the result of studiously imitating Western models. The social pathology depicted is real, however, the kind of pathology of which Westerners often assume we have a monopoly. We do not.

The greatest significance of the film in Russia might well be its function as a safety valve, letting off steam from all those years of bitter frustration. In the 1960s, radical philosopher Herbert Marcuse, thinking deep thoughts out in California, came up with the concept of "repressive tolerance," meaning that the freedoms people appear to enjoy in Western society are merely a more insidious form of repression. This is a theory to which I've never subscribed.

But we may now try out Marcuse's theory on Russia. Is the release of *The Burglar* an example of "repressive tolerance" on Moscow's part? Or of real tolerance? In fact, the old-fashioned "safety valve" metaphor seems to tell us more than Marcuse. But will this safety valve ensure safety? The same week I saw *The Burglar,* hundreds of thousands of Balts were allowed to demonstrate in Estonia, Latvia, and Lithuania calling for (previously unheard of) secession from the Soviet Union.

A few years ago, blood would have run in the streets. But the fear factor seems to be dropping fast. We can only wait to see what happens next.

12

Fidel and Vanity Fair *Get Married: The Havana Film Festival*

H ERE I WAS worried about poor old Fidel Castro, portly, grizzly, the romantic young revolutionary turned ideological dinosaur. But *Vanity Fair* has saved him! It carries on the cover of its fifth-anniversary issue "Sisters in Glitz" with a supremely airbrushed photograph of Jackie and Joan Collins. And right in there with the Collins girls is glamour coverage of the Havana Film Festival and glitzy Fidel Castro.

The Festival, I learn to my astonishment, is concerned with politics as well as movies. But that's okay, because it has glitzy politics, glitzy parties, glitzy artists. Novelist Gabriel Garcia Marquez, Fidel's "best friend," is not your frugal kind of leftist, you understand, but has five luxurious homes on three continents.

At the Festival, which Garcia Marquez attends as head of Cuba's Film Foundation, the daiquiris flow like water at parties for honored overseas guests, with heavy security forces to keep out the lower orders. No threadbare Cubans off the street, please.

Now offhand you wouldn't think Fidel Castro was a terrific candidate for glitzhood. He has reduced Cuba from the third richest country in Latin America to destitution, its basket-case economy kept afloat by $5 billion a year from the Soviet Union. He hires out his young men to serve as Soviet mercenaries in Africa, and if they're crippled or get AIDS they don't come back. All this to preserve in Cuba a rationed pauperism which

283

allows women to buy one bra or one pair of panties per year. One or the other.

Nor does Fidel have the sexiness of Mikhail Gorbachev with his sparkling talk of *glasnost,* attempting to rejuvenate the unproductive Soviet economy by introducing market mechanisms borrowed from capitalism. Fidel stands firm against pandering to the petty materialism of the Cuban riffraff, keeping his eye fixed on the bright star of Leninism.

For Cuba is the Western Hemisphere's Albania—which is every bit as worthy of the glitz treatment as Cuba. It's really unfair. Here Albania is as fossilized as Cuba, no *glasnost,* no *perestroika.* But Cuba has a whole series of unfair advantages.

Havana has been enticingly Sandinista-ized, you see. It has the support of airheads in Hollywood and elsewhere who, intimidated a few years back, have reverted with slight changes of phrasing to the 1960s conviction that "America is the greatest force for evil in the world today." Anyone who opposes America is consequently irresistably sexy.

Breeze through *Vanity Fair*'s heady advertising. Ultima II: "For the woman who dares leave civilization behind" (in the background a helicopter landing on a tropical beach). Saks Fifth Avenue: "Saks understands. The nonstop potential of soft-suiting." Marshall Field's: "The soothing infusion of icy pastels strewn over neutral. Call it emotional architecture if you will" (blouse: $395). Calvin Klein, Gucci. Tiffany, Giorgio Armani, Fendi, Lalique, Yves Saint Laurent, Chanel, Louis Vuitton. Lancôme: "revolutionary micro-bubbles dispersed in two revolutionary formulations" (two "revolutionaries").

Now what on earth, you are thinking, do women who can afford $395 blouses, dress themselves in emotional architecture, treat their skin with revolutionary microbubbles, and whose idea of the tropics is landing on a beach in a private helicopter, see in Fidel Castro? Fidel has proclaimed that money for these goodies comes from merciless *gringo* exploitation of Latin America. And most of these women, after all, are *gringos.* Furthermore, Fidel has established a regime whose only "nonstop potential" seems to be repression and miserable poverty.

As a moral action, it seems to me, these *gringo* ladies, if they're sincere, should give up the soothing infusion of icy pastels strewn over neutral and go forward with the vanguard of the proletariat to a single pair of panties every two years.

But this line of reasoning misses the magic that makes a magazine for superior people work. Superior people want to wear superior clothes, superior makeup, superior perfume, go to superior places like Paris, London, Rome. But they're also ineluctably drawn to superior *ideas,* by which I mean ideas not shared by the vulgar.

Every scruffy Marielito knows he's better off in an American prison than free in Cuba. *But is a reader of* Vanity Fair *not superior to a scruffy Marielito?*

So the magazine sent a giddy female reporter to the Havana Film Festival, which she covered as a kind of moral society event—which is like an ordinary society event except that everything is morally thrilling.

U.S. film director Oliver Stone won an award—not for *Platoon* but for *Salvador,* which all of 150 people in the United States saw, I think, but which supports dashing Marxist-Leninist rebels against the U.S.–supported government. At a reception we shake the hand of Fidel himself! (Beautiful women swoon.) Then the hand of Garcia Marquez! Then the Nicaraguan vice-president! Salvadoran revolutionaries! Uruguayan revolutionaries! A Canadian television crew is there with Margaret Trudeau! Robert Redford almost came!

Our reporter gives a breathless account of the wonders of Communist Cuba and how everything bad in the Western Hemisphere is the doing of the United States. She gives no sign of seeing a single film at the festival or of speaking Spanish, spending all her time at luxury hotels for foreigners and at lavish parties given at palatial houses for official guests of the state.

Marxist sea breezes cool the night lawns. Marxist pigs are roasted over open fires. Glasses of *mojitos* are handed over tables groaning with Marxist delicacies. We dance the samba, the mambo, the cha-cha-cha, the merengue. "I haven't partied like this since I was a kid," says a fetching American creature. "And there aren't even any drugs going down."

But who needs drugs at this, the advent of Marxist glitz? As savored by the superior people who read *Vanity Fair*.

13

Art Hysteria: The Modern's "Committed to Print"

TIRED? FRAZZLED? Worn out by politics? Have I got the art show for you!

Art hasn't been the same since Andy Warhol's Brillo pads and Campbell's soup. But oughtn't it still contain something serene, tranquil, timeless, that lifts you out of yourself, helps you along life's weary way?

I'm in this sort of mood, so to escape the smashing cymbals of electioneering in New York I duck into Manhattan's celebrated Museum of Modern Art. The Cézanne show? I hesitate, then follow the crowd into what is plainly the hot show of the season, "Committed to Print." Photostats, silk screen, offset, wall posters, billboards, "body prints" made by people covering themselves with paint and pressing against a big piece of paper, they're all art now.

But "committed" to anything beside print? Well, with William S. Paley, David Rockefeller, and Mrs. John D. Rockefeller III among the trustees it can't be anything subversive. In addition, the show is funded by the New York State Council on the Arts and National Endowment for the Arts. It's almost official, America's finest, a celebration of America.

The first thing that catches my eye is a print of the U.S. flag, but distorted, misshapen. The catalogue tells me the distortion is an "eloquent statement of forboding and concern." Forboding about what, for goodness sake?

Part of a nearby lithograph, "Cold Light," reproduces the

287

front page of a newspaper with the headlines: *"William Calley, Laos, Red Chinese."* Next is a map of the United States with the inscription: *"The United States of Attica. Founded by the American People on September 13, 1971, at Attica Prison, N.Y., Where 42 Men Gave Their Lives in an Heroic Struggle for Freedom. The Judson Three."* But who were the Judson Three?

We have an etching of six pistols with "phallic associations," the catalogue says, then a print of *El Grito de Rebelde* ("Cry of the Rebel"), a man bound and blindfolded on the cover of a periodical called *Toward Revolutionary Art.* The print is from a photograph of an Iranian political prisoner circa 1974, thus a prisoner of the Shah. Which is to say the prisoner might be one of those terrific people who gave us the Ayatollah Khomeini, and who took all those American hostages in Tehran, and who, on occasion, are still heard screaming, "Death to America!"

My eye begins to weary a little, but I slog on: masses marching under a red banner, El Salvador, Uruguay, the Dominican Republic. If you read Russian: "Thank you, Comrade Stalin, for our daily bread." (I repeat: "Stalin.") There's a really good one with a boxer being punched out and the slightly mysterious legend "We get exploded because they've got *money* and *God.*" Fortunately I have the catalogue which explains, *"exploded* calls to mind *exploited* in the context of 'money' and 'God.' "

"The face of a boxer receiving a blow to the head," it reads, "dramatizes the implied act of exploitation and gives it a violent dimension. The work as a whole intimates that the success of one group is, almost by definition, at the expense of another." I wonder if the curator ever studied modern economics, or if he checked any of this out with Mr. Rockefeller.

We next have racial oppression in "both the Third World and our own cities," gay repression, Chicano repression, sexist repression, just plain repression, *La Lucha Continua* ("The Struggle Continues"). And this is just the first room.

In the second room, "Governments/Leaders," I see repellent evocations of Richard Nixon, Lyndon Johnson *(LBJ Murderer),* and Ronald Reagan, plus a timely explanation of what's wrong with the world. We have a huge poster with, filling the top half, the word "Cause" superimposed on the U.S. Capitol building, and, filling the bottom half, "Effect" superimposed on a mass grave with thousands of human skulls. The message—subtly insinuated—is that the United States government causes death.

I'm beginning to think this show is a little one-sided when I catch sight of another American flag. But in place of the red stripes are printed words: "The American People are the only people who can interpret the American flag, a flag which does not belong to the people to do with as they see fit. Should be burned and forgotten. Artists, workers, students, women, Third World peoples. You are oppressed. What does the flag mean to you? Join the people's answer to the repressive U.S. government and state laws restricting our use and display of the flag."

There is room after room of this stuff. America, in case you haven't gotten the idea, is vicious, violent, racist, sexist, exploitive, repressive. Nuclear weapons and power are bad. God is bad. But with war, it depends. If there's a revolution and you're a Marxist-Leninist, and hence on the side of the people, war is good. But if it's war against urban guerrillas, rural guerrillas, other Marxist-Leninists and hence against the people, war is bad.

Take Nguyen Van Tro, executed in 1964 for attempting to murder Defense Secretary Robert McNamara in Saigon and here memorialized. He is very good. McNamara is bad.

Near the end is an aquatint of a crying Statue of Liberty, reflecting "the complexities of the American experience." The artist is quoted as saying "I think Liberty has a great deal to cry for."

Which leaves me puzzled about one thing. A large number of contributors to the present show came from all over the world: Iran, Lithuania, Brazil, Holland, Argentina, Sweden, Venezuela, China, Spain, Ireland, Chile, France, Uruguay, England, South Korea, West Germany, and Cuba. If America is such a foul, repressive place, *why have all these artists come here to live?*

If Luis Cruz Azaceta thinks America is so awful, he can always go back to his native Cuba, which is not only free of all the evils he finds in the United States but where, I understand,

Fidel Castro just adores protest art. Hans Haacke could live an idyllic life in East Germany. Young Soon Min could attain ultimate freedom in North Korea. If I felt like these people, I wouldn't stay here a minute.

14

Eggs for the Soviet Omelette: The Russian Avant-Garde of the 1920s

I MAGINE AN EXHIBITION on the Jewish Holocaust that showed only smiling children, happy families, bucolic picnics, comfortable homes with serene people, connubial, cozy. You say to the person who organized the exhibition: "But it has only happy people." And he answers: "Yes, we decided to show how happy the Jews were *before* the Holocaust."

Such an exhibition might leave you with a peculiar, suspended feeling. Of course everyone knows what happened to Jews once they were given into the tender care of Heinrich Himmler. But do people know what happened to avant-garde Russian painters of the first decades of this century once Stalin controlled Soviet life in the 1930s?

In his preface to the Hirshhorn Museum's splendid show of "Russian and Soviet Paintings, 1900–1930," Robert McCormick Adams, secretary of the Smithsonian Institution, tells us that cultural exchanges between America and the Soviet Union are steps toward "mutual understanding." But the show's cut-off date of 1930 gives us precious little understanding of what happened to Soviet painting, or Soviet painters, when the artistic ice age descended. There's not a clue to their fate in either the show or the catalog.

The oldest Communist one-liner is: "You can't make an omelette without breaking eggs." Once upon a time in Russia, a defender of the Soviet system delivered the line to a visiting

Romanian novelist and revolutionary, Panait Istrati, who was disillusioned with what he was seeing in the Soviet motherland. Unfortunately, few remember Istrati's quick rejoinder: "I can see the broken eggs. Where's the omelette?"

The Russian show at the Hirshhorn, while still revealing no omelette (which, according to recent admissions from the Kremlin, would be rather hard to find), at least shows us what Russia's artistic eggs were like before they got broken. For all its Jews-before-the-Holocaust feeling, it is a remarkable exhibition.

The avant-garde culture that flourished in the Russian Empire in the early part of the century, continuing into the first years of the Bolshevik regime, was one of the great modern movements, dynamic, vibrant, turbulent, varied. The best-known names in the West are Kandinsky, Chagall, Malevich, Rodchenko, and Goncharova, but there were many schools: Suprematism, Rayonism, Cubo-futurism, Constructivism, Neo-primitivism. In its timing and variety, modernism in Russia most closely paralleled that in Germany.

Both Russia and Germany made breakthroughs in absolutely all the arts. In both, many of the artists were politically active. And the modern movements in both countries were suddenly crushed by a totalitarian power: in Germany, Hitler's National Socialism, in Russia, the Soviet variety. Yet with the exception of celebrated expatriates like Chagall, and despite its intrinsic interest, Russia's modern movement has remained comparatively unknown in the West, and this precisely because Soviet authorities have kept so much of it in basements under lock and key.

The leading Russian artists of the pre-1917 period generally shared a belief in the coming political revolution. At its triumph they were ecstatic, seeing limitless freedom in the destruction of the old order. The new authorities, in fact, at first elevated the avant-garde to a height never attained anywhere before or since, and for a time Soviet modernism had behind it the full force of the state.

It lasted only a few years. Already in the late 1920s the Soviet regime began to denounce modernism as inaccessible to "the masses," preferring what Maxim Gorky admitted was the "consoling lie" of Socialist Realism. Some of Russia's great modern artists died in the 1920s. Others fled or disappeared in Stalin's purges. Of the fifty-seven painters in the present show (from the collections of the Tretyakov Gallery in Moscow and the State Russian Museum in Leningrad), a full quarter fled the Soviet Union. The last resting place of two others is unknown.

Painters either accepted to work in the "Socialist Realism" style, featuring muscled, heroic, Soviet man—an "inspiring example to the masses"—or were forced out of their profession. Entire artists' studios were destroyed. Chagall, Kandinsky, and Goncharova fled abroad.

Gustav Klutsis was accused of not showing the "class enemy" in his posters and was sent into the Gulag where he died. Dmitri Grinevich openly rejected Socialist Realism, refused to join the Union of Soviet Artists, and spent eight years in the Gulag. He fought in World War II in a penal battalion.

Alexandr Rodchenko was expelled from *October,* his official art unit, and spent the last twenty years of his life in isolation and obscurity. Kazimir Malevich, the father of Suprematism (his best known work in America is "White on White" in New York's Museum of Modern Art), resisted pressure for many years but finally brought himself to produce the official art he despised.

But one of the most tragic figures is the gifted Pavel Filonov, a particularly determined artistic refusenik. Forbidden to exhibit his paintings, he found work as a janitor, caught pneumonia, and, weak from hunger, collapsed in the snow during the 1941 siege of Leningrad and froze to death. The State Russian Museum in Leningrad has over 400 of his paintings and drawings, preserved with devotion by his sister. They have never been exhibited. Two of his paintings, unearthed at last for America, are in the current show. [In 1988 a large retrospective of his work was shown in Moscow and Leningrad, and in 1990 in Paris.]

It is sad to think how enthusiastically most of these artists first supported the Bolshevik Revolution. But we had a stranger if less generous example in Paris, where Pablo Picasso became an ardent Communist during the Stalin period, at a time when Moscow still condemned his work as degenerate and kept his paintings in the Hermitage cellar. Although Picasso knew this, and lived until 1973, he allowed himself to become an ornament of the world Communist movement. He never bothered to visit the Soviet Union.

15

The Ruckus Over Jesus: Scorsese's The Last Temptation of Christ

S ATAN APPEARED UNTO ME in the form of an innocent child. And he spake unto me, "Make thee a movie of the life of Jesus, showing him as a man, loving women." And I said, "No, it would be blasphemy." And Satan said, "He will have a loving wife and children, even as any man." And I said, "No, I would burn in Hell." And Satan said, "I'll offer you a three-picture deal at Universal, with ten percent of the gross and a million dollar guarantee if you bring the picture in under seven million." And I said, "Let me think it over."

Satan offered the same deal to Martin Scorsese, who, being under the spiritual influence of Nikos Kazantzakis (*Zorba the Greek*), the world's most famous Greek after Michael Dukakis, didn't hesitate a minute.

And lo, it came to pass that the movie adaptation of Kazantzakis's *The Last Temptation of Christ*—co-starring in the romantic roles Willem Dafoe (*Platoon*'s good sergeant) and Barbara Hershey (*A World Apart*'s lady Communist)—became in America the theological event of the year. Dafoe and Hershey play that devoted couple Jesus and Mary Magdalene, not often portrayed in this connubial light, which is causing a bit of a ruckus.

I approach the subject of *The Last Temptation of Christ* with deep prejudice, having actually seen the movie and read the book, which is a pretty dumb book (the Greek novel, not the New Testament). But what else do you expect of a man who acquired, to warm his aged bones, Melina Mercouri, later Greek culture minister, but then a young actress determined to make something of herself? Earlier, Kazantzakis was much given to sins of the flesh, God and Satan struggling in him daily.

Yes, I was outside the Ziegfeld Theatre at one o'clock Friday afternoon for the first public showing of *The Last Temptation of Christ,* a member of that churning mass, those struggling to get into the movie, and those demonstrating against it: fundamentalist Protestants, Catholic Old Believers, Mormons, Greek Orthodox, Orthodox Jews, with banners and giant placards, *"Lord Jesus, never in 2,000 years of Christian civilization have such defaming insults been hurled at Thee before such an immense public."* I still haven't figured out what the Jews were doing there.

The news media gave saturation coverage to the event, while in Hollywood leading film directors—Warren Beatty, Sidney Pollock, Peter Bogdanovich—spoke earnestly of freedom of expression, which might have been more impressive if any of them had been Christian. The arguments they advanced would have been more convincing if they'd been defending a remake of that great Nazi anti-Semitic epic, *The Jew Süss,* for example, thereby clearly identifying themselves with the hallowed doctrine, "I disagree with what he says, but I'll fight to the death for his right to say it." But this didn't seem to occur to them.

Kazantzakis was a Seeker. Born in 1883, he was first a Greek nationalist against the hated Turk. Then came a Christian-mystic period when he prayed for six months on Mount Athos trying to achieve direct contact with the Savior. Unsuccessful, he became a disciple of Nietzsche—who loathed Christianity, considering it a religion for weaklings.

In time Kazantzakis repudiated Nietzsche for Buddha, then Buddha for Lenin. He "sang lovingly" for a time about the Soviet Union. "For there in Russia," he wrote, "the new myth of God will assume flesh and blood. From there will come our salvation." While continuing to dream of an ideal system he called "metacommunism," he was finally disappointed in garden-variety Communism and returned to Christianity.

In *The Last Temptation of Christ,* Kazantzakis with rare

confidence "supplemented" what he considered the obviously incomplete account found in the Gospels, adding "noble and passionate" embellishments "befitting Christ's heart." "Words which we do not know He said I have put in His mouth," wrote Kazantzakis, explaining that if it weren't for the obviously mediocre intellectual quality of the Disciples, Christ patently "would have said them."

At the appearance of the book, theologians were shocked by the human "temptations" attributed to Jesus. Kazantzakis's answer was an appeal to higher authority: himself. "While I was writing this book, I felt what Christ felt," he explained. *"I became Christ* (his emphasis). And I knew definitely that great temptations, extremely enchanting and often legitimate, came to hinder him on his road to Golgotha."

We are plainly dealing here with a conceit rarely encountered in this world. Kazantzakis is not really anti-clerical, or even irreligious. I've seen on the stage in Paris basketballs thrown through the crown of thorns. I've seen in Belgium Christ's Passion displayed from the point of view of Barabbas. I've seen a famous Austrian play called *The Council of Love* in which the members of Holy Trinity are shown inventing venereal disease. Kazantzakis does none of these things. He simply, confidently, in a spirit he imagines to be utterly Christian, refashions Jesus in his own image.

Jesus's human character is apparent from the start of the film, but it's the last thirty minutes that set many people's teeth on edge. Jesus's "last temptation" is when, on the cross, he imagines what it would have been like to live the life of an ordinary man. We see Jesus and Mary Magdalene making love. They apparently aren't made for each other, Mary Magdalene is killed off, and Jesus then marries Mary, Lazarus's sister. He dallies with still another sister of Lazarus, Martha. But he and Mary have children, grow old. And finally His dream ends, and Jesus returns to the cross and dies for our sins.

Opinions of church men vary considerably. Paul Moore, Episcopal Bishop of New York, who is never unfashionable, thinks *The Last Temptation* is "right on." John Cardinal O'Connor of New York declined to boycott the film but said "sensible" people would avoid it. I say *The Last Temptation of Christ* is a handsomely made film, rather stupid, blasphemous, of course, and a monument to the extraordinary self-infatuation of Nikos Kazantzakis.

16

PBS at the Bat: Nestor Almendros's Nobody Listened

And somewhere men are laughing,
And somewhere children shout,
But there is no joy in Cuba.
Mighty Castro has struck out.

S UCH, AT LEAST, is the opinion of Cubans, whose hopes were
high when *glasnost* and *perestroika* broke out in the Soviet
Union. Marvelous to behold, it is also the opinion, however
newly espoused, of at least a few of those bubbly ecstatics who
make up the American artistic Left.

Fidel Castro's 1988 speech on the anniversary of his attack on
the Moncada Barracks was the occasion of widespread disappointment among long-suffering Cubans. With reform sweeping
over the Communist world, they'd hoped change might be
coming in Havana too.

But Castro was categorical. There was no need for glasnost in
Cuba, he declared in his three-hour speech. "If someone has a
toothache," he asked, "why should he wear a cornplaster?"
Cuba must not imitate the Soviet Union in its experimentation
with capitalist mechanisms but rely on the "purity" of its
ideology.

The word of the hour in Havana is "rectification," a return to
rigid doctrine after Castro's own limited experiment with free
market techniques for marketing farm produce. He decided
material incentives were corrupting Cuba and Cuban agriculture
and ordered them ended, along with bonuses for productive

workers. Although moral incentives have never created a successful economy yet, anywhere, that's the only kind of incentive *el lider* will now allow.

Proximity to the United States, which is waiting to "swallow Cuba like a ripe fruit," was used by Castro as another reason for not trying free-market techniques. He has now strictly curtailed the importation from Russia of Spanish-language editions of Soviet periodicals, and banned the liberal *Novidades de Moscu (Moscow News)* completely.

The notion of Moscow as a source of dangerous capitalist subversion for Havana takes some getting used to. But at least a fragment of the American artistic class has picked up the notion that Castro—once so vibrant, so new, so exciting—is now an "establishment" dictator, or worse, a fossil.

The dynamism of Russia's Mikhail Gorbachev has thrilled artistic Americans, and Castro suffers by comparison. He also suffered by comparison with Nicaragua's Sandinistas, who had the advantage of freshness.

The New York Public Theater's annual *Festival Latino* might be a bellweather. Normally a political playpen where a mere socialist would pass for right-of-center, the festival this year [1988] featured *Nobody Listened,* a brilliant, deeply moving documentary film on the brutal repression that Castro has brought to Cuba.

Greenwich Village intellectuals watched as Huber Matos, Eloy Gutíerrez-Menoyo, and other legendary comrades of Castro relived in the film the total extinction of liberty under the former boy revolutionary, the merciless prison beatings, executions, the country's endless, grinding poverty. Spanish speakers in the house laughed with contempt at footage from a French television documentary in which Castro extolled the virtues of his revolution.

Nobody Listened was personally presented by the Public Theater's director, Joseph Papp, and Americas Watch's Aryeh Neier, with on stage several of the film's principal personages. They included Gutíerrez-Menoyo, who commanded the anti-

Batista guerrilla forces in the Sierra del Escambray and later served twenty-two years in Castro's prisons, to be freed only after the direct intercession of Spanish President Felipe Gonzalez. Also on stage was Ariel Hidalgo, released from a Cuban prison only five days earlier after being adopted as a "prisoner of conscience" by Amnesty International.

Nobody Listened, later shown at the Kennedy Center in Washington, was directed by Nestor Almendros and Jorge Ulla, the former one of the world's greatest cinematographers—from the films of François Truffaut and *Sophie's Choice* to *Days of Heaven* (for which he won an Academy Award). Almendros's earlier documentary on Cuba, *Improper Conduct,* although extremely well received in some quarters, was violently attacked in others as "one-sidedly" anti-communist.

This time around there have been fewer attacks. New York's *Village Voice,* which speaks with authority south of Manhattan's Fourteenth Street, violently condemned *Improper Conduct* but is singing the praises of *Nobody Listened,* which has the same politics. The key here, of course, might be the change in attitude of Moscow, which no longer approves of Fidel Castro.

The last prominent holdout of the "one-sided" school of detractors of *Nobody Listened* is the Public Broadcasting Service. Over the years PBS has aired an absolutely staggering number of documentaries obsequiously favoring Marxist movements and regimes. One PBS official told Almendros openly and coldly that PBS "didn't do" anti-Communist documentaries.

A pretense of fairness obtained for a time, however, and, rather than flatly reject *Nobody Listened,* PBS looked for a pro-Castro documentary to pair with it for "balance." Are we to understand, if it were the 1930s, that an anti-Nazi documentary would have to be balanced by a film enraptured by the accomplishments of Adolf Hitler? Curious as it is to recall, Hitler had far more economic accomplishments to his credit than Fidel Castro.

It's nonetheless worth taxpayers' attention that PBS—which has a long history of infatuation with brutal Marxist regimes the world over—is at this point more protective of Fidel Castro's miserable Marxist-Leninist system in Cuba than Joseph Papp and the *Village Voice*.

The title *Nobody Listened*, of course, pertains to Cubans very much like the cultural bureaucrats of PBS. Many Cubans wouldn't listen when warned about the totalitarian Left, and got Fidel Castro. At the price of bourgeois freedoms, Castro promised boundless prosperity, but he expunged one without delivering the other, turning Cuba from the third richest country in Latin America into a pauper state dependent on Soviet handouts.

Note: Since this was written, PBS first told Nestor Almendros that *Nobody Listened* could definitely not be shown on PBS because it is too "one-sided." PBS later reversed itself, but as of July 1990 the film has not been shown.

17

The Film Director as Nazi: Ingmar Bergman

Q UESTION: WHEN IS a Nazi not a Nazi? Answer: when he is Ingmar Bergman, especially if one thinks the Swedish film director is a genius.

This at least seems to be the view of one of our deeper thinkers, Woody Allen. And I hope I'm not addressing poor unfortunates who think Woody Allen is a mere comic, for in his own view, and perhaps that of many, he ranks somewhere between Schopenhauer and Kierkegaard.

In his essay on Ingmar Bergman's autobiography, *The Magic Lantern,* beginning on page one of the *New York Times Book Review,* Allen refers in turn to: Søren Kierkegaard, German Expressionism, Sergei Eisenstein, Surrealism, the Gothic, Carl Dreyer, Anton Chekov, Augustus Strindberg, and Franz Kafka. So it's clear we are dealing with a person of some culture.

It almost entirely escapes the attention of Woody Allen, however, who is rumored to be Jewish, that Ingmar Bergman, his idol and favorite filmmaker, was in his younger years a fervid Nazi. By which I mean until Bergman was about thirty-five—and long after the armies of Adolf Hitler were defeated and Hitler himself dead.

Bergman's Nazi past is far from concealed in his book. Nor is Woody Allen the only reviewer to pass it by in silence. This is curious after innuendoes of anti-Semitism forced the resignation of one major and some quite minor officials from George Bush's campaign staff, events that utterly dominated the political news

303

just before Hurricane Gilbert, which in the orderly rationality the anti-Semitic commotion somewhat resembled.

And if Fred Malek's resignation weren't enough, one has only to recall Ronald Reagan's visit to the cemetery at Bitburg to realize how anything tainted with the Nazi past can set off a force three gale. The most absurd of all these incidents was the resignation from the Reagan White House of Jack Kohler upon discovery of the fact that, before fighting in the U.S. army against Hitler, he'd belonged to some sort of Nazi Cub Scouts at the responsible age of nine.

And yet, Ingmar Bergman, in those stirring prewar days visiting Hitler's Germany, was a full-grown Nazi and idolator of Adolf Hitler. He shouted *Heil Hitler!* with the Nazi mobs, he admits, fervently raising his arm in the Nazi salute, losing himself in the wonderful energy of the packed masses, loving the *Führer* himself.

The film director's older brother was one of the founders of Sweden's Nazi Party. His father voted for Swedish Nazis. Many of Ingmar's teachers and pastors were Nazis. His family's closest friends were strong supporters of the "New Germany." For years, simply put, Ingmar Bergman and all his Swedish relatives and friends were on Hitler's side, ecstatic at his triumphs and saddened by his defeats.

When a flood of pictures of Hitler's death camps was released to the world at the end of the war, Ingmar Bergman, "like so many others," he writes, charged heatedly that they were lying Allied propaganda.

Nor was he quick to change his mind. Other Swedish sources (this is not in his book) report Bergman's first fall-back position was the moral equivalence of Hitler and Churchill. And it was only well into the 1950s, with the director in his mid-thirties, that it sank in on our artistic film genius that Adolf Hitler was actually a bad person and had done some mischief in this world.

Here is Ingmar Bergman in *The Magic Lantern* (Viking) on his visits to the magic world of Nazi Germany:

I had never seen anything like this eruption of immense energy. I shouted like everyone else, held out my arm like everyone else, howled like everyone else, and loved it like everyone else.

During our nightly conversations, Hannes (a German friend) explained how the Germans had created a bulwark against Communism, and how the Jews had sabotaged this bulwark, and how we must all love the man who had shaped our common destiny and decisively welded us together into one will, one strength, one people.

Hannes hung a photograph of Hitler above my bed so that I would always have the man before my eyes, so that I should learn to love him in the same way as Hannes and the Haid family loved him. I loved him too. I fell headlong into an atmosphere glowing with idealism and hero worship, and an aggressiveness which to a great extent was in harmony with my own.

A *portrait of the artist as a young Nazi.* But has Ingmar Bergman really changed that much, judging by his still somewhat odd reactions in the presence of Jews and his artistic support for the Palestinian cause? One could make the case that the man has never had a sensible, humane day in his life.

A common but not much recognized human trait is the difficulty most people have in feeling positive and negative emotions toward the same object. Thus if one adores Ingmar Bergman as a film maker, even if one is Woody Allen, it is painful to think that he was for a long time a rabid Nazi and anti-Semite, and one avoids the subject. When there is no conflict, it is easier. If one is an ardent Left-liberal, for example, it is with a full heart and great lung power that one denounces anti-Semitism in the Bush or Republican ranks.

This, of course, suggests that the charges of anti-Semitism are something of a pretext, and that one's basic commitment has nothing to do with anti-Semitism at all. Nazi-schmazi.

18

The Romance of Cocaine: Tequila Sunrise

A H, THE SHIMMERING, scintillating, evanescent glamour of cocaine. The romance. The magic. Ah, the glamour of drug addiction, the thrilling glint of needles in the moonlight, the spine-tingling excitement of cop killings, drive-by shootings, of slaughtering inane bystanders, the divine surge of the rush, the mystery, the heady romance. Or did I say that already?

Or perhaps you're one of those stodgy stick-in-the-muds who think that drug addiction is a squalid and menacing business, that it's ruining the lives of millions every year, and that Americans are terrified and consider it their number one national problem. While I think Marion Barry's a fun guy to have for mayor of Washington, perhaps you feel there's something vaguely discreditable about him paying all those visits to the Ramada Inn.

Well, you obviously haven't seen *Tequila Sunrise,* the season's most romantic movie, with its entrancing evocation of the cocaine high life of Los Angeles's South Bay, which is what insiders call the southern half of Santa Monica Bay. The northern half—Malibu, Pacific Palisades, Santa Monica, Marina del Rey—everybody's heard about already. But south of the airport? Manhattan Beach? El Segundo? Hermosa Beach? Redondo Beach? Torrance? Palos Verdes? South of LAX (the airport) lies romance.

Speedboats and yachts cruise the moonlit waters of the bay laden with cocaine and bundles of $15 million in romantic greenbacks. Legendary drug kingpin Mel Gibson lives in a romantic beachfront villa and drives a romantic Porsche. But is he really retired from the narcotics trade after sacrificing fifteen years of his life so that his fellow South Bay residents can go to bed stoned? That's the big mystery.

Beautiful Michelle Pfeiffer runs a romantic restaurant, the gathering place for everybody who's anybody in South Bay. Michelle is romantically intimate with both Gibson and Kurt Russell, head of the L.A. Police Department narcotics section, but without ever giving you the slightest feeling she's promiscuous or low-down.

Because *Tequila Sunrise,* in addition to the romance of cocaine, is about friendship. Gibson and Russell went to high school together, and even though life has taken them along different paths—Gibson to luxury and riches in the narcotics trade, Russell to trying to throw Gibson in jail—they've remained fast friends.

Don't expect me to make sense out of this movie. It has more than a murky plot. It is solid murk. Gibson is also fast friends with Raul Julia, a legendary Mexican drug kingpin who is definitely not retired. Raul Julia has two identities: Carlos the King of Crack, and a Mexican police honcho—who turn out, amazingly, to be the same person.

Well, *Tequila Sunrise* has everything: smooching, cocaine sniffing, gourmet dining, yachting, moonlight over Santa Monica Bay, a bit of cops and robbers, bang bang, you're dead, more cocaine. A little recreational cocaine never did anyone any harm, did it? But perhaps the best way to give the moral structure of this movie is to explain who are the good guys and the bad guys.

Even apart from his fifteen years of community service providing South Bay with cocaine, Mel Gibson is most definitely a good guy. He's the nicest, his eyes are bluest, he's adorable with his kid and at the end he quite deservedly gets the beautiful girl, Michelle Pfeiffer. Raul Julia is also a good guy, warm, caring, entertaining, a loveable drug trafficker.

Kurt Russell is kind of betwixt and between. On the up side, he's remained close friends with Gibson during all the drug years. On the down side, well, he's a cop, which makes him necessarily unappealing. Understandably, he doesn't get the girl.

I've no mixed feelings about a fourth character, however, undoubtedly the worst guy in the movie: a bloodhound of a narc from the federal Drug Enforcement Agency, who pants throughout the film to put narcotic traffickers behind bars. There is very little to be said in defense of this DEA person, who is really Mr. Odious.

An interesting geographical fact about South Bay, which is a lily-white district replete with Mercedes and BMWs, is that inland a bit lies an area that the local press refers to neutrally as "south central" Los Angeles, which is code for poor and black. Only one part of it is known throughout the nation: Watts.

South Central L.A. has been hit by the crack epidemic like no place in the world, with some twice as many gang murders per capita as Washington. There are no black people in *Tequila Sunrise*, of course. And I think it's absolutely marvelous of Robert Towne (*Chinatown*), who wrote and directed this movie, to create, so close to an area where cocaine is chewing up people's lives most savagely, a ritzy world in which the exact same controlled substance is chic.

I admire the man for not getting in a panic about this "drug war" business, too. And if one day two cars should careen past Towne's swimming pool for a drive-by execution, I hope he'll take it romantically. He's a puny, sickly person though, the kind that whimpers, which might take some of the fun out of it for him.

A film critic from the *Washington Post*, in a city where cocaine is also not unknown, fell into raptures over *Tequila Sunrise*, calling it "irresistible," the "sexiest, most intelligent Hollywood movie in a long time." I hope that he, too, wouldn't whimper, which would be neither sexy nor intelligent. It would really spoil the mood.

Note: In view of the nation's current "War on Drugs," it would appear from *Tequila Sunrise* that much of Hollywood is definitely not "on board" for the war. From the fact that not a single one of the nation's major film critics noted that the film conveys a rather sympathetic attitude toward casual drug use (condoned by the liberal culture), as well as toward even drug trafficking, one might infer that the country's movie reviewers—as opposed to its editorial writers—are not on board for the war either.

19

The Politics of Sentimentality: Charlie Chaplin

I ASKED JOHN WAYNE, in his last years, how he felt about the
old days in Hollywood. He said that thinking about them, "I
have a warm feeling in my heart." When I sought his opinion of
Charlie Chaplin, he answered with no enthusiasm that Chaplin
was "a pleasing comic," but no match for Groucho. Wayne
obviously had a cold feeling in his heart for Charlie Chaplin.
Why?

With the American media in an orgy over the 100th birthday
of Chaplin, probably called a genius to his face more than any
man in history, with pundits now hailing Chaplin as an eternal
symbol of the "little fellow," the underdog, the undying spirit
of the human heart, it's worth wondering if the whole thing
hasn't gotten overblown.

In theatrical release today, by common agreement, Chaplin's
films would do no business at all. Most are silent. But above all,
except for his early one- and two-reelers (the original basis of
his world celebrity), they're mawkish. If audiences today saw
them in their entirety, instead of snippets on television, they'd
find them filled with treacly pathos. And not just today. Chaplin's films have been dated in their sentimentality for fifty years.

What is being presented as the collective consciousness of the
race on Chaplin is in fact the view of a special class. One
wouldn't know this from the current media frenzy, but Chaplin
had (and has) many detractors. Pablo Picasso, no less, said,
"When he starts reaching for the heart strings, maybe he im-

presses Chagall, but it doesn't go down with me. It's just bad literature." And there was a time, for quite different reasons, when most Americans sincerely hated Chaplin.

In the late 1940s, America had just been through a draining war. It had won. Patriotism was high. But a new enemy had emerged, Stalin's Soviet Union, perceived overwhelmingly by Americans as a new threat.

Charlie Chaplin had done little during World War II, either for America or for Britain (he had remained a British subject). He never visited his native London to lend moral support during the Blitz. He never entertained the troops, either British or American. Between tennis games at his luxurious home in Beverly Hills, he conceived of a single wartime venture: ardent support for Communist causes.

Five months after Pearl Harbor—although he later presented himself as a pacifist—Chaplin called vociferously for an immediate Allied invasion of Europe, a Soviet demand of the time. He called Moscow sympathizers at pro-Soviet rallies "comrade," and told them he wasn't a Communist but was "pretty pro-Communist." He supported numerous Communist-front organizations. Moscow appreciated Chaplin's ornamental value and in 1946 invited him aboard a Soviet ship. Chaplin obliged by referring to U.S. customs officials as "the Gestapo."

Chaplin's reaction to Western military victory in 1945 was to make *Monsieur Verdoux,* the story of a celebrated Frenchman (Landru) who made a vocation of marrying, and then murdering, rich widows. Perversely (this was his pacifist period now), Chaplin used *Verdoux* as a vehicle for denouncing arms and armies, saying the only difference between them and Verdoux, who murdered ladies for profit, was one of scale.

Moreover, Verdoux had earned our special indulgence, Chaplin explained, because he was forced into murdering ladies by the collapse of capitalism. Chaplin, critics noted, had been gung-ho for war in defense of Moscow, but turned into a self-described "peace-monger" when it came to defending the West against this same Moscow, now in an expansive phase, which had gobbled up half of Europe. Chaplin's sexual penchant for sixteen-year-old girls also did his reputation little good. It was an era when America held its movie stars to standards of behavior now applied to cabinet appointees, and the anti-Chaplin explosion was predictable.

Later, from his fifteen-room, twelve-servant, thirty-seven-acre estate in Switzerland, Chaplin was vindictive. His *A King in New York* (1957) is perhaps the most spitefully anti-American film ever made. And, after leaving America, Chaplin systematically banned U.S. newsmen from all his press conferences and screenings.

In his early days Chaplin was very gifted, nimble, fast, a wonderful mimic. I truly like him, however, only in his early short movies, when he's often a rascal. His feature-length films, beginning in 1921, are marred by the most cloying sentimentality: *The Kid, Gold Rush, City Lights*. With *Modern Times,* moreover, Chaplin begins to think, alas, condemning the industrial age. *The Great Dictator,* in which he spoofs Hitler, is an embarrassment.

Chaplin's sentimentality and his politics are linked. Those familiar with show-business know that comedians, with some exceptions, are cold people, often clinical depressives. "Sentimentality," by definition, is an outpouring of false emotion—for sentimental people do not feel much genuine emotion, wallowing in substitutes. ("You're a wonderful audience; I love you all.") Chaplin's object of political sentimentality was "Russia," which he never visited. What the world does not need, I would suggest, is a thinking comedian.

In one respect, however, Chaplin was ahead of his time. American and British armies fought to keep him safe in World War II, but he felt no loyalty. He announced defiantly that he was above narrow "patriotism," that he was a "citizen of the world." Since most members of today's U.S. media are also "citizens of the world," with no demonstrable loyalty to the country which assures them safety and freedom, I'm not surprised they like Charlie Chaplin's moral principles just fine.

20

Heavy Thinking in the Afternoon: Oprah Winfrey and Shirley MacLaine

TIRED? STRESSED? CONFLICTED? Right-brained? Suffering from dis-easement like Jim Wright? Need to accelerate your consciousness? Shirley MacLaine has the answer.

Sometimes I feel I'm not really getting to the heart of America. Here I come back from this *meshugaz* in Cuba, and think deep thoughts about the birth of Charlie Chaplin and death of Abbie Hoffman, and visit my dentist, who has strong opinions. Soon I'll be leaving for Europe, where I'm going to have to do a lot of explaining. And still I'm not sure what this darn country is about.

So in my quest for understanding I decide to *go deep,* and plunge into the heart of darkest daytime television to the Oprah Winfrey Show, where I find Shirley MacLaine. The last time Shirley and I met she was ecstatic about a perfect world she'd just visited: Mao Tse Tung's China. Red Guards were beating "capitalist roaders" to death in the streets, tens of millions of Chinese were starving, and Peking's subsequent rulers said Mao's Cultural Revolution was absolutely horrible, but Shirley didn't notice.

Shirley has now changed her field of expertise to the sacred writings of the Hindus. She's also been studying the "Tibetan masters," who are Buddhists actually, but what the heck. Our culture is so "stressed," "conflicted," and "rightbrained"

(Shirley is left-brained) that we need all this stuff, she says. Our culture absolutely must "access" it or we'll get sick."

What we've first got to understand is the *chakras*. We've each got within us seven of these things, says Shirley, seven "spinning wheels of energy," seven "centers of consciousness."

We have, in order: the "base" or "fear" chakra (base of spine), "sexuality" chakra (guess where), "emotion" chakra (pit of stomach), "heart," or "love" chakra, and chakras for communication (throat), vision (head), and Divine Force (Shirley waves her hands high up).

Now here's the genius part. *Each chakra has a color.* "We all have a rainbow inside us!" Shirley cries happily. Seven colors! And they help you "align yourself." Because this is going to make a better you! What did you think?

Let's say you have trouble with your boss, says Shirley. It gets you in the solar plexus, right? Now what you do is *isolate it.* Then: "Use yellow! Visualize yellow!" Shirley cries. *"Go within,* and *wash that area with a meditative approach with yellow."* It's amazing how this works, she says.

Or say a lover has left you, says Shirl. You're feeling it in the heart chakra, right? Green? So you *go within the heart energy center and wash it with a meditative approach with green.*

Suppose you're having an argument with a loved one. You mix! You meditate in green (love chakra), and at the same time also in blue (communication chakra). "After a while you get very adept at this," she says. "It's amazing." Furthermore, all these chakras vibrate to musical notes, says Shirl, bursting into a musical scale beginning with middle C.

Oprah, an amiable person, is gamely trying to work out a fusion of Shirley's Hinduism with Christianity, but looks quizzical when Shirl objects strenuously to calling God "Him." Says Shirl: "I would prefer to call it "God-Goddess-All-There-Is." Shirl says we're all part of God-Goddess-All-There-Is.

Now I won't tell you I browse through the Hindu scriptures every night. The *Vedas* go on forever. The *Mahabharata,* with more than 90,000 couplets, is the world's longest poem. The *Bhagavad Gita* is a Sanskrit epic in which Krishna gives Prince Arjuna a million reasons why he should fight in a coming battle.

Krishna spews out a lot of arguments in the *Bhagavad Gita* but I'll be darned if I can find Shirley's seven colors, or how to meditate in green and blue while arguing. What I find in the *Vedas,* however, is what Shirley's not telling you about Hinduism: that man has no immortal soul, and that there is no God of mercy or forgiveness. For, if you're a Hindu, a man's sins are never forgiven—indeed, there's no one out there to do the forgiving.

In your next life, if you're good, you may be born in Beverly Hills, of course, but maybe as a cockroach. In Hinduism you have *karma,* a long series of reincarnations, and at the end, with great good fortune, *mukti,* liberation from the necessity of rebirth: nothingness.

So, adopting Hindu theology, I'd hazard a guess that in her next life Shirley MacLaine will be a chicken. And then, if she's a bad chicken, an ant. And then, if she's a really good ant, she might never be born again. But here's the relevance of all this to our ordinary American life:

Speaker Jim Wright, to help him through his time of troubles, has taken up Transcendental Meditation, which comes out of the same Hindu books Shirley's been reading. And I'd say he's having trouble in the fear, emotion, communication, and head chakras, and should consequently be meditating simultaneously in red, yellow, blue, and indigo.

Try it, Jim! Wash those energy centers with a *Hindu technicolor meditative approach!* You'll leave that Ethics Committee behind in your dust. And in your next incarnation, I should say, you'll be a Texas prairie dog. Either that or, why not? Nothing.

No Pearly Gates, Jim. No Lord in all His glory. No life everlasting. You take your choice, Jim. You go with the Shirl and the Hindus or you go with us.

Note: I do not know Jim Wright, but the end of his political career, while not necessarily disproving the validity of Hindu doctrine, might suggest that he was perhaps meditating in the wrong colors.

21

Burning the Flag and Robert Mapplethorpe

E GGED ON BY the Supreme Court, would I burn Robert Mapplethorpe?

The man's dead already, remember. I'm no murderer. That great voice is silenced, that great eye blinded, that great catamite taken from us by AIDS. When will we get another Corcoran-class photographer to take divinely aesthetic pictures of a "black man urinating into a white man's mouth" (as sympathetically reported by U.S. family newspapers), or of the photographer himself in full posterior nudity being penetrated anally by a bullwhip (likewise)?

Mapplethorpe's untimely departure leaves our civilization poorer, I'm telling you. I'm lucky I saw his full show in sophisticated, cosmopolitan Philadelphia before the yahoos of Washington started imposing on great art the aesthetic tastes of Peoria.

I wouldn't dig him up, I'm no grave robber either. But inspired by the Supreme Court's ruling allowing the burning of the American flag as free expression, I'm just imagining Mapplethorpe's dead body lying around someplace, and me seized with a desire to express myself.

Greg Johnson cried: "Red, white, and blue, I spit on you," and I could yell, "Mapplethorpe, you're a dork." That's pretty thin gruel though. So I think I'd sprinkle him with kerosene and burn him up.

Now there are emotional people in this country who attach a

319

sacred character to a dead person's remains and to burial. (You noticed how often those who condemned flag burning were called "emotional.") But the ACLU will explain to you that burial, as a religion-derived custom, has no legitimacy as church and state are separate in this country. Preserving dead bodies, moreover, is obviously ethnocentric. Hindus burn their dead. Parsees expose them to be eaten by vultures. Are our customs superior?

So, peacefully, harming nobody, expressing myself freely in the constitutional way that makes us so different from Hitler's Germany, Stalin's Russia, Khomeini's Iran, and Deng's China (all invoked in sanctifying both the Mapplethorpe show and the right to burn the flag), I'd burn the guy up. I think I'd beat the rap, too. Or it would be interesting to find out.

And I have a secret weapon: *art*. If I wanted to do more than win over the Supreme Court, if I craved the support of the entire intellectual community, I'd set fire to this Mapplethorpe not as self expression but as *performance art*—a kind of performance that even the NEA hasn't heard of yet. I'd invite all the curators and art critics, announcing that this isn't recommended for children, and burn Mapplethorpe, creating a new art form.

And I'd do my darnedest to get a $15,000 grant from the National Endowment for the Arts, like Andres Serrano, who did the renowned Christ in urine. (It amazes me that Greg Johnson didn't have an NEA grant to burn the flag in Dallas.) *Then* with my $15,000 grant, let those polyester-suited, philistine yokels try to stop me. Ho, ho! Every freedom-loving artist worthy of the name would rush to my support! I'd really shame the bumpkins then.

Because the artistic community has its own eleventh commandment: *Thou shalt grant federal funds to art that's too intellectual for you to understand, you rube.* This keeps high-class art out of the hands of the rabble, who are too coarse to appreciate it and can't tell Marcel Duchamp from a marcel wave. But would I actually get my $15,000 grant to burn Robert Mapplethorpe? Because there's a flaw in my argument, and I'm man enough to admit it.

In Chicago I could get official sponsorship for an American

flag displayed on the floor with an invitation to walk on it. I could get official support for art demeaning almost any of this country's institutions: sexual, political, or religious. But could I demean gays? Women? "Inferior races"?

Because this whole controversy has taken place as if those favoring the Mapplethorpe show (and the right to burn the flag), those shuddering at "censorship," were supporting absolute freedom and the total separation of art from content. But the most ruthless censorship takes place before art even comes close to reaching the public. Is every novel written published? Every play produced? Every painting exhibited? Above all, in museums? The moral pieties of our culture barons just happen to be different from those of ordinary Americans. They censor, in darkness, every day.

Public money goes into any amount of junk-art gleefully and maniacally denigrating everything that ordinary people hold sacred—which seems to be the point. And all I want to do, in a spirit of moral uplift, is burn Robert Mapplethorpe's corpse if I find it lying around someplace. But will the NEA fund me? Bitter laughter.

Mapplethorpe himself admitted to drawing inspiration from the pornography shops of Manhattan's Forty-second Street: "Basically I'm selfish. I did them [his "sex pictures"] for myself—because I wanted to. I wasn't trying to educate anyone. I was experimenting with my sensibilities."

Faced with a credo of such egocentricity I'm even provisionally prepared to adopt it—conveniently reversing myself since it spares me the need to even express anything. In burning Robert Mapplethorpe all I have to do is experiment with my sensibilities.

Actually I don't care if I have to buy the kerosene myself. If I find this guy's body lying around I'm going to burn it.

22

Mad Manichaeanism: Summer Blockbuster Movies

THE BLOCKBUSTER MOVIES of summer—often decried as the season when the apparent age of movie-goers declines to twelve—are in fact engaged in a Manichaean struggle over the nature of evil.

Ghostbusters II presents evil as a pink sludge coursing through a Manhattan sub-sewer and causing all that is vicious, venomous, and hateful about New York life. *Batman,* which begins with an opening sequence in a decayed Gotham taken over by drifters, hookers, and muggers, lays its degeneracy at the feet of a Satanic figure called ''the Joker'' (Jack Nicholson).

The latest *Indiana Jones,* not very originally, makes the locus of evil Hitler and the Nazis. And *Lethal Weapon 2,* set in a contemporary Los Angeles hardly more realistic than the fantasy 1930s of Indiana Jones, casts white South Africans as modern Nazis. I'm a pink sludge man myself, but I suppose reasonable people can differ.

Batman, Indiana Jones, Ghostbusters, and *Lethal Weapon* seem slotted for the summer's Big Four. And Manichaeanism, for those who care, is a historic religious faith which viewed the world as a dualistic struggle between God and Satan, the forces of light and the legions of darkness.

What distinguished Christianity from Manichaeanism, which has surfaced many times as a Christian heresy, was that the Manichees (St. Augustine was a Manichee before his conversion), rejected as repugnant the Christian notion of sin. For a

Manichee, man's miseries are caused not by sin but by simple contact with the material world, the realm of Satan. The individual bears none of the blame.

In the wake of the huge bicentennial celebration of the French Revolution, we might recall that the *philosophes* of France's Enlightenment, so influential with the revolutionaries, agreed with the Manichees in repudiating the doctrine of Original Sin. For the *philosophes,* man is naturally good. He is held back by the state (Rousseau), church (Voltaire), or private property (Gracchus Babeuf, much honored in Moscow). If these malign institutions can only be gotten rid of, man will attain happiness.

Interestingly, this belief system has never been accepted by the popular culture, which has always had its Satanic figures. Even in the age of schlock, Conan Doyle had his Doctor Moriarty, Sax Rohmer his Fu Manchu, Ian Fleming his Doctor No and successors. But are the legions of light and darkness struggling for your soul and mine? That is the question.

Steven Spielberg, director of *Indiana Jones, E.T.,* and *The Color Purple,* is entirely a creature of light. Or so he thinks. He took a very sardonic view of American patriotism in *1941* (a turkey), and of earthlings in general in *E.T.* (a hit), and it's gripping to see Spielberg, a prudent man, boldly going after such a safe target as Adolf Hitler.

But the one wicked thing we actually see Hitler do is burn Karl Marx's *Das Kapital.* This would be a stirring indictment except that at the period of the movie Hitler was contracting his Holy Alliance with Josef Stalin. Does Spielberg know this? The Hitler-Stalin alliance wasn't his idea, Spielberg might plead. He bears none of the blame. Which is the Manichaean cop-out.

In *Lethal Weapon,* the South African successor-Nazis are extremely wicked. A South African "minister of diplomatic affairs" maintains a fortified hill villa on Mulholland Drive in movie-star country from which he runs a monster cocaine ring. Now whatever reproach you make against South Africa, it doesn't traffic in narcotics. Nor do South African planes strafe Americans on California beaches. *Lethal Weapon 2,* you see, is somewhat fanciful.

The vilification of cocaine trafficking, moreover, is quaint for those familiar with Hollywood, which is shot through with cocaine use. In fact, the last film of *Lethal Weapon*'s star, Mel Gibson, was *Tequila Sunrise,* a positive narcotic trafficker's anthem. Gibson, as an honorably retired trafficker, gets the girl. And the movie's only really obnoxious people are DEA agents. How does Gibson feel about his quick change from hero drug trafficker (retired) to hero of the war against drugs? Would he plead Manichaeanism?

In *Batman,* the Lucifer figure (Jack Nicholson) steals the show, but perishes in the last reel, naturally. All ends well when Batman applies himself, and crime, prostitution, and rudeness vanish from the streets of Gotham. Meanwhile, in *Ghostbusters,* Bill Murray and his friends conquer the most ominous evil of all, the pink sludge.

All these films have diabolic figures: Hitler, the Joker, South Africans. Even the pink sludge has a man-like accomplice, a Carpathian ghost named Vigo. But the heroes, and most people in these movies, are without sin. Only in *Ghostbusters* are ordinary people bad, when they fall under the spell of the pink sludge. And you can hardly blame them.

If these film directors were true Manichaeans, of course, they wouldn't have beach houses in Malibu. They'd know, as Manichaeans, that the material world is the realm of Satan and they'd abjure earthly pleasures. They'd know that their women, shopping on Rodeo Drive, are Satan's instruments, seducing man so that the day of his emancipation from darkness and material things will never come.

Listen. It's summer. It's hot. These movies are awful. I'm trying to give these guys some class. If they don't read Augustine, don't blame me.

Note: In the closing days of the season, *Honey, I Shrunk the Kids* beat *Ghostbusters II* by a nose. What Augustine would say to such a development I wouldn't care to speculate.

23

Whose Vietnam? Casualties of War

THE DOGS OF WAR are loose again in the movies, particularly in an impressive new film called *Casualties of War*, which has enraged many Americans who led the "peace" movement against the war in Vietnam. In *1984*, George Orwell's O'Brien proclaims: "Who controls the past, controls the future." And so, after *The Deer Hunter, Coming Home, Apocalypse Now, Full Metal Jacket,* and *Platoon,* the battle is on again over whose "Vietnam" is to enter the national mythos.

Positively gargling blood is Frances FitzGerald, whose *Fire in the Lake* won every prize in sight when it was published in 1972. The book predicted Vietnam would be "cleansed by the flame of revolution," and it went into positive ecstasy over the coming "discipline of the revolutionary community." Judging by the tidal waves of refugees, when the "revolutionary community" came into being it was just a tad less blissful than the dreamers had imagined. So FitzGerald has a lot of blood to gargle.

Writing in the *Village Voice,* she is blazingly incoherent, calling the whole film "excruciating sadoporn." (The almost priggishly discreet rape is about sixty seconds of screen time.) In the movie the entire event, FitzGerald says, might be a "revolting dream of the impotent Michael J. Fox [the actor]—and of the United States."

In 1969 the *New Yorker* published a long story about American grunts raping and murdering a Vietnamese girl. Since GIs raped girls in World War II without making the pages of the *New*

Yorker, I considered the story in 1969 "more anti-war stuff." Director Brian DePalma, then a little nobody (never a member of the radical Left incidentally), didn't agree, and twenty years later he's brought the story to the screen with a particularly compelling performance from Sean Penn as the sergeant commanding the squad that did the deed.

We have, first of all, a real war: nasty, brutish, and long. Crawling through a strange, sweaty country filled with vermin, boobytraps, and snipers, American infantrymen get blown away all the time. One dies horribly from stepping on a land mine. Brownie, a jovial black squad member, two days before his return to "the world," is killed by a sniper.

Sergeant Meserve (Penn) is hard as nails, decorated, calloused but not about his men. In a firefight, he saves the life of PFC Eriksson (Michael J. Fox). The real Sergeant Meserve, called by his commanding officer the "best combat soldier" he'd ever seen, was nominated for a Bronze Star for crawling out under fire to bring back one of his men, lying wounded and helpless.

Stricken by Brownie's death, the sergeant becomes convinced, with some evidence, that all Vietnamese they encounter are Viet Cong, women included. When the whorehouse district in a nearby town is declared off limits, two of them kidnap a local Vietnamese girl and take her with them on long-range patrol deep into enemy territory. They rape her, and when her coughing threatens to give them away, kill her.

It's not a pretty business. The real "Eriksson" (all names are changed), very religious, is horrified by the rape and murder and, against advice of lieutenant and captain, reports the event to authorities. But in infantry combat, as perhaps nowhere else, a man's life depends on his comrades whether they rape women or not. And for a soldier to turn in his squad leader—one who saved his life—is a kind of military sacrilege.

The real Sergeant Meserve and three other soldiers were court-martialled by the Army, did up to five years in Leavenworth (ten in the movie), and were discharged dishonorably. Their whereabouts are unknown. For his own protection, "Eriksson" changed his residence and identity. And all five have disappeared, like dust in the wind, no more tangible now than if they'd fought for the Blue or the Gray at Gettysburg, leaving behind only their story. Brave soldiers, fighting a terrible war, did a terrible thing and were punished for it. What is there about this to enrage Frances FitzGerald and her friends?

I will tell you. Attitudes toward Vietnam have changed radically since the 1970s, when smug campus war resisters spat on returning soldiers and called them "baby killers." Now, although the "peace" people have had their way in Central America, avowed hatred for the United States and U.S. soldiers has gone out of fashion. For most of these antiwar people the style is now to "love" America so much they can't bear to have it do the least thing disagreeable, and they see Americans who fought in Vietnam not as monsters but as victims.

This applies to *most* antiwar people. There are others—like FitzGerald—who still can't stand to see American soldiers in Vietnam portrayed as human beings, behaving in the beastly way soldiers often do in combat, but fighting a dangerous war, courageous, grieving when their buddies are killed.

Audiences in packed movie houses (and the lines are long) have a lot of sympathy for Sergeant Meserve and his squad, fighting for their country in a strange land, good soldiers who, amid the horror of war, do a terrible thing. FitzGerald's blood must run cold at the words of actor Michael J. Fox, speaking of the jungle, the exhaustion, the danger: "You can almost see why they did it."

What the public might find harder to see is why Frances FitzGerald, wealthy, a child of privilege, while America's poor were in Vietnam fighting for their country, turned against her own people.

24

The Year of the Orgasmic Woman: When Harry Met Sally

REMEMBER THE "Year of the Woman"? A portentous affair, even unto the lofty heights of the United Nations? Are you ready now for the "Year of the Orgasmic Woman?" Because it's arrived. Oh, yes it has.

Talk in women's magazines has been rumbling along for years now about "orgasmic women," and "non-orgasmic women," with loud demands for female orgasm as some kind of human right. *Cosmopolitan* and other women's magazines have made an industry of it.

Now two hit movies, *When Harry Met Sally* and *sex, lies, and videotape* (the latter winning highest honors at the illustrious Cannes Film Festival) have brought the subject over the great divide into the realm of light conversation. I don't know if we've reached the stage of "Have you had any good orgasms lately?" but it might be coming.

I have a shady past. Not the military part. That was terrific. But in the dark days of the counter-culture, as a refugee from the radicalism then raging in journalism, I took shelter for a time as contributing editor of *Cosmopolitan*, which I curiously never include with the high-prestige publications in my resume. They'd picked me out of the pages of the Tom Wolfe–Clay Felker *Esquire,* then a magazine dealing with manly subjects, and the senior staff meetings under Helen Gurley Brown were exhilarating.

We "girls" (the word was still in use) talked about how to get a man, and whether to take the sexual initiative, and foreplay, and afterplay, and a lot about orgasms. The atmosphere was like, *"orgasms now!"* and the language was inspirationally dirty. The managing editor and I were the only men and kept our mouths shut.

I had a connection around that time with *Playboy,* too, so I was kind of a hired gun, but it seemed to me these ladies should turn to me as an oracle on what men would think of them if they took this or that daring sexual initiative. They didn't though. And now everybody knows anyway. Steamy female discussions once confined to the hallowed halls of the Argonaut Building on Manhattan's Fifty-seventh Street are now cocktail conversation all over America. Thus the old order changeth.

Witnessing the Soviet invasion of Czechoslovakia exactly twenty years ago (Red Army tanks clanking through the streets), but also meeting charming Czech women (dutifully), I've never found it easy to answer questions involving disparate categories like nowadays: which is worse, Communism or cocaine? Or: what do women want, equal pay or orgasms? It depends on the woman, I guess. Who knows? Not me, I assure you.

Take *When Harry Met Sally.* The way women talk about these things now in public! The big scene, featured in all press accounts and running for weeks in coming attractions, is Sally (Meg Ryan) "faking" an orgasm.

Not in bed, you understand, but in a delicatessen, with people all around, and *loud,* with lots of thrashing about and hysterical cries of "Oh, God! Oh, God!" She's proving her point, that men can be fooled. Earlier, in a roadside diner, she bellows contentiously to a chance acquaintance, "I do too have good sex!" So it seems this is something you can talk about now with people you scarcely know. Like: "Do you have good sex?" "Pretty good. How about you?"

Which is exactly the tone of *sex, lies, and videotape.* We have John and his wife Anne, who is "frigid," which is what we used to say before "non-orgasmic." She has a hot-pants younger sister named Cynthia who's sleeping with John, Anne's husband, who's an adulterer, I suppose. When along comes Graham, a friend of John's from many years back.

Graham enters bathed in celestial light, a kind of sex angel, soft-spoken, unthreatening. Anne in all simplicity tells him that sex for her is a big nothing, and Graham, gentle and honest, tells her sweetly that he's impotent. He was disappointed in love, so he's developed this innocent hobby of videotaping young women who masturbate in front of his videocam. Afterwards he plays back the cassettes to remind him of the old days, I guess.

Now frankly I think this Graham is a little kinky, not just a nice guy waiting for the Right Girl to come along. Nor do I think Anne will find happiness with a gentle, soft-spoken man addicted to videotapes of women masturbating. I just don't think they're made for each other. I'm obviously wrong though, because at the end of the film they're sitting lovingly together in the rain, him with his potency recovered, her orgasmic.

And Graham destroys all the tapes! Donna, Diane, Diana, Deborah, Delia, Doris, Denise . . . And that's just the D's. They trusted him, and where's his loyalty? All their tender delivering of themselves wasted just so the movie can have this lovey-dovey ending. *Both* movies have lovey-dovey endings.

Because they're "women's movies." Harry's a "political consultant" but you never see him consult. Sally's a reporter but you never see her report. In women's movies, only the boy-girl part counts. But *sex, lies, and videotape* and *When Harry Met Sally* are both big hits—hits for your New Woman.

A young female person I hardly know told me in the elevator the other day that she loves professional wrestling. She spends hours gazing at it on television and adores watching the men. I didn't ask her anything else because I was afraid she'd tell me.

25

Treason Redux: Le Carré's
Russia House

A T NEW YORK'S BLOOMINGDALE'S—as part of that idealistic
institution's bridge-building to Moscow—you can buy a
loaf of imported Russian bread for $6. While for $19.95 at
American booksellers you can buy John le Carré's new *Russia
House,* now being praised to the skies as the book finally ending
the Cold War. Of the two, I think the bread is both a better
bargain and decidedly less bad for you.

For one thing, the bread has the sour taste and the grainy,
bumpy bits of real Russian bread. It's the genuine article. It
comes from Russia. While *Russia House* is supremely ignorant
of Russia. It's thin, mushy, "peace" drivel worked up by a
pretentious thriller writer out of surly antipathy toward his own
society and a strange obsequiousness toward its adversaries.
Russia House also defends—even champions—treason.

The book is getting rave reviews from Soviet officials, quoted
in all U.S. advertisements. This in itself is piquant, as who
would want Moscow's views on Western intelligence services—
when the Soviet Union has habitually issued blood-curdling lies
about such comparatively mundane subjects as its own economy? Would you expect the Kremlin to praise an espionage
novel that doesn't serve Soviet purposes?

There is a misperception about John le Carré propagated by
the U.S. news media, now busy crying up *Russia House* as the
biggest thing since *War and Peace.* John le Carré is indeed a
creature of the Cold War but, contrary to what's being reported,

Russia House represents no really new departure. Le Carré's approach has *always* been to demean the intelligence services of both Britain and America, reserving a particular aversion for the latter.

From his first successful book in 1963, *The Spy Who Came in From the Cold,* the burden of le Carré's whole argument—carried by really negligible literary skills—has been what Jeane Kirkpatrick calls "moral equivalence" (I prefer "moral symmetry"). It should be obvious that a writer who ignores the free, open pattern of our society and places it on the same level as the closed, coercive secretiveness, which has unfortunately been the Soviet pattern, is carrying water for Moscow.

What should be obvious, however, was not. It is now. With *Russia House* le Carré has broken into the open. While preserving some of the mannerisms of the moral-symmetry mode (the KGB is still not very nice), le Carré's hatred of Britain, America, and the West is such as to establish him now as emphatically pro-Soviet. In his new book, he entirely justifies high treason on the part of its protagonist, a minor publisher with a special relationship with the British Secret Service. It's the story of a traitor, similar in some ways to the notorious Kim Philby, but with Philby's behavior now presented as exemplary.

Oh, our hero commits treason for "love," you understand, for "peace," for human brotherhood. But he delivers into the hands of the KGB a supposedly hugely important, ultra-secret document—at which point, furthermore, he defects to Moscow. No matter how shoddily *Russia House* is written, this is what is commonly called treason.

To tell his tale of a traitor-hero, le Carré has assembled a cast of characters that make cardboard seem pretty well-rounded stuff. We have Barley, our publisher, tall, fifty something, "gracefully clumsy," saxophone-playing. We have Katya, a Russian woman, heart-stoppingly beautiful, heart-stoppingly devoted, heart-stoppingly noble. She can cook, too. I'm sure that at some time in his life le Carré has met a real woman, but you'd never suspect it from this depiction. We have Yakov, a Russian scientist, the most brilliant man in Russia, who guarantees us that the Soviet "defense-industrial complex" is totally impotent and Moscow therefore harmless.

A device: it is to save Katya from KGB unpleasantness that Barley commits treason. He strikes a "bargain" with the KGB. He delivers the secret document in exchange for a KGB promise that it will lay off Katya. Given the arrogance and aggressivity of America, the reader understands that Barley's treason will also promote peace, make the world safer, and improve the quality of saxophone playing.

Treason is the book's *raison d'être*, the high point, the big scene, after which Barley tootles off to Lisbon, where in the final pages he serenely awaits Katya, since he tells us the KGB (a truly quaint idea) has never broken its word.

From his willful ignoring of intelligence procedures and persistently feeble grasp of human motivation, I've suspected for some time that le Carré's years in British intelligence were spent as a dry-as-dust statistical analyst or code clerk, and that he knows as much about intelligence as he knows about saxophones. As far as I am concerned, *Russia House* proves it.

In contrast, I bought a loaf of Bloomingdale's Russian bread and it's really not bad. Compared to le Carré, even the sign in the window is soaring prose:

Perestroika Comes to Bloomie's Bakery. In the spirit of the new openness between the USSR and the USA, Bloomingdale's Bakery will be flying in: *Peace Bread From Moscow.*

Bloomie's has *borodinsky,* a "sour rye with a highly compacted crumb flavored with coriander seed." And another bread, *rjanog,* which is "perfect to serve with smoked salmon."

The trouble with le Carré's *Russia House* is that it's got no sourness and no highly compacted anything. I've tried it with smoked salmon and it's still terrible.

Note: That the central episode of *Russia House* is an act of treason, an act which le Carré presents as highly praiseworthy, has been almost entirely overlooked by the media. ABC News honored le Carré as "Person of the Week" and *Newsweek* made him the object of a celebratory cover story. As a national media response to a widely publicized book endorsing treason, this is remarkably supine.

26

Madame Butterfly's Revenge: M. Butterfly on Broadway

THE SCALES FELL from my eyes. Here I'd been thinking of this bizarre French sex-and-security scandal from the Western point of view, even the French point of view. Bernard Boursicot, a French diplomat, was not only nailed for treason a few years ago on behalf of Communist China, but the love of his life—a Beijing Mata Hari with whom he had been having an affair for twenty years—turned out to be a man.

Oh, there was ribald laughter at Montparnasse and Deux Maggots, not to mention the Café de Flore. The DST (*Défense de la Sécurité du Territoire*) didn't think it was humorous at all, mind you, and hit Boursicot like a ton of bricks, trying him in camera at a special state security court, the kind of thing that would give the ACLU the willies, which is why France has no ACLU. And we probably never will know what treasonable documents Boursicot passed along to his lady love (if "lady" is the term). Boursicot was found guilty of high treason.

And then I saw *M. Butterfly*, the one new unsubsidized American play to be launched on Broadway during the season, later to win the Pulitzer Prize for drama. Thanks to Art, the muse imparted to me profundities hidden from the eyes of irreverent Frenchmen, and I saw the episode in its true light.

This moving story reveals at last the truth about relations between East and West. The plain fact is that the West has always thought of itself as *male,* and the East as a submissive *female,* just dying to be dominated and conquered and otherwise

339

kicked around. This is what General Westmoreland thought in Vietnam, as the play carefully explains to us. But it's an illusion, that's what it is.

And the French diplomat Boursicot is a perfect symbol of this illusion, mistaking Vietnam's General Giap, and Japan's Tojo, and that Chinese Red Army that clobbered us near the Yalu in North Korea, as delightful young ladies in a Bangkok massage parlor. *Monsieur Butterfly* is really an inspirational work, bringing together, as the author admits himself, all that is false in "racism, sexism, and imperialism."

Now I will level with you. In the homosexual subculture—for I have my sources—when a woman sues for divorce after ten years of marriage because she's just discovered her husband is a woman, it's the subject of much hilarity. And even more so when a man discovers—horrors!—that his wife is a man. I will say no more.

But on Broadway we are in the realm of Art, which sees through such superficialities. *M. Butterfly,* for example, melds Japanese and Chinese cultures into one, which is some trick. I'd also thought those fragile Japanese lotus blossoms that sank the U.S. fleet at Pearl Harbor had dissipated any doubts of Japanese virility. A whole series of abrasive actions, including destroying the Russian Fleet at Tsushima and invading China, should really have dissipated them already. Then we faced the Chinese ourselves in Korea. And the rampaging Red Brigades in Mao's Cultural Revolution didn't seem very feminine. Also take a look some day at Thai boxers.

The trouble with me is I've been around too much, not only Tokyo and Beijing, but also Naples, where I once saw the San Remo Opera Company do Puccini's *Madame Butterfly* with that cad of a U.S. naval officer Pinkerton. Perhaps because I was serving at the time in the U.S. Sixth Fleet, I've always considered this one of Puccini's most ludicrous plots—although *Girl Of The Golden West* is also good for some giggles.

In the opening scene of *M. Butterfly* on Broadway—now get this—a female star of the *Peking* Opera is singing Puccini's *Japanese* opera *Madame Butterfly* in *Italian*. Boursicot (his name changed to Gallimard) falls head over heels for this delicate Italo-Nippo-Chinese flower. But all is artifice designed to exploit his racist-sexist-imperialist piggery! And in case you had any doubts about what kind of man this Frenchman is, he sides with the United States in Vietnam.

Gallimard spends a fast twenty years with this crazy Chinese drag queen. In the mad, "revolutionary" year of 1968, Peking Intelligence even sends her to join him in Paris, where, interestingly, there are great posters up reading *"Front Populaire"*— presumably still around from Léon Blum's day thirty years earlier. "She" produces a baby. I don't know. She walks off stage and comes back with a baby.

Finally the DST smells a rat. Peking? Mao? The fanaticism of the Cultural Revolution? And this Chinese opera singer turns up in Paris? Then there are those missing classified documents. And they discover that Mister Butterfly is not a girl.

But, boy, the tongue lashing you're in for then. You fool, you're probably as bad as Gallimard. Mr. Butterfly, now revealed as a puny male, shouts a lot in his thin voice about how the West thinks that it's masculine, and that the womanly East wants to be dominated. But Gallimard was snookered! That's what he was. By a hardworking little Chinese drag queen playing for twenty years on his overweening sexism, racism, and imperialism!

Gallimard can't take it any more. I can't take it any more. Gallimard dresses himself in Japanese women's robes, checks the yen-franc rate, I assume, and performs that well-known Sino-Nippo-Italian custom, hara-kiri. The emasculation and suicide of the West! In real life, Mr. Butterfly is deported to China while Gallimard (Boursicot), as far as I know, is still in the slammer.

David Hwang, who wrote all of this, is the son of a wealthy Shanghai-born banker who says he loves his adoptive country, America. His mother loves America. His parents wanted their son to have the best of everything and so sent him to Stanford and Yale. He studied with Sam Shephard and Joseph Papp, won Guggenheim, Rockefeller, NEA, and NYSCA fellowships. But old-fashioned patriotism doesn't take a playwright far in those circles.

Now David Hwang probably speaks Chinese. If the West is so sexist, and racist, and insufferable, and repulsive, so in need of being taken down a peg, why doesn't he give People's China a whirl? I've seen hovels in Xian and farther west that I'm sure he'd find adorable.

If he stepped out of line at the wrong time he might get beaten to death. But, hey, no place is perfect.

Note: Re getting killed in China, I would be curious to have Hwang's view of the massacre at Tiananmen Square. Was the Beijing government racist? Imperialist? Sexist? Who was in drag? Hwang is certainly well qualified to speak.

27

The FBI, the KKK, and a Sartrian Marxist: Costa-Gavras's Betrayed

H OW WOULD YOU MAKE a movie about Al Capone, showing the mobster was a very bad person, but nowhere near as bad as the FBI's Eliot Ness, Capone's nemesis? Or look at it another way. Let's suppose you hate America—not that you mind summering in the Hamptons and hobnobbing with Park Avenue radicals, but that you hate America on principle as a racist-imperialist country, the hobgoblin of correct-thinking Marxists everywhere. How would you make a movie showing American society as so corrupt and vicious that it produces a nationwide organization of neo-Nazi white racists—but so rotten that the FBI, which smashes this Nazi-racist organization, is even worse?

I'm talking about Costa-Gavras's new hysterico-Marxist folly *Betrayed*, with Debra Winger and Tom Berenger: a film so snarled, so convoluted, so crazed, and so illogical that movie critics—"F" students in political science to a man—are amazingly giving it the slamming it deserves.

Mind you, if Costa-Gavras had set his film in Greece, Uruguay, or Chile, the locations of his early triumphs (*Z, State Of Siege, Missing*), reviewers in their high-minded ignorance would probably have believed every word. But he made the tactical error of setting *Betrayed* in America, about which even movie reviewers know enough to realize Costa-Gavras is lying as fast as he can roll his camera.

Now you and I know there's no such thing as a Communist.

343

And if there were one, nowadays he wouldn't go around America spouting gobblygook from *Das Kapital,* but adopt the idiom of any group which, in whatever way, diminishes the United States. This is the New Moscow Line, often expressed these days as "Up With a Perfect America!" Which is to say down with the actual, real America and any America any of us will ever see.

In France, Costa-Gavras is plain-spoken. He has identified himself as a "Sartrian Marxist," and since late philosopher Jean-Paul Sartre defined *himself* as a "Communist fellow-traveller," the statement is fairly clear. In fact, Costa-Gavras and his original mentors, movie stars Simone Signoret and Yves Montand, had a long history of supporting Communist causes. Signoret has died and Montand has undergone a serious conversion. *"Nous étions des cons!"* (we were dopes), he now says about his Communist period. But Costa-Gavras chose a more flexible option.

When you see Costa-Gavras in Paris, there are no evasions. He's your straight, mind-numbing Marxist. Whatever Moscow says—updated periodically of course—is good enough for him. But whenever he flies to America he converts to free enterprise in the plane in mid-Atlantic. This time he told the *Washington Post* his earlier self-description as a Sartrian Marxist was "playful." He takes Americans for political illiterates, and fair is fair, he's usually right.

Thus his latest movie, *Betrayed,* is about racism, anti-Semitism, and fascist plotting in the American heartland, let's say Nebraska. The publicity says it's a "powerful, provocative, and frightening story of divided loyalties, love, and personal betrayal."

First "love." Debra Winger is an undercover FBI agent who falls in love with Tom Berenger, an all-American farmer she's supposed to have under surveillance. He's really very sweet, and adorable with his motherless children. Unfortunately he engages in the recreational sport of kidnapping blacks with his white buddies, turning them loose at night, and hunting them down with dogs and shotguns.

Some people play golf. The English upper classes go fox hunting, a famous "blood sport." Tom and his dogs have their own blood sport: black hunting. When asked for a real-life example of this, Costa-Gavras replied "Howard Beach."

With Tom, Debra visits a grand camp meeting with flags waving—American flags, Confederate flags, and the flags of Nazi Germany. The crowd wears KKK robes and sings "Amazing Grace," and we realize with horror that all of these elements together make up an American fascist front: the KKK, Nazis, Christianity, and American patriotism. Tom, of course, was decorated in Vietnam.

And all these American fascists have a dream, a computerized version of Charles Manson's old dream. Linked throughout the country by computer terminals—for there are millions of these American fascists—they plan to stage riots, "kill all the Jews and niggers," and seize power, giving the green light to nuclear energy, banning abortion, and reestablishing prayer in the public schools. They're that vicious.

But Debra loves Tom, because he does have this adorable side. Which is more than you can say for the FBI, whose regional director, John Heard, is unrelievedly nasty, cold, and cruel. Even black FBI men are nasty. Nonetheless, the FBI breaks this Nazi-KKK-Pat Robertson conspiracy wide open.

Which you'd suppose is a good thing. But no! That's where those "divided loyalties" from the ads come in. Debra hates these KKK Nazis with their prayers in the public schools—but the FBI is even worse! The FBI "uses" her against that cute Tom Berenger, who's only planning a coup d'état. "You used me!" Debra cries to the regional director of the FBI. "You betrayed me!"

That's where the "betrayal" comes in, thereby giving the film its title. The FBI betrays this innocent young agent into trapping a really very sweet racist murderer.

If you find this story slightly dippy, dear reader, think back over the rabidly anti-United States *Missing,* with Jack Lemmon and Sissy Spacek, which after all won an Academy Award. With the same man in charge, Costa-Gavras, but with you necessarily less informed, *Missing* gave as true a picture of Chile as *Betrayed* does of America.

But if only thirty-two people see *Betrayed,* producer Irwin Winkler will still be happy. Bowed with riches and guilt from the success of the *Rocky* series, he will sleep the sleep of the morally redeemed in far Beverly Hills. For he will have done his bit to awaken America to the true danger to our country: fascism.

People may say what they like about communism being brutal, economically regressive, and morally corrupt. And they may dream fond dreams about Hitler being gone and fascism discredited. But the threat to our country will always come from the Right, and from the Right alone. And if there aren't enough fascists in America, well, Irwin and Costa will make them up.

Note: Betrayed was a commercial fiasco. It says something about the mindset of Hollywood, in an age when the average movie costs $20 million and must be seen by some seven million people to turn a profit, that such a film as *Betrayed* even gets financed.

28

Britain's Loony Left: Letter to Brezhnev

THE MOVIES! I thought to myself. I've been away in Russia; I must catch up with the new movies. My heart sank a little when I saw that the most highly touted new film in New York was a ritzy British import called *Letter to Brezhnev*. It sank a little further when I saw it had been a successful play in London, which these days makes me wary.

I'd just returned from the Soviet Union, which, to be brief, is the pits. I was sick of it: bugging, calling from public phones, people scared to talk, the country class-ridden, rotten with corruption, the populace drab, the *nomenklatura* callous, with its life of secret luxury. Why should I have to see a movie that had anything to do with the Soviet Union? It seemed very unfair.

Still, the film's reviews were dithyrambic. "Exhilarating and refreshing." "Heart-piercing sweetness and hope." "Zesty." "Hilarious and heartbreaking." "A terrific movie." "Exuberant, sassy and dynamic." And this not just from the *Village Voice,* but from the *New York Times,* the *New York Daily News* and that arbiter of intellectual taste, *People* magazine. And the film was playing in Manhattan on Third Avenue across the street from Bloomingdale's, so it wasn't intended for the oppressed masses. It was very up-market, for the Bloomingdale's shopper, the latest thing in fashionable ideas about the Soviet Union.

I could not believe this movie before I saw it. I could not believe it while it was flickering before my eyes. And even now that I've seen it, I can't believe it.

The film was made before Chernobyl, obviously. It probably was booked into the theater before Chernobyl. But it was raved about by these dippy film critics after Chernobyl. And the airheads in the audiences were caught up in the romance of the Soviet Union—laughing gaily at the anti-Western jokes straight from the Amtorg Joke Book—all after Chernobyl, which you'd think might have made them a little less exuberant, sassy, and dynamic. But let us begin.

We are in Liverpool. In fact, we never get out of Liverpool, which is wondrously clever, you see, because it's far easier to sustain exhilarating, refreshing thoughts about the Soviet Union in Liverpool than when in the Soviet Union. Anyway, we're in Liverpool.

Before us are two young, romantic, female Liverpudlians. They are working girls, proletarians, a bit on the *lumpen* side. One stuffs chickens in a meat-processing plant, the other is on welfare. Despite their modest position in life, the two girls display an elaborate feminine wardrobe—a new dress or coat in almost every scene—good quality materials, stylish cut. The taste is a bit garish, but it's their taste.

The girls spend their evenings hopping from one affluent-looking discotheque to another, along with other young working-class Liverpudlians. The home of the girl on welfare is snug, comfortable, well-kept. There is no sign of poverty anywhere. When the girls spend a night at a hotel, it, too, is snug and comfortable, freshly painted, in Tudor style, for all the world like the hotels at Stratford-on-Avon. The shockingly high level of material comfort enjoyed by these English proletarians—and one of them on welfare—would, I should think, make the film highly unwelcome in the Soviet Union.

The authors of *Letter to Brezhnev*, however, seem to be under the distinct impression that these girls are oppressed. Stuffing chickens is beneath human dignity, apparently. In a better world, chickens would stuff themselves. The two girls are not identical. One seems to be after a Guinness record for sexual promiscuity and is a habitual thief of the lighthearted, happy-go-lucky kind one doesn't often meet in life. The other is more "romantic." Both are foul-mouthed. Both urinate in public, and in front of the camera. In a better world, no doubt, they would urinate in private. One tearfully maintains she is happy with her life: fornicating, drinking vodka, and stuffing chickens. But we, godlike, peering into her soul, understand that she is not. Furthermore, we have a cure.

Enter romance in the persons of two Soviet merchant seamen. Our two girls, in adjoining hotel rooms, spend "a night of love" with these adorable creatures. The more romantic girl, Elaine, is smitten, exchanges vows, writes a personal letter to Leonid Brezhnev, and becomes determined, despite all efforts to dissuade her, to emigrate to the Soviet Union to rejoin her Soviet sailor. Motive?

Here *Letter to Brezhnev* grows slippery. When asked directly, Elaine swears in her surly way that her motive is "love." She loves this Russian sailor. But the film is after a Guinness record of its own. It's absolutely loaded down with anti-Western, pro-Soviet dialogue, cracks, and "jokes," enough, you might say, to sink their sailors' ship. In the midst of her well-dressed, well-fed, disco-hopping misery, Elaine blurts out: "Living in Russia can't be worse than here." (But it can, dear, and above all for you.) And again: "I don't have anything here to give up."

She asks her Russian sailor about the Soviet food shortages she's read about in the British papers. This lovable person answers: "But that's what our newspapers say about you!" So, you see, perfect symmetry. The Soviet press says there are shortages in Britain, and there aren't. And the British press says there are shortages in the Soviet Union, and there obviously aren't any there either. Plainly there are no shortages in either country. It's pure chance, I think, that the film doesn't tell us about the enviable safety record of the Soviet nuclear-power industry.

Much of the film's affection for the Soviet Union is conveyed by the extreme nastiness of the people who attempt to dissuade Elaine from emigrating. They range from her family and other Liverpudlians to a newsman and a member of the Foreign Office, which will plainly stop at nothing. One ugly number says the Russians "invade countries and deprive them of their basic human rights," which gets a big laugh from the audience, as the

Russians plainly do no such thing. Reports of Soviet misbehavior have evidently been invented by Rupert Murdoch.

Elaine is told that in the USSR people have "no freedom," that they "can't speak against the system," to which she answers that she's tired of hearing all this from people who "don't know bugger-all about the place." She tells her mother, "Go knit yourself an Iron Curtain," which also gets a good laugh. When reminded that she speaks not a word of Russian, that her future husband will be at sea, and that she will be totally isolated among a people about whom she knows nothing, she reverts to love. She loves him.

And love conquers all! That nice Mr. Brezhnev sends Elaine an airplane ticket. She is filled with hope, sure she is on her way to a better world. "One must simply believe in Russia," she says. Her girlfriend, the all-in sex champion of Merseyside, tells her, in tears, trembling, "You're right." Almost the movie's last words are Elaine's heartfelt "I am lucky," just before her airliner takes off and the film, prudently, ends.

No Soviet Union, you see. Cagey, cagey. That might spoil it. We have to get along with these Soviets, you know. We must all do our best to have exhilarating thoughts about Soviet Union.

Note: Letter to Brezhnev was released in the United States in early 1986, not long after the ascension of Mikhail Gorbachev. Now that under *glasnost,* economic and other miseries of the Soviet system are the object of violent criticism in Moscow itself, and that the film's Leonid Brezhnev is vilified daily, held responsible for every Soviet failure from corruption, brutality, and economic regression to the collapse of houses during the Armenian earthquake, I cannot imagine what the Britons who made *Letter to Brezhnev* could possibly say in defense of their film, or what the U.S. movie critics who adored it could say to justify their unqualified, ecstatic reviews. Perhaps they're all busy forgetting the whole thing ever happened. I would not want to guarantee that their political judgment has in any way improved.

29

The Sneaky Side of Pacificism: *Spielberg's* Empire of the Sun

THERE IS A WONDERFUL little child inside film director Steven Spielberg. He admits this himself. Unfortunately this wonderful little child cries at night, pathetic little whimpers, because Spielberg has never won an Academy Award despite all the director has done for the cause of peace.

Spielberg is pressing on earnestly however, and CBS gave him fabulous publicity with a prime-time, full-hour documentary on the making of *Empire of the Sun,* a movie which the director himself tells us is a "universal message of peace for now and future generations." Spielberg apparently decided he has heretofore been too subtle and unassuming. He's made millions, you understand, but serious people haven't given him the recognition that is his due, never looking beneath the surface to see his movies' true portent. That hurts a guy.

The director was bitterly disappointed in 1983 when his great peace movie, *E.T.,* washed out at the Academy Awards. It was so unfair because *E.T.* had everything. Starry-eyed, from the innocent child's point of view of course, it showed that we don't live in a hazardous world at all but a gentle, benevolent universe where only American authority figures are vile. It should have had Academy members weeping unashamedly.

But the "peace vote" was underhandedly snatched away that year by *Gandhi,* which wasn't much more realistic than *E.T.* but had a lot of pseudo-history behind it. Spielberg got a gold medal

351

for *E.T.* from an association at the United Nations, and I saw the tears in his eyes, but it wasn't the same as an Academy Award. The lesson was not lost on the director, however, and in *Empire of the Sun* he decided to get pseudo-history on his side.

Spielberg is ill-equipped to handle real history, because he has what the French call a "purely cinematographic culture." Simply put, if something hasn't been the subject of a movie he hasn't heard of it. He doesn't seem to read at all.

Consequently, although he based *Empire of the Sun* on an autobiographical novel by J. G. Ballard, an Englishman who lived through the events of the movie in his early teens, Spielberg recounts with some astonishment that before Pearl Harbor, Shanghai had this curious place filled with Europeans called the "International Settlement." He seems never to have heard of "treaty ports," "extraterritoriality," "war lords," Japan's first or second Chinese "incidents," or the fact that in European enclaves in China—in the case of Shanghai, the heart of the city—Chinese writ simply did not run.

Chinese history for Spielberg is a delightful blank. Although he knows about Japanese Zeroes, of course, because Hollywood made movies about Pearl Harbor and the war in the Pacific.

In *Empire of the Sun* Spielberg shows us a map of Shanghai with this mysterious "International Settlement" clearly demarcated, but not a clue that right next to it, part of the French Empire, was another part of Shanghai also governed by Europeans, the "French Concession." Nor does the film contain a clue that in this period most Europeans in Shanghai were in fact Russians, refugees from the Bolshevik Revolution. No one has ever made a movie about them, apparently.

The story of *Empire of the Sun* is simple enough. It is the story of the "odyssey into manhood" of a wealthy English boy in Shanghai, twelve years old at the beginning of the film, fifteen at the end. Separated from his parents, he is interned by the Japanese when, after Pearl Harbor, the International Settlement is taken over by the Empire of the Sun. The boy has a threadbare collection of odyssey-into-manhood adventures. It is all from the child's point of view, at which Spielberg is so wonderful, people tell him.

Now you might be wondering what a lily-livered wimp like Spielberg is doing making a movie showing *anything* positive coming out of a fighting man's war, even victory. In his elephantine *1941*—one of the biggest and most expensive fiascoes in Hollywood history—Steven Spielberg made his feelings about patriotism abundantly clear. Even immediately after the attack on Pearl Harbor, he relentlessly and with a deathly humorlessness attempts to ridicule everyone who comes to the defense of his country.

In dealing with American characters in *Empire of the Sun,* Spielberg runs true to form. All Americans, naturally, are abominable. But the key to this movie lies elsewhere. A Japanese air base adjoins the internment camp of our rich little English boy, Jim. And Jim becomes enamored of . . . Japanese Zero pilots. The enemy.

How interesting! Since Steven Spielberg doesn't read books, he probably doesn't realize that he nakedly displays a trait common to most pacifists—verifiable in every country occupied in World War II by Nazi Germany. For one of the pacifists' least appetizing characteristics—pathologically inhibited as they are about the use of force in their own defense—is that they tend to idolize and thrill to brutal violence when committed by their enemies. Marcel Déat, the Frenchman who, as World War II approached, wrote perhaps the most famous pacifist tract in history, *Die For Danzig?,* held high office under the German Occupation. He went over to the Nazis within days, as did all French "pacifists" of the 1930s, every one. No one has made a movie about them either, I gather.

So the American pilots who turned back the Japanese fleet at Midway were a bunch of imbeciles and louts. But the Japanese of that war, who conducted death marches, routinely killed prisoners, and frequently tortured them for pure entertainment, ah, they were gorgeous people. Glamorous, too, when you come to think of it. From a child's point of view, of course.

Do you read me, Crazylegs? If this country is overrun militarily in our lifetime (which I strongly doubt), Steven Spielberg will worm on his belly to lick the conqueror's jackboots. Not that I bear him any ill will. He is what he is.

Note: Empire of the Sun was another one of Spielberg's fiascoes. He really should stay away from war movies.

30

Can Jesus Save Madonna?
"Like a Prayer"

A LL YOU GUYS are futzing around about ephemeral stuff, here today and gone tomorrow: an airline strike, who's going to be the next U.S. secretary of defense, the decline of the Soviet Empire. But I've been concentrating on the cosmic truths contained in Madonna's brand new, world-premiere video, like the dark night of the soul, and why man was placed on earth, not to mention Our Savior, and whether He's forgotten us. And if you have any cosmological, theological, or teleological questions left after this video, "Like a Prayer," I really don't know what they could be.

Before the titles you see Madonna fleeing across a barren wasteland with burning crosses to let you know what a bleak, hopeless world this is, with the KKK and skinheads and all. She falls, prostrate, with the shoulder strap of her bra showing. Because this video is not only going to explain the relationship of man and God, it's going to set you straight on sex, gang rape, feminism, racism, police brutality, judicial injustice, salvation, and the stigmata. Because Madonna gets the stigmata. I didn't tell you that right off because I was afraid you'd run away in alarm.

In her dark night of the soul, Madonna spies a country church with the windows glowing warmly. Hope! It looks like a Protestant church from the outside, but when she gets inside it's a Catholic church because Madonna was brought up Catholic.

Nor does she start dancing around in her underwear right away either. She begins like the lead soprano at the Folies Bergeres singing "Ave Maria." "Life is a mystery. Everyone must stand alone." But then: "I hear You call my name." Wow. Gooseflesh.

Behind a grill in this Jesuit-style church is a black Jesus. Why not? What the hell? And he's crying. I mean, it's only a statue of Jesus, but real glycerine tears are coming out of his eyes. Why? Ah, hah! We don't know yet. Meanwhile the music has moved to rock and Madonna is thrashing about like a klutz to: "In the midnight hour. I can feel your power." And Jesus, who maybe doesn't like rock, turns from a statue into a real live person and walks out the door of the church, biblical robes and all.

This is when Madonna gets the stigmata. Because she misses Him.

Now we get the social protest part. Four white skinheads are raping a girl, at least that's what it looks like, but run away when they see the cops. Whereupon Jesus enters the scene in civvies, and naturally hastens to succor the poor girl. But when the cops get there, *they arrest Jesus!* Wouldn't you know?

In the meantime, Madonna has been flying around through the air, and when she comes down we change churches again, because she falls straight into the arms of a Protestant Episcopal black woman priest. But who can sing and dance like blazes. The woman priest and her pentacostal choir riff along, "Just like a prayer. You know I'll take you There."

And Madonna is saved. At least I think she's saved. She's throbbing and flailing about with every inch of her partially clothed body, down on the ground, and up in the air, and if that isn't Salvation I don't know what is. Then Jesus in his New-Testament suit suddenly appears again and kisses her. On the mouth. You heard me. At this point for some reason the wax Jesus statue cries tears of blood. Hmm.

Then we have an epilogue. The grill protecting the wax Jesus in the church is transformed into the iron bars of a police lock-up. And in that police lock-up is Jesus in civvies again. So there's still racial injustice, even with Madonna saved.

But then there's an epilogue to the epilogue! Everyone appears on stage for curtain calls at the end of the show! We have the cop and the skinheads and the girl who got raped, jiving away. And Madonna and Jesus jiving away, too. Then a big maroon curtain with "The End" on it comes down and you think, what the hell is this?

Listen. Christianity has gotten soft. Italy has banned Madonna's "Prayer" video, but in the good old days—when Pope Innocent IV felt as strongly about Christian doctrine as the Ayatollah Khomeini feels about Moslem doctrine—Madonna would have burned at the stake for this.

The last Christian to be executed for blasphemy was the Chevalier de la Barre in France in 1766, only ten years before the U.S. Declaration of Independence. He failed to doff his cap when passing a religious procession following the Holy Cross.

And when the Pope dissolved the Knights Templar, Jacques de Monay, commander of the order, was broken on the wheel. He confessed to blasphemy, then recanted. Rather than save his life by confessing falsely, he burned alive at the stake, crying out in warning to the Pope: "We will meet again before the court of the Lord."

No rock music then.

Note: Madonna's "Like a Prayer" album sold over 10 million units, and she is the world's highest paid female entertainer. At a pre-tax 1989 income of $23 million, she ranks between Sylvester Stallone and Sugar Ray Leonard.

31

Culture's Mega-Stalinist: Brecht and The Threepenny Opera

DOES THIS STING PERSON actually earn his living singing? On the evidence of his performance in Bertolt Brecht's *Threepenny Opera* at Washington's National Theatre, it would seem implausible, his voice so weak and thin, recalling over the years a timid version of my brother singing in the shower. He's that good.

You say that in 1988 Sting made *Forbes*'s list of the world's highest paid entertainers? Pulling down in pre-tax profits something like $14 million? Ah, the technical wizardry of digital recording. Rock concert amplifiers like the crack of doom. Guaranteed lifetime hearing impairment.

But Sting has given all that up. He's gone intellectual, you know, concerned with preserving tropical rain forests and saving the planet from such scourges as global warming and capitalism. Perhaps amplifiers might in some undiscovered way interfere with the mating season of the Brazilian parakeet, so Sting went through the first week at the National Theatre "unmiked." You couldn't hear a word he said, and later when he was miked you realized how well off you were.

And capitalism! Wow! Sting, baby, I'm really glad you caught up with that insidious pestilence. Now that a day doesn't pass in Moscow without the Soviets saying that their system is economically regressive and unworkable, that they're compelled to introduce market mechanisms, and that Stalin was the worst murderer since Genghis Khan, I think it's really neat that you decided to honor Bertolt Brecht, the cultural world's most vibrant Stalinist.

With thousands of East Germans flooding westward over the Hungarian border, how remarkably up-to-date of Sting to bring us fresh winds of change from 1950s ultra-Stalinist East Berlin, where I actually interviewed Bertolt Brecht in his last days, which was instructive. The *Dreigroschenoper (Threepenny Opera)* was first produced in Berlin in 1928 under the Weimar Republic, of course, so I suppose Sting was bringing us fresh winds of change from pre-Hitler Germany's Communist Party, which adamantly refused to join with Socialists or anybody else to form a common front against the Nazis, calling Socialists "social Fascists," in fact. Brecht was a fervent proponent of every single one of the Comintern's dicta, then and always, and so scathing were the *Dreigroschenoper*'s attacks on what the enemies of German democracy called *Das System* that over its five-year Berlin run the show might have done its bit to undermine confidence in Weimar and help replace it with—Adolf Hitler.

How's that for a Brazilian parakeet, Sting, baby? And when Hitler came, did Brecht flee to Stalin's joyous Soviet Union that he'd been touting so rapturously? Heck, no. He went to suffer the capitalist *Schweinerei* of Pacific Palisades, California, and only returned to (East) Berlin after World War II, when the authorities made him the royally subsidized Dramatist Laureate of German Communism.

During the East Berlin workers' riots of 1953—the first rising against Communism in all Eastern Europe—Brecht denounced the demonstrators as "fascistic, war-mongering rabble" and gratefully thanked Soviet troops and tanks for their "swift and accurate intervention." He was a slavish Stalinist and consistently displayed the most extraordinary cowardice. Pablo Picasso was a Communist, but his politics scarcely got into his painting, while Brecht's plays are brimming with Soviet agitprop.

Did the innocent audience at the National Theatre know any of this? Did George Bush, who sat through the whole miserable opening night? Get with it, George, baby! Don't be afraid.

Brecht's political approval rating is zero. After all, Kurt Weill—whose wonderful music was appallingly performed in Washington—broke with Brecht because he was "tired of setting Karl Marx to music." What kind of approval rating has Karl Marx?

With Sting still reminding me of my brother, this time in his masterful performance as Greed in a Sunday School morality play (age 12), and with the rest of the show's cast dizzyingly amateurish, what was this *Threepenny Opera* all about? Why, bourgeois and criminals being the same! How's that for a zinger? The musical explains that in this capitalist world:

> A man can only live by resolutely
> Ill-treating, beating, cheating other blokes.
> A man can only live by absolutely
> Forgetting he's a man like other folks.

As opposed to Stalin's Gulag, you see, which imprisoned nine percent of the Soviet population and terrified the rest out of their wits, but where guards naturally treated inmates with exquisite kindness. Sting, however, saved all his bitterness for the bourgeoisie. Witness the play's last number, in which Sting passionately cursed "the coppers, sons of bitches." That's bourgeois coppers, you understand.

Me and Bertolt Brecht: I was a respectful young man. He was a very old geezer, it seemed to me, and not a bit de-Stalinized. We talked about his play *Happy End* (the German title), and I deferentially pointed out that in English we say "happy ending." Brecht said absolutely not. It was "happy end." We talked about Shakespeare, whom he considered his precursor, a leader of the "bourgeois revolution." Thinking he couldn't have read much Shakespeare, I didn't even answer that one.

Brecht called his work the "non-Aristotelian" theater. He told me he didn't want his audiences to experience "catharsis" or "pity and fear" (Aristotle's words), but to emerge from his plays thinking hard and debating the plays' politics. At least in this, I've followed his instructions faithfully.

Brecht's poetry and language in German have a special expressionist flavor, and the music of Kurt Weill—entirely responsible for the *Dreigroschenoper*'s success, I'm convinced—is marvelous. But Brecht's plays are wooden, stilted, browbeating, tediously devoted to his kindergarten Marxism. Brecht was a contemptible, fawning toady to the greatest tyranny in history, that murdered, not millions, but tens of millions. He rendered it servile homage from beginning to end, in his life and in his plays.

Not far from East Berlin's glorious Stalinallee, Brecht told me that he wanted to be remembered for enlightening people about social and political circumstances, for his politics. And that's just how I remember him.

Note: National Public Radio gave an admiring interview to the translator of this new *Threepenny Opera*. Having elegantly rhymed "happy" with "crappy," the translator fervently assured listeners how "close" we all were to Brecht, and reminded us of how concerned Brecht was with "artistic freedom." For the most groveling follower of the Stalinist line in artistic history this was falsification on a truly breathtaking scale, but the NPR interviewer seemed to believe every word.

32

A Broadway Flop Goes
Downmarket: CBS's Pack of Lies

IS TELEVISION CULTURE? High culture? Low culture? Broadway these days is low culture, I think. Which is lower? How about Hallmark Greeting Cards? Are they culture? At least they'd be patriotic, you'd think, in a low sort of way. But are they?

To answer such thought-provoking questions, CBS and the Hallmark Hall of Fame have brought all you millions of wonderful Americans, fresh from its two-year-old flop on Broadway, *A Pack of Lies*, the most sincere, heartfelt plea for treason on behalf of the Soviet Union that has ever been presented to the American public.

You thought, what with the commotion about U.S. Marine guards in Moscow, and the Walker case, and the bill in Congress to introduce the death penalty for espionage in peacetime, that treason had a bad name and the American people were up in arms about it. Well, it just shows how wrong you were. And I've written a little verse I'd like the Hallmark Greeting Card people to consider my application for employment:

> Roses are red
> Violets are blue
> The KGB's sweet
> And so are you.

On the other hand, I'm a prudent person. And just in case the American side wins I'm mailing to the FBI—but still addressed to Hallmark, of course—a companion verse:

Commies are Red
Cowards not new
Traitors will die
And so will you.

To be impartial, you see. Because a man has to keep himself covered on both sides.

I confess here to a special interest. According to the show's producer, Arthur Cantor, I am the man who killed *A Pack of Lies* on Broadway. Writing in the *New York Times,* I said the play was a prime example of what I call "Treason Chic," the proposition that treason is a justified and even admirable act provided it is "principled," done to serve some high purpose— in this case Communism. The show promptly died.

But the brouhaha in New York intellectual salons! Even the great Irving Kristol, socially positively cherubic, assured me that I'd been too harsh and that Arthur Cantor was absolutely "apolitical." A conservative colleague from the *New York Times* editorial board (for there are such) insisted strenuously that *A Pack of Lies* was "just a good show!" When I pointed out that it was loaded to the gunwales with special pleading for Communism and pro-Soviet treason, he objected that those passages in the play "had no credibility!" By this standard, Hitler's *Mein Kampf* was not anti-Semitic because his arguments had no credibility.

So to remove any lingering ambiguity for the great American television audience out there, CBS and Hallmark added to their drama a special last scene, spelling out my exact point in words of one syllable. But first, my Communist History Minute:

Once upon a time there were two New York Communists called Julius and Ethel Rosenberg, who were charged with nuclear espionage for the Soviet Union, convicted, and executed. But there were two other interesting New Yorkers around at the time named Morris and Lona Cohen. Just as the trap was being sprung on the Rosenberg spy network, the Cohens escaped the FBI dragnet and, leaving family and friends, disappeared forever. Disappeared as the Cohens, that is. With brand new forged identity documents, they soon appeared in London as two Canadians named Helen and Peter Kroger.

Resuming their old tricks, they were nailed by MI-5 as a key part of a tremendous Soviet espionage operation called the Portsmouth Naval Secrets Case—Portsmouth being a center of submarine and anti-submarine warfare, and our undersea missiles being the "inviolable" leg of our nuclear deterrent. The Krogers were condemned to long prison terms, were later exchanged with the Soviet Union, and when last heard from were living in Poland, although what they think of recent developments in Warsaw I wouldn't know. But the final stage of MI-5 surveillance of the Krogers in England was conducted from the home of Wilfred Search, a British aircraft engineer with a high security clearance who displayed consistent, patriotic willingness to cooperate with MI-5.

But many years later enters playwright Hugh Whitemore, a new breed of Englishman, cravenly eager to carry the white flag of surrender in case, my goodness, any difference should arise between his country and the Soviet Union. Whitemore fictionally "rethought" the Kroger-Search relationship. The Krogers had committed high treason, betrayed their country, their adoptive country, their family, their friends, all that. Perhaps Britain would one day have to capitulate to Soviet authority. Fair enough. But on the other hand, didn't Ruth Search "betray" her friend Helen Kroger by letting MI-5 operate that stakeout? Which was worse? This was a real thumb-sucker.

The Broadway play preserved some drab relics of "dramatic tension." The two Krogers held the stage with long soliloquies on why they became Communists—undiluted Moscow agitprop. But these soliloquies are cut for television as perhaps emphasizing that these people really *are* agents of the KGB. And Ruth Search, now "Barbara Jackson" (Ellen Burstyn on CBS), flings herself from one edge of the screen to the other in agonies of neurotic self-flagellation.

But you could see the great mind of Hallmark pondering: perhaps those dummies out there in boobland still won't get it. Perhaps they'll think that high treason is still a far more vile act than allowing police surveillance of Soviet agents. Perhaps they'll remember that betraying your country is betraying your native land, home, friends, kin, schoolmates, everything an ordinary human being holds close. In times gone by, for such an act, men's hearts were ripped beating from their breasts.

So Hallmark and CBS added this fabulous last scene: Julie Jackson, Barbara's teenage daughter, visits her Auntie Helen Kroger (Terri Garr) in prison. Auntie Helen is without makeup, her hair unkempt. Because she's been betrayed, and when you're betrayed you don't have the heart to wash your hair. Julie reproves Auntie Helen a little for fibbing, but our Soviet agent, both smug and haughty, makes the following rousing declaration: *"I don't regret what I did! We believed in it!"*

Having thus cleared herself morally, Auntie Helen, now the aggrieved party, turns bitterly censorious: *"All those years, the possibility that your mother would knife me in the back never occurred to me! I'll never forgive her for that!"*

In tears, Julie caves in, gets off some miserable, contrite lies about her mother dying a month later, presumably of remorse, but sobbing that her mother thought of Soviet-agent Helen "every night!" And the credits roll.

So you see how simple it is? All of you who were worried about Marine guards and Mount Alto and Soviet bugs in the new Moscow Embassy? If Mrs. Walker hadn't knifed Mr. Walker in the back, and our security people hadn't knifed our Marine guards in the back, and our Moscow Embassy technicians hadn't knifed the Russians in the back by doing electronic checking, it would be a far better world.

High treason's okay now. Haven't you heard? It's these dastardly knifings in the back that are really corrupting our society. I'm going to write a Hallmark greeting card about it.

I've been debating with myself for years now which is lower, Broadway or television. Everyone in television would rather be in the movies. Television actors want to be movie actors. Television directors want to be movie directors. Television writers want to be screenwriters. And not just for the money, but because they'd be ascending to a higher artistic realm, with more time, more break-downs, more takes, higher polish. So television's relationship to the movies is clear.

On the other hand, to argue the case for Broadway's lowness, those who don't go regularly to the New York theater have no idea of its appalling general level. The list of smash Broadway hits that have been humiliating movie disasters for reasons of mawkishness or plain cretinism is long: *1776, Annie, Hair, A Little Night Music, A Chorus Line*. Nowadays Hollywood rarely even tries to make films of Broadway hits any more. (This is also true of most recent best-selling novels, whose stories have many times proved themselves simply too idiotic once set before a movie camera.)

Pack of Lies brings us new evidence, however. It was a resounding flop on the stage, and frankly, even given the power of the *New York Times,* I think it would have failed without my intervention. But *Pack of Lies* was welcomed by CBS and Hallmark as a Sunday Night Movie with open arms.

So Broadway audiences might retain some vestigial common sense after all. Whereas television audiences, although made up of millions of good, patriotic American people, seem to watch the "boob tube" in a particularly debased state of mind. It's free, or seems free. They don't have to get dressed, or go out, or park the car. And what with interruptions for commercials and the distractions of children, beer, and going to the bathroom, they appear to take in their "television movies" in such an indiscriminate haze that they'll swallow just about anything.

33

Jane Fonda Saves Mexico: Carlos Fuentes's Old Gringo

JANE FONDA, queen of the exercise tapes, met one day in moral cloudland Mexican novelist Carlos Fuentes, the great literary revolutionary and personal friend of Daniel Ortega and Fidel Castro. Together Jane and Carlos resolved to make a magnificent movie celebrating the Mexican Revolution, *The Old Gringo,* from a novel Fuentes was writing about the classic American writer Ambrose Bierce.

Bierce (*Tales of Soldiers and Civilians, The Devil's Dictionary*) disappeared mysteriously in Mexico in 1913. But it was a decision of some audacity to fictionalize him as a romantic sympathizer of Pancho Villa and the Mexican Revolution (with something of the same attitude as John Reed toward the Bolshevik Revolution), as Bierce—brilliant, witty, acerbic—was the most intensely conservative figure that American literature has produced.

A teenager in the Civil War, Bierce rose from drummer boy to brevet major in the ranks of the Union Army. He fought at Shiloh and Chickamauga, was twice wounded and twelve times cited for valor. And all this without any particular feeling for the Union cause, and none whatever for the abolition of slavery. He sympathized, in fact, with the Confederacy, and was disgusted by the Reconstruction imposed on the South.

After the war Bierce became a celebrated San Francisco newspaperman, forming a literary circle which included Mark Twain, Bret Harte, and Jack London, and was later mentor to

H. L. Mencken. Stephen Crane said of one of Bierce's stories, "Nothing better exists. It has everything." Edmund Wilson called Bierce an unregenerate reactionary and, indeed, the man who defined revolution as an "abrupt change in the form of misgovernment," and aborigines as "persons of little worth found cumbering the soil of a newly discovered country," can lay fair claim to this description. His skillful, eerie short stories and startling essays are still there in libraries for all to read, and the list of his aversions is long.

For Ambrose Bierce—tall, handsome, soldierly, sardonic—loathed and despised (a partial list): socialism, anarchism, feminism, the "emancipated woman," liberalism, organized labor, and reform. He thought America was going to the dogs with the influx of immigrants from southern and eastern Europe (and you can imagine how he felt about people who had the misfortune of not even being white). He favored "shoot-to-kill" orders to quell riots, selective breeding to improve the race. "Despotism" in his books was an approbatory word. The role of government, he felt, was to restrain the "rabble." He didn't have a democratic bone in his body.

Working for William Randolph Hearst as a renowned journalist, Bierce is presented in *The Old Gringo* as opposed to his employer's policy on the Spanish-American War. Which is precisely correct. But why did he oppose it? Because Spaniards were a "civilized and chivalrous race," he wrote, in contrast to the Cuban insurgents, "mostly Negroes and Negroids, ignorant, superstitious, and brutal exceedingly."

It tells you a great deal about the trustworthiness of Carlos Fuentes that he should take such a man as Ambrose Bierce (Gregory Peck in the film) and introduce him in fictionalized form as a soppy, sentimental, revolution groupie.

The Old Gringo is another one of these vapid, flaccid, wildly overrated Latin American novels. It's a string of impressionistic scenes with foggy narrative connectives, heavy borrowings from other Mexican writers (Martin Luis Guzman, Jesus Sotelo Inclan), noble abstractions presented as the "common people," and wholesale misrepresentations of Mexican history. The movie is all too faithful.

Northern Mexico, where the novel and film take place, had no land problem, no conflict between hacienda and peasant, no ponchos, and no mezcal. So Fuentes, to give color to his vaporous impressions, simply lifted the southern Mexican agrarian rebellion of Emiliano Zapata ("Land and Freedom!") with its mezcal-drinking, poncho-wearing Indians (all described by Sotelo Inclan in his book about Zapata), and transported it bodily to the north, to Pancho Villa country, closer to the Rio Grande and, as it were, to his readers.

Jane Fonda, the film's star and producer, plays a prim American governess-turned-sexpot, liberated from all her inhibitions by these wonderful, earthy, illiterate Mexican "whores" (the film has a kind of sterilized carnality). Ambrose Bierce falls in love with her. She falls in love with one of Pancho Villa's illiterate generals. Ambrose Bierce beds down a wonderful, lusty Mexican prostitute, joyous as only the common people are joyous. I'm telling you, this Mexico is one sexy country. Audiences at the Cannes Film Festival giggled, but what do they know?

We see a Mexican general executed by Pancho Villa himself, dying fearlessly, crying, *Viva la Revolucion!* Faithful to the *revolucion* to the end! At Fuentes's level of veracity, you leave the movie not even convinced there's such a country as Mexico.

To kick the film off, however, PBS ran a rhapsodic, one-hour, prime-time documentary on Carlos Fuentes himself. In addition to showing Fuentes's celebrity toadying, the documentary, like *The Old Gringo,* gets off some real whoppers. It tells us that 1968 was a big year for Fuentes, who roams the world's glamour spots like an "elegant gypsy." In Paris, students rose in heady revolt but there was "brutal repression" (false). Whereupon Fuentes moved on to Prague, where there was another protest movement followed by more repression (Soviet tanks). The documentary tells us that Carlos Fuentes condemns both repressions equally.

But in Paris, after the student demonstrations, General de Gaulle called an election and, on an 80 percent turnout, won a stunning landslide victory with 80 percent of the vote. So if the repression was "brutal" it was exactly as brutal as most Frenchmen wanted it to be. And Prague? After the Soviet invasion there was no election, and if a free election had been held Communist authorities wouldn't have gotten 2 percent of the vote. An "equal" condemnation by Fuentes of a notorious Soviet invasion and of a democratic government with massive popular support seems odd.

Carlos Fuentes, assisted by PBS, is essentially a purveyor of a bogus Mexico for the Martha's Vineyard set. As for Jane Fonda, having done so much to bring happiness and freedom to Vietnam and Cambodia, and to raise female consciousness with her workout tapes, one might think she could spend more time with her daughter Vanessa, who, hours after attending the Manhattan premiere of *The Old Gringo,* was arrested and charged with loitering to purchase drugs.

But saving a daughter from drug addiction would have been selfish, I think, when Jane Fonda has millions and millions of people depending on her in Latin America alone. El Salvador! Honduras! Mexico! The *compañeros* must rise up! Throw off the yoke of gringo imperialism! Saving a daughter, you must admit, would be pretty small potatoes compared to that.

34

Was Shakespeare Alienated? *Branagh's Anti-War* Henry V

S ZEKSPIR did it!
This is the way they spell Shakespeare in Poland, where, so international is the world these days, I first read of the earth-shaking "anti-war" movie of *Henry V.* Yes, William Szekspir himself, the leading classical dramatist not only of English speaking lands, but of Poland, Russia, Germany, and the entire West, is the culprit, the man originally responsible for historical distortions in this heroic play. I caught up with Laurence Olivier's *Henry V* in Shanghai, where it played with Chinese side-titles, so you can see this is important.

Olivier's triumphalist film of 1944 bore little resemblance to England's historic warrior King Henry V and to Agincourt, his greatest victory, and Kenneth Branagh's perverse "anti-war" version bears far less. But Shakespeare's Elizabethan depictions of both king and the 1415 battle were wide of the mark as well.

No, Henry V was not attacked as he left the field at Agincourt by a bevy of grieving mothers—as in Branagh's "anti-war" version. He did not wander about endlessly with a dead soldier over his shoulder like some undertaker. The aftermath of the battle was not a lament or dirge (this is really ridiculous), for Agincourt was a stunning English victory, a dazzling feat of arms, won at a remarkably low cost in lives.

But Shakespeare's Agincourt and Henry V, although patriotic, were by no means historically accurate. A feature of this medieval battle was not the French "killing of the boys" in the English baggage camp, but wholesale slaughter by the English of their French prisoners—and this in two stages.

The first, ordered by the king when afraid his numerous and ill-guarded captives might pick up discarded weapons and attack anew from the rear, had some military justification. The second, when English bowmen wandered over the field killing fallen French men-at-arms not worth holding for ransom, had none.

But if you expect Shakespeare to have expanded on brutal behavior by his own countrymen (he barely alludes to the first slaughter and mentions the second not at all), you've come to the wrong playwright. For that matter, before the modern age— which I would begin in the eighteenth century—you could find no playwright, painter, or poet in any country who would attack the sacred heroes of his own people. And it was not a question of patronage.

Despite today's almost unshakable view of the artist as "critic" and "alienated" (a belief doubtless deeply ensconced in the mind of actor-director Kenneth Branagh), before the modern period artists weren't the least alienated. Like all artists before them, they celebrated the absolute values of their own religion and people, were what we would call today "ethnocentric."

But Shakespeare, celebratory enough but a man of the English Renaissance, gives us little notion of the historical Henry V, a man still deep in the Middle Ages.

War, not horse racing, was the medieval sport of kings. Kings and noblemen fought for diversion, honor. As in the perilous pastimes of duels and jousting (France's Henri II was killed jousting), kings didn't really need much reason to fight. Henry V's conscious models were King Arthur and other mettlesome chivalric heroes. For no ideal or principle, with no qualms whatever, he launched an invasion of France in the Hundred Years War that few today would think worth the cost in blood.

Henry's father had fought for Christendom in Lithuania with the Teutonic Knights. The son planned to lead a new Crusade to the Holy Land. Dying in the field after Agincourt, Henry fervently wished—his dying words—to rebuild the walls of Jerusalem. His unarmored common soldiers fought mainly for plunder, not even hinted at by Shakespeare.

Born while Chaucer wrote *The Canterbury Tales,* Henry V spoke what linguists call "Middle English," a blend of Anglo-Saxon and Norman French. The humanist, Elizabethan speeches given him by Shakespeare, called by London wits the "high point of English football oratory," are exhortational marvels, but of Henry's spoken language we would not understand a word.

The night before Agincourt, where some 6,000 Englishmen cut to pieces a French force four times their number, killing thousands while taking at most 500 casualties (Shakespeare says 29 dead), the entire English army, served by a legion of priests, devoutly confessed, heard Mass, and took communion. The king himself heard Mass three times in succession. Before entering battle his soldiers knelt, crossed themselves, and, praying, took into their mouths handfuls of the earth in which that night they might lie. It was ancient ritual, tribal, almost as strange to Shakespeare as to us.

Wrestling *Henry V* into a protest against modern wars in the Falklands and Vietnam was an absurd undertaking. It's a minor play of Shakespeare, famous in our time mainly because, with the headiness of victory in World War II, it was such a triumph for Olivier. Kenneth Branagh, who could only have decided to do his movie in order to piggy-back Olivier, ended up with one of the most curdled classical films in years. In the battles of the Middle Ages, knights and royalty rode chargers; they didn't fight on foot. They wore clanking protective armor, and certainly didn't tussle bare-headed like English schoolboys on a rugger pitch.

With Branagh's adolescent slouch and daring gift for innovation, I would suggest he try his hand at Shakespeare's *Henry VI,* son of Henry V. Not as the eponymous king, mind you, but as his enemy, Joan of Arc, who the decade after Agincourt launched the victory campaign that finally drove the English from France.

When they got their hands on Joan, the English burned her at the stake, of course, and Shakespeare, for whom it was England all the way, treats the famous saint most discourteously, calling her a strumpet and a witch. But that's the challenge. Kenneth Branagh as Joan of Arc, made famous by Ingrid Bergman! He triumphs over Shakespeare! Hears voices! Talks to the Virgin Mary personally!

Why not? It makes as much sense as this one.

Index of Names

377